T0389147

Violence and the Caste War of Yucatán

Violence and the Caste War of Yucatán analyzes the extent and forms of violence employed during one of the most significant indigenous rural revolts in nineteenth-century Latin America: the Caste War of Yucatán in the tropical southeast of Mexico. Combining the results of historical, anthropological and sociological research with the thorough investigation of primary sources from numerous archives, the book ascertains that violence was neither random nor the result of individual bloodthirstiness but in many cases followed specific patterns related to demographic, economic, political and military factors. In addition to its use against the enemy, violence also played a role in the establishment and maintenance of order and leadership within the ranks of the contending parties. While the Caste War has been widely considered a conflict between the whites and the Maya, this book shows that Indians and non-Indians fought and died on both sides.

Wolfgang Gabbert is Professor of Development Sociology and Cultural Anthropology at the Leibniz University Hannover in Germany. He is the author of *Becoming Maya: Ethnicity and Social Inequality in Yucatán since 1500* (2004) and *Creoles: Afroamerikaner im karibischen Tiefland von Nicaragua* (1992).

CAMBRIDGE LATIN AMERICAN STUDIES

General Editors
KRIS LANE, Tulane University
MATTHEW RESTALL, Pennsylvania State University

Editor Emeritus
HERBERT S. KLEIN
Gouverneur Morris Emeritus Professor of History, Columbia University and Hoover
Research Fellow, Stanford University

Other Books in the Series

115. *For Christ and Country: Militant Catholic Youth in Post-Revolutionary Mexico*, Robert Weis
114. *The Mexican Mission: Indigenous Reconstruction and Mendicant Enterprise in New Spain, 1521–1600*, Ryan Dominic Crewe
113. *Corruption and Justice in Colonial Mexico, 1650–1755*, Christoph Rosenmüller
112. *Blacks of the Land: Indian Slavery, Settler Society, and the Portuguese Colonial Enterprise in South America*, Weinstein/Woodard/Montiero
111. *The Street Is Ours: Community, the Car, and the Nature of Public Space in Rio de Janeiro*, Shawn William Miller
110. *Laywomen and the Making of Colonial Catholicism in New Spain, 1630–1790*, Jessica L. Delgado
109. *Urban Slavery in Colonial Mexico: Puebla de los Ángeles, 1531–1706*, Pablo Miguel Sierra Silva
108. *The Mexican Revolution's Wake: The Making of a Political System, 1920–1929*, Sarah Osten
107. *Latin America's Radical Left: Rebellion and Cold War in the Global 1960s*, Aldo Marchesi
106. *Liberalism as Utopia: The Rise and Fall of Legal Rule in Post-Colonial Mexico, 1820–1900*, Timo H. Schaefer
105. *Before Mestizaje: The Frontiers of Race and Caste in Colonial Mexico*, Ben Vinson III
104. *The Lords of Tetzcoco: The Transformation of Indigenous Rule in Postconquest Central Mexico*, Bradley Benton
103. *Theater of a Thousand Wonders: A History of Miraculous Images and Shrines in New Spain*, William B. Taylor

(Continued after the Index)

Violence and the Caste War of Yucatán

WOLFGANG GABBERT
Leibniz University Hannover, Germany

CAMBRIDGE
UNIVERSITY PRESS

University Printing House, Cambridge CB2 8BS, United Kingdom

One Liberty Plaza, 20th Floor, New York, NY 10006, USA

477 Williamstown Road, Port Melbourne, VIC 3207, Australia

314–321, 3rd Floor, Plot 3, Splendor Forum, Jasola District Centre, New Delhi – 110025, India

79 Anson Road, #06–04/06, Singapore 079906

Cambridge University Press is part of the University of Cambridge.

It furthers the University's mission by disseminating knowledge in the pursuit of education, learning, and research at the highest international levels of excellence.

www.cambridge.org
Information on this title: www.cambridge.org/9781108491747
DOI: 10.1017/9781108666930

© Wolfgang Gabbert 2019

This publication is in copyright. Subject to statutory exception and to the provisions of relevant collective licensing agreements, no reproduction of any part may take place without the written permission of Cambridge University Press.

First published 2019

Printed in the United Kingdom by TJ International Ltd. Padstow Cornwall

A catalogue record for this publication is available from the British Library.

Library of Congress Cataloging-in-Publication Data
NAMES: Gabbert, Wolfgang, author.
TITLE: Violence and the Caste War of Yucatan / Wolfgang Gabbert.
DESCRIPTION: Cambridge, United Kingdom ; New York, NY, USA : Cambridge University Press, 2019. | Series: Cambridge Latin American studies | Includes bibliographical references and index.
IDENTIFIERS: LCCN 2019008499 | ISBN 9781108491747 (alk. paper)
SUBJECTS: LCSH: Yucatán (Mexico : State) – History – Caste War, 1847–1855. | Violence – Mexico – Yucatán (State) – History – 19th century. | Political violence – Mexico – Yucatán (State) – History – 19th century. | Mexicans – Warfare – Mexico – Yucatán (State) | Mayas – Warfare – Mexico – Yucatán (State)
CLASSIFICATION: LCC F1376 .G15 2019 | DDC 972/.6504–dc23
LC record available at https://lccn.loc.gov/2019008499

ISBN 978-1-108-49174-7 Hardback

Cambridge University Press has no responsibility for the persistence or accuracy of URLs for external or third-party internet websites referred to in this publication and does not guarantee that any content on such websites is, or will remain, accurate or appropriate.

To Ramón Berzunza Pinto†
eminent scholar and valued friend
and, as always, to Ute

Contents

List of Illustrations		*page* ix
Acknowledgments		x
Introduction: Caste War Violence – Prospect and State of the Art		1
	PART I VIOLENCE AND WAR	15
1	Violence in Anthropological and Sociological Perspective	17
2	Violence in Organized Groups	23
	PART II VIOLENCE IN YUCATÁN BEFORE AND BEYOND THE CASTE WAR, 1821–1901	31
3	The Context	33
4	Misery and Everyday Violence: Lower-Class Rural Life	38
5	Political Violence before and beyond the Caste War	48
	PART III THE CASTE WAR AND VIOLENCE: AN OVERVIEW	59
6	The Beginnings	61
7	A War of Attrition	68
8	Rebel Consolidation	79
9	The End of Rebel Autonomy	85
	PART IV VIOLENCE AND THE GOVERNMENT FORCES	91
10	Government Forces	93
11	Violence and Suffering within the Government Forces	104
12	Violence by Government Forces against Others	117

viii *Contents*

PART V VIOLENCE AND THE KRUSO'B   147

13 The Social Composition of the Rebel Movement   149
14 Of Loot and Lumber: the Kruso'b Economy   152
15 Kruso'b Politics and Religion   159
16 Violence among the Kruso'b   192
17 Kruso'b Violence against Outsiders   207

PART VI INTRICACIES OF CASTE WAR VIOLENCE   247

18 Civil War, Ideology and Motivation   249
19 Kruso'b and Soldiers: Parallels and Contrasts   264
20 Caste War Casualties   269
21 The Caste War in Broader Perspective   276

Appendix 1 Rebel and Kruso'b Attacks   282
Appendix 2 Attacks by Government Forces   300
Appendix 3 Kruso'b Attacks on Pacíficos   319
Bibliography   321
Index   338

Illustrations

MAPS

3.1 The Yucatán peninsula in the second half of the nineteenth
century *page* 32

TABLES

3.1 Men liable to taxation (aged between 16 and 60), 1845   35
10.1 Soldiers with Maya surnames in National Guard and army
units   100
15.1 Causes of death of major rebel leaders   177
17.1 Captive employment   224

FIGURES

7.1 Caste War defense work in Iturbide   69
9.1 Generals Bravo and Cantón and the commanders and officers
of the battalions that occupied Chan Santa Cruz, 1901   86
9.2 Federal and National Guard soldiers in Chan Santa Cruz,
1901   89
14.1 Chan Santa Cruz in the 1860s   156
15.1 Clothed cross in Yucatán   172
17.1 Church in Chan Santa Cruz, 1901   223
17.2 Northeastern corner of the central plaza in Chan Santa Cruz,
1901   226
17.3 Caste War fortifications in Bacalar   236
18.1 Captives in Chan Santa Cruz and Tekax massacre   254

Acknowledgments

The drama of the Caste War in Yucatán attracted my attention many years ago when I read Nelson Reed's pioneering study on the topic. From the very beginning, I was puzzled by what moved people to commit gross acts of violence. Tackling this riddle and completing this book has taken quite some time, however, as research and writing were frequently interrupted by other academic commitments. Over the years, the support and encouragement of many people made this project viable. Although I mention but a few, my thanks go to all of them. I am particularly grateful to Paul Sullivan, who shared his encyclopedic knowledge of the Caste War and generously provided me with copies of some rare documents. His painstaking reading of a manuscript version of this book helped to sharpen my arguments and avoid a number of factual errors. Beyond this, his own work on the Caste War has been an inspiration. John Chuchiak made transcripts of several letters from Caste War rebels available to me unstintingly. Nelson Reed, Matthew Restall, Terry Rugeley, Rajeshwari Dutt, Romana Falcón and Raymund Buve provided me with helpful comments on papers and manuscripts that have become part of this book. The work of Georg Elwert had a lasting impact on my understanding of conflict and violence. Any remaining errors of fact and interpretation are, of course, mine. Michel Antochiw, Othón Baños Ramírez, Ramón Berzunza Pinto, Bernd Hausberger, Ueli Hostettler, Esteban Krotz, Laura Machuca, Barbara Pfeiler, Ella Fanny Quintal Avilés, Teresa Ramayo Lanz, Vera Tiesler and Lorraine Williams Beck provided intellectual and practical support in Mérida, Campeche and Mexico City. Grateful thanks also go to the directors and archivists at the Archivo General de la Nación and the Archivo Histórico Militar of the

Acknowledgments

Secretaría de la Defensa Nacional in Mexico City, the Archivo General del Estado de Yucatán and the Centro de Apoyo a la Investigación Histórica de Yucatán (now Biblioteca Yucatanense) in Mérida, the Archivo Histórico del Arzobispado de Yucatán in Conkal and the Archivo General del Estado de Campeche in Campeche. As on other occasions, it was a real pleasure to work with Sunniva Greve on the polishing of my prose.

My greatest debt is to Ute Schüren who, following her own inquiry on Yucatán's past, shared most research stays in Mexico and beyond, critically commented on earlier versions of my manuscript and helped me to express my thoughts more clearly and in a more ordered fashion.

Financial support for some of the archival research this book is based on was provided by the Deutsche Forschungsgemeinschaft.

I am very grateful for permission to reprint several photographs from the *Album fotográfico: Recuerdo de la excursion del sr. gobernador a Sta. Cruz de Bravo* (Mérida 1901) from the Crescencio Carrillo y Ancona collection held by the Biblioteca Yucatanense in Mérida, figure 14.1 from Nelson Reed's *The Caste War of Yucatán*, copyright © 1964 by Nelson Reed, © renewed 1992 and figure 18.1 courtesy of the Tozzer Library, Harvard University.

Introduction

Caste War Violence – Prospect and State of the Art

The Prospect

The nineteenth century was a particularly violent period in Latin American history. The wars of independence against Spain between 1810 and the mid-1820s brought devastation to many regions. In contrast to the relative stability of three hundred years of colonial rule, the newly independent countries were shaken by countless military coups, civil wars and popular rebellions. Society was militarized to a substantial degree since large sections of the male population participated in warfare. The collapse of colonial institutions and the long absence of a strong central government took its toll. Although the wars of independence brought freedom from colonial rule, they did little to improve the living conditions of the masses. Working conditions for laborers remained oppressive, while commercial agriculture, often devoted to export crops, expanded at the expense of peasant farming. Beyond this, the new elite of Spanish-speaking Creoles, as those of alleged Hispanic descent born in the Americas were called, dismantled the colonial laws that had partially protected the communal property of the rural, mostly indigenous, population, a move that led to widespread social unrest.[1]

Mexico was no exception to this state of affairs. A succession of more than fifty governments "ranging from monarchy or dictatorship to constitutional republicanism" headed the state between 1821 and 1857.[2] Dozens of rural uprisings unsettled the country, particularly since the 1840s.[3] These were frequently depicted by contemporary elites as racial

---

[1] See, for example, Bakewell 2004:411–442; Ohmstede 1988:14, 19; Lynch 1992:407.
[2] Cockroft 1990:62.   [3] For the uprisings, see González Navarro 1976 and Reina 1980.

Introduction

or caste wars, that is, indigenous revolts against the rest of the population.[4] The so-called *Guerra de Castas* or Caste War of Yucatán in the tropical southeast of the country, the focus of this book, was among the most important of these rural insurgencies in nineteenth-century Mexico for at least three reasons:

1. Its duration and magnitude. In its most intense phase from 1847 to the mid-1850s, it assumed the character of a full-blown civil war that affected large sections of the regional population. The conflict continued up to the beginning of the twentieth century in the form of guerilla warfare and raiding.

2. The tremendous loss of human life and material resources. The population of Yucatán dropped by more than 40 percent between 1846 and 1862 alone.[5] Thus, even in its civil war phase, the Caste War lasted longer and claimed more victims than most other wars and rebellions in nineteenth-century Mexico.[6]

3. Its consequences. After initial success in 1847–8, the rebels, who mostly stemmed from the Maya-speaking lower classes, were forced to retreat to the isolated southern and eastern areas of the Yucatán peninsula (today Quintana Roo) where they established independent polities. The rebels and their descendants became known as *kruso'b*, which in Yucatec Maya simply means "the crosses," a term derived from the religious cult that emerged among them in 1850. The cult centered on idols in the form of a cross that were imputed with the ability to speak.[7] Supported by this ideology, the rebels succeeded in maintaining their independence from the governments of Yucatán and Mexico for half a century.

---

[4] The term caste (*casta*) had two related meanings in colonial Mexico. In the narrow sense it referred to people of presumed mixed ancestry, such as mestizos or mulattoes, while in the wider sense it meant any population group in the colony, including Spaniards and Indians (e.g., DHY:99, 114). Following Independence, the term was mostly used in the sense of "race" to distinguish between Indian and non-Indian castes.

[5] Editorial, *RP*, September 11, 1867, 3–4. See Chapter 20 for a more detailed discussion of war casualties.

[6] See Chapter 21 for a brief comparison of the Caste War and other contemporary wars and insurgencies.

[7] Although several sources mention that more than one cross was venerated, the cult has become known as the Speaking (or Talking) Cross. This book uses the plural form only if indicated in the documents.

Introduction

"There is only one remedy for this war: war to the death, war without quarter."[8] This statement by an army officer in the early 1850s describes the nature of the Caste War in a nutshell. The general level of violence was indeed high during the war. Even Mexican General Severo del Castillo, director of the campaign against the Caste War rebels in the mid-1860s, had to admit that "barbarous and cruel actions were as common among whites as they were among Indians." Prisoners were occasionally mistreated or killed on the spot, and houses, property and fields destroyed.[9] Some examples indicate the spectrum of atrocities committed: Caste War rebels captured by government forces during an expedition to Bacalar in 1850 were brought to the village of Kankabchén and hanged from a scaffold, their bodies dragged by cavalrymen (*cosacos*) and flung onto a small square on the road to rancho Dzelcacab.[10] When the army attacked the rebel hideout Bolonná in late March 1855, it caught seven or eight of the defenders, who were then "put to the sword." Later, the soldiers summarily executed two captives from an ambush.[11] The rebels, for their part, frequently killed prisoners captured in combat.[12] Non-combatants likewise suffered from their outrages during assaults. When Becanchén was raided in late December 1855, for example, the rebels set fire to the village, and killed sixteen men and women, while others were burned to death in their houses.[13]

Although violence tends to appear chaotic, random and irrational, this book takes as its starting point that certain patterns, motives and underlying causes of rebellions and civil wars such as the Yucatán Caste War go beyond individual meanness and brutality. As Stathis Kalyvas, adopting ideas from Goethe and Shakespeare, puts it: "There is logic in madness and hell has its laws."[14] My hope is to bring at least some order into the apparent chaos of the fighting, looting and killing that characterized the Caste War. This order cannot be deduced from such general factors as

---

[8] Cámara Zavala 1928, part 11.

[9] GCY:37 (quote). For the killing of rebel prisoners, see J.J. Mendes to Comandancia de la 4a division en operaciones, Izamal, July 20, 1848, in M.F. Peraza to General en Jefe, Mérida, July 22, 1848, AGEY, PE, G, box 68; M.F. Peraza to General en Jefe, Valladolid, May 9, 1855, *EO*, May 15, 1855, 2–3; Suárez y Navarro, [1861] 1993:164. For more evidence on these issues, see Chapter 12. Rebel violence is discussed in Chapter 17.

[10] Baqueiro 1990, 4:103.

[11] M.F. Peraza to General en Jefe, Valladolid, March 30, 1855, AGEY, PE, G, box 100.

[12] See, for example, Ligeros apuntes de algunos episodios del sitio de Valladolid ministrados por un testigo presencial, 1848, CAIHDY, M, XLIII.1847–1849/27.

[13] Movimiento de los Bárbaros, *UL*, December 28, 1855, 4.   [14] Kalyvas 2006:388.

4   *Introduction*

poverty, oppression or racial hatred but can only evolve from careful consideration of the specific social contexts and dynamics of the violent acts concerned. I am somewhat skeptical, however, of trends in the sociology of violence that plead for a shift from "why" questions that look for reasons to "how" questions that concentrate on performance, since these minimize the importance of searching for causes. The late Trutz von Trotha denied, for example, that an understanding of violence could be found "in any 'causes' beyond the violence." In his view, the key to violence lay "in the forms of violence itself."[15] By stressing performance, nevertheless, von Trotha and others hint at a significant point, namely, that violence should be examined as a process and often a highly dynamic one at that.[16]

The following chapters are an attempt to gain a deeper understanding of the drama of the Caste War that haunted Yucatán for more than fifty years by elucidating both the structural features of politics, society and the economy (such as colonial heritage, political instability and the grabbing of peasant or national lands by the elites) and, as far as the sources permit, the situational factors that facilitated or fostered the use of violence within and between the contending parties. Although gaps remain, the available information allows for the partial reconstruction of key events and processes, of patterns of violent behavior and of the social, political and ideological context of acts of violence. Among other things, different types of violence will be discerned (internal versus external). Beyond this, tentative hypotheses on the meaning of violent action can be formulated.

Of course, no single book can do justice to the bewildering complexity of participants' motives, actions or reactions and the intended or unintended consequences of their deeds in a conflict such as the Caste War. Furthermore, several imbalances in the existing sources are reflected in this volume. Firstly, the book concentrates on the perpetrators rather than the victims of violence.[17] Secondly, it is predominantly a book about violence and men. There are several partly interrelated reasons for this. While women actively participated in rebellions in colonial Mexico, as William Taylor has shown, and took part in armed conflict in the formal

---

[15] Trotha 1997:20; see also p. 22; Sofsky 1996; Baberowski 2016:20–26, 136–39. Collins's (2008, 2009) argument seems to lead in a similar direction.

[16] Trotha 1997:21–22; Baberowski 2016:31–35, 139.

[17] These roles cannot always be separated unambiguously. The ill-treatment and exploitation of Yucatecan soldiers by their superiors is a case in point (see Chapter 11).

Introduction

role of soldiers in some societies – think of the female warriors in the West African Kingdom of Dahomey – they are heavily underrepresented as victimizers in most historical cases of collective violence.[18] As for the Caste War, little is yet known about the part women played in the conflict, not least due to the male bias of the sources, where women mostly appear as victims of male violence associated with rebel or army assaults. As Georgina Rosado Rosado and Landy Santana Rivas argue, however, it is conceivable that at least some women played a leading military, political and religious role among the Caste War rebels.[19]

Such lacunae notwithstanding, this book endeavors to provide critical data and make the Caste War accessible to the comparative study of civil wars, rebellions and collective violence.

Existing Scholarship on the Caste War

A book about violence during the Caste War in Yucatán may appear trite at first glance. What could be more obvious, more "natural," than violence in a bloody confrontation that lasted more than fifty years and took the lives of thousands? This apparent banality might explain why so little work has hitherto been done on the topic. While the general course of the war is well documented,[20] I know of no major in-depth study that concentrates on the violence of the Caste War, with the exception of pioneering work by Paul Sullivan (1997a; 2004), the books of Martha Villalobos González (2006) and Terry Rugeley (2009), and several studies of my own.[21]

Nelson Reed's *The Caste War of Yucatán* (1964) is without doubt the most widely read modern study of the conflict. With its many reprints,

---

[18] For Mexico, see Taylor 1979:116, 125, 127; for Dahomey, see Edgerton 2000. For a recent interesting discussion on the relation between gender and war, see Das 2008.

[19] Rosado Rosado and Santana Rivas 2008.

[20] See, for example, the contemporary works of the Yucatecan historians Baqueiro ([1878–1887] 1990) and Ancona ([1879/80] 1978) and the later studies of Reed (1964; 2001), Berzunza Pinto ([1965] 2001], Bricker (1981), Rugeley (1996; 2009), Careaga Viliesid (1998) and Dumond (1997).

[21] While analysis of the ethnic composition of the contending parties is provided in Gabbert (2004b and 2004c), my articles in 2005 and 2014 examine the role of violence in the rebel political organization and its economy. Robins (2005) compares some aspects of Caste War violence with the Pueblo revolt of 1680 and the Great Rebellion in Peru from 1780 to 1782, considering all of them revitalization movements that combined millennialism with a genocidal impulse. The memory of the Caste War among present-day descendants of the kruso'b is discussed in Sullivan (1984; 1989), Grube (1998), Montes (2009) and Hinz (2011; 2013).

6   *Introduction*

translation into Spanish and publication of a revised edition (2001), it drew the attention of a broader international public to the war in a hitherto remote and little-known region of Mexico. This highly readable book offers a lively account of the course of the war and of crucial aspects of rebel, social and religious organization, which will be discussed in detail in Chapter 15. War-related violence as such, however, is not analyzed in detail. The first part of Reed's book is entitled "The Two Worlds of Yucatán" (The Ladino World and the Mazehual World), highlighting the separation of non-Indians and Indians in the region. In line with this conception, Reed basically considered the Caste War a result of Maya resistance to Ladino oppression, an interpretation that continues to prevail in part of the academy and the wider public.[22]

Terry Rugeley (1996) and Don Dumond (1997), in contrast, argue that the municipal level saw intensive interaction between Indians and non-Indians (vecinos), including intermarriage, and that members of both categories participated jointly in numerous political and sometimes military affairs. While Rugeley concentrates on the decades preceding the outbreak of the conflict, Dumond offers a detailed encyclopedic account of the war, including material on hitherto rarely studied rebel groups in the south of Yucatán (*pacíficos del sur*). Careaga Viliesid (1998) discusses military confrontations up to the late 1860s and provides an extended account and interpretation of the kruso'b cult up to the 1990s. Hence, all three books present vital information on the causes, origins and development of the war, as well as on several aspects of rebel religious organization, but do not focus on Caste War violence as such.

---

[22] See, for example, Reed 1964:47–49; 2001:54–56. Several later scholars also ascribe an essentially ethnic or racial element to the war. See Buisson 1978:8, 21–22; Bartolomé 1988:179; Montalvo Ortega 1988:301, 314; Quintal Martín 1988:13; Bracamonte 1994:109–146. Robins recently imputed "exterminatory objectives" to the kruso'b and considered rebel actions consistent with "genocide" (Robins 2005:11, see also pp. 2–3, 8, 84–95, 164). Other scholars stress the class aspect of the conflict and see it as a peasant rebellion (Orlove 1979; Chi Poot 1982; Dumond 1997). They generally equate peasant and Indian, however, and therefore largely retain a dichotomous interpretation of the conflict. Montes (2009) rightly emphasizes that class relations were molded by the elite racist ideology in colonial and post-colonial Yucatán. His conceptualization of race and ethnicity nonetheless remains fuzzy; he fails to discern between ethnic (or racial) categories and communities, and pays insufficient attention to the complex relationship between social categories as ideological constructs and their ascription to people on the ground. He infers the "identity" of Caste War rebels as "Maya" from the racist ideology and racist practices prevalent among Yucatecan elites. Montes thus ends up with a dichotomic interpretation of the war as driven by the struggle of "the Maya" against Ladino oppression (see, especially, pp. 19, 51–52, 77–86, 186–187).

Introduction 7

The works of Paul Sullivan, Martha Villalobos González and Terry Rugeley are of particular importance here in addressing crucial aspects of Caste War violence. In his groundbreaking article, Sullivan (1997a) offers the first systematic study of major aspects of kruso'b warfare, such as the number, timing and duration of raids on the Yucatecan frontier, the rebel economy and the motivations of leaders and the rank-and-file to participate. His marvelous book *Xuxub Must Die* (2004) provides additional data on kruso'b raiding and the nature of rebel leadership in his meticulous analysis of one rebel assault in the 1870s. Villalobos González (2006) further deepens our understanding of the rebel economy and rebel politics in her study of the exploitation of forest resources as a major source of revenue. The exploitation of forest resources permitted the preservation of rebel autonomy for five decades, on the one hand, but became a bone of contention among the leadership, on the other, resulting in divisions and, at times, violent conflict among and between the different groups.

Rugeley's voluminous study from 2009 is a shrewd and detailed treatment of Yucatán's history from the independence era in the 1820s to the establishment of authoritarian rule in Mexico by Porfirio Díaz and the beginnings of a henequen (sisal) boom in Yucatán in the 1880s. His ambition is to fill a persistent research lacuna and to rectify what he considers the "ethnohistorical apartheid" that plagues existing scholarship, the fact that we know "more about the rebels' maroon world than about the larger Yucatecan society and how it pulled out of the wreckage and went on."[23] As Rugeley shows, not all of the region was affected by the Caste War in like manner, and conflict with rebels and their descendants became less and less important as time went on. Although violence plays a major role in his account, it is not the main analytical thrust. In contrast to the present study, which also analyzes developments in the rebel territory, he focuses on social and political institutions in areas controlled by the government.

Unlike existing scholarship, forms and patterns of violence take center stage in the present book. Violence is a reality that is molded by economic, political and social features and, in turn, molds numerous aspects of people's lives. While there is an obvious overlap in terms of sources used and topics discussed in relation to existing studies, the particular focus of this book leads to different emphases, the scrutiny of matters not exhaustively analyzed so far and, consequently, to partly divergent conclusions on key issues such as the constitutive role of internal and external violence

[23] Rugeley 2009:5.

Introduction

in the political organization of the rebels, the logic involved in killing or sparing individual categories of captives (men, women, children, upper class, lower class), and the function of internal and external violence in the government forces, on the one hand, and among the rebels, on the other.

While the Caste War is often seen by the wider public and part of scholarship as a conflict between two unitary actors, that is, the whites and the Maya or the army and the rebels,[24] it will be shown here that Indians and non-Indians fought and died on both sides. The book discusses the violence between the contending parties but also the use of force in their own camps.[25] As will be argued, violence was instrumental in shaping the social organization of the conflict groups. In addition, the nature of the war changed through time and, for some participants, violence became a means of "production" as much as of destruction. While large sections of the population suffered greatly during the war, violent acts provided others with a source of income, prestige and power.

This book is the result of an interdisciplinary endeavor that combined the painstaking investigation of primary historical sources with an explicit discussion of findings from the anthropology and sociology of violence. While the latter provided the conceptual tools to order and analyze the myriad of empirical data and allowed for the formulation of hypotheses for their interpretation, the former helped to maintain a sense of the complexities, contradictions and contingencies of social reality. Beyond this, the book is a conscious attempt to link Caste War studies to the anthropology and sociology of violence and war, and to make this case more accessible to comparative social science research. The relationship between violence and political organization and their commonalities and particularities in both conflict groups (Caste War rebels and government forces) is discussed and correlated with the results of comparative studies of armed groups.

The Sources

This book is based on the study of extensive unpublished documents from various archives in Mexico City (Archivo General de la Nación, AGN; and Archivo Histórico Militar, Secretaría de la Defensa Nacional,

---

[24] Cf. Villalobos González 2006 and Paoli Bolio 2015 for recent examples.

[25] I make no distinction between unjust violence and violence as the legitimate exertion of force, since the evaluation of certain acts as legitimate or illegitimate is frequently disputed by both participants and observers.

Introduction 9

AHM), Mérida (Archivo General del Estado de Yucatán, AGEY; and Centro de Apoyo a la Investigación Histórica de Yucatán, CAIHDY, now Biblioteca Yucatanense), Conkal (Archivo Histórico del Arzobispado de Yucatán, AHAY; and Archivo Carrillo y Ancona del Seminario de Yucatán, ACASY) and Campeche (Archivo General del Estado de Campeche, AGEC), and published primary sources such as the official newspapers of the states of Yucatán and Campeche from the 1840s to the end of the nineteenth century. Many of the sources provide data on the damage caused by rebel assaults, the course of military expeditions, and occasionally a body count of putative rebels who were captured, wounded or killed. They offer comparatively little detailed information on specific contexts, however, or on the performance of individual acts of violence. Nevertheless, numerous military reports contain descriptions of armed engagements. Statements by captured rebels and former prisoners of the insurgents give major insights into everyday life, including the role of violence.

With respect to the Caste War, the researcher faces a problem familiar from the study of insurgencies of subaltern groups in general, namely, that the overwhelming majority of the sources stems from the pen of rebel adversaries. There are, however, some written statements by insurgents, including internal military and mundane communications, proclamations of the Speaking Cross habitually signed with "Juan de la Cruz" (John of the Cross), letters to the government and correspondence with priests, officials and others. These provide at least a glimpse of their worldviews.

Of course, none of these sources can be taken at face value but should be critically interrogated for their ideological background and political or personal aims, such as inflating enemy losses to promote one's military success. The problem of biased or entirely false accounts is particularly acute in conflict and war, since accusations of undue violence are made regularly to discredit the adversary. Only rarely are we lucky enough to come across documents that reveal such attempts, as occurred with reference to the nature of the Caste War. While the Yucatán government depicted the conflict in its public discourse as a race war, in which the Indian population set out to exterminate the peninsula's non-Indian inhabitants, the governor explicitly denied this claim in a classified document from 1847 I found in the state archive in Mérida.[26] We are frequently less

---

[26] See Chapter 18.

Introduction

fortunate, however, and do not have the necessary sources at our disposal to verify accounts of violence. While statements by adversaries should thus be treated with caution, other people may also have an interest in inventing or distorting evidence. Such is the case, for example, with the story of a farm hand who presented himself in Mérida in 1862 as Isidoro Chan from the town of Pisté. He informed the authorities that he had been kidnapped by the kruso'b in a raid on the said town and described in gruesome detail some of the atrocities they had committed. Having entangled himself in contradictions, however, it transpired that he had never been to Pisté and that in reality his name was Isidoro Tun. He had invented the story to disguise the fact that he was a fugitive peon from a hacienda near Tixpéual.[27] The main tools at our disposal for veracity control of our sources are the examination of logical consistency, the search for internal contradictions and, where available, cross checks with other accounts of the same event.

The Structure of the Book

Part I briefly discusses the results from the anthropology and sociology of violence that seem most significant for the topic of this book. These help to understand the dynamics of the Caste War and to recognize the key structural and social contexts in which violent acts evolved. Rather than interpreting it as an irrational outburst of atavistic instincts, violence should be understood in most cases as a multi-faceted means to achieve certain ends. It can be used to obtain material gain, establish dominance or express ideas. Violence and war have strong transformative qualities, so that the political, social or ethnic composition of the contending parties and their motives for fighting can undergo change over time. In addition, the reasons why leaders take part in the struggle may differ radically from those of the rank and file.

Part II gives a short description of Yucatán's key social characteristics in the nineteenth century, allowing the reader to place subsequent chapters in their historical context. The persistence of colonial structures and the enduring importance of racist arguments in the elite discourse following Yucatán's independence from Spain in 1821 are fundamental to understanding the conflicts that led to the outbreak of the Caste War and its interpretation by numerous contemporary observers as a racial

---

[27] Rugeley 2009:149–150.

Introduction

fray. It is shown, furthermore, that for many Yucatecans violence was part of everyday life beyond the rebellion, particularly in the countryside. Widespread destruction and cruelty to combatants and non-combatants alike had been common in previous insurgencies and wars, and re-emerged in the frequent uprisings and coups that haunted Yucatán during the Caste War.

Part III provides a chronological outline of the principal events and phases of the uprising and serves as a guideline and contextualization for the more topical discussions in subsequent chapters. The chapters in this part discuss the origins of the Caste War in the strife between two Yucatecan political factions in 1847 and describe the advance of the rebels up to mid-1848, their retreat to the southeast of the peninsula due to internal discord and the arrival of government troop reinforcements. Particular attention is given to the most intense combat period that saw a ruthless counter-insurgency campaign lasting until the mid-1850s. The rebels were indomitable, however, and created independent polities whose autonomy endured until 1901, when Mexican forces finally crushed rebel resistance in a massive military offensive.

Parts IV and V discuss the structural and situational features that fostered violence both within and between the contending parties. Internal violence played a crucial role when it came to enforcing order and military discipline, as a deterrent against desertion or to gaining and preserving status and power among the rebels. In addition to military considerations in the narrow sense, the need to procure food by harvesting enemy cornfields, for example, or the quest for enrichment by looting or putting prisoners to work often triggered external violence. Both rebel and government forces were guilty of strategic massacres and other atrocities in a show of force or an attempt to demoralize the enemy and, at times, of situational carnages as acts of hatred and revenge.

While material incentives partly provoked violent behavior in soldiers, Part V argues that the use of force by and among the kruso'b cannot be understood in isolation from their political organization or their economy, which was based on looting Yucatecan settlements and lumbering in the area under their control. When the original military and social organization became untenable as a result of death, destruction, flight and dispersal during the war, the religious cult of the Speaking Cross provided solace and hope, and an alternative organizational focus. Allegiance to the town of origin and a number of chiefs endowed with traditional legitimacy as community leaders was replaced by identification with the cult and fealty to potent warriors. Rebel leaders began to legitimize their violent deeds as "orders from the cross." Beyond this, the use of force was an essential component of the emerging political structure, which could be described as strongmen rule (*caudillaje* or caudillo politics).

Part VI summarizes the main results of the empirical chapters and asks what they reveal about earlier characterizations of the Caste War as a racial or class conflict. In addition, it provides an overview of the magnitude of the casualties suffered in the conflict, combatant and noncombatant alike. The chapters in this part also consider general conclusions to be drawn from the empirical material on violence in the Caste War in particular and in insurgencies and civil wars in general. Army and rebel violence show both striking similarities and a number of differences. Force was used, for example, to maintain internal discipline and order. Over and above, violence served both military and economic ends. The acquisition of booty was a key motive for violent action in both groups. In kruso'b society, however, violence was far more relevant as a constitutive feature of its political structure than in the case of the army, which was embedded in a more sophisticated bureaucratic structure.

The Appendices provide vital information on the dynamics of the Caste War. The voluminous tables summarize the quantitative information I found on rebel assaults and army attacks. Concise and in chronological order, they represent most of the data on which this book is based. Although some minor events may be missing due to a lack of relevant data, to my knowledge this is the most detailed and most extensive compilation on these issues up to now.[28] It presents information on targets, military strength, the number, gender and status of victims (Indian or non-Indian), the amount of booty taken, and the losses and casualties suffered by the respective attackers. These facts allow us to grasp the changing nature of the war and gain key insights into the structure of individual rebel assaults on Yucatecan and pacífico settlements, on the one hand, and army thrusts into rebel territory, on the other.

---

[28] Sullivan (1997a, I:cuadro I) provides considerable information on rebel assaults from 1853 to 1886. An almost identical table, with some additional data on looted cattle, is published in Villalobos González (2006:281–285). None of these charts include data on rebel leaders, the gender and status of Yucatecan victims or the booty obtained by the kruso'b. Sullivan also gives some information on other rebel and army campaigns (1997a, I:cuadro II and II:cuadro II).

Note to the Reader

All translations of foreign language quotations are mine; emphasis is in the original unless otherwise indicated. The spelling of Yucatec Maya follows the CORDEMEX dictionary (1980) or what is used in the sources. Variations in the orthography of the primary sources cited have been respected. The use of accents and the spelling of personal and place names may therefore vary. Authors did not distinguish consistently, for example, between "b" and "v" in Spanish.

PART I

VIOLENCE AND WAR

Despite its apparent concreteness, defining "violence" is a complex affair, since it refers to a certain form of human interaction with potentially different intentions, perceptions and assessments of a specific situation. Scholars also employ the term to denote instances of physical or mental harm. Johan Galtung even extended the meaning of "violence" to include structural features such as poverty, exploitation and discrimination.[1] Although this is part of a laudable effort to denounce the exploitation of human beings by their own kind, I think it curtails the term's usefulness as an analytic category, since the range of occurrences it embraces is too diverse. In addition, it becomes indiscernible from phenomena typically subsumed under the categories of oppression, exploitation or discrimination. Hunger, for example, can either be the result of structural forces, such as high market prices for edibles that prevent the poor from buying them, or of denying people access to food through the use of physical force as in the case of looting or destroying the crops of a peasant village. While both processes can lead to starvation of the victims, their structure, duration and visibility differ considerably. I will therefore confine my discussion to instances of physical force and define violence as interaction "in the course of which at least one of the parties intentionally and against the will of its counterpart takes action that causes or could cause physical harm."[2]

[1] Galtung 1969, 1990.   [2] Gabbert 2004a:97.

I

Violence in Anthropological and Sociological Perspective

Although violence is not the most common method of conflict processing, it is certainly the most dramatic in its immediate impact on the human body and the mind. It seems to be a phenomenon intrinsic to human society from the outset. In the words of French anthropologist Georges Balandier: "In the beginning was violence, and all history can be seen as an unending effort to control it."[3] Violence is frequently regarded as an outbreak of atavistic impulses or urges, as antisocial and deviant.[4] Anthropology and other social sciences have shown, however, that the use of force tends to follow certain rules, is culturally shaped and has consequences that are not merely destructive. Conflict and violence cannot therefore "be dismissed as exceptional, irrational, immoral, meaningless, a sign of social pathology, or the result of either the actions of 'evil men' or the putative presence of 'violent instincts.'"[5] Rather than addressing acts of violence as sudden outbursts of human nature, the present study treats them as cultural products whose frequency, forms and meanings cannot be understood in isolation from their specific social and historical context. Violent acts may seem appallingly similar in terms of injury, destruction and death but they are shaped by ideas, meanings and logics that differ from one collectivity to another and change over time.[6]

---

[3] Balandier 1986:499.
[4] See, for example, the classic formulation of that view by Lorenz (1974).
[5] Sluka 1992:24.
[6] See also Coronil and Skurski 1991:289; Sluka 1992:24; Krohn-Hansen 1997:235; Trotha 1997:33.

The late David Riches wondered why actors opted for violence so often despite the risks involved, the difficulty of controlling it, its social disapproval in many circumstances and its status as merely one option. Contrary to established opinion, he conceived violence essentially as a means to achieve certain ends.[7] "Inherently liable to be contested on the question of legitimacy," violence is particularly apt to express opposition. It is highly visible and requires "relatively little by way of specialized equipment or esoteric knowledge."[8] Since it operates both instrumentally (causes change in the social environment) and expressively (dramatizes certain ideas), actors find it attractive:

The expressive function of acts or images of violence capitalizes, firstly, on the visibility of violence, and secondly on the probability that all involved – however different their cultural backgrounds – are likely to draw, at the very least, some basic common understanding from the acts and images concerned. These two properties of violence make it an excellent communication vehicle.[9]

This, of course, does not deny the occurrence of misunderstandings about the concrete meaning of certain acts of violence. Burning down one's house or killing one's kin, however, can hardly be misread as acts of friendship.

Georg Elwert, like Riches, considered violence in most cases a means–end rational action strategy. Of crucial importance is his distinction between, firstly, kinds of violence related – up to a point – to instinctively steered processes, secondly, instrumental varieties based precisely on the exclusion of such elements and, thirdly, strategic forms that employ others as instruments of violence. As Elwert rightly pointed out, it is the third form that is most important among humans.[10] Instinct-related aspects of violence should therefore be distinguished analytically from instrumental aspects. Furthermore, when exploring the motives for violence, we must differentiate between the immediate perpetrators and the "strategists" behind them.

Although conflict and violence are frequently perceived as negative and as pathological traits in society, Lewis Coser, following Georg Simmel, developed a more agnostic view. He showed that conflicts can have "positive functions," at least for certain actors or groups.[11] Conflicts

---

[7] Riches 1986:12; see also Kalyvas 2006:28; Eisner 2009.
[8] Riches 1986:11; see also Kalyvas 2006:25–28.   [9] Riches 1986:11–12.
[10] Elwert 1997:86–87.
[11] Coser 1956, 1967; Simmel [1908] 1995. See also Gluckman's work (1955) on the integrating effects of the feud. Durham (1976) argues that war is adaptive under

In Anthropological and Sociological Perspective

have the power, for example, to strengthen, or even establish, group identity and cohesion.[12] In the words of Schiefenhövel, "Martial aggression is a means of cementing the boundary with 'the other' and thereby one's own identity, especially in critical situations."[13] In a similar vein, Jenkins considers killing "the ultimate form of categorization."[14] Aggression toward outsiders holds the group together. As Simmel and Coser have argued, the expression of hostility toward outsiders allows social relations within the group to be maintained even in contexts of stress. It constitutes a safety valve that provides "substitute objects upon which to displace hostile sentiments as well as a means of abreaction of aggressive tendencies" in order to release tension.[15] It is perfectly possible that a struggle is taken up to preserve or reorder the structure and cohesion of the group rather than to achieve certain ends with regard to the adversary.[16] Hence dealing with the consequences of violent acts calls for a distinction between their effect within the group concerned and those on other groups. The group-preserving function of violence may, in the course of the conflict, override the original material or strategic motives. Violence should therefore be studied historically and in terms of process. As mentioned earlier, it has the potential to develop its own momentum, one that is only loosely related to factors such as the economic or political circumstances responsible for its onset.[17] Beyond this, the temporal dimension is important in several ways:

Firstly, people perform violent acts more readily once they have become routine, making their recurrence more probable.

Secondly, socialization practices can foster the inclination to employ violence.[18] Contrary to the widespread assumption (at least among the broader public) of the "violent nature of man," the late Walter Goldschmidt (1989) rightly asserted the cultural nature of war, stressing

---

conditions of competition for scarce resources in pre-state societies. Balandier (1986:507–509) lists the precolonial Mawri in Niger as an example of a society that prefers war to peace. War contributed significantly to group cohesion by reducing the internal exploitation of tributary peasants by warriors, since the former were party to the spoils of new campaigns.

[12] Coser 1956:34, 87, 104; Simmel [1908] 1995:284–290.   [13] Schiefenhövel 1995:359.
[14] Jenkins 1997:65; see also Schlichte 2009:63–64.
[15] Coser 1956:155; see also pp. 39–40, 164 n. 16.   [16] Coser 1956:105.
[17] Riches 1986:9; Trotha 1997:18, 21. Feldman, for example, noted the "growing autonomy of violence as a self-legitimating sphere of social discourse and transaction" in the conflict in Northern Ireland in the twentieth century (1991:5, cited in Krohn-Hansen 1997:236).
[18] Cf., for example, Chagnon's (1983) work on the Yanomamö. See also Schiefenhövel 1995:357.

the significance of child-rearing and positive reinforcement in the making of violence-prone warriors: "[T]he society shapes natural human capacities and potentialities to its accepted purposes, reinforcing some and suppressing others. It does this by systematically rewarding and punishing, by indoctrinating youth, creating role models to be emulated, and honoring those who perform well with special prestige and influence."[19]

Cultural norms imply encouragement or restraint of the capacity for aggressive behavior in socialization but also inform ideas of when and against whom the use of force is seen as legitimate. They furthermore indicate how violence is to be realized, the tools to be employed, the adequate degree of force in specific situations and the modes of killing considered acceptable, honorable or particularly cruel.

Thirdly, violence changes the perception of time profoundly. Long-term planning becomes increasingly obsolete and the here-and-now gains in significance.[20]

Fourthly, violence as a "memory-shaping reality" (*erinnerungsmächtige Wirklichkeit*) reorganizes the past, the present and the future. Tradition and folklore are dominated in many groups by narratives of violence, war, triumph and defeat. Histories of violence constitute the main routes of identity formation through, for example, the "invention of tradition" in contemporary ethnopolitics.[21] Memories of the Caste War still play a key role in the self-perception of rebel descendants in today's Quintana Roo and their dissociation from Spanish- and Maya-speaking populations in the Yucatán peninsula.[22]

Fifthly, prolonged conflict has a crucial effect on the structure of the groups involved. As Coser pointed out:

Groups which are engaged in continued struggle [with other groups] tend to lay claim on the total personality involvement of their members so that internal conflict would tend to mobilize all energies and affects of the members. Hence such groups are unlikely to tolerate more than limited departures from the group unity. In such groups there is a tendency to suppress conflict; where it occurs, it leads the group to break up through splits or through forced withdrawal of dissenters.[23]

---

[19] Goldschmidt 1989:24; see also Schlichte 2009:59. Ember and Ember (1994:620) found that socialization for aggression was a likely consequence of war, leading to higher rates of interpersonal violence. Values, child-rearing and reinforcement practices in a particular society may, of course, differ greatly from one group to another.

[20] Trotha 1997:25; Schlichte 2009:58, 61–62.

[21] Trotha 1997:26; see also Baumann 2009.

[22] Several seminal studies have analyzed the historical consciousness of rebel descendants. See in particular Sullivan 1984; Montes 2009; Hinz 2013.

[23] Coser 1956:153.

In Anthropological and Sociological Perspective

The anthropology and sociology of violence contribute to understanding acts that seem particularly irrational and cruel, such as the killing of women and children. David Riches suggested that the perpetrators legitimize these acts as a form of tactical preemption designed to forestall the "indirect threat" posed by women and children, and their emotional and economic support for enemy fighters.[24] In addition to instrumental considerations, such as weakening the morale of the enemy and their material bases by depriving the fighters of a female labor force and emotional support, and destroying their families and their future, the expressive quality of violence is important. As Ruth Seifert has shown, gender-specific violence such as mass rape is in many instances an integral part of the struggle rather than a marginal excess committed in a war situation. Not only does it harm the women affected, it can also be interpreted as an attempt to humiliate male opponents, whose masculinity is questioned if they are shown to be incapable of protecting their wives and daughters. Thus, a hierarchy of male dominance is established on both sides and enemy morale undermined through the abuse and objectification of women.[25]

While tactical preemption is "the initiating purpose (or 'primary meaning') of violence" in merely a minority of instances, it is crucial to legitimizing the perpetrators' use of force.[26] In fact, the idea of tactical preemption is so malleable that it can be employed to justify almost any kind of atrocity. Its legitimizing capacity is confined solely by the norms of the dominant group, such as the belief that "real men" refuse to fight women and children or that killing non-combatants violates the warrior ethos.

Although violence is more than the chaotic explosion of aggressive urges and the underlying logics of certain patterns can be uncovered, there will always be major puzzles that remain unsolved. Apart from instrumental and strategic calculations, emotions and contingencies are vital to *some* acts of violence. Factors that lead to the use of force are, for example, revenge, fear or the desire for respect and recognition.[27] The use of violence is particularly attractive to people who lack other means to establish a personal identity, acquire status and gain the respect of

---

[24] Riches 1986:6.   [25] Seifert 1995:25–29; 1996:35–37; see also Schiefenhövel 1995:349.
[26] Riches 1986:5, 7.
[27] For the role of these factors in war, see, for example, Schlichte 2009:79–82; Eisner 2009:48–53; Kalyvas 2006:60.

22   *Part I: Violence and War*

others.[28] Demonstrations of physical strength, courage or cruelty enable those who lack economic or social capital to present themselves as valuable associates.[29]

Although human beings have an innate capacity for fighting (as well as for cooperative behavior), combat is of necessity an exceptional situation involving an enormous amount of stress, especially if it occurs hand-to-hand or at close quarters. Sorokin characterized the mental condition of fighters as "abnormal, high-voltage emotionality." Fear of being maimed or killed, the combatant's "all-pervading and dominant emotion," calls for neutralization by "counter-forces such as the sense of duty, courage, shame, and the fear of being shot in the back," which in turn leads to a "terrible inner struggle."[30]

Many other emotions are aroused, such as *intense compassion for and commiseration* with killed and wounded companions, *rage and hatred* toward the enemy; *exaltation* in victory and utter *despair* in defeat; *admiration* for heroism and *reprobation* of cowardice; *indignation* at ignoble actions and *approbation* of noble ones; *satisfaction* with the faithful discharge of duty and *repentance* for failure. These and many other emotions are incessantly aroused by war and revolutionary situations. They all attain high-voltage intensity; they all rapidly come and go, rendering the whole emotional life highly turbulent and unstable. The disturbance is further reinforced by hundreds of trying conditions inseparable from war and revolution: the lack of necessities and elementary comforts; dirt and filth; the sight of ruin and destruction, including the corpses of the victims; pain from wounds and privations; the environment of prison and concentration camps; anxiety for the safety of dear ones; and the like.[31]

Moreover, emotional and strategic motives for violence often go together. As Coser, following the lead of Simmel, remarked: "It is useful to hate the opponent." Affective energy can be mobilized for the struggle to achieve certain ends, such as defeat of the enemy, and "is likely to strengthen the parties to the conflict."[32] The motivation to use force can differ among the perpetrators. Violence may be a strategic tool for leaders, for example, but expressive for their followers.[33]

---

[28] Coser 1956:78–80; see also Lifton 1996:92–93.   [29] Riches 1986:13.

[30] Sorokin 1942:22–23. See also Goldschmidt 1989:17–19; Hughbank and Grossman 2013:495. For the possible traumatic consequences of fighting and killing, notably at close quarters, see Grossman (1996:31, 43–44, 59, 61–62).

[31] Sorokin 1942:25, emphasis in original.   [32] Coser 1956:58.   [33] Kalyvas 2006:26.

2

Violence in Organized Groups

Organized groups of combatants such as warrior bands or armies are shaped by violence in at least two ways. One is their capacity to exert force against outsiders when, for instance, enemies are attacked or the squad is defended against external aggression. Violence is also frequently applied to group members, a general point exemplified by an event that occurred during the Caste War. While justifying the death sentence imposed by one of his commanders on the spearheads of an army mutiny in the town of Tihosuco in 1851, General Rómulo Díaz de la Vega, commander-in-chief in Yucatán, expressed an idea that to a certain degree seems valid for all armed forces:

I feel deeply sorry about the punishment Colonel Rosado has imposed on the ringleaders of the sedition, but it was highly necessary because if crimes such as the one that concerns us here are left unpunished, subordination and military discipline, without which it is impossible to command masses of armed men, would cease entirely.[1]

The threat of force and its actual use are crucial to upholding discipline in any organized group of combatants, since a certain amount of coordination, and thus subordination, is indispensable to minimizing peer risks during the struggle and creating conditions for maximum success. The degree of coordination and subordination and how it is guaranteed can vary considerably, of course, depending, among other things, on the structure (e.g., internal hierarchy and distinction of roles) and size of the

---

[1] R. Díaz de la Vega to MGM, Peto, August 25, 1851, AHM, XI/481.3/3259.

armed groups, the type of weaponry used, the incentives to fight and the perceived legitimacy of the struggle as such and the leaders in particular.[2] The stronger the motives of individual combatants to fight, the lesser the amount of disciplinary force threatened or employed.

Several methods are used to control combatant fear. Prevalent in this context are drugs (mostly alcohol), routinization (training, military drill) and rituals (to guarantee victory, to render combatants invulnerable or to purify killers).[3] In addition, the inhibition to kill other human beings must be overcome. As numerous studies show, humans are not natural born killers. Instead "in the brains of healthy members of the human race, we appear to have a powerful resistance to killing our own kind."[4]

Most participants in close combat are literally "frightened out of their wits," as the saying goes. Once the arrows or bullets start flying, combatants stop thinking with the forebrain (that part of the brain which makes us human). Instead, their thought processes localize in the midbrain, or mammalian brain, that primitive part of the brain generally indistinguishable from that of an animal. At this point, the trust in one's training, equipment, and fellow warrior become [sic] the essence of how a person acts in the chaos known as combat.

In conflict situations, this primitive, midbrain processing can be observed in a consistent trend toward resisting and avoiding killing one's own species.[5]

This trend is strongest in hand-to-hand combat. It abates when the victim has his back turned to the perpetrator as if in flight, when weapons are used or when the enemy is at a distance, since "the farther away you are the easier it is to kill."[6] Consequently it is much more difficult to slay an enemy with a knife or machete than to kill hundreds by dropping a bomb from a plane. Herbert Kelman has tried to answer the question of how "normal" people can participate in massacres and even kill the defenseless. He identified three major psychological processes: 1. the routinization of violent acts; 2. a context where victims are systematically dehumanized; and 3. authoritarian situations where the actor does not

---

[2] See, for example, Simmel ([1908] 1995:350–352) and the discussion on hierarchy and organization in armed rebel groups in Schlichte (2009:144–177). There is a vast array of possible motives for fighting, among them defense, enrichment, ideology and personal loyalty to a leader.

[3] Goldschmidt 1989:19–22; Grossman 1996:132, 270–273. See also Hoffman (2011:224–251) for an interesting interpretation of the use of war magic in Africa.

[4] Hughbank and Grossman 2013:498. See also Grossman 1996:xiv, 1–4, 11, 16, 22, 27–28, 97–98, 118, 253.

[5] Hughbank and Grossman 2013:497.

[6] Hughbank and Grossman 2013:499–501 (quote from p. 500).

Violence in Organized Groups

consider himself responsible for his deeds.[7] The routinization of violence reduces the need to make decisions and facilitates repression of its implications. The focus lies on the details. The "task" can be subdivided into small steps executed "automatically." Thus, repressive institutions such as armies are mostly characterized by a complex division of labor that leads to diffusion of responsibility and mutual affirmation of the normality or legitimacy of the deeds performed.[8]

Ethological studies have shown that in several species, including humans, "empathy is biased toward the in-group."[9] As Schlichte rightly argues, "there is always a distinction between the rules that apply to the group and those that apply to non-members." Boundaries between members and non-members harden in the course of conflict, group images become more stereotypical and norms become "rigid moral orders that in turn allow for further violence." Violent conflict reinforces and radicalizes the distinction between insider and outsider.[10] Frequently, the enemy is not simply considered different but almost as belonging to a different species. This dehumanization of opponents is an important factor in the development of extreme forms of violence and massacres, as Kelman has stressed: "Thus when a group of people is defined entirely in terms of a category to which they belong, and when this category is excluded from the human family, then the moral restraints against killing them are more readily overcome."[11] Cultural, social, moral, mechanical or physical distance helps the killer to dismiss the humanity of the victim. Killing is easier when the victim is seen as culturally alien, socially different (e.g., as belonging to a different caste or class), deserving of his fate, hit from a distance or perceived through a technical instrument (such as a night-vision or computer screen device).[12]

Participation in violent acts and massacres is enhanced when these are "explicitly ordered, implicitly encouraged, tacitly approved, or at least permitted by legitimate authorities."[13] The need for individuals to make personal judgements in these situations is reduced, bringing a different

---

[7] Kelman 1973:38–52. See also Grossman 1996:186–192, 252, 255–256; Bandura 1999; Baberowski 2016:28–29, 41–42.

[8] Kelman 1973:39–44, 46–48; see also Hinton 1996:827–828; Hughbank and Grossman 2013:505.

[9] De Waal 2013:xiv.   [10] Schlichte 2009:66.

[11] Kelman 1973:49. See also Lifton 1996:92; Grossman 1996:252, 255; Bandura 1999:200–201.

[12] Grossman 1996:158–170.

[13] Kelman 1973:39. See also pp. 40–46; Grossman 1996:143–145.

26   *Part I: Violence and War*

sense of morality into play. People may assume they have no choice but to obey orders and thus shift responsibility for their acts onto their superiors. Numerous studies indicate that, in general, the strongest motive for fighting is not hate, fear or ideology but group pressure and the desire to gain the recognition of comrades and leaders, the reputation of the group or the will to contribute to its success.[14] It should be kept in mind that massacres and other atrocities are frequently committed as a deliberate warfare strategy rather than a spontaneous act by combatants running wild. Their object is to scare people, to induce them to flee or to break the will of the enemy. Beyond this, atrocities create a strong bond between the perpetrators and their commanders, thus binding them more firmly to the group cause. Shared guilt leaves little room for reconciliation with the adversary and prevents those inclined to surrender from doing so.[15]

VIOLENCE IN CIVIL WAR

While the concept of war is frequently reserved for interpolity violence, warfare can be defined for the present purpose in the broadest sense as "a particular type of political relationship between groups, in which the groups use, or threaten to use, lethal force against each other in pursuit of their aims." Unlike other types of violence, war is made by organized collectivities, not individuals.[16] As Kalyvas points out, war is a "social and political environment fundamentally different from peace in at least two crucial ways." The constraints are many and the risks incomparably higher for everyone involved: "It is one thing to vote for a political party but quite another to fight (and possibly die) for it."[17] War situations increase polarization of the participants concerned, heighten uncertainty and alter expectations.[18] Violence in a counter-insurgency war, in particular, can become habitual, "the normal mode of behaviour": "In such a situation one reacts to any kind of surprise or threat with immediate violence."[19]

---

[14] Grossman 1996:89–90, 149–152; Hughbank and Grossman 2013:502–505.

[15] See, for example, Grossman 1996:207–211.

[16] Harrison 2002:561 (quote); Ferguson 1984:3–5. See Cohen (1984:330) for the narrow conceptualization of the term. While the definition employed here is far from precise and avoids specification of the size and structure of the groups involved as well as the extent of combat and casualties, it stresses the social nature of war and seems sufficient for the aims of this book.

[17] Kalyvas 2006:38.   [18] Kalyvas 2006:38.   [19] Lifton 1996:92.

Violence in Organized Groups

Civil wars differ from interpolity wars insofar as the contending parties are *"subject to a common authority at the outset of the hostilities."*[20] They frequently imply guerilla tactics and counter-insurgency strategies that are particularly savage, with a disproportionate share of non-combatant victims. In addition, the violence here is "more intimate," often among people with a high degree "of closeness and peaceful interactions."[21] This may be due to the fact that, apart from armies, irregular forces play a vital role, blurring the boundary between combatants and non-combatants. In addition, as Coser has suggested, the closer the relationship between the participants, the more intense the struggle. Since hostile feelings in this context are normally suppressed to a significant degree, they can accumulate over time, intensifying the conflict once it breaks out.[22]

Kalyvas recently stressed the dynamic character of collective violence and criticized civil war research for its primary focus on the determinants of the conflict's "onset, duration and termination, and its effects" rather than on the struggle per se.[23] This seems particularly lamentable since civil war, as in other cases of enduring violence, is driven by its own momentum, which in turn can lead to fundamental changes in the composition of the contending parties or their motives for fighting. Why the war broke out in the first place may become secondary or even obsolete in the course of the conflict. Different actors have different motives for joining the struggle. Events on the ground may not be driven by the master cleavage. Settling old grudges with neighbors, exploiting opportunities for self-enrichment and other local or personal motives, for example, can be important contributing factors.[24] Kalyvas highlights war as a phenomenon that "transforms individual preferences, choices, behavior, and identities" and violence as the principal channel through which it "exercises its transformative function."[25] He provides a succinct summary of further dynamics that can lead to the generalization of violence and atrocities in civil wars. The breakdown of established political order "reveals or creates a culture of generalized brutalization" and "gives rise to undisciplined armed groups that prey on civilians." The "endless spiral of retaliation" stems from the absence of law enforcement, while lack of security leads to massive preemptive violence. Violence is almost omnipresent, social control eliminated, peaceful skills unlearned and new violent skills acquired. This environment sees the rise to prominence of

---

[20] Kalyvas 2006:5, emphasis in original.
[21] Kalyvas 2006:11; see also pp. 330–334; Valentino, Huth and Balch-Lindsay 2004.
[22] Coser 1956:68.   [23] Kalyvas 2005:93.   [24] Kalyvas 2006:3–5; Schlichte 2009:78.
[25] Kalyvas 2006:389.

"people with a propensity for violence" and the emergence of "vested interests in the use of violence." Contrary to most interstate wars, civil wars brutalize both civilians and soldiers with "unremitting exposure to violence."[26] Furthermore, civil wars afford ample opportunity for what Kalyvas has called "indirect violence," when the force of the contending parties is tapped by civilians in pursuit of their own aims. Hence, as Kalyvas has rightly stressed, non-combatants should be considered agents in their own right: "While political actors 'use' civilians to collect information and win the war, it is also the case that civilians 'use' political actors to settle their own private conflicts."[27] Civilians may try, for example, to exploit one of the contending parties to settle old scores by falsely denouncing a hated neighbor as an insurgent supporter. While Kalyvas's remarks help to see civilians not merely as objects or victims of war, the case should not be overstated. The strategies he mentions are not open to all non-combatants and room to maneuver is limited for most of them.

The form and degree of violence employed by the contending civil war parties ties in with economic factors such as the sources tapped to ensure material survival. The methods of procuring the necessary resources vary markedly in the degree of force required. Resources can come from external allies such as neighboring states or diaspora communities abroad. One example is the Irish community in the United States and its support for the Irish Republican Army (IRA) in the twentieth century. In this case, little or no force was required. Members of the diaspora, however, can be pressed into contributing to the group cause. If these sources are absent or inadequate, the contending parties are obliged to live off the land they occupy, implying a far greater degree of violence. This involves depriving people who are unwilling to support them with food, valuables or land. Hence, insurgents plunder government-controlled areas, prey on the population in contested territories or those under their control, and attempt to set up enterprises to exploit resources or realize productive activities.[28] Similar holds for the regular armed forces when the government is unwilling or unable to secure their provisioning. Reliance on plunder or illegal trading activities seems to go hand in hand with a high level of violence toward non-participants of the contending parties (brutality against civilians, terrorist methods, forced recruitment) as well as toward those within the group (strong discipline, severe sanctions, combatant conditioning).[29]

---

[26] Kalyvas 2006:55–56.   [27] Kalyvas 2006:14; see also pp. 36, 343–350.
[28] See, for example, Rufin 1999.   [29] Rufin 1999:44.

CONCLUSION

Violence and war are extremely complex phenomena that need to be studied from different angles. As this and the previous chapter have shown, violence can have a variety of forms (affective, instrumental and strategic), functions (change of environment, dramatization of ideas), meanings (revenge, demonstration of dominance) and motives (rage, greed, the quest for liberation). Thus individual acts of violence are the outcome of a complex interplay of factors that either conflict with or mutually reinforce one another. Rage, for example, can drive combatants to avenge their dead comrades by slaughtering war prisoners despite orders from their superiors to spare their lives in an attempt to de-escalate the struggle. Commanders, too, exploit sadistic individuals by letting them do the dirty work of torturing captives to obtain information. It is therefore nigh to impossible to sort out the factors that lead to the final outcome in single instances of violence. The study of multiple cases, however, reveals certain underlying patterns.

With the exception of self-harm, violent acts imply at least two parties, i.e., victims and victimizers, who are normally implicated in some form of social relationship (competition, envy, domination). As the anthropology and sociology of conflict have shown, however, to grasp the rationality behind violent acts it seems important in a number of cases to examine their effect on the perpetrators rather than on the victims. Scapegoating, demonstrating ruthlessness toward internal competitors for leadership or committing atrocities to bind participants more strongly to the group cause are some examples that come to mind.

Insurgencies and civil wars such as the Caste War in Yucatán are not singular events in sequence but rather interrelated chains of violent acts. While situational factors and contingencies are of major importance, individual deeds can only be understood as elements of a comprehensive process with its own momentum. The original motive for the struggle may become less significant or entirely irrelevant in the course of the conflict. As we will see, the practical necessities of warfare on the ground, such as adequate provisions for soldiers, can carry more weight than any strategic plans the leadership might pursue.

PART II

VIOLENCE IN YUCATÁN BEFORE AND BEYOND THE CASTE WAR, 1821–1901

The caste war, that is to say, barbarism as against civilization, do you know what this means? A threat, a constant menace to the interests of the district; a threat and a menace that must be destroyed at all costs, otherwise it will be the cancer that slowly erodes the guts of the district …. It is necessary, it is urgent, it is imperative that we combine our efforts, focus on destroying the savage, defeat him, bring him war to deliver him civilization thereafter … It is a shame that in the age of electricity and steam power a handful of savages keeps progress and the Enlightenment in check.

That is why we should all work … to save society threatened by the barbarian's incendiary torch and destructive axe. … Marching as one man to destroy the Indian, the Indian … who is born lying, grows up stealing and dies cheating. That is why it is necessary … for the sword of Hernan Cortez to join the civilizing propagator [*propagadora civilizadora*] of Las Casas.[1]

This quotation from a report on the Chenes region in the southern part of the Yucatán peninsula aptly summarizes key elements of the elite discourse during the Caste War. The conflict emerged as a struggle between civilization and barbarism epitomized by the Indian rebels. The latter were portrayed as treacherous and murderous savages, and their struggle as archaic and particularly brutal. The rebels, on the other hand, denounced government forces for their merciless and indiscriminate slaughter of insurgent combatants, as well as of women and children.[2] Indeed, ruthless violence was common in the Caste War. As the following pages will show, however, the massive use of force had already become established practice in Yucatecan rebellions and civil wars prior to this and persisted parallel to the war in the course of political infighting among

---

[1] R.J. Piña: "Revista de los Chenes" (Part 1), *LD*, March 17, 1871, 3.
[2] See, for example, F. Chan and V. Pec to Bishop Guerra, November 30, 1849, EHRY 3:358.

the elite. For many Yucatecans, particularly among the lower classes, violence became an integral part of everyday life both before and beyond the Caste War.

MAP 3.1 The Yucatán peninsula in the second half of the nineteenth century (after Dumond 1997:312)

3

The Context

While the characterization of the Caste War by the elite as a racial struggle against progress is grossly misleading, as will become clear in later chapters, it reflected the post-colonial nature of the Yucatecan society. The structure of the population in the region, its economy and hegemonic worldview were the product of three centuries of Spanish colonial rule in a relatively poor and isolated part of the Viceroyalty of New Spain. Colonial society was always more complex than the rigid dichotomy between conqueror and conquered or Spaniard and Indian (or Maya) permits. Neither the Spaniards nor the Indians were homogeneous populations but instead stratified internally into nobles and commoners. In addition, Yucatán harbored significant numbers of people of African descent.[3] Beyond this, colonial law and daily practice distinguished between those of presumed mixed ancestry, such as between mestizos and mulattoes. The colonial quadripartition of Spaniards, Indians, Africans and mixed, however, dwindled to a dichotomous system of thought and administration when Yucatán gained political independence from Spain in 1821 (as part of what then became Mexico). This system differentiated between non-Indians (*vecinos*) and Indians (*indios, indígenas, maya*). The *repúblicas de indios* (Indian republics), established

---

[3] People of alleged full or part African descent made up between 0 and more than 34 percent of the population in the Yucatecan parishes in the early nineteenth century. Restall undertakes the first systematic treatment of the Afro-Yucatecan role in colonial Yucatán and provides information on their numerical strength in the parishes (2009, especially pp. 296–303).

34 *Part II: Violence in Yucatán, 1821–1901*

during the colonial era as administrative units for the indigenous tribute-paying population, survived for several decades. Although formally abolished in the liberal constitution of 1841, in reality the repúblicas continued to operate, having been re-established by law in 1847. They persisted as administrative entities in the state of Yucatán until 1868 and in the state of Campeche, which had separated from Yucatán in 1858, until 1869. Nevertheless, the terms indio and indígena still appeared in official documents until at least the late 1880s.[4] Everyday speech reflected the administrative dichotomy between Indian and vecino, although the Spanish-speaking elite often considered it a "racial" and not merely a legal differentiation. The terms *yucateco* (Yucatecan) and *blanco* (white) were also used to imply the opposite of Indian or Maya. Yucatec Maya remained the language of preference among the Indians, as it had been in the colonial period, but was also the mother tongue of many vecinos, predominantly in rural areas and small towns. Hence Maya surnames (such as Chi, Chan or Puc) served as key indicators of the distinction between Indians and vecinos.[5] According to census data, Indians made up almost 70 percent of the entire population of Yucatán on the eve of the Caste War, as illustrated in Table 3.1 Percentages were even higher in the central and eastern *partidos* (districts) of Hopelchén (Chenes), Tekax, Yaxcabá, Peto and Valladolid, whereas in the western parts of the peninsula, the percentage of Indians was much lower.[6]

Agriculture remained the backbone of Yucatán's economy in the nineteenth century, as it had been in the colonial period. Sugar and, somewhat later, henequen emerged as the major cash crops. The henequen plant found ideal conditions in the drier climate of the north and west of the peninsula, where large haciendas became the core area of cultivation. Fiber made of henequen leaves supplied raw material for the production of ship riggings, cordage and twines, among other things. By the mid-1840s, henequen had already surpassed cattle in importance as a commercial

---

[4] Censuses still classified people as indios and vecinos in the late 1880s. See, for example, Municipalidad de Tekax, Padron general Cuartel 3, 4, 5, 1887, AGEY, PE, P, box 246.

[5] The Maya language also possessed a dichotomous structure of social categories. *Masewal* (commoner) or *otsil* (poor) generally referred to members of the in-group, while those from the out-group were referred to as *ts'ul* (foreigner, gentleman, rich man). For a discussion of the social categories in colonial and post-colonial times and the corresponding legislation, see Gabbert 2001; 2004c:62–64, 78–79, 111–115; Restall 2009:90–109. For surnames used to distinguish Indians from vecinos see, for example, Regil and Peón 1853:293. As a rule, Indian and Maya were not used as self-identification.

[6] See also Cline 1950, II:65; V:154–156; Remmers 1981:83–85; Lapointe 1983:30–31, 41, 49, 57; Bracamonte 1994:113.

The Context

TABLE 3.1 *Men liable to taxation (aged between 16 and 60), 1845*

District	Partido	Vecinos	%	Indios	%	Total
Mérida	Mérida	5,749	44.21	7,254	55.79	13,003
	Ticul	2,659	32.06	5,635	67.94	8,294
	Maxcanú	1,172	22.10	4,131	77.90	5,303
	Tecoh	2,665	33.78	5,224	66.22	7,889
Subtotal		12,245	35.50	22,244	64.50	34,489
Izamal	Izamal	3,786	31.13	8,377	68.87	12,163
	Motul	3,794	36.49	6,603	63.51	10,397
Subtotal		7,580	33.60	14,980	64.40	22,560
Valladolid	Valladolid	2,856	16.73	14,216	83.27	17,072
	Tizimín	2,501	29.30	6,036	70.70	8,537
	Espita	1,780	29.51	4,251	70.49	6,031
Subtotal		7,137	22.56	24,503	77.44	31,640
Tekax	Tekax	3,093	24.20	9,688	75.80	12,781
	Yaxcabá	1,839	19.77	7,463	80.23	9,302
	Peto	4,129	25.66	11,962	74.34	16,091
	Bacalar	719	29.02	1,759	70.98	2,478
Subtotal		9,780	24.06	30,872	75.94	40,652
Campeche	Campeche	2,840	62.62	1,695	37.38	4,535
	Seybaplaya	1,179	50.60	1,151	49.40	2,330
	Carmen	1,995	91.77	179	8.23	2,174
	Hecelchakán	2,585	37.39	4,328	62.61	6,913
	Hopelchén	1,912	24.66	5,841	75.34	7,753
Subtotal		10,511	44.34	13,194	55.66	23,705
Total		47,253	30.88	105,793	69.12	153,046

Source: My calculations based on "Censo de 1845" in Regil and Peón (1853).

article. Sugar, in contrast, was primarily produced on estates in the northern districts of Espita and Tizimín, and in the hitherto sparsely inhabited borderlands of the interior. The environs of Peto, Tekax, Bolonchenticul and Hopelchén alone constituted between two-thirds and three-quarters of the area under cultivation (see Map 3.1).[7] Most of the rural peasant population cultivated corn, beans, squash and root crops such as cassava (yuca) and sweet potato on their *milpas* (swidden fields) in the bush, which

---

[7] Cline 1947:50–52; 1948a:82–83, 86, 89; 1950, V:339–340; Remmers 1981:197–200.

were relatively close to their *ranchos* (hamlets), villages or towns. Corn and beans played a vital role in both subsistence and sales.[8]

Given the key role of agriculture, land, labor and water were crucial factors in the regional economy. Water was both precious and scarce due to an almost complete lack of rivers and lakes in the north of the Yucatán peninsula. People were therefore obliged to satisfy their water needs from the few available sources, i.e., wells, *cenotes* (natural sinkholes), cisterns and natural or artificial reservoirs (*aguadas*). Hence, control of this resource became a key component of the local power structure, allowing landlords to attract workers to their estates.[9] Control of the few water sources was a frequent bone of contention between indigenous communities and private landowners, especially after Independence. With the consolidation of land ownership, the old custom of common waters that prevailed during the colonial regime was lost. Hacienda owners began to prohibit the use of resources on their privatized lands, expelling the cattle of indigenous communities and small ranchers, and banning hunting and wood-cutting. Natural water sources were appropriated and peasants forced to pay for access with labor or corn.[10]

Land *as such* was not scarce in nineteenth-century Yucatán. Vast areas of unoccupied soil existed, notably in the sparsely settled eastern and southern parts of the region, most of which was covered with dense tropical forest. Given their potential for cash crop cultivation, plots close to human settlements, rare water sources or the few routes of communication were highly valued. Indeed, successive governments of independent Yucatán attempted to bring more soil into commercial production by permitting private entrepreneurs to claim supposedly unused national lands (*baldíos*), areas that also served as army pay instead of cash. Since the 1850s, governments had been restricting the *ejidos* (common town or village lands), exerting constant pressure to have them sectioned into privately owned plots. This affected the poor and the landless in particular, who had hitherto used some of the national and village lands to make a living. Unsurprisingly, land policies entailed endemic conflict.[11] Privatization of the soil had advanced in the 1840s in the northwest (the Mérida and Izamal districts) leaving between 65 and 75

---

[8] For an overview of Yucatán's economy on the eve of the Caste War, see Remmers (1981:147–279).

[9] See, for example, Martínez de Arredondo 1841:218–219; Cline 1950, V:340.

[10] Bracamonte 1993:36, 41.   [11] Patch 1990; Rugeley 2009:271–277.

The Context

percent in the hands of individuals. In the south and east of the peninsula, in contrast, land privatization was in full swing.[12]

Human labor was possibly the most critical resource for the establishment of commercial agriculture.[13] Henequen plantations required permanent weeding and almost constant harvesting, rendering them incompatible with peasant milpa agriculture. Commercial sugar plantations also presupposed a permanent supply of field hands, who had to be present for weeks at a time for the harvest in the dry season (December to May) and were therefore unable to tend to their own fields.[14] Vast areas of uncultivated land were still available for independent peasant production in regions outside effective government control in the eastern and southern parts of Yucatán. A great number of peasants preferred to live scattered in the forest close to their swidden fields beyond the towns and villages, as they had done in the colonial period. This allowed them to evade the payment of onerous religious contributions and civil taxes, and working for a landlord.[15] The flight of countless peons and the concomitant loss of manpower was an ongoing problem for landlords. Consequently, landowners and the government deemed certain forms of compulsion indispensable to combating tax evasion and the farm hand scarcity. The idea behind restoring the repúblicas following Independence on July 26, 1824, was "to contain the dispersion of Indians in the forest and procure an honest occupation that makes them useful to themselves and to society."[16] Apart from the habitual access to water and debt peonage, landlords went to considerable lengths to attract laborers and keep them. This took the form of paternalist practices such as paying for weddings and funerals of their peons or acting as godfather to their offspring.[17]

---

[12] Remmers 1981:121; Bracamonte 1993:37–38.

[13] See, for example, Busto 1880, 3:35–36, 256, 262–264.

[14] Strickon 1965:46, 50–51, 53–54; Wells 1984:219–220.

[15] See, for example, C. Buendia to Tesoreria General de Yucatán, Ticul, May 5, 1847, AGEY, PE, G, box 65; DAME:386, 451–452; SGY:annex 28; Méndez 1870:380; Patch 1990:57–60. Civil and religious head taxes were particularly burdensome and unjust since they had to be paid irrespective of individual income or wealth. For the regulation of contributions and taxes in Yucatán, see Suárez Molina 1977, 2:98–99; Rugeley 1996:25–31 and Dumond 1997:87–88.

[16] PG 1:135; see also Art. 22 of the Ley para el régimen interior de los pueblos, October 7, 1850, APP 3:479; Gabbert 2004c:62.

[17] See, for example, P. Regil y Peón to Emperador, Mérida, November 10, 1865, AGN, G, SI, vol. 46, file 14; Norman 1843:71–72; Morelet 1872:106; Suárez Molina 1977, 1:163; Joseph and Wells 1988:224; Gill 2001:189–190. See Peniche Rivero (1999) for a stimulating discussion on the ambivalence of coercion and attraction in relations between landlords and farm workers.

4

Misery and Everyday Violence: Lower-Class Rural Life

The works of Howard F. Cline and Terry Rugeley provide rich detail on several aspects of daily life in nineteenth-century Yucatán.[1] Major studies on the living and working conditions in the henequen haciendas also exist.[2] However, a comprehensive study of everyday life in the region with particular reference to the inhabitants of cities, towns and villages has still to be written. Filling the void here would exceed the scope of this book. The following pages pursue the more humble aim of showing that beyond wars and rebellions, violence was a constant in the daily lives of most Yucatecans. This background provides clues to what was considered normal or expected behavior and should make it easier to understand why, for example, acting violently was not a remote form of settling affairs and why fleeing to the bush or joining the rebels were attractive options to many lower-class Yucatecans.

Life was grim for the lower classes in nineteenth-century Yucatán. Their situation varied considerably depending on whether they lived in urban or rural environments, whether they were self-employed or not and whether they lacked or had access to some means of production.[3] Permanent farm workers on the haciendas had at least minimal food security, since they received corn rations in addition to a salary paid in cash, script or metal chips accepted only in the *tiendas de raya* (hacienda

---

[1] Cline 1950; Rugeley 2001a and 2009.
[2] See the literature cited in the rest of this section.
[3] I will confine my discussion here to the living conditions of the rural lower classes, since they are of the greatest relevance to the topic of the book. For a description of the various groups of laborers on the haciendas, see Suárez Molina (1977, 1:155–158).

Misery and Everyday Violence 39

shops).[4] Their lives, however, were under strict supervision. Landlords regulated their marriages and as a rule did not allow marriage to a peon from another hacienda, in which case the estate owner was obliged to pay off any debts the designated spouse might have.[5] Farm workers did not enjoy freedom of movement, especially when indebted to their masters.[6] Due to poor diet, peons and their families often suffered from vitamin deficiency diseases such as pellagra, which caused weariness, skin damage and mental disturbance. Given their harsh living conditions, farm laborers were wont to take refuge in alcohol, attempt to escape or commit suicide.[7] In addition to state institutions, bounty hunters were frequently hired to track down evaders and bring them back to the fold.[8]

Peasant living conditions in villages and towns varied in terms of access to land, which was even more restricted in the second half of the nineteenth century due to legal reforms directed at individualizing the corporate land holdings mentioned earlier.[9] Unlike farm workers, villagers and their daily lives were subject to less control by superiors. Although compulsory labor was officially prohibited in 1824, it persisted in practice, with villagers forced to work for government officials or private citizens, to transport travelers or toil in road construction and maintenance.[10] Indians were ordered to cultivate a cornfield of sixty *mecates* (2.4 ha) every year, supposedly "for their own benefit" according to a law from 1850 on the prevention of "vagrancy and idleness." In reality, the law was used as a pretext to force Indians unable to fulfill this obligation due to lack of land into working agriculturally for others.[11]

---

[4] J. Vargas et al. to Emperador, Mérida, February 5, 1866, CAIHDY, M, LIII.1866/2/4/14; Suárez Molina 1977, 2:296, 298–300, 303; Joseph and Wells 1988:221, 239–244.

[5] Stephens [1841] 1969, 2:417–418; [1843] 1963, 2:146; Arnold and Frost 1909:331; Peniche Rivero 1999:29–30.

[6] Suárez Molina 1977, 2:281–284; Wells 1984:220; Peniche Rivero 1999:20.

[7] Maler 1997:48–49; Wells 1984:231; Joseph and Wells 1988:252–253 and 1990:109–110. For a more positive evaluation of peon living conditions, see Suárez Molina (1977, 2:303–306).

[8] See, for example, Suárez Molina 1977, 2:300–303; Wells 1984:224–225.

[9] See, for example, Wells 1984:221. For privatization policies and peasant resistance against these measures in the 1840s, see Güemez Pineda (2005a:263–310).

[10] Suárez Molina 1977, 2:292–293, 295. See several examples in Güemez Pineda 2010:216–240. Road maintenance was part of the compulsory work expected from every man liable to the head tax until 1875. Any man not willing to do the work personally was at liberty to pay for a substitute (Suárez Molina 1977, 1:144–147).

[11] Ley para el régimen interior de los pueblos, October 7, 1850, APP 3:479; see also J. Vargas et al. to Emperador, Mérida, February 5, 1866, CAIHDY, M, LIII.1866/2/4/14; Suárez Molina 1977, 2:296; Güemez Pineda 2010:230, 238.

40   Part II: Violence in Yucatán, 1821–1901

In both rural and urban areas, Indians and other poor people taken into the masters' household as children (*criados*) provided most of the domestic services. A government report deplored the "enormous abuses" of this practice with reference to the acquisition and treatment of criados.[12] They were given free food, clothing and accommodation but their wages were meagre.

Physical force intensified the severity of these living conditions, in particular for the lower classes and dependents, i.e., wives, children, criados and other domestics, all of whom were subject to patriarchal authority. As in most parts of the world at that time, violence was a day-to-day affair in nineteenth-century Yucatán. Beatings were seen as a normal child-rearing practice in both families and schools. Yucatán's civil code from 1871, for example, established that a father had the power to correct and punish his children "temperately and moderately." The law extended this faculty to the authorities, who were, if necessary, to "help fathers in the exercise of this power in a prudent and moderate manner."[13] Domestic violence toward wives was also prevalent. As a contemporary observer reported for the Maya-speaking lower class, a husband's right to flog his wife "for the most insignificant fault in preparing his meal or in other domestic chores" met with general approval.[14]

Lower-class males suffered physical aggression at the hands of superiors and were beaten regularly by hacienda overseers and parish priests. As a popular proverb had it: "Indians only hear with their buttocks" (*Los indios no oigan sino por las nalgas*).[15] Many observers held the opinion that "as a corrective to this race, still immersed in the grossest ignorance, floggings are absolutely necessary to make them comply with their social duties."[16] This attitude found its expression in legislation. The law re-introducing the repúblicas indígenas in 1847 had already established the use of corporal punishment for disobedient Indians with the words: "If advice fails to make them [the Indians] docile and

---

[12] Report of José M. Peón, agent of the Ministerio de Fomento, Mérida, May 23, 1854, quoted in Suárez Molina 1977, 2:318.

[13] Gobierno del Estado 1871a:53 (Art. 396 and 397). Whipping, however, was forbidden in public and private schools in 1846 (Medidas ..., September 22, 1846, APP 3:53).

[14] García y García 1865:xx.

[15] Stephens [1843] 1963, 1:82. Granado Baeza (1989:57) phrased it in 1813 as follows: "The Indian does not hear or understand with his ear but with his back" (*El indio no oye ni entiende por la oreja, sino por la espalda*). See also Bracamonte 1994:111, 191, 197; Gill 2001:71, 171.

[16] García y García 1865:lxii; see also Arnold and Frost 1909:324.

Misery and Everyday Violence 41

submissive, the prudent correction their temper and customs require is to be employed."[17] Whipping was not confined to Indians but likewise applied to vecino peons.[18] The terms Indian and peon are used interchangeably in numerous contemporary statements.[19] This allowed the Yucatecan elite to present the authoritarian relations of production and the merciless living conditions on the haciendas as indispensable to counteracting the "natural idleness" of the allegedly Indian farm hands. Thus, exploitation and oppression were embellished to the point of civilizing acts.[20] Employers could legally sanction domestics and farm hands with corporal punishment in Yucatán until 1871, when the liberal government formally established equal civil rights for adult males, and new civil and penal codes "recognized not one invidious distinction among men, neither that of servant, nor master, nor Indian."[21] This notwithstanding, it remained standard practice and was rarely sanctioned.[22] One landlord's legal representative defended his client's persistent whipping with the following argument:

[T]he Constitution only prohibits flogging as a penalty. Thus, it deprives the courts and the civil and military authorities of the power to apply lashes granted by the old laws as punishment or a penalty for crime, but in no way prevents parents, masters, etc., using more effective corrective measures to prevent domestic faults ... and as an example to others who belong to that intimate society rightly called domestic.[23]

This reasoning was not as absurd as it might seem at first glance. The owner and the administrator of the hacienda were both responsible by law for maintaining "peace and order" and sanctioning their peons' supposed offenses (e.g., failure to comply with labor demands, absence from the

---

[17] Ley ... para el régimen de los indios, August 27, 1847, APP 3:151.

[18] See, for example, Causa criminal contra Enrique Mena, Umán, Mérida, October 13, 1846, AGEY, J, PN, vol. 39, file 37.

[19] In actual fact, peons were generally Maya speakers. This language, however, was too widespread to be suitable as a trait of distinction between Indians and non-Indians. Besides, the Spanish surnames suggest that many farm hands did not regard themselves as Indians and were not considered as such by some of their contemporaries. See Gabbert 2004b:95; 2004c:75–78.

[20] Cf., for example, Regil and Peón 1853:300–301; P. de Regil Peu et al., Mérida, March 26, 1878, in Busto 1880, 3:256.

[21] Gill 2001:57. This date was comparatively early. In Germany, for example, the manorial right to corporal punishment was not abolished until 1918 (Lüdtke 1983:279).

[22] See, for example, Gill 2001:59–60, 175–177, 195–196, 210; Peniche Rivero 1999:21; Joseph and Wells 1988:234–236; Flores 1961:478–479.

[23] Causa a José María Aranda por injuria real, AGEY, J, box 91, 1872, quoted in Peniche Rivero 1999:21.

42 *Part II: Violence in Yucatán, 1821–1901*

hacienda without leave, lack of respect) with arrest or, at least up to 1871, corporal punishment.[24] The Civil Code of Yucatán from 1871 established that landlords had a duty to "admonish the servant for his faults and, if these were minor, to emend him as if he were his tutor."[25] In fact, the authority of the master or his overseer over the workers and their families was almost "absolute." As Stephens wrote: "He settles all disputes between the Indians themselves, and punishes for offences, acting both as judge and executioner."[26] Being prosecutors, judges and inflictors of punishment at one and the same time left the door wide open for arbitrariness of all kinds by landowners and administrators, with Gill even ascribing them "life-and-death power."[27] Indeed, landowners generally had a close, frequently kin relationship with the political and legal authorities. They faced little risk of legal retribution and, if necessary, authorities could be bribed.[28] The complaint made by four farm workers to the municipal president about the justice of the peace in Seyé exemplifies the tight cooperation between landlords and the authorities. The latter had designated the farm hands to public works and sentenced them to twenty-five lashes for having asked their employer, Francisca Lugo, for the *carta cuenta*, a document recording the amount farm laborers owed their masters. The laborers evidently considered paying off their debts and leaving their current employer, much to the chagrin of the latter, who was unwilling to accept this against the backdrop of a farm labor shortage.[29]

Peons reacted to the harsh living conditions and abuse by landlords and overseers primarily with what James Scott has called "everyday forms of resistance," such as foot dragging, pilfering, false compliance, desertion, sabotage and arson.[30] Cattle theft, in many instances by farm workers, was the most common crime against property in Yucatán.[31] In considerable contrast to village peasants, farm laborers rarely brought their complaints to court, given the strict control of their lives and the habitual close relations between hacienda owners and officials of the government and the law.[32]

---

[24] Ley para el servicio en los establecimientos del campo, Campeche, November 3, 1868, *EP*, November 6, 1868:2; see also Suárez Molina 1977, 1:163; Gill 2001:195.

[25] Gobierno del Estado 1871a:294 (Art. 2570, 2).   [26] Stephens [1841] 1969, 2:415.

[27] Gill 2001:106.

[28] Baerlein 1913:150, 160, 197; Wells 1984:225; Joseph and Wells 1988:237–238; Peniche Rivero 1999:21.

[29] P. Ortega Palomo to Gobernador, Acanceh, September 6, 1879, AGEY, PE, JP Acanceh, box 210B.

[30] Scott 1989; see also Joseph and Wells 1988:248–254.

[31] Regil and Peón 1853:295; Güemez Pineda 1987:70, 79, 115–116, 118, 121.

[32] Joseph and Wells 1988:236–237.

Misery and Everyday Violence

There was, at least ideologically, a direct link between domestic violence and corporal punishment as exercised by the masters, since the relationship between landlord and peon was conceived as patriarchal. Christopher Gill has argued convincingly that patriarchy was "a key factor in the violence endemic to Yucatecan society."[33] Members of the Spanish-speaking elite, especially landlords, saw the peons and their families as childlike and thus deserving of corporal punishment. The male elite also felt free to engage in voluntary or forced sexual relationships with lower-class females. Lower-class males, notably peons or peasants, had little opportunity to defend the honor of their wives and daughters. They were indeed trapped in a contradiction. On the one hand, they claimed their rights of authority as patriarch of the family but, on the other hand, were denied adult status. Thus, hacienda owners addressed their laborers as *palitzil* (boy) irrespective of their age and beat them like children.[34] Domestic violence in peon households may have functioned as an outlet for the frustration and anger this contradiction must have caused.[35] Men tended to demonstrate their masculinity by exercising violence toward their peers or their wives and children. The consumption of cane liquor, sold freely at the hacienda's tienda de raya or town store, often triggered these aggressive acts.[36]

Violence and corporal punishment were of course employed beyond the confines of haciendas and the legally permitted range. Whipping, the stocks or breaking stones were the standard colonial punishments applied to Indian commoners by the *batabo'b* (sing. *batab*), as the caciques or governors of the *repúblicas de indígenas* were known.[37] The practice of whipping continued after Independence, with some batabo'b using it to sanction their subjects for trivialities.[38]

Vecino government officials were no better and repeatedly disciplined villagers with lashings.[39] On September 2, 1880, for example, José Pilar González accused the *jefe político* (district head) of Ticul, Sabino Piña, of jailing him incommunicado for six days and punishing him with 200 canings. Piña had suspected González of maliciously detonating some of the bombs distributed in the surroundings of the town to warn the

---

[33] Gill 2001:93.   [34] Gill 2001:7.   [35] Gill 2001, especially pp. 92, 166–169, 177.
[36] Gill 2001:199–200; Joseph and Wells 1988:239.   [37] García y García 1865:xlix-li.
[38] See several examples in Güémez Pineda 2010:234 and Rugeley 2009:225.
[39] See Güémez Pineda (2010:220, 225, 227, 236) for several examples implying justices of the peace.

44   *Part II: Violence in Yucatán, 1821–1901*

inhabitants of possible assault by Caste War rebels.[40] Another case in point is that of Rafael Castillo, a judge charged with abuse of a young woman in 1886. Justina Rufina Aké had entered his house as a wage worker. When her master had "cruelly whipped" her for some unknown reason, she fled, taking refuge in the house of Eleuteria Sánchez. Castillo ordered that Justina be returned to his home. Some time later, he beat her with his staff "to the extent that it cracked on her body," forcing her to flee to the town of Peto. Castillo tracked her down and had her brought back to his home once again, where she was kept against her will.[41] The sources do not tell us what ultimately happened to Justina or how long she was confined to the judge's house.

CRIME

Violence not only occurred in the form of maltreatment by superiors but also in the context of disorder and delinquency, such as male brawling. A survey from 1853 provides a glimpse of the number of crimes in mid-century Yucatán. Most of the offenses involved bodily harm, which the report ascribed to "passion and the furor of rage." Drunkenness was a common cause of offenses against individuals. Injuries were usually inflicted with a machete, which the rural folk, "small and adult," carried at their side like "an ordinary piece of clothing."[42] Sanctions for homicide tended to be mild. Those found guilty frequently got away with less than six years imprisonment.[43] Indians appeared in legal documents as delinquents five times less than the rest of the population.[44] The reason for this imbalance in the rate of delinquency among the various population groups is unknown. However, several possible explanations come to mind. The percentage of crimes and delicts reported was far higher in cities and

[40] Expediente relativo a la acusacion de José Pilar González, July 3, 1882, AGEY, PE, C, box 362, file 76.

[41] F. Galera to Gobernador, Tekax, December 15, 1886, AGEY, PE, C, box 236.

[42] Regil and Peón 1853:294; see also Joseph and Wells 1988:249–250.

[43] Joseph and Wells 1988:251. The Criminal Code of 1871 established "forced labor" sanctions of ten to twelve years for homicide, eight to ten years for the offender if the killing was the result of a brawl and four to six years if it was self-defense (Art. 460–461). The killing of adulterers by a male or female spouse remained free of sanction if he or she found them "in the act of adultery or in preparatory and proximal action." Similar applied in the case of having slain a person caught in flagrante or "in preparatory action" with a daughter, niece, sister or daughter-in-law. Although not explicitly stated in the law, this referred to the illegitimate sexual relations of female relatives only. See Gobierno del Estado 1871b:93–94.

[44] Regil and Peón 1853:293.

Misery and Everyday Violence 45

towns, where most officials resided, than in rural areas, which were home to the majority of Indians. In addition, it is likely that many instances of crime on the haciendas remained unreported and were dealt with directly by landlords or overseers. It can also be assumed that the majority of disputes and crimes in villages and hamlets were taken care of locally without the involvement of legal institutions. Implicating the latter would have meant considerable expense in terms of time and money. Beyond this, the judicial system could hardly be considered a neutral power situated above the litigants but rather as an extension of elite rule, given the generally intimate relationship between landlords and government officials mentioned earlier. Furthermore, frequent changes of government (see Chapter 5) seriously affected the credibility of the judicial system. Each new government replaced the judges and appointed magistrates "selected from the narrow circle of its followers." Hence the legal system lost its independence and respectability. "Not just once but many times ignorant and corrupt magistrates and judges have clutched the balance of justice with their hands," a contemporary observer complained.[45]

The political unrest that plagued Yucatán and the rest of Mexico not only brought with it the proliferation of violence in rebellions and civil wars, but also led to the flourishing of banditry. While assault and robbery in the countryside was already rife in most of Mexico, a report in 1853 stated that armed highway robberies and muggings were "unknown or very rare" in Yucatán.[46] As late as 1861, these heavy crime levels seem miraculously to have been significantly lower in Yucatán than in other parts of Mexico. General Suárez y Navarro reported to the federal government in 1861: "The people of Yucatán are docile and restrained. Robberies and homicides occur on a very small scale compared to their number and frequency elsewhere." He estimated that no more than fifty delinquents had been imprisoned for serious crimes at that time.[47] This was soon to change, however, and overland travel became increasingly unsafe.[48] Gangs of deserters or bandits, known as *gavillas* (gangs of thugs), began marauding in the countryside, sometimes in quite large groups. On June 12, 1866, for example, between forty and fifty deserters attacked the villages of Baca and Mocochá, killing several inhabitants.[49]

---

[45] Suárez y Navarro [1861] 1993:179.   [46] Regil and Peón 1853:294.
[47] Suárez y Navarro [1861] 1993:180.
[48] See, for example, C. Baqueiro to CGE, Hopelchén, October 20, 1856, AGEY, PE, G, box 103.
[49] Attack, *PODM*, June 13, 1866, 4.

46   *Part II: Violence in Yucatán, 1821–1901*

The gavilla issue became acute in both Yucatán and the rest of the country following the collapse of the Habsburg Empire of Maximilian I and the re-establishment of Republican rule in Mexico in 1867.[50] The establishment of Maximilian's empire was the outcome of the conflict over the settlement of Mexico's foreign debt, which had led to military intervention by Spain, Great Britain and France in 1861 to enforce payment. France, however, pursued more ambitious aims that sought the installation of a dependent monarchy in Mexico. The Spanish and British troops withdrew as soon as the far-reaching goals of the French became clear. In 1864, Maximilian was proclaimed emperor of Mexico backed by the then French emperor Napoleon III and the Mexican conservatives, who had fought against the liberal government of Benito Juárez since 1857 in the *Guerra de Reforma* (Reform War). What followed was several years of bloody war against foreign intervention and the Mexican emperor, which also affected Yucatán. After the defeat of Maximilian I and his execution in 1867, Juárez reduced the Mexican army from 60,000 to 20,000 men. Many of the soldiers dismissed joined the marauding bandits. Military requisition gave way to plunder. For the most part, gavilla leaders were former officers or imperial civil servants, now heading groups of decruited soldiers and peons.[51] Infringements originated from the gavillas, but also came from unexpected corners. Such was the case in 1881, when two peasants were assaulted and robbed by a passing detachment of active soldiers on the road between Kanasín and Mérida.[52]

While manslayers generally faced mild punishments, as mentioned above, group assaults and muggings around the countryside were sanctioned with rigidity. As early as 1848, highway robbery involving groups of four or more holdup men was punishable by martial law in Yucatán.[53] A national decree in 1858 established that all highwaymen apprehended in flagrante delicto deserved the death penalty within three days.[54] The 1873 *Ley de salteadores y plagiarios* (holdup men and kidnappers)

---

[50] See, for example, J.L. Guerra to Gobernador, Umán, August 23, 1873, *RP*, August 27, 1873, 1. See also M.F. Peraza to General en Jefe, Valladolid, [April] 1855, AGEY, PE, G, box 100.

[51] Bazant 1991:43–48; Rugeley 2009:288–291.

[52] A. Gorocia to Gobernador, Mérida, October 10, 1881, AGEY, PE, box 219.

[53] Decreto, Santiago Méndez, Maxcanú, February 14, 1848, AGEY, PE, G, box 68.

[54] See Art. 15, Decreto, *GS*, June 9, 1858, 1–2.

Misery and Everyday Violence

repeated the sanction. Documents show that this was no empty threat, since assaultants in Yucatán were indeed shot under martial law.[55]

These draconian sanctions and rapid executions failed, however, to put an end to gang assaults. Many former soldiers were accustomed to taking what they needed along the way during the years of rebellion and civil war. Whether this was labeled requisition or robbery made little difference to them. Much seems to have been a matter of opinion during these wars. What one party considered legitimate requisition to secure troop provisions was condemned by the other as downright robbery. Beyond this, arms abounded and alternative ways of making a living were either scarce or highly unattractive, such as endless hours of drudgery in the henequen fields under hot sun for miserable pay and, at worst, ill-treatment by landlords or overseers. The limited capacity of the police and the courts to enforce the law undoubtedly contributed to the spread of violence. Evidence suggests a prevailing climate of impunity in many areas. In 1866, for example, two men led a small group into the town of Dzilan. Presenting themselves as government commissioners, they arrested two Frenchmen on counts of desertion and theft, led them to the graveyard and hanged them. As discovered later, the murdered men, Juan N. Poth and Emilio Barteloot, belonged to the Mexican (Imperial) army and had indeed stolen valuables from their superiors and deserted. The would-be commissioners were two of the officers affected. Having taken "justice" into their own hands, they returned to Mérida as if nothing had happened and were molested by none.[56]

---

[55] See, for example, Comandancia Militar de Motul, Luis G. Jaime, July 17, 1873, *RP*, July 21, 1873, 2; G. Palomino to Gobernador, Mérida, May 1, 1876, *RP*, May 3, 1876, 3.

[56] J.M. Morales to Comisario Imperial, 7a división, Mérida, August 16, 1866, AGN, G, dossier 2001, box 2497, file 2.

5

Political Violence before and beyond the Caste War

Nineteenth-century commentators and numerous later scholars have implicitly or explicitly depicted the Caste War as a struggle of outstanding brutality. The Yucatecan historian and governor Eligio Ancona, for example, accredited the conflict "titanic dimensions" and "terrible episodes" of a kind found at best in the antiquity. "Blood ran from one extreme of the peninsula to the other amidst the flames stirred up by the conflagration of towns and the shouting of savages rejoicing in the middle of destruction."[1] While contemporaries tended to stress the particular barbarity of the "savage Maya rebels," later authors were quick to denounce the excessive repression Indians suffered at the hands of non-Indians.[2] A closer look, however, at the historical antecedents of the Caste War and the political conflicts that took place in Yucatán simultaneously, albeit unrelated, leads me to tone down the idea of the extraordinariness of violence in that rebellion.

Intense political mobilization marked the first half of the nineteenth century throughout Mexico. The military adopted a leading role in the course of the bloody contentions that accompanied the movement for independence. The crisis and subsequent demise of the colonial regime gave rise to sharp polemics against colonial oppression and heated debates about the nature of the emerging political order. Should Mexico become a federal republic or a unitary state ruled by a strong central government? Was democracy the rule of the people, including the lower classes, or should political participation be confined to property owners and "men of

---

[1] Ancona 1879/80, 4:14.
[2] Cf., for example, Baranda 1867; Ancona 1879/80, 4:5–15; González Navarro 1970.

Political Violence before and beyond the Caste War

reason," as more conservative thinkers suggested?[3] Beyond this, the challenge to monarchical rule in Europe as a result of the French Revolution and in Latin America following independence from Spain shattered the basis of political legitimacy. Authority could no longer count on traditional legitimacy based on the genealogy of kings or noble birth and was now "in the eye of the beholder," as Will Fowler aptly phrases it. "It could be questioned, challenged, overcome, and ultimately appropriated," so that authority "was there for the taking, and the strongest bidder could take all if he played his cards right in what had become a dog-eat-dog world."[4]

Institutional instability, the growing power of the military and the politicizing of the town government with the introduction of elections triggered a proliferation of violent struggles throughout the country. Yucatán was no exception. Political unrest, coups and rebellions were endemic and *pronunciamientos* (pronouncements) became a common form of articulating protest. The pronunciamiento was an act of defiance "whereby a garrison or town council declared its insubordination to the national and/or regional government and threatened to use violence if the authorities did not attend to its grievances."[5] As a rule, the comparatively small group of *pronunciados* issued a petition specifying their complaints and demanding that these be settled by the government. They hoped that other towns or garrisons would declare their support and force the authorities to negotiate. While not all pronunciamientos became full-blown uprisings or coups, some degenerated into bloody revolts.[6]

Yucatán had no deep-rooted militarist tradition. No major uprisings took place during the colonial period and on the whole the transition to independence was relatively peaceful. The army was "more a pleasant club than an instrument of defense or destruction," as Howard Cline remarked, at least for the local gentlemen in the officer ranks.[7] This began to change in the 1830s, when the military became the most important political actor in the region as a result of changes to the organization of local militias (National Guard) and the dispatch of military commanders and governors from the centralist government in Mexico City. Military rule prevailed in Yucatán from 1829 to 1837 without

---

[3] Cf. for the more conservative view of Mexico in general, Mora [1836] 1965, 1:280–281; and for Yucatán, Sierra O'Reilly [1848–51] 1994, 1:199; 2:276.

[4] Fowler 2010b:xxv.   [5] Fowler 2012b:xxiv.

[6] See the edited volumes of Will Fowler (2010a and 2012a) for conceptual discussions and empirical examples of violent political protest in nineteenth-century Mexico.

[7] Cline 1950, II:72; see also V:132.

50 Part II: Violence in Yucatán, 1821–1901

interruption.[8] Yucatán's relations with the central government were hotly disputed (federalism versus centralism). The regulation of import duties, the amount of payments to the central authorities and the supply of soldiers and money for Mexico's war with Texas, which had sought independence since 1836, were some of the controversial issues. This led to pronunciamientos against the centralist Republic and, beginning in 1840, Yucatán declared itself independent several times (1840–3, 1845–6, 1847–8).[9]

As mentioned earlier, politics was distinguished by rapid change of government, frequent coups, and a marked institutional instability that lasted into the final quarter of the century in Yucatán, as in the rest of Mexico. Twenty-six governors alternated in office in the twenty-five years from 1848 to 1873.[10] No less than six governors replaced their respective predecessors between July 1857 and early 1860. According to a contemporary observer, governors "ascended and descended with the pace of scoop wheel buckets." He continued as follows:

> The revolutionary uprisings succeeded in a scandalous manner in Yucatán, and passions were unleashed with more fury than ever. The governors came to be counted, not for months, but for days, and we can already add, for hours, because it happened that two governors turned up on the same day, one taking possession in the morning, leaving the post at noon to his successor.[11]

Political instability resulted from several factors. There was no bourgeoisie to speak of, nor was there a strong middle class, both potential bearers of a broader nationalist project. For decades after Independence, no social group, ideological current or political faction commanded sufficient strength to pursue its interests in the face of rivals or put its vision of society into effect.[12] The clergy, possessor of vast real estate, the military (the national army and the local militias) and the hacienda owners figured as the main power groups. Lack of funds limited the capacity of the government and administration to act. In Yucatán, with its rickety economy, which still had to be adjusted to the new political context, the state remained the largest single employer. Thus, the governorship, leading political positions and public employment constituted a highly esteemed

---

[8] Negrín Muñoz 1991:42–48.

[9] General Rivas Zayas to Presidente Bustamente, Campeche, August 25, 1839, EHRY 1:266–270; Betancourt Pérez and Sierra Villarreal 1989:82–83; Negrín Muñoz 1991:48–59; Rugeley 2009:39–41.

[10] Wells 1996:216. [11] GCY:115, 131 (quote).

[12] For Mexico in general, see Wolf and Hansen 1967:177; Fowler 1995:307.

Political Violence before and beyond the Caste War 51

prize. Even control of the town councils was much sought-after, since these bodies auctioned licenses for such public services as tax collection, meat and grain supplies and the construction of public buildings, all of which provided a welcome source of income and profit.[13] Independence brought, among other things, republican and democratic institutions, including elections and municipal self-government. Ballots occurred frequently at all levels, among them town council (*ayuntamiento, cabildo*) elections. Few institutions, however, guaranteed voting freedom and fairness. Local elections in particular tended to be fraught with manipulation of results, intimidation of voters and other abuses.[14]

From the late 1830s to the 1850s, political conflicts in Yucatán were determined by the struggle between two liberal squads, each grouped around a leader. While Santiago Méndez for the most part represented the interests of the city of Campeche, Miguel Barbachano acted on behalf of Mérida's elite.[15] Since political parties with a firm organization and ideology were non-existent, major political actors depended on multiple chains of vertical alliances linking politics at the peninsular, regional and local level. These included ties to the lower classes in the towns and villages of the hinterland, mainly secured by local elites such as the batabo'b in the case of Indians and by militia officers, officials (e.g., justices of the peace, jefes políticos), landowners, businessmen and priests, among others, in the case of vecinos.[16] This predominance of personalistic politics and loyalties was a direct result of rapid social and political change and institutional weakness. Given their flexibility, patron–client relations seemed advantageous in this environment. They filled the void and provided at least a modicum of security and trustful relations, since impersonal guarantees for life, status and property were either weak or absent.[17] Political groupings displayed the characteristics of what has become known as "factions" in the anthropological debate: contentions and

---

[13] For Yucatán, see Rugeley 2009:20–22.

[14] For Yucatán, see, for example, Bellingeri 1995; Rugeley 1997:476–479; 2009:23; Güémez Pineda 2005b:94–99. Local town councils in independent Mexico were formally established in 1825. During centralist rule from 1834 to 1840, town officials were appointed rather than elected.

[15] Cline 1950, V:619–622; Betancourt Pérez and Sierra Villarreal 1989:57–59, 111–113; Negrín Muñoz 1991:59–62.

[16] See also Rugeley 2009:23, 28. The role of caciques in local and regional politics and networking is discussed extensively in Dutt (2012).

[17] For the factors that fostered the predominance of patron–client relations, see the classic works of Weingrod (1968), Scott (1972), Stuart (1972), Lemarchand and Legg (1972), and the recent overview in Hicken (2011).

fighting did not arise between different classes. Instead, the conflict groups cross-cut strata by integrating members of different social positions, such as landlords and peons, members of the elite and the urban poor. These groups or networks were only visible as collective actors in instances of conflict over control of resources, labor or loyalty. Recruitment relied on certain principles, including kinship, *compadrazgo* (ritual coparenthood), friendship, patron–client ties and indebtedness. The leaders constituted the point of coalescence for members of such diversity. Ideological differences played only a minor role, if any, and most factions fought for power, status and resources within the existing social order, their often-revolutionary discourse notwithstanding.[18] Consequently, political allegiances and ideological standards shifted frequently and were altered to match rapidly changing circumstances and the actors' personal interests. Since factions rely on personal relationships and loyalty is exchanged for safety, patronage or material gain, they are inherently unstable. Once a leader forfeits his ability to guarantee protection or resources by losing power, influence, property or his life, the henchmen look for more attractive strongmen to follow. This applies largely to the supporters of politicians, military units operating in Yucatán, and Caste War rebels.

The organization of the military in Mexico and Yucatán was a key contributing factor to the proliferation of violent conflict since Independence and, with the exception of brief periods, saw the coexistence of two kinds of military units. The regular formations were part of the Mexican army and subordinate to the *Ministerio de Guerra y Marina* (Department of War and Marine) in Mexico City. Each state (or department during the centralist reign) was obliged to contribute a specific number of men to the army.[19] During the periods of Yucatecan Independence, the state maintained its own regular military units of professional soldiers, the so-called permanent forces, who obeyed the governor's orders. In 1841, for example, these units comprised half an artillery battalion stationed in Campeche, an infantry company in Carmen, a cavalry company in Mérida and a "light

---

[18] For faction characteristics, see Nicholas 1965; Alavi 1987; Lynch 1992:404–406.

[19] Mühlenpfordt [1844] 1969:396–398. In the 1840s, the country was divided into eighteen military districts. The federal (or central) units were stationed in barracks in prominent places such as Mérida, Campeche and Carmen Island. The army contingents in military districts were therefore composed of locally recruited soldiers and, where necessary, supplemented by units sent from the country's capital.

Political Violence before and beyond the Caste War

battalion" (*El Ligero*) consisting of six infantry companies "to cover the points for which they are destined."[20]

Apart from regular armed forces, the federal states and local town governments commanded their own local militia units (since 1848 referred to as the National Guard) consisting of male citizens of a certain age (mostly from sixteen to fifty) who were not exempt from military service.[21] Each district was to organize one or more local militia battalions of light infantry composed of between one and eight companies of draftees. The battalions were headed by a colonel generally stationed in the district seat (*cabecera*).[22] The number and strength of the companies varied considerably from one town to another and from one period to another, ranging from 150 to fewer than 20 men.[23] The militia or National Guard allowed the federal states to defy the central government militarily. Even municipal governments were in a position to muster their militia companies should the politics of the state administration adversely affect fundamental local concerns. In other words, any conflict of interest could easily revert to violent strife.

The particular organization of the militia strengthened the soldiers' local and personalistic loyalties. Companies consisted of men from individual towns headed by a captain. Militia regulations conceived soldiers as citizens, at least in theory. In certain periods, this implied that soldiers elected their officers, sergeants and corporals, who were then approved by

---

[20] Organización de la fuerza permamente, April 13, 1841, APP 2:121–122. Each company was to have seventy-five soldiers, eight corporals, two cornets, one sergeant first degree, two sergeants second degree, two sub-lieutenants, one lieutenant and a captain. The permanent infantry still consisted of one battalion (*batallón ligero permanente*) in 1848 (Organizando la fuerza permanente de infanteria, June 8, 1848, APP 3:211–212).

[21] For regulations on exemptions, see Chapter 10.

[22] Reglamento de la milicia local, 1832, APP 1:54–55; Reglamento de la milicia local, August 6, 1842, APP 2:197–198. According to the regulation of 1842, each militia company was to have eighty-one soldiers, twelve corporals, two cornets, one sergeant first degree (permanent), four sergeants second degree, two sub-lieutenants, two lieutenants and a captain. For Mexico in general, see also Richthofen 1859:455–456; Chust and Serrano Ortega 2007:100, 104–105.

[23] Rugeley 2009:69. The National Guard battalion of the Ticul district rose from 339 men in nine local units with 14 to 70 members in 1856 to 899 men organized into eleven companies ranging from 60 to 109 men in 1878, for example (Estado general de la fuerza disponible, Ticul, November 26, 1856, AGEY, PE, G, 1856, box 103; Batallon del partido de Ticul, Ticul, March 17, 1878, AGEY, PE, PM, box 202). The National Guard battalion of the Maxcanú district consisted of 408 men organized into four companies in the major towns (Maxcanú 127, Halachó 97, Opichén 99, Chocholá 80, and 5 staff) in 1873 (J.A. Cepeda Peraza to Gobernador, Tekax, December 23, 1870, *RP*, December 26, 1870, 1).

54   *Part II: Violence in Yucatán, 1821–1901*

the government in line with the militia regulations of 1841. The state government, however, continued to appoint the battalion commanders.[24] Eligibility assured that the upper ranks came, as a rule, from the local elite. As of 1832, for example, candidates for the position of captain were required to have property worth 2,000 pesos, 400 pesos of annual revenue or a profession.[25] In addition, the *alcaldes* (mayors) organized, and in many instances rigged, elections to the advantage of their favorites. Beyond pay and status, officer positions were attractive because they bestowed on those concerned the power of leading an armed force and, as will be seen later, gave them access to soldiers' labor. The militia system created a powerful bond between soldiers and their officers, who frequently became local strongmen. "Men and officers forged a shared bond," as Rugeley aptly remarks, "one that superseded matters of national loyalty, and which was an essential ingredient in the coming civil wars. Soldiers marched behind a particular man, not a constitution or national cause."[26] This was also true for the federal army. Due to the size of Mexico and poor communication channels, regional commanders enjoyed a substantial degree of autonomy. The weakness of the central government and its inability to ensure an adequate and regular supply of troops also demanded independent action and the more or less legal appropriation of goods. According to Escalante Gonzalbo, the army was a collection of clienteles: "As a unit it appeared only in the budgets, in practice obedience had to be negotiated with each troop and the interests of each commander considered." Soldiers and commanders rarely adhered to institutional loyalties or solid ideological orientations. Officers were wont to see troops as a resource for negotiation with the state and pursuit of their particular interests. For the soldiers of the army

---

[24] Sobre organización de la milicia local, April 5, 1841 and Reglamento de la milicia local, August 6, 1842, both in APP 2:119–120, 196–210; Nueva organización de la milicia local, March 27, 1847, APP 3:109–111; Reglamento provisional, Guardia nacional de Yucatán, Mérida, November 8, 1849, CAIHDY, F, VI.1847/24; Reglamento para la organización de la guardia nacional expedido en 11 de septiembre de 1846 y mandado observar por decreto de 14 de enero ultimo, Mérida, February 1856, CAIHDY, F, XI.1856/28; Bases para la organización de la guardia nacional de Yucatán, México, April 16, 1851, AHM, XI/481.3/3255. For Mexico in general, see Richthofen 1859:456; Chust and Serrano Ortega 2007:96, 106; Thomson 1991:280.

[25] Representación de Tomas de Castro, May 12, 1841, AGEY, PE, M, box 46, file 30. The regulations of 1842 established that a commander or officer of the local militia was merely required to have "an exercise, profession or industry allowing them to live honorably" (Reglamento de la milicia local, August 6, 1842, APP 2:209).

[26] Rugeley 2009:42; see also pp. 39, 41.

Political Violence before and beyond the Caste War 55

and the National Guard, on the other hand, military units provided protection and opportunities for pillage in addition to the promise of pay.[27]

The frequent civil wars among Yucatecan political factions in the 1840s led to vast mobilization of the lower classes as combatants. Arms were easily available to large sections of the population, as they were frequently distributed by the government or its opponents and the use of force had become a standard means of political struggle.[28] These trends were reinforced by Yucatán's fight against the centralist Mexican government, which resulted in Yucatán's declaration of independence in 1840. Negotiations over reintegration were to no avail. Hence the Mexican government sent an expeditionary force of several thousand men to Yucatán in 1842 to bring the dissenting state into line.[29] Bloody battles and a months-long siege of Campeche by the invaders ensued. In an attempt to mobilize Yucatecans hitherto exempt from military service, the state government issued a decree on March 27, 1843, calling for guerilla units to support the Yucatecan forces in their struggle against the Mexican army. It promised rewards in the form of land and tax exemption to anyone who joined the guerillas:

Each citizen, regardless of class, is entirely free to form guerilla units of between five and fifty members.... These [units] will burn the ships, magazines, artillery, arms and provisions of the enemy [the invading Mexican army], destroy the quarters and settlements where they live or render them useless, poison their wells, mine the roads, and block paths that could facilitate access to other places. Furthermore, they are to burn and level the trees, brushwood, and woods in the vicinity of the enemy.[30]

The decree legitimized the formation of armed groups and the use of force outside regular military units and undoubtedly contributed to the generalization of violence, the cruelty of the fighting and the high number of victims.[31] Similar provisions were made by the Mexican government during the war with the USA in 1847–8 and by President Benito Juárez against the French invasion in 1862.[32] Thus, the confiscation of goods and

---

[27] Escalante Gonzalbo 1993:166 (quote), 181–184.   [28] Rugeley 1997:483, 485–486.

[29] Rugeley 2009:39–41, 45–51; Betancourt Pérez and Sierra Villarreal 1989:85–93; Baqueiro 1990, 1:77–118.

[30] APP 2:240–242; see also Nuevos premios de campaña, August 26, 1842, APP 2:215–216.

[31] For the heavy losses see, for example, Ancona 1879/80, 3:423–425, 434; Betancourt Pérez and Sierra Villarreal 1989:91.

[32] Thanks to Raymond Buve (personal communication), who brought this parallelism to my attention.

56   Part II: Violence in Yucatán, 1821–1901

valuables by force, the destruction of property, physical violence, and even acts of extreme cruelty were by no means unique to the Caste War but rather the habitual concomitant of warfare in mid-nineteenth-century Mexico. The pattern persevered in the numerous rebellions and civil wars between local elite factions that haunted Yucatán while the Caste War was in full swing.[33] One example is the uprising led by Pablo García against the Mérida-based government of Yucatán under Pantaleón Barrera, a prelude to the division of the peninsula into two states of the Mexican Federation (Campeche and Yucatán). The war began on August 7, 1857, and devastated the western parts of the peninsula for five months. During this period the Campeche newspaper *El Espíritu Público* published a regular column entitled "Depredations of the Barbarians," accusing not Caste War rebels but Mérida government troops of countless atrocities:

The city of Campeche has within it the war of barbarians, because it not only fights against invaders who make war without quarter, but also steal from and brutally destroy abandoned houses, they murder unarmed defenseless citizens purely for the pleasure of seeing the floor stained with human blood.... [In the hacienda Huayamon] they tied up fourteen servants ... stripped their families of garments, destroying everything they could not carry and take with them.... In the various inroads made by the enemies and the encounters they have had with the troops of this city, the Campechans had occasion to observe that it is the machete of the savage that is wielded in the enemy camp regardless of class; they are waging the same war against the armed forces as they are against women and children.[34]

According to a report published in a Campeche newspaper, a unit of the Mérida forces entered the Chibic hacienda on the night of December 16, 1857, where they slew a servant with machetes, took possession of cattle and horses, and wreaked the "usual destruction of their vandal raids."[35] Government troops were even accused of rape,[36]

---

[33] See, for example, J.F. de Ciero to juez de 1a instancia de Tekax, hacienda Tixcacal, January 22, 1847, AGEY, PE, J, box 66; V. Rivero to Gobernador, Valladolid, April 16, 1847, AGEY, PE, G, box 64; R. Huerte et al. to Presidente, Mérida, July 10, 1873, and letter from Vecinos de Timucuy, July 9, 1873, both in AGN, G, sec. 2a 873 (6) 7 (51); Rugeley 2009:49–51.

[34] Depredaciones de los bárbaros, *EP*, October 23, 1857, 3; see also October 30, 1857, 4; November 6, 1857, 4. See also La bolsa, ó la vida y la bolsa, *EP*, November 10, 1857, 4; Suárez y Navarro [1861] 1993:374.

[35] P. Garcia and P. Baranda to Jefatura Politica, Campeche, December 18, 1857, *GS*, December 28, 1857, 3.

[36] See, for example, Una proclama modelo, *EP*, November 13, 1857, 3.

Political Violence before and beyond the Caste War

and of shooting captured Campeche soldiers "without any formality."[37] García denounced Governor Barrera's reaction to his uprising to the minister of state in Mexico City as follows:

> In his foolish delirium he tried to stifle it with fire and blood, ordering the most cruel and barbaric war against the District of Campeche ever recorded in our annals, cutting down, pillaging, killing and burning in the name of freedom, order and justice.... The District of Campeche sustained five months of fighting and suffered excessive murders and robberies.[38]

Although these statements certainly contain more than a smattering of political propaganda, it is fair to claim that they at least hint at the ruthlessness with which this civil war was fought, most probably on both sides.[39] Another example of the cruelty of civil wars and insurrections in Yucatán is the struggle for Yucatán governorship in early 1861 between Agustín Acereto and Lorenzo Vargas. Acereto's son Pedro accused Vargas's troops of having burned and ravaged his father's haciendas "worse than the barbarians [Caste War rebels] would have done." He furthermore blamed Vargas for having burned several of the prisoners he had taken.[40] In December 1861, two officers of the government forces, headed since November by Liborio Irigoyen, were ambushed, shot on horseback by followers of Pedro Acereto and "cut to pieces with cruel machete blows, as were their horses." When Pedro's brother, Antonio Acereto, arrived at the government camp in Pixoy several days later to discuss options to bring the hostilities to an end, he was killed instantly by infuriated soldiers with machetes, apparently in retaliation for the ambush.[41]

A third example is the mistreatment of Pablo Garcia, who had become governor of the state of Campeche after its separation from Yucatán, and of his companion, Francisco Negroe, following their capture by insurgents in 1873. They were forced, among other things, to walk barefoot for long distances and left without food. The scourgers demanded a ransom of 5,000 pesos to be handed over by a fixed time or both prisoners would be executed.[42]

---

[37] Un nuevo combate, *EP*, November 10, 1857, 4.

[38] P. García to Ministro de Estado, Campeche, April 9, 1859, AGN, G, leg. 935, box 1 (1121).

[39] This conclusion is supported by Baqueiro 1990, 5:4–5, 10.

[40] Crónica del Estado, *EC*, February 18, 1861, 3.

[41] L. Irigoyen to MGM, Mérida, January 24, 1862, AHM, XI/481.4/8924; Baqueiro 1990, 5:175, 185–186.

[42] J. Coronado to Gobernador, October 11 and 12, 1873, *RP*, October 15, 1873, 3.

CONCLUSION

As shown in the preceding pages, many Yucatecans experienced violence in different contexts before and parallel to the Caste War. The use of force was an integral part of socialization practices, as well as of gender and labor relations. Requisition, a frequent euphemism for plundering, was a common method of provisioning military units. As will be seen in many instances, there was no fundamental difference in the behavior of Caste War rebels and that of political insurgents during civil wars or the armed gangs found marauding in the countryside since the late 1860s. At times it was difficult to establish who had committed a crime or assaulted a hacienda or a village.[43] All kinds of cruelty took place in the struggles against the Mexican invasion as well as in contests between Yucatecan elite factions long before the Caste War began. Why had violence become so widespread in mid-nineteenth-century Yucatán? Several factors come to mind. Members of the lower classes were both victims and perpetrators of violence. Devoid of other resources, the use of physical force was the most obvious if not the only option in many situations, as in the case of self-defense or the appropriation of food and other basic necessities for survival. These deeds were typically carried out by groups of men under conditions of stress, such as in an army squad during a campaign, circumstances that must surely have stimulated the incidence of violence. In addition, given the weakness of legal institutions, the risk of being sanctioned for violent deeds was almost nil. Large numbers of lower-class males were mobilized for the countless pronunciamientos and civil wars, thus allowing physical force to become routine. Beyond this, guns were available to many in the course of these struggles, which facilitated the use of violence, for example, in highway robberies.

---

[43] See, for example, T. Aznar Barbachano to Gobernador de Belice, Campeche, July 11, 1863, *LNE*, July 27, 1863, 2–3; D. Burau to MGO, Mérida, August 7, 1866, AGN, G, SI, vol. 33, file 27.

PART III

THE CASTE WAR AND VIOLENCE: AN OVERVIEW

Although violence was a common feature of the Caste War through-out its course, it was not uniform, varying in its frequency, forms and dimensions. The incentive to use force altered in accordance with the actors and contexts concerned, and changed over time. The following is a rough chronological overview of the principal events of the Caste War and serves to contextualize the more topical discussions in Parts IV, V and VI. It will be described how the Caste War began in July 1847 as the excrescence of one of the many civil strifes that plagued Yucatán in the first decades after Independence, how the rebels advanced successfully on all fronts in the initial months of the struggle, and how they were forced to retreat in mid-1848. The consolidation of autonomous rebel polities in the southeast of the peninsula, the frontier war that lingered on for decades and the final defeat of the rebels in 1901 will also be addressed.

6

The Beginnings

The origin of the violent conflict that became known as the Caste War cannot be understood in isolation from Yucatán's relations with the Mexican Republic and the political rivalry between Miguel Barbachano and Santiago Méndez and their respective liberal factions. In November 1846, Governor Barbachano agreed to reintegrate the state of Yucatán, which had gained independence again in 1845, into the Mexican Republic. At the time, Mexico had entered the war with the United States on the Texas issue and was therefore willing to make concessions to Yucatán. But not all Yucatecans applauded Barbachano's decision. Opposition was particularly strong in Campeche, Méndez's stronghold, since rejoining Mexico put an end to the peninsula's neutrality in the conflict with the USA. The harbor blockade lurking in the wings would have led to grave interference with the city's main source of income, that is, the import and export of goods. The Campeche city council reacted promptly with a putsch against Barbachano's government on December 8, 1846.[1] Six weeks later, on January 22, 1847, Barbachano's troops were obliged to surrender and Domingo Barret, one of Santiago Méndez's henchmen, became provisional governor. Barbachano's followers, however, were little inclined to accept this state of affairs and prepared their own insurrection to reconquer the governorship for their leader and the jobs they had lost in the public administration for themselves. The attempted rebellion in Mérida on February 28, 1847, collapsed after two weeks and the insurgents accepted the amnesty proclaimed by

---

[1] Pronunciamiento, Campeche, December 8, 1846, EHRY 1:349–353; Baqueiro 1990, 1:152–157.

62   *Part III: The Caste War and Violence: An Overview*

the government on March 9.[2] This by no means prevented Barbachanistas from summoning supporters for their cause.

While recruitment of the Maya-speaking lower classes, including legal Indians, as soldiers for civil wars between Yucatecan elite factions or draftees for struggles with the central government, either by force or with the promise of less dues, had been common practice since the late 1830s, Barbachano's vecino and Indian henchmen proved particularly successful in that endeavor.[3] They pledged to reduce the hated poll tax and offered life-long tax exemption to anyone prepared to take active part in the overthrow of the Barret government. In addition, they addressed a topic of central importance to the peasantry – the growing shortage of land due to privatization of communal lands and baldíos. They likewise promised to abolish the legal basis for expropriation and award indemnification to affected communities.[4]

The political situation remained extremely tense for several months. The election for governorship was held on July 18, 1847. Santiago Méndez won and was to replace Barret in September. Serapio Baqueiro, author of the most detailed nineteenth-century political history of Yucatán, clearly doubts the fairness of the ballot, exclaiming "when has a political party, with no law other than its flag, managed the popular vote as it should? When have elections in this case ceased to be a joke [*un sarcasmo*] on the people. Naturally this deceit [*sarcasmo*] would newly excite the followers of Barbachano."[5] Conspicuously, a cacique conspiracy against the Barret government was discovered in the vicinity of Valladolid just after the election. Barret and the local jefe político portrayed it as the prelude to a general uprising of the "barbarous and savage Indians" against the white race.[6] Evidence of this was thin, to say the least, and one of the supposed ringleaders, Manuel Antonio Ay, the cacique of

---

[2] Amnistía, March 9, 1847, APP, 3:107–108; Baqueiro 1990, 1:192–208, 2:216–217.

[3] See, for example, Baqueiro 1990, 1:228, 230–231, 234, 370; Ancona 1879/80, 4:17, 24; Norman 1843:227; Stephens 1963, 2:160, 226, 229; Reed 1964:126. Indians were still recruited to fight in insurrections and civil wars in later years, even at the height of the Caste War. See, for instance, F.M. Cossa to Gobernador, Valladolid, July 24, 1873, *RP*, August 1, 1873, 1.

[4] Pronunciamiento, February 28, 1847, APP 3:104–106 and EHRY 1:367–369. A key legal basis for land expropriation was the Ley sobre enagenación de terrenos baldíos, April 5, 1841 (APP 2:116–119).

[5] Baqueiro 1990, 2:220.

[6] E. Rosado to D. Barret, Valladolid, July 22, 1847, AGEY, PE, G, box 65; Proclama del gobernador provisional Barret, Mérida, August 5, 1847, EHRY 1:373–375. See also Chapter 18.

The Beginnings 63

Chichimilá, denied the charge at his trial, as did other rebel leaders later, and instead indicated that poll tax reduction as promised by Barbachano was the reason for the uprising.[7] Evoking a race or caste war was most likely a political ploy to divide Barbachano's vecino and Indian sympathizers and influence non-Indian opinion, capitalizing thereby on the involvement of several Indian caciques in the conspiracy. Barret's appeal for unity in the face of the alleged threat of an "Indian war of extermination against whites" was tantamount to denouncing insurrection of any kind against his government as a plot against the very roots of civilization, since it merely played into the hands of "barbarous savages." Fomenting a "race war" was indeed a severe charge for any political movement in a post-colonial society such as that of Yucatán, where people categorized as Indians made up the bulk of the population and the elites felt threatened by a possible insurrection of the exploited masses.[8] In fact, several Barbachanistas tried to divest themselves of the suspicion of favoring a racial uprising and subsequently joined the government in its alleged struggle to defend civilization against Indian barbarity.[9]

Government officials did their best to quickly back their portrayal of the plot with racial discourse and concrete deeds. The commander of Valladolid voiced his conviction that the district could only be saved by "immediately shooting any Indian conspirators and their chiefs." Which is exactly what happened. Within days, Manuel Antonio Ay was sentenced to death by a military court and publicly shot in the plaza of Valladolid on July 26, 1847.[10] In the hunt for Cecilio Chi, another supposed ringleader, government troops entered his home in Tepich two days later and, as a future commander-in-chief phrased it, "committed a number of excesses." Villagers were mistreated, some of their belongings stolen, an Indian girl of ten or twelve years of age violated and the *casa real* (local court house) burned. Several suspected rebels were shot the

---

[7] Quintal Martín 1986:33, 35; Baqueiro 1990, 1:227–228; A. Sel and F. Cob to F. Rosado, Yaxkopil, January 29, 1848, EHRY 2:278; Bricker 1981:96.

[8] See Gabbert (2004c:48–51) for a fuller account of Caste War antecedents and the fear of an "Indian uprising" in Yucatán.

[9] See, for example, Baqueiro 1990, 1:239–241.

[10] The quote is from E. Rosado to D. Barret, Valladolid, July 22, 1847, AGEY, PE, G, box 65. For the trial against Ay, see Quintal Martín 1986 and Baqueiro 1990, 1:228–230. Reed (1964:57) suggests that Ay was dealt with differently than former rebels, who often got away with imprisonment or exile or were pardoned, since he was the first to be condemned to death, an indication that Indians received special treatment. Be that as it may, vecino leaders of pronunciamientos were frequently executed in later years. See, for example, GCY:94.

64   *Part III: The Caste War and Violence: An Overview*

next day.[11] Between late July and early August, alleged followers of Jacinto Pat, another cacique suspected of being involved in Manuel Ay's conspiracy, were jailed and flogged "cruelly and barbarously" every day; their corn was also stolen. Pat's own hacienda was looted and his wife and daughters arrested.[12] During the subsequent weeks, hundreds of supposed Indian adherents of the rebellion were jailed and publicly flogged. Many were executed.[13] Retaliation came hot on the heels of these outrages. In response to the repression or attracted by the Barbachanistas' political plan, a wide insurrection movement against the government began to emerge, backed by a section of Barbachano's vecino followers and the henchmen of various Indian leaders. Several groups of insurgents began fighting for their own objectives including lower taxes and religious dues, free access to land and equal rights.[14] The uprising began in the surroundings of Valladolid in eastern Yucatán. Soon, most of the Maya-speaking lower class in the center, around Sotuta, and in the southern borderlands of Tekax and the Chenes region joined the rebellion, mobilized by their patrons or caciques.[15] Although the insurgents and their leadership included vecinos, the government was quite successful in depicting the rebels collectively as Indians and labeling the uprising a race or caste war.

From the summer of 1847 to the spring of 1848, Caste War rebels on all fronts were mostly on the offensive. One possible reason for the weakness of government defenders was the poor coordination of their efforts. Up to the appointment of General Sebastián López de Llergo on March 7, 1848, government forces of the still independent state of Yucatán had no central command, leaving officers to act in isolation.[16] In addition, towns and troops attacked by the rebels rarely possessed sufficient arms or

[11] The quote is from GCY:30; see also Baqueiro 1990, 1:235–236.

[12] GCY:33, 34 n. 8.

[13] See, for example, C. Carrillo, alcalde 1°, Tihosuco, July 30, 1847, AGEY, PE, J, Juicios a indígenas sublevados, box 65; P. Uicab to Gobernador, Mérida, August 1, 1848, AGEY, PE, G, box 67; GCY:28; Ancona 1879/80, 4:44; Baqueiro 1990, 2:28–33; Reed 1964:63–64, 102; Rugeley 2009:82–83.

[14] Heller 1853:285, 287; Ancona 1879/80, 4:18–27, 44; Baqueiro 1990, 1:222–237; 2:20, 28–33, 35–36, 58, 220–226; Reed 1964:57, 63–64, 102; Bricker 1981:95–97.

[15] Baqueiro 1990, 1:224–225; 3:8; Ancona 1879/80, 4:18, 31, 36, 74–75, 77, 137; Reed 1964:48, 76; Lapointe 1983:67–69. Cline (1947:49, 58; 1950, II:76) saw land loss or its threat, the more business-like nature of the sugar haciendas and consequently less paternalist social relationships in the frontier regions, where sugar production had only recently been introduced, as the chief factors underlying the uprising. See Patch (1990) for a meticulous study of the agrarian situation before the rebellion and a critical evaluation of Cline's hypothesis.

[16] GCY:46.

The Beginnings

ammunition.[17] Beyond this, the Barbachanista sympathizer Colonel José Dolores Cetina launched several pronunciamientos in the second half of 1847, which distracted government troops from their struggle against Caste War rebels.[18] As a result of the latter's advance, numerous inhabitants of the eastern towns and villages fled their homes to supposedly safer areas in the west, a premature move according to government opinion, and at times without any real threat.[19] This led the government to pass laws sanctioning such behavior.[20] A great number of people fled to northern Belize, where they established new settlements.[21]

The situation got out of control and became so desperate for the government, now led by Santiago Méndez, that the latter saw no alternative but to resign in favor of his archrival, Miguel Barbachano, on March 25, 1848.[22] Barbachano was still on good terms with some of the Caste War rebel leaders, particularly Jacinto Pat, and thus seemed the more likely candidate to negotiate an end to the fighting. He did in fact reach a peace agreement with Pat. Besides abolishing poll tax and ending the expropriation of community lands and baldíos, the "treaty of Tzucacab" stipulated that Barbachano was to be governor for life, with Pat designated lifetime "Governor of all Indian Captains" of Yucatán.[23] These arrangements, however, were neither acceptable to the Yucatecan elite nor to Barbachano's political rivals. Curtailing the privatization of baldíos and community lands would interfere with the expansion of

---

[17] P. Ramos to SGG, Campeche, May 6, 1848, AGEY, PE, G, box 67; Gobernador to Comandante General de Marina del apostadero de la Havana, Maxcanú, March 21, 1848, AGEY, PE, G, box 67; T. Vazquez to Gobernador, Abalá, May 20, 1848, AGEY, PE, G, SGG, box 67; J. López Llergo to General en Gefe, Mérida, August 1, 1848, AGEY, PE, G, box 67.

[18] Ancona 1879/80, 4:49–59, 85.

[19] For a complaint about such "cowardice," see Secretario del Gobernador to Jefe Político de Campeche, n.p., May 1, 1848, AGEY, PE, G, box 67.

[20] Consejo del Estado, Mérida, February 5, 1848, AGEY, PE, GB, box 69.

[21] Cal (1983:49) speaks of 1,000 refugees in northern Belize for July 1848. In 1851, it was estimated that between 10,000 and 12,000 refugees from Yucatán resided in Belize (Cámara Zavala 1928, part 8). Since the source addresses them as "defenders," the figure could refer to males only. Other sources estimate the number of Yucatecan refugees in northern Belize at 14,000 in 1855 (CGE to MG, Mérida, February 24, 1855, AGEY, PE, G, box 100), 20,000 in 1856 (Villalobos González 2006:181), 12,000 to 15,000 in 1858 (Superintendent to Governor, Jamaica, June 22, 1859, R. 65, ABH:225) and more than 14,000 in 1863 (F. de la Vega et al. to Obispo, San Esteban, February 2, 1863, AHAY, G, O, box 447, file 2).

[22] Nombrando Gobernador del Estado al señor don Miguel Barbachano, Maxcanú, March 25, 1847, APP 3:200.

[23] Tratados de Tzucacab, Tzucacab, April 19, 1848, EHRY 2:313–316.

66   Part III: The Caste War and Violence: An Overview

plantation agriculture, seen as the mainstay of future economic development. Lifetime governorships for Barbachano and Pat would for many years have stood in the way of any aspirants to these leadership positions, since the former was merely forty years old and the latter about fifty. At the same time, many of the rebel leaders and their followers had lost faith in Barbachano and other Yucatecan politicians. Time and again, political factions had mobilized the Maya-speaking lower classes to fight in civil wars and struggles with the central government, promising reductions in taxes and religious fees and the repartition of land.[24] Promises that were indeed rarely kept. In addition, constant battles notoriously drained the public treasury so that special taxes were imposed on the population again and again.[25] Pat was thus forced by his rebel companions to resume fighting, and the struggle continued.[26]

In the spring of 1848, the insurgents dominated large areas of the peninsula and more than 30,000 people sought refuge in Mérida and Campeche.[27] Despite the widely held notion that the rebels were on the verge of expelling non-Indians from the peninsula, no real threat existed for the west and northwest, as Rugeley argues convincingly. Campeche's city walls had a strong defense, while the rebels lacked the artillery and military training to seriously jeopardize it. Their offensive came no closer than Ticul in the south and Izamal in the east of Mérida.[28] At the time, the insurgents counted probably between 25,000 and 30,000 men.[29] The government had mobilized forces of similar size, among them no fewer than 10,000 *hidalgos*, as "loyal" Indians were called, a term indicating noble status during the colonial period.[30]

---

[24] See, for example, Nuevos premios de campaña, August 26, 1842 and Decreto dispensando de la contribución civil y religiosa, April 12, 1843, both in APP 2:215–216, 242; Baqueiro 1990, 1:28–28, 33, 228, 230–231, 234, 370; Ancona 1879/80, 4:17, 24; Norman 1843:227; Stephens [1843] 1963, 2:160, 226, 229.

[25] See, for example, Decreto estableciendo una contribución personal, March 17, 1843, APP 2:238–240.

[26] Baqueiro 1990, 2:176–183.

[27] Baqueiro 1990, 2:202–203. GCY (p. 57) and Ancona (1879/80, 4:132) estimate the number of refugees between 30,000 and 40,000, whereas González Navarro (1970:86) suggests more than 80,000 in Mérida alone; 6,000 people fled to Campeche in 1848 (Negrín Muñoz 1991:74).

[28] Rugeley 2009:66–67.

[29] Los indios bárbaros, *LNE*, December 3, 1864, 2–3. Dumond (1997:106) estimates the total rebel population at over 50,000 and probably more than 15,000 combatants in late 1847.

[30] Carrillo y Ancona 1871:68. The size and composition of the government forces will be discussed in more detail in Chapter 10.

The Beginnings

The fortunes of war began to change in mid-1848. The rebels, surprisingly for many, withdrew to the east and government forces gained the upper hand. While contemporary observers referred to this as "the powerful intervention of a providential Being,"[31] more mundane causes were probably decisive. The rebels faced the major challenge of supplying their troops with provisions but, for reasons to be discussed later, found little support among the Maya-speaking lower classes in the north and west of the peninsula (the districts of Campeche, Mérida and Izamal).[32] Following his return to power, Barbachano immediately informed the Mexican president of the critical state of the Caste War and requested both financial and military assistance. Between 1846 and 1848, the Mexican government made a futile attempt to prevent the forced annexation of the country's northern territories by the expansionist USA. The end of the Mexican–US war in February and the payment of fifteen million dollars compensation to Mexico for lost territory gave the central government financial and military leeway, allowing it to respond favorably to Barbachano's request for money, arms, ammunition and later military units. Yucatán returned to the Mexican Federation in August 1848.[33] Strengthened by these reinforcements, government troops advanced toward the east of the peninsula and finally reconquered Valladolid and Tihosuco in December. By that time, the rebels had suffered defeat on all fronts, having been pushed back to the sparsely populated area between Cape Catoche and Bacalar.

---

[31] GCY:58.   [32] Apuntes ... Manuel Antonio Sierra, EHRY, 2:368, 370–371.
[33] GCY:64–65; Baqueiro 1990, 2:103–104; 3:36–43; Bazant 1991:22, 26.

7

A War of Attrition

Battles between large combat units characterized the first phase of the war from July 1847 to the end of 1848, when rebel forces attempted to conquer the area controlled by the government. The insurgents mobilized large detachments, at times amounting to several thousand combatants, if government sources are to be trusted. Between 1,500 and 2,000 men assaulted Tihosuco in November 1847, for example, while 4,000 attacked Chemax and 10,000 Ichmul in December of the same year. In January 1848, 5,000 rebels besieged Valladolid, which was evacuated on March 15. In February, 15,000 rebels beleaguered Peto. Bacalar was conquered by 12,000 rebels in April 1848.[1] Late 1848, however, saw a shift in the nature of the war. According to a contemporary observer, it transmuted into "an eternal war with no quarter," assuming "a more bloody and fierce character." This second phase no longer saw large battles but a "guerilla war in which engagements were daily and everywhere but with no conclusive result."[2] At times rebel units totaled 1,000 or 2,000 combatants, but in most cases did not exceed several dozen or a few hundred men.[3]

General Manuel Micheltorena, who was sent from Mexico to organize the struggle against the rebels as *Comandante General del Estado* (commander-in-chief), arrived in Campeche on February 5, 1850. He pursued a twofold strategy. On the one hand, he institutionalized a line of military posts (*cantones*) along the front stretching from Iturbide in the southwest to

---

[1] J.E. Rosado to Gobernador, Valladolid, December 9, 1847, AGEY, PE, G, box 64; GCY:35–36, 40, 43, 50.
[2] GCY:72, 74.   [3] See Appendix 1.

68

FIGURE 7.1 Caste War defense work in Iturbide. Photograph by Wolfgang Gabbert.

Cruzchén in the district of Valladolid in the northeast, while other military units constantly persecuted the rebels, destroying their resources in areas beyond the front line.[4] On the other hand, he persevered in his attempt to negotiate an end to the war. Peace commissions had already been sent to dialogue with the rebels in late 1849 and convince them to cease fighting. Several military units failed to abide by the ceasefire, thwarting any attempt to attain peace.[5] Even Komchén, the headquarters of prominent rebel leader José María Barrera, suffered an assault in this context that saw more than a hundred of his followers slaughtered. Barrera himself was forced to leave his possessions behind, barely managing to escape.[6] During their excursions, government forces murdered hundreds of alleged rebels and their families. Rebel leaders lamented the indiscriminate killing of combatants, and of innocent women and children.[7] The frustrated leader of the peace commissions, the priest José Canuto Vela, noted in his diary on November 23, 1849:

The post from Becanchén brought bad news: massacres of Indians, outbreak of hostilities by some of our forces. Bad prospects for my mission. Our men of war do

---

[4] Baqueiro 1990, 4:30, 135–136; GCY:73.   [5] See Chapter 12.   [6] Baqueiro 1990, 4:73.
[7] Letters from Florentino Chan and Venancio Pec to Bishop Guerra and the Governor of Yucatán, November 30, 1849, EHRY 3:357–361.

70   *Part III: The Caste War and Violence: An Overview*

not think or foresee that the looting and killing of Indians puts us at the border of the worst evil, the duration of the war.[8]

Understandably, the rebel leaders felt betrayed. In a letter to the *corregidor* (chief magistrate) of the Petén in Guatemala, who had also endeavored to mediate a peace agreement, they complained of the Yucatecan government's duplicity. Shortly after responding positively to several letters from Vela's commission to make peace, the military sent troops to capture the rebel leaders, who consequently doubted the genuine willingness of the government to reach a settlement.[9]

While government forces maintained pressure on the rebels, it was impossible to launch a decisive campaign that would crush them once and for all. The Caste War rebels, for their part, raided the extended front line and besieged exposed points such as Kampocolché, Tihosuco, Saban and Bacalar.[10] Until the mid-1850s, they struggled hard to avoid extermination. In 1849, when two of their most important chiefs (Jacinto Pat and Cecilio Chi) were killed, "anarchy reigned."[11] Their successors were José María Barrera, Florentino Chan and Venancio Pec. None of these men, however, possessed the necessary prestige or influence to unify the rebel movement, which was now composed of several thousand followers and fragmented into an "infinity of bands."[12] This even led to skirmishes among them.[13] Pressure on the rebels increased when the government launched offensives between January and May 1850. Even Barrera's new headquarters Kampocolché was taken.[14] Barrera and his men were forced to flee to the forests. Accounts differ on the details. It seems clear, however, that they established a new settlement around a cenote that

---

[8] Cited in Baqueiro 1990, 3:237.

[9] V. Pec, J.M. Barrera and V. Reyes to Modesto Mendez, n.l, n.d. [1851], AHM, XI/481.3/3257.

[10] M. Micheltorena to MGM, March 28, 1851, AHM, XI/481.3/3257; GCY:72–73, 77.

[11] S. López de Llergo to MGM, Mérida, October 12, 1849, AHM, XI/481.3/2914. Apparently, Cecilio Chi was murdered by his secretary for personal reasons in the spring (probably May) of 1849. Jacinto Pat was slain by Venancio Pec in September of the same year. See Chapter 16.

[12] GCY:80; see also Ancona 1879/80, 4:275; Baqueiro 1990, 4:49, 58. A list of rebel leaders and the number of their adherents from April 1850 suggests that 85,091 people rebelled against the government at that time (Lista de capitancillos indios, M. Micheltorena to MGM, Mérida, April 4, 1850, AHM, XI/481.3/2914).

[13] Letter from F. Chan, B. Pec, B. Novelo, n.p., n.d. [1849], AHM, XI/481.3/2914; Letter from B. Pat, Mahas, July 19, 1850, CAIHDY, M, XLII.1850–1866/11.

[14] Baqueiro 1990, 3:221–223; 4:65–73. Several letters from rebel leaders provide a glimpse of how they perceived this disastrous situation (Cartas de capitancillos indígenas, December 1849–March 1850, AHM, XI/481.3/2914).

A War of Attrition

allegedly harbored two or three miraculous crosses with the power of speech. Here they founded a religious cult. The place became known as Chan Santa Cruz or "Little Holy Cross" and attracted hundreds of rebels, who in turn began to form villages in the vicinity during the autumn of 1850.[15] Subsequent years witnessed the emergence of a religious, military and social organization that integrated numerous local groups. The rebels usually referred to themselves as *cristiano'b* (Christians), *otsilo'b* (poor) or *masewalo'b*, while the term kruso'b (crosses), in comparison, was a rare occurrence.[16] It is this last term, however, that has become standard in the literature to refer to the eastern branch of Caste War rebels and will therefore be employed in the following pages.

For the divided and almost routed rebels, the new Cult of the Speaking Cross became a vital cohesive element. The proclamations of the crosses, generally signed "Juan de la Cruz," offered an interpretation of their destiny and presented past defeats as sanctions for having offended God's orders,[17] but they also inspired hope for a better future. Beyond this, veneration of the crosses provided inhabitants of different villages and followers of different leaders with a common ideological point of identification.[18] In fact, this new cult encouraged the rebels to continue fighting. Government sources noted that the "barbarians" had acquired new courage,[19] and were "determined to win or die, overcoming difficulties and despising dangers."[20] In the months to come, however, it was the rebels who faced major reversals, dashing, at least for the moment, the hopes provided by the crosses. The army attacked Chan Santa Cruz on March 23, 1851, and in the course of the expedition took two of the crosses venerated by the kruso'b, killed the idols' "patron," and captured

[15] M. Micheltorena to MGM, Mérida, April 2, 1851, AHM, XI/481.3/3257; Baqueiro 1990, 4:118–123. See Chapter 15 for a more extended discussion of the cult.

[16] See, for example, Cartas de capitancillos indígenas, December 1849, AHM, XI/481.3/ 2914; Traduccion de once manuscritos de lengua maya, April 2, 1851, AHM, XI/481.3/ 3257; Proclamation of Juan de la Cruz, in Bricker 1981:188–207; Libro sagrado, in Chi Poot 1982:277–294; Juan de la Cruz, Chan Santa Cruz, February 1, 1850, CGC:68; for kruso'b cf. J.M. Barrera to V. Pec and A. Puc, 1852, San Cristóbal, June 6, 1852, CAIHDY, M, XLII.1850–1866/25; Libro Sagrado, in Chi Poot 1982:285.

[17] See, for example, Juan de la Cruz, X-Balam Nah, Xocen, Xcenil, December 11, 1850, in Villa Rojas 1945:162.

[18] See, for example, letters 5 and 9 in Traduccion de once manuscritos de lengua maya, April 2, 1851, AHM, XI/481.3/3257.

[19] Comandancia General de Yucatán, February 8, 1851, AHM, XI/481.3/3255.

[20] M. Micheltorena to MGM, Mérida, January 10, 1851, AHM, XI/481.3/3255.

72   Part III: The Caste War and Violence: An Overview

2,000 prisoners.[21] Government forces found the bodies of numerous rebels who had died of starvation; scores of families surrendered to the troops.[22] In addition, many of the leaders were either dead or captured. In early April, most insurgents were prepared to capitulate. According to Micheltorena, only rebel commander Bonifacio Novelo was determined to continue the struggle.[23] In the spring of 1851, more than 1,200 people residing in the rebel area presented themselves to the army within a mere six weeks. When General Micheltorena handed over chief command of Yucatán to his successor, General Rómulo Díaz de la Vega, he went so far as to declare in a letter to the Minister of Defense that the war was over. Only "some remnants" of the rebel forces persisted "as always in the case of wars that have lasted so long."[24] This judgement was more than a little flawed.

General Rómulo Díaz de la Vega, who arrived in Mérida on May 29, 1851, divided government forces into "mobiles" and "sedentaries" to ease the strain on soldiers who had served a considerable amount of time in military camps or combat squads. He ordered the abandonment of several advanced military posts and sent the sedentary units to their hometowns to maintain public order and repel any unexpected rebel invasions. Active forces were to be relieved every four months.[25] Colonel Rosado, commander of the front line, was ordered to build five National Guard battalions of 600 men each, subdivided into three brigades (under General Cadenas and the Colonels Rosado and Molas). These were to replenish the garrisons in cantonments, where vecino numbers did not suffice for a sedentary guard with the strength to defend the front line. The remaining soldiers were divided into platoons to conduct "incessant raids" on Caste War rebels.[26] In general terms, Díaz de la

---

[21] M. Micheltorena to MGM, Mérida, April 2, 1851, AHM, XI/481.3/3257; Ancona 1879/80, 4:316–317.

[22] M. Micheltorena to MGM, Mérida, April 24, 1851 and R. Díaz de la Vega to MGM, Mérida, June 26, 1851, both in AHM, XI/481.3/3257; J.E. Rosado to CGE, Cruzchén, May 6, 1851, AHM, XI/481.3/3258; R. Díaz de la Vega to MGM, Mérida, June 12, 1851, AHM, XI/481.3/3256. See also Appendix 2.

[23] M. Micheltorena to MGM, Mérida, April 24, 1851, AHM, XI/481.3/3256.

[24] M. Micheltorena to MGM, Mérida, May 17, 1851, AHM, XI/481.3/3258. In less than two weeks, 358 people presented themselves to the troops in Cruzchén alone (Relación de los indígenas presentados, Cruzchén, May 6, 1851, in J.E. Rosado to CGE, Cruzchén, May 6, 1851, AHM, XI/481.3/3258).

[25] Baqueiro 1990, 4:151, 155–156, 159; Bases para la organización de la guardia nacional de Yucatán, México, April 16, 1851, AHM, XI/481.3/3255.

[26] Instrucciones á que debe sugetarse el Sr. Coronel Don José Eulogio Rosado, Mérida, July 4, 1851, AHM, XI/481.3/3256.

A War of Attrition

Vega sustained the dual strategy initiated by his predecessor. While he undertook to revive the peace commissions under Canuto Vela, constant pressure was to be exerted on the rebels in the form of continuous incursions.[27] In the spring of 1852, the general organized a major offensive that penetrated deep into rebel territory. The intensity of the thrust and its probable impact on the rebels are vividly described by Díaz de la Vega:

They are filled with terror for being persecuted and harassed everywhere, realizing that they have no village to hide that will not be discovered; that neither the rough forest nor the distance to our line [of defense] can save them from persecution; that they cannot pursue their agricultural work in peace since our soldiers attack them when and where least expected, destroying them, killing those who resist and taking as prisoners those who do not seek safety in hasty flight.[28]

The three-month government offensive resulted in the death of 296 rebels and the capture of 985 males and 832 females.[29] Another major blow to the insurgents was the blocking of their major supply route from Belize through Chichanhá.[30] The rebels there had already signed a peace treaty with the Yucatecan government on August 19, 1851. The kruso'b from Chan Santa Cruz attacked the village to bring its residents back into line.[31] Government troops ousted the kruso'b forces in Chichanhá in March 1852,[32] and the village remained disputed for some time.[33] Demoralized by recurrent army attacks, numerous rebel groups in the south (among others, from Icaiché, Lochhá, Macanché, Mesapich and Xkanhá) led by José María Tzuc signed another peace agreement with the government on September 16, 1853.[34] At the same time, many southern rebels disagreed with Tzuc's peace policy and

---

[27] See, for example, R. Díaz de la Vega to MGM, Peto, May 11, 1852, AHM, XI/481.3/3300; see also Chapter 12.

[28] R. Díaz de la Vega to MGM, Peto, May 11, 1852, AHM, XI/481.3/3300.

[29] Relacion de los muertos, prisioneros y recogidos, R. Díaz de la Vega to MGM, Peto, May 11, 1852, AHM, XI/481.3/3300.

[30] For Chichanhá's importance for the trade with Belize, see, for example, M. Micheltorena to MGM, Mérida, April 13, 1850, and Version al castellano de cuatro escritos que tomaron á los rebeldes, September 11, 1850, both in AHM, XI/481.3/2914; M. Micheltorena to MGM, Mérida, April 2, 1851, AHM, XI/481.3/3257; Corregidor del Petén a coronel Baqueiro, Flores, July 13, 1851, EF, August 10, 1851, 4, in AGN, G, sin sección, box 391, file 5.

[31] Noticias de la campaña, SDN, October 8, 1851, 4; Dumond 1997:186–187.

[32] R. Díaz de la Vega to MGM, Peto, May 11, 1852, AHM, XI/481.3/3300.

[33] J. Cadenas to General en Gefe, Division Vega, Campeche, March 29, 1853, AGEY, PE, M, box 178, file 104; J.E. Rosado to General en Gefe, Peto, May 24, 1853, AGEY, PE, M, box 182, file 34.

[34] Gobernador de Yucatán to MGO, Mérida, November 19, 1853, AGN, G, sin sección, box 416, file 10; GCY:97–101; Dumond 1997:192–197. The so-called pacíficos del sur

74   *Part III: The Caste War and Violence: An Overview*

resettled with their families in the area controlled by the kruso'b.[35] The rebels remained on the defensive there and were attacked even in their core area by government forces. According to prisoners taken by the military, many of the rebels were "bored with the life they were leading, without resources neither food nor ammunition and no hope of a decisive victory."[36] The government, on the other hand, was unable to mete out this decisive blow. Chan Santa Cruz and the surrounding areas were repeatedly attacked during the years that followed.[37] Each time, however, the rebels regrouped after the soldiers' withdrawal. Maintaining pressure on the rebels for extended periods proved impossible. Díaz de la Vega repeatedly begged the state and federal governments for reinforcements, albeit to no avail.[38] In addition, soldier morale declined dramatically following a number of failed expeditions into kruso'b territory in 1854 and 1856 with heavy losses. Beyond this, life in the military camps was characterized by abysmal living conditions and abuse by officials (see Chapter 11). An experienced officer drew a lively, if somewhat desolate, panorama of the military situation in the frontier garrisons, describing them as "threatened daily by constant attack from the enemy camp" and at "risk of succumbing."[39]

The failure of Díaz de la Vega and his predecessor, Micheltorena, to bring the Caste War to a conclusion was due to several economic and political factors. The war imposed heavy financial burdens on both public and private budgets. Manning cantonments and barracks, and upholding pressure on the rebels with mobile units called for a large number of soldiers and the National Guard.[40] This impacted on the Yucatán economy, aggravating the labor shortage. Díaz de la Vega's reorganization of government forces in 1851 was a response to landowner complaints that military service meant labor shortages, "restoring thousands of hands to

---

(the peaceful of the south) enjoyed autonomy de facto until the end of the nineteenth century. Later, they were gradually integrated into the state of Campeche as a result of intensified commercial and administrative relations and road construction. For the history of the pacíficos, see Castro 2001 and Schüren 2003.

[35] La cuestion de colonias militares en Yucatán, *EP*, May 29, 1868, 3–4. This source estimates the number of men who joined the kruso'b at between 4,000 and 5,000.

[36] M.F. Peraza to General en Jefe, Valladolid, April 3, 1855, *EO*, April 20, 1855, 1–3.

[37] J.M. Novelo to Mayor General de la Division, Peto, September 24, 1855, AGEY, PE, G, 1856, box 103; see also Appendix 2.

[38] R. Díaz de la Vega to MGM, March 26, 1852, AHM, XI/481.3/3300.

[39] J.M. Novelo to Mayor General de la Division, Peto, September 24, 1855, AGEY, PE, G, 1856, box 103; see also Appendix 1.

[40] Baqueiro 1990, 4:136. Of the 893 men liable to pay the religious contribution in Motul, 316 rendered military service in August 1850, for example (Matrícula del pueblo de Motul, Motul, October 1, 1850, AHAY, G, O, box 436, file 15).

A War of Attrition 75

agriculture and the crafts."[41] Lack of funds for military equipment and army provisions was a permanent dilemma. In 1855, for example, monthly military expenses amounted to 28,000 pesos, not counting the cost of weapons, belts, ammunition and other war materials, leaving the state "incapable of providing soldiers with footwear or clothing." In addition to 6,000 pesos for monthly civil expenditures, state needs totalled an annual 408,000 pesos. The treasury's annual income amounted to merely 350,000 pesos, mainly derived from the custom houses in Campeche and Sisal, and the sale of government bonds, leaving a deficit of 58,000 pesos in 1855 alone. In addition, the government had accumulated a debt of 59,500 pesos from earlier deficits and owed 93,000 pesos to merchants for anticipated import duties and loans obtained from a number of landlords.[42] Beyond this, frequent changes of government led to inflationary treasury expense, with each new governor obliged to reward his clients for their support. As Mexican General Juan Suárez y Navarro exposed in a report to the central government in Mexico City, each new Yucatecan administration issued offices and granted promotions, turning cities and towns into "deposits of chiefs and officers who mostly enjoy undue salaries." The new rulers acknowledged the nominations made by their predecessors and lavished jobs on their own minions so generously that "to say most [public] income is consumed by the payment of militia chiefs and officers not assigned to specific corps would be no exaggeration."[43] The recognition of former power-holder appointments and promotions was clearly an attempt to appease the beneficiaries and prevent them from rejecting the new administration.

The growing divergence of economic and political interests between western and northwestern Yucatán and the frontier regions constituted another major obstacle to mounting a resolute campaign against the kruso'b. The rapid advance of the rebels in the first ten months of the Caste War had convinced most Yucatecans that defense demanded financial and, if necessary, personal sacrifice. The more eastward the rebels were driven, however, the less urgent the additional sacrifice of lives, time and money appeared to many Yucatecans, particularly in the western and

---

[41] R. Díaz de la Vega to MGM, March 26, 1852, AHM, XI/481.3/3300.
[42] In 1865, the monthly military budget for Yucatán alone (without Campeche and Carmen) reached 54,424 pesos (Presupuesto, P. Rivas y Peon, Mérida, October 28, 1865, AHM, XI/481.4/9987).
[43] Suárez y Navarro [1861] 1993:176–177.

76   *Part III: The Caste War and Violence: An Overview*

central parts of the state.[44] In contrast to towns, villages, haciendas and farms close to the kruso'b zone of influence in the southeast, the political and economic centers around Mérida and Campeche, which were sufficiently remote, no longer felt threatened by rebel attacks.[45] The destruction of the sugar industry in the frontier regions as a result of the Caste War led to concentration in the west and northwest on the cultivation of henequen, the second promising export product. In 1879, the cultivated area saw an increase from 640 hectares in 1845 to 45,200 hectares.[46] Hence, Yucatán's elite considered firm military action less urgent.[47] While the line of cantonments along the frontier was strong enough to impede a massive rebel advance toward the west, the front line was too broad to be defended in its entirety, leaving scores of unprotected settlements potential targets for rebel assaults.[48]

The years between the early 1850s and 1864 witnessed an endless series of mutinies, rebellions and changes of government, often provoked by the conflict of interest between Mérida and the frontier regions.[49] This considerably weakened efforts to protect the frontier and defeat the Caste War rebels. In February 1853, for example, a group headed by Colonel Cetina, who had a personal conflict with his former leader, deposed Barbachano from office as governor. In turn, the latter's henchmen incited a rebellion in September in Tizimín and fought until they were ultimately routed on December 10.[50] As in other cases, troops were withdrawn from the front line for this civil war, either to defend or fight against the government. The defeat of the pronunciados made it impossible to resume defense of the frontier as before, since military units were frequently dispersed or transferred to other parts of Mexico.[51] Military activities were thus mostly confined to defending the front line. Even the number of cantonments had to be reduced to twenty-two, leaving many towns and

---

[44] See, for example, M. Micheltorena to MGM, Mérida, August 5, 1850, AHM, XI/481.3/2914; M. Micheltorena to MGM, Mérida, January 10, 1851, AHM, XI/481.3/3255; E. Rosado to CGE, Tihosuco, January 24, 1851, in Comandancia General del Estado de Yucatán (Impreso), Mérida, January 31, 1851, AHM, XI/481.3/3255.

[45] Rugeley 2009:121.

[46] Cline 1948b:41; see also 1948a:82–83; Remmers 1981:376–391.

[47] See, for example, Angel 1997:529.

[48] J.M. de Vargas to MGM, Mérida, January 13, 1859, AHM, XI/481.3/7504.

[49] GCY:115.

[50] GCY:93–94; Ancona 1879/80, 4:334–337. For the background, see Rugeley 2009:110–111.

[51] GCY:94–95. See, for example, M. Peraza to CGE, Valladolid, January 12, 1856, AGEY, PE, G, box 103; D. Burau to MGO, Mérida, September 9, 1866, AGN, G, SI, vol. 33, file 27; J.D. Capetillo to Gobernador, Tekax, February 25, 1879, *NE*, March 7, 1879, 3.

A War of Attrition 77

villages abandoned.[52] Peto and its surroundings, now unprotected by outposts such as Kancabchén, became the target of repeated kruso'b attacks.[53] Peto and Tihosuco were the only barracks of any significance in the southern line of defense, although here, too, the situation was grim. Peto had no more than ninety-two army soldiers and sixty National Guards, an "insignificant" number given the need to defend a sprawling town surrounded by numerous rural settlements. The situation was no better in the fortified garrison of Tihosuco. The 200 soldiers stationed there "had almost no weapons and the few they had were often useless in an active campaign. There were no bayonets whatsoever." The 150 cartridge belts at hand were damaged so that much of the gunpowder was lost.[54] Arms and ammunition were lacking in other places as well and, in a letter to the minister of defense, the state's commander-in-chief considered the armament of Yucatán's army "absolutely useless."[55] The lack of arms and ammunition in the cantonments was not simply the result of insufficient funds but, at least in a number of cases, of a conscious policy of curtailing the military capacity of the frontier garrison for fear of insurgencies against the ruling party in Mérida.[56] As if all this was not enough, Campeche's struggle from 1857 to 1862 to separate from Mérida and become an independent state in the Mexican Federation was a further drain on military detachments from the frontier settlements and cantonments.[57]

These drawbacks notwithstanding, Yucatán's government was not without success in the struggle against Caste War rebels. Governor Irigoyen made an offer of amnesty in December 1858. The date set to surrender passed without response and government forces made incursions into the northeast in the initial months of 1859. This prompted several rebel groups in the area to enter into peace talks. A treaty was

---

[52] S. Mendez to Ministro del Estado, Mérida, December 15, 1855, AHM, XI/481.3/4820; J. M. de Vargas to MGM, Mérida, January 13, 1859, AHM, XI/481.3/7504; GCY:95; Cámara Zavala 1928, part 11.

[53] G. Ruiz to SGG, Tekax, February 18, 1855, AGEY, PE, G, box 101.

[54] J.M. Novelo to Mayor general de la division, Peto, September 24, 1855, AGEY, PE, G, 1856, box 103.

[55] CGE to MG, Mérida, [February 9] 1855, AGEY, PE, G, box 100. See also CGE to MG, n.p., February 11, 1855, AGEY, PE, G, box 100; M. Peraza to CGE, Valladolid, January 12, 1856, AGEY, PE, G, box 103; J. Oxtoll to Gobernador, Tekax, October 9, 1858, AGEY, PE, G, box 115; L. Irigoyen to MGM, Mérida, August 30, 1862, AHM, XI/481.4/8772; Comisario Imperial, D. Burau to MGO, Mérida, September 9, 1866, AGN, G, SI, vol. 33, file 27; J.D. Capetillo to Gobernador, Tekax, February 25, 1879, NE, March 7, 1879, 3.

[56] See, for example, P. González to Emperador, Mérida, November 27, 1865, AGN, G, SI, vol. 44, file 69.

[57] See, for example, J. Cadenas to MGM, Mérida, August 28, 1857, AHM, XI/481.3/5440.

78 *Part III: The Caste War and Violence: An Overview*

finally signed on October 2, 1859.[58] The pacified rebels who settled in Kantunil were known as *pacíficos del norte* (the peaceful of the north) and, similar to the pacíficos del sur, became bitter enemies of their former allies, who in turn considered them traitors.

[58] Dumond 1997:215–217; L. Irigoyen to MGM, Mérida, March 11, 1859, AHM, XI/481.3/7114.

8

Rebel Consolidation

In contrast to the pacíficos del norte, rebel groups in the southeast were not prepared to surrender. Despite their precarious situation, threatened by hunger and with little hope of final victory, they were determined "to die rather than submit to the orders of the government."[1] This steadfastness was due not least to their favorable geographical position compared to that of their northern ex-peers, since it was more remote from the clutches of the government and closer to Belize as a source of arms, ammunition and other crucial provisions. Freed from constant persecution by army squads, kruso'b society consolidated in the late 1850s. Chan Santa Cruz and other villages in the surroundings and in the direction of Bacalar were transformed into more solid settlements.[2] The kruso'b gradually regained the initiative in the struggle with Yucatán and maintained it up to the end of the century.[3] The reduction in military pressure opened up new opportunities to assault frontier settlements.[4] In contrast to the first phase of the war, and as a result of their reduced military capacity, the rebels refrained from the notion of conquering or controlling territory. Instead, they developed a pattern of surprise attacks to loot cattle, pigs, mules, horses and valuables, selling them in Belize in exchange for arms, ammunition and other essential supplies.[5] In the 1860s, Yucatecan

---

[1] P.A. Gonzalez to Gobernador, Yokdzonot, January 25, 1855, *EO*, February 16, 1856, 1–3.
[2] See Chapter 14.   [3] Sullivan 1997a, I:3.
[4] Los indios bárbaros, *LNE*, December 3, 1864, 2–3; GCY:72–74, 94, 102–104, 175; Sullivan 1997a, I:3.
[5] See, for example, J.M. Novelo to General en Jefe, Pachmul, January 2, 1855, *EO*, January 23, 1855, 3–4, and Chapter 17. For details on the kruso'b economy and the relationship with Belize, see Chapter 14.

80   *Part III: The Caste War and Violence: An Overview*

military defense consisted of two lines of cantonments that converged in Tihosuco. Major garrisons existed in only a few places, such as Valladolid and Peto, with smaller command posts at several intermediate points. Confronted with raiding parties of 600 or 800 rebels who had negotiated the woods in the space between two cantonments, the soldiers "could do nothing." Each garrison alone, comprising eighty to a hundred men, proved inadequate for confrontation with the kruso'b, according to an anonymous Yucatecan report:

> When the force of the principal garrison was placed in movement and came to fill out its ranks with the stations in order to form a strong column and to strike with great success, the Indians had already had time to withdraw.... If some intrepid officer went to an encounter with insufficient forces ... or if some small party on the march from one station or another entered into an unforeseen skirmish with them, then our troops were certain to be defeated.[6]

The rebel attacks on Bacalar constituted an exception to the pattern of surprise assaults, pillage and withdrawal. This Yucatecan outpost interfered with kruso'b trade with Belize, representing a permanent threat to their supply of indispensable goods. Bacalar was assaulted several times, finally conquered in 1858 and held by the kruso'b for decades. In addition, the kruso'b achieved major military victories over attacking government forces, capturing scores of guns, ammunition and other equipment. In January 1860, a major incursion into Chan Santa Cruz of almost 3,000 men led by Pedro Acereto ended in disaster. Serapio Baqueiro qualified it as "the most ignominious and bloody defeat of the Yucatecan arms." It was so shameful that no official communique on the "gloomy event" was published. The kruso'b captured ammunition, harnesses, supplies and more than 2,000 firearms.[7] In fact, government troops were unable to reach the kruso'b core area around Chan Santa Cruz again until 1901. A thrust of several hundred soldiers failed to get further than Kampocolché in June 1864.[8]

The imperial interlude from 1864 to 1867 strengthened the rebel position even further. The struggle between adherents of Maximilian and republicans, who rejected the French invasion and imperial rule, absorbed considerable financial and military resources in Yucatán, as in the rest of Mexico. The emperor sent José Salazar Ilarregui as Imperial commissary accompanied by an army to take over the administration of Yucatán in

---

[6] Anonymous 1878:89.
[7] Baqueiro 1990, 5:117–127, quote from p. 127; Aldherre and Mendiolea 1869:78–79.
[8] La Redacción, *LNE*, July 1, 1864, 3.

Rebel Consolidation

September 1864. Ilarregui decreed dissolution of the National Guard and issued a proclamation in November inviting the rebels to lay down their arms and recognize the Mexican Empire. The rebels responded promptly with attacks on eighteen villages, hamlets and haciendas, now unprotected due to dissolution of the National Guard, and the capture of numerous prisoners. In their wake, they left fifty-five dead and twenty-four injured.[9] When the Mexican General José María Gálvez launched a counterattack with the aim of subduing the rebels in May and June 1865, his troops were besieged in Dzonot and Tihosuco by 2,000 or 3,000 rebels. More than 400 of the 1,000 to 1,400 Mexican and Yucatecan soldiers were killed or wounded. Artillery, ammunition and all types of baggage were lost to the kruso'b.[10] This disastrous defeat demoralized the Yucatecan troops yet again.[11]

Like his predecessors Micheltorena and Díaz de la Vega before him, the new commander-in-chief in Yucatán, General Severo Castillo, repeatedly begged the government for reinforcements since he had no more than 1,400 soldiers at his disposal, less than half the number (2,900) he deemed necessary to defend the frontier. Even this small armed force included auxiliaries and non-combatants of all kinds, such as musicians.[12] Campaigns by Yucatecan liberals in 1866 and 1867 to end Maximilian's rule further drained military units from the already weak frontier garrisons.[13] In addition, the kruso'b launched several major attacks and rebel success attracted new followers. Alarming news in the district of Valladolid indicated that Indian families from several towns had left and were heading for Chan Santa Cruz to join the rebels. No reasons were given, but fear of a new "general conflagration" of Indians was gaining

---

[9] GCY:134; Proclama del Excmo. Comisario Imperial á los Jefes y habitantes de Chan Santa Cruz y de las otras poblaciones anexas, Mérida, noviembre de 1864, *LNE*, November 23, 1864, 1–2; La Redacción, *LNE*, December 3, 1864, 3–4; Relacion de los muertos y heridos hechos por los indios sublevados en los ranchos Kakalná, Thuul y el pueblo de Tzucacab, Peto, November 29, 1864, and Relacion de los muertos y heridos que hicieron los indios sublevados en los puntos que se expresa, Peto, December 1, 1864, both in *LNE*, December 3, 1864, 4.

[10] J. Salazar Ilarrequi to MGM, Ticul, June 22, 1865, AHM, XI/481.4/9976; J. Salazar Ilarregui to J. de Dios Peza, Mérida, June 24, 1865, CAIHDY, M, XLVII.1864/21; GCY:135–137. Dumond (1997:292, based on Molina Solís 1927, 2:382–386) gives 1,000 soldiers as the size of the expedition.

[11] P. Regil y Peón to Emperador, Mérida, November 10, 1865, AGN, G, SI, vol. 46, file 14.

[12] S. Castillo to MGM, Mérida, July 4 and October 17, 1865, both in AHM, XI/481.4/9987.

[13] See, for example, Negrín Muñoz 1991:92–93; Rugeley 2009:243–247.

82   Part III: The Caste War and Violence: An Overview

ground among the general public.[14] Furthermore, a major section of the pacíficos del sur resumed fighting against the government and in 1868 carried out attacks on Yucatecan settlements in coordination with the kruso'b.[15] Loot from their raids brought the kruso'b firearms of good caliber.[16] In 1869, kruso'b leader Crescencio Poot even mocked the government: "If the government has no ammunition, ask me and I will give two or three hundred thousand cases and shells and grenades, whatever you want; do not bother to ask in Mexico ... Merida will fall and all of Yucatán will be ours."[17]

Poot's threat to conquer the entire peninsula, however, was merely a bluff to discourage the government from organizing new campaigns against the rebel area. While the kruso'b had acquired impressive skills to fend off attacks on their territory, their capacity for offensives remained limited. Assaults on haciendas and towns were realized with relative ease and even sieges of frontier garrisons lasting for weeks were possible. In August and September 1866, for example, 3,000 kruso'b beleaguered Tihosuco once gain.[18] The conquest and permanent control of larger areas, not to mention the entire peninsula, however, was way beyond rebel military strength and administrative capacities. Escaped prisoners reported in June 1869 that the kruso'b were preparing a major campaign on Valladolid with possibly 2,000 to 3,000 fighters.[19] Nothing of the kind took place in reality. Instead, several smaller settlements (e.g., Tacchibchén, Yaxcabá) were assaulted by approximately 1,000 men in early July.[20]

After the disaster of 1865, it would take years before the army made incursions into rebel territory. Colonel Traconis approached Cobá in March 1870 and advanced toward Tulum, Muyil and Chunpom in January 1871. Nicolás Urcelay reached San Antonio Muyil in August 1872.

---

[14] Prefecto político to Comisario Imperial, Mérida, October 1, 1866, AGN, G, SI, vol. 33, file 27. Possible motives for joining the kruso'b are discussed in Chapter 17.

[15] J.A. Cepeda to Gobernador, Tekax, March 11, 1868, RP, March 16, 1868, 1.

[16] See, for example, J.M. Novelo to M.F. Peraza, Tekax, March 10, 1858, GS, March 15, 1858, 4; F. Medina to Gobernador, Ticul, August 2, 1867, RP, August 9, 1867, 1.

[17] J.C. Poot, J.A. Cobá, A. Ek, C. Novelo, T. Moreno, A. Chablé, J. Aguilar, Tibolon, July 1, 1869, EP, July 27, 1869, 3–4.

[18] See Appendix 1.

[19] R. Novelo to CGE, Valladolid, June 22, 1869, RP, June 25, 1869, 2–3.

[20] Various letters to Gobernador, July 2 and 3, 1869, RP, July 5, 1869, 2; Los bárbaros en el Oriente, EP, July 9, 1869, 4.

Rebel Consolidation

Little came of these incursions.[21] Traconis conceded explicitly that "little of material importance" had occurred during his 1871 thrust and instead claimed "great moral advantages":

This time the Indian rebels have understood that we can wage the same war they wage; that we can invade them as they invade us; that we can destroy their villages as they destroy ours; that we are able to chase them in the middle of their forests they believe to be impenetrable ... and above all, they remain quite convinced that the forces of the government fight with faith, with unwavering courage and no holds barred.[22]

It is more likely, however, that the kruso'b were less than impressed. They showed little resistance to these expeditions, preferring to withdraw deeper into the bush after minor skirmishes. Although Traconis advanced with 1,000 soldiers and 300 hidalgos, he took no more than eleven prisoners, among them three women and five children. He claimed to have inflicted numerous casualties (injured and dead) on the rebels but did not provide exact numbers or other details.[23] The circumstances make his claims questionable, since he met with little resistance and ousted rebels wherever he found them. It is highly improbable that the rebels would have had the opportunity to carry off all their dead and wounded.

The advances of Traconis and Urcelay were to be the last major military actions against the kruso'b for almost three decades. The reasons for this reluctance resembled those of the past. The Yucatecan government shied away from the immense cost of a decisive blow to the kruso'b.[24] Most people still detested serving in the National Guard and landlords endeavored to obstruct the potential drain on their workforce to the cantonments. Kruso'b attacks did not affect the economic and political core regions of the state, as mentioned earlier, and rebel raids became less and less frequent. The survival strategies of the kruso'b had changed significantly. Their economy no longer relied on booty from Yucatecan

---

[21] D. Traconis to Gobernador, Valladolid, March 22, 1870, *RP*, March 25, 1870, 2; Diario de la columna de operaciones, Valladolid, February 20, 1871, *RM*, February 26, 1–2 and March 1, 1871, 2.

[22] D. Traconis to Gobernador, Valladolid, February 17, 1871, *RM*, February 24, 1871, 1–2.

[23] Movimiento militar, *RP*, January 25, 1871, 4; D. Traconis to Gobernador, Xocen, February 6, 1871, AGEY, PE, M, box 293, file 40; Relacion que manifiesta los prisioneros de guerra, Valladolid, February 7, 1871, *RP*, February 15, 1871, 1.

[24] A government committee estimated the campaign expenses at 200,000 pesos per month in the 1870s. At that time, the annual income of the states of Campeche and Yucatán amounted to approx. 107,000 and 232,000 pesos, respectively (Dictamen de las comisiones de guerra y defensa contra los bárbaros sobre la pacificacion de Yucatán, Mexico, 1873, CAIHDY, F, XXV.1873/5; Busto 1880, 1:xii, lxxv).

84   *Part III: The Caste War and Violence: An Overview*

towns to finance their purchases in Belize. Instead, rent paid by British entrepreneurs for the right to exploit the rich logwood stands controlled by the kruso'b gained in significance.[25] As Paul Sullivan has shown, forty-seven of the fifty-one assaults that can clearly be attributed to the kruso'b between 1853 and 1899 occurred prior to 1875. Only four or five incursions into Yucatecan territory took place after 1874 (two in 1875, one or two in 1879 and one in 1886) despite the fact that generally even garrisons in major towns were small.[26]

[25] See the detailed discussion in Chapter 14.
[26] Sullivan 1997a, I:3. My count differs slightly from Paul Sullivan's. I acknowledge two raids in 1879: see Appendix 1. Only forty soldiers were present in Peto, for example, in 1885 (D. Vazquez to Gobernador, Peto, February 7, 1885, AGEY, PE, M, box 232).

9

The End of Rebel Autonomy

The beginning of the twentieth century coincided with the end of kruso'b autonomy. The authoritarian Mexican President, Porfirio Díaz, sent regular armed forces under General Ignacio Bravo to Yucatán to attack the Caste War rebels. The massive and long campaign began in 1899. Protected by three Mexican army battalions and Yucatecan militia units, peons drove a path into the area controlled by the kruso'b with clearings of up to 300 meters in width to avoid assault. Military posts were set up every ten kilometers. Although they provided some resistance, the kruso'b were unable to stop the advancing government forces. The military campaign endured for three years. Chan Santa Cruz was occupied on May 4, 1901 (see Figure 9.1). Twenty-seven "battles" – in reality light gunfights – took place with no army casualties recorded.[1] In April 1902, the federal territory of Quintana Roo was established in the area once controlled by the kruso'b. Chan Santa Cruz, renamed Santa Cruz de Bravo (today Felipe Carrillo Puerto), became the capital. While many rebels left for Belize, others retreated deeper into the dense forest. In the course of the year, the army destroyed most of the remaining rebel settlements and milpas. Only a few isolated groups remained.[2]

---

[1] Reed 1997a:8; Dumond 1997:390–395. While likewise stressing the impact of disease, Wells, in contrast, mentions heavy army losses during the campaign: "Four thousand soldiers were struck with malaria during the course of the war to drive the *cruzob* out of their stronghold. More than two thousand Yucatecan soldiers perished during the fighting. Disease and fatigue were greater killers than the *indios*" (1985:105, emphasis there).

[2] Dumond 1997:397–399.

FIGURE 9.1 Generals Bravo and Cantón and the commanders and officers of the battalions that occupied Chan Santa Cruz, 1901. By permission of the Secretaría de la Cultura y las Artes del Estado de Yucatán, Biblioteca Yucatanense, Fondo Audiovisual.

Economic, political and military factors led to the ultimate defeat of the Caste War rebels. Firstly, the kruso'b suffered substantial population losses due to illness, such as fever and dysentery.[3] Secondly, several coups cost important leaders their lives, further weakening the rebels.[4] Thirdly, severe fluctuation in henequen prices forced Yucatecan entrepreneurs to consider diversifying their investments. This increased the economic pressure on rebel territory since several commercial companies were keen to invest in agriculture or exploit forest products in the northeast of the peninsula and the areas hitherto controlled by the kruso'b. As early as 1876, Yucatecan entrepreneurs began cutting dyewood, gathering chicle and vanilla, and cultivating sugar cane and tobacco in the northeast. The growing demand for raw materials for the European textile industry led to a boom in dyewood exports.[5] The southern borderlands to Belize, however, were still in the hands of the Caste War rebels and exploited by British companies. Many

---

[3] See, for example, Correspondencia, *RP*, August 5, 1874, 4.   [4] See Chapter 16.
[5] Lapointe 1983:148–150, 153–159; Dumond 1997:377; Villalobos González 2006:160–162, 254–258, 268–271.

The End of Rebel Autonomy

Yucatecans began to wonder "what prosperity the state might attain if it possessed the eastern forests, where not only dyewood abounds but also an infinity of other precious woods."[6] A newspaper article envisioned the various advantages to be gained by conquering rebel territory, including "immense fertile lands," new ports open to foreign trade but "first of all, the legitimate and secure possession of a vast expanse [of territory] covered with thousands of trees of precious woods that will deliver truly fabulous profits."[7] In addition, landlords speculated about access to the labor force in the rebel area.[8] These interests coincided with plans by President Díaz to advance the country's economy by promoting the production of agrarian cash crops and the exploitation of natural resources for export. Thus, the federal government was now more inclined to contribute substantially to a final campaign against the kruso'b.[9]

Another important factor was the termination of the protracted diplomatic conflict between Great Britain and Mexico over the latter's boundary with Belize. The presence of British subjects on the Latin American mainland had already infuriated Spain, which saw it as an infraction of its sovereignty during the colonial period. A last attempt to subdue the British settlers in Belize by force had failed in 1798. The status of the settlement and its boundaries with the republics of Mexico and Guatemala following Independence, however, remained disputed. When the Caste War broke out, the British were in an uncomfortable position. Most of the time, the regular military force belonging to Belize amounted to no more than 200 or 300 men.[10] These small British forces were not able to control its northern and western boundaries effectively, to stop the arms trade conducted by several Yucatecan refugees and Belizian merchants with the kruso'b, as demanded time and again by the Yucatecan and Mexican governments, or to defend the territory against a possible rebel invasion. In fact, Caste War rebels were not considered trustworthy and conflicts occurred several times when they impinged on British soil to pursue deserters or claim rent from those lumbering or cultivating along the rebel side of the border.[11]

---

[6] Noticias de Yucatán, *EE*, March 7, 1896, in Wilhelm 1997:76.

[7] La recuperación del territorio maya, *EE*, May 28, 1902, in Wilhelm 1997:333.

[8] Katz 1959:1017–1018; Wells 1985:98, 100.   [9] Careaga Viliesid 1990:124–130.

[10] See, for example, Cámara Zavala 1928, part 9; Ch. Leas: "Belize or British Honduras," 1863, reel 2 and A.C. Pindle to Ch. Hale, Belize, September 18, 1872, reel 4, both in TULAL, MIC 736.

[11] For examples of these hostilities, see Cal 1983:93–95, 108, 120, 124–125. Belizian settlements and lumber camps were also repeatedly attacked by pacíficos from Icaiché (Cal 1983:113, 115, 139–203).

Consequently, the inhabitants and institutions of Belize viewed the kruso'b with ambivalence, as a potential threat, on the one hand, and a force that permitted their entrepreneurs to exploit the rich wood stands on the Mexican side of the border, on the other.[12] Hence, the British government and the Belizian authorities endeavored to maintain friendly relations with the kruso'b but openly shunned backing the rebels in order to avoid a serious conflict with Mexico. In 1867, President Benito Juárez severed diplomatic ties with any country that had maintained relations with Maximilian. This included Great Britain, which had transformed the settlement of Belize into the formal colony of British Honduras on May 12, 1862. Diplomatic relations between Mexico and Great Britain were suspended until the 1880s, giving the British less reason to take account of the Mexican position.[13] The situation began to change when relations between the two countries were resumed and negotiations to solve the pending issue of boundary regulation got underway in 1884. Two Mexican gunboats appeared on the Caribbean coast prompting kruso'b leader Aniceto Dzul to ask Queen Victoria to annex the rebel territory. The government of the United Kingdom of Great Britain declined the request, instead offering mediation with Mexico to reach a peace agreement.[14] The dispute between Great Britain and Mexico was finally settled with the Spencer-Mariscal Treaty of 1893, which established the Río Hondo as the international boundary of Belize. While the aim of the British was to guarantee their sovereignty over Belize, Mexican President Porfirio Díaz was lured by the richness of the rebel territory. In 1898, the Mexicans stationed a pontoon at the mouth of the river to suppress the trade in arms and supplies. This ended free trade between the settlers of Belize and the kruso'b, and ultimately cut the rebels' lifeline.[15]

Important changes in weaponry and the improved equipment of the Mexican army constituted a third vital factor. Army and militia officers fought with pistols and swords, while the rank and file were armed with machetes, bayonets and muskets at first and as of 1853, with percussion

---

[12] Ch. Leas to S.M. Seward, Belize, September 5, 1863, TULAL, MIC 736, reel 2. For a meticulous analysis of the relationship between British institutions in Belize and the kruso'b, see Cal 1983, particularly chapters I and II. Villalobos González considers the relationship between the kruso'b and the British less ambivalent (2006, especially pp. 36–45).

[13] Cal 1983:114, 118, 126.   [14] Villalobos González 2006:249–250, 254, 258, 268–272.

[15] Careaga Viliesid 1990:123–133; Dumond 1997:361–363, 378–379.

FIGURE 9.2 Federal and National Guard soldiers in Chan Santa Cruz, 1901. By permission of the Secretaría de la Cultura y las Artes del Estado de Yucatán, Biblioteca Yucatanense, Fondo Audiovisual.

rifles. Officers were often mounted.[16] The flintlock muskets employed both by the kruso'b and their enemies in the initial years of the war failed to work in the rain, a frequent occurrence in the long wet season from May to October, leaving bayonets and machetes as the only serviceable weapons. Modernized military technology, however, began to work against the rebels. Breech-loading guns were not widely adopted by the kruso'b since they required specialized, industrially manufactured ammunition. As a result, many rebels persevered with muzzle-loading, single-shot rifles.[17] While these were more cumbersome to handle and had a lower firing rate, ammunition was cheaper and could be produced by the marksmen themselves from raw products such as powder and lead. The Mexican forces

---

[16] Reed 1997a:3; Informe sobre el plan de campaña del Gral. Castillo, J.L. Uraya to Emperador, n.p., [November 27] 1865, AGN, G, SI, vol. 44, file 69; Batallón Ticul, Armamento, February 9, 1882, AGEY, PE, box 220.
[17] Dumond 1997:393; see also p. 529 n. 16.

90   *Part III: The Caste War and Violence: An Overview*

under General Ignacio Bravo, in contrast, were equipped with modern Mauser rifles, Hotchkiss cannons and machine guns (see Figure 9.2).[18] It was thus modern technology, employed in a resolute and coordinated campaign by both Yucatecan and federal armed forces, that ultimately put an end to kruso'b autonomy.

[18] La guerra contra los mayas en Coatzacoalcos y Veracruz. Los mayas no resistirán, *EE*, September 24, 1899, 1, in Wilhelm 1997:130; B. Reyes to capitán de la fragata M. Azueta, n.p., March 1, 1901, AHM, XI/481.4/14652; Declaración del indigena presentado José Zacarias Ciau, April 16, 1902, AGEY, PE, GM, box 374; Reed 1997a:8.

PART IV

VIOLENCE AND THE GOVERNMENT FORCES

The threat or use of violence in attack or defense is the raison d'être of all military organizations. Physical force is primarily directed against the enemy but likewise applied to members of one's own group to establish and maintain internal hierarchies, enforce decisions by superiors and discipline subalterns. The following discusses external and internal violence. While the subsequent chapter addresses these issues in relation to Caste War rebels, the current chapter deals specifically with government forces. In order to visualize the heterogeneity of those who fought the Caste War rebels we begin with a brief description of each group.

IO

Government Forces

The Caste War brought several changes to the military. Firstly, the scheduled strength of government forces varied considerably in the course of the war, increasing from around 4,800 men at the beginning of the struggle to 17,000 in the early 1850s.[1] Due to recruitment problems, however, which we shall discuss, forces in active service were much smaller in number. In 1855, for example, a mere 5,000 men stood "at daggers drawn [*en pie de guerra*]."[2] In 1863, the operations division amounted to four infantry battalions and an artillery brigade of 1,942 men, with the addition of twenty-four cantonments manned by a total of 1,492 soldiers.[3] Secondly, combat units became more diverse. The armed forces that fought against the Caste War rebels were a heterogeneous mix. Regular government units included Federal Army detachments sent from Mexico City after Yucatán's reintegration, an infantry battalion (*El Ligero*) and minor artillery, and cavalry detachments of Yucatecan soldiers. The majority of those who fought against Caste War rebels, however, were drafted to the militia (or National Guard) battalions established in major Yucatecan towns and served for different periods of time according to shifting

---

[1] Organizando la fuerza permanente de infanteria, June 8, 1848, APP 3:211–212; Reed 1997a:3. The National Guard alone comprised 16,000 men in 1852 (M. Micheltorena to MGM, Mérida, August 5, 1850, AHM, XI/481.3/2914). Its strength rose to some 800 officers and 19,000 soldiers in 1894 (Rugeley 2009:314).

[2] CGE to MG, Mérida [February 9] 1855, AGEY, PE, G, box 100.

[3] Division de operaciones. Estado que manifiesta la fuerza que debe tener la expresada, Mérida, July 30, 1863, *LNE*, August 10, 1863, 1. The number of cantonments was later reduced. A document from 1866 mentions only fourteen localities with a garrison along the frontline, which was covered by a total of 2,480 men and surprisingly included Mérida (F.G. Casanova to Comisario Imperial, Mérida, May 19, 1866, AGEY, PE, M, box 254, file 19).

94   *Part IV: Violence and the Government Forces*

military needs. In the early years of the war, the Yucatecan government also hired several hundred US mercenaries.[4] Small units of cosacos, "country men covered with leather mounted on local horses," were particularly feared by the rebels "for the promptness and the facility with which this cavalry could pursue them." Without the usual lances, helmets and harness, they were more efficient than the regular cavalry under local conditions, especially on level land.[5] In general, however, they played a minor role since they were not eligible for guerilla warfare in dense jungle.[6] Volunteers were recruited for special campaigns when the need for additional combatants arose.[7] Furthermore, local vecino or Indian men waged their own war against the rebels.

The coexistence of a variety of armed forces, the strong reliance on draftees, the presence of volunteers in military units and the participation of people who fought the rebels on their own led to several problems and became an obstacle to central strategic planning and the enforcement of military discipline. National Guard units were subordinate to the political authorities and the state government. This meant that army commanders had no authority over them, thereby complicating military coordination.[8] Yucatán's commander-in-chief reported to the minister of defense in 1865, for example, that most troops consisted of men with insufficient military training and equipment.[9] Flintlock and percussion rifles of assorted calibers frequently coexisted in the same battalion and called for different types of ammunition. Army officers from other parts of Mexico faced immense difficulties when it came to training Yucatecan

---

[4] For the presence of US mercenaries, see M. Micheltorena to MGM, Mérida, August 5, 1850, AHM, XI/481.3/2914; Baqueiro 1990, 3:98, 111; GCY:66; Reed 2001:122–126.
[5] P.A. Gonzalez to Gobernador, Yokdzonot, January 25, 1855, *EO*, February 16, 1855, 1–3; Gacetilla, *LRP*, September 22, 1862, 2–3.
[6] Reed 1997a:3.
[7] M. Micheltorena to MGM, Mérida, June 20, 1850, AHM, XI/481.3/2914; S. Castillo to MGM, Mérida, May 2, 1865, AHM, XI/481.4/9976; several lists from July 1866 in AGEY, PE, M, box 257, file 48; GCY:105.
[8] See, for example, Art. 3 of Nueva organización de la milicia local, November 8, 1849, APP 3:282. The practical impact of this legal situation was somewhat mitigated by the fact that, beginning with Rómulo Díaz de la Vega, Yucatán's governorship was placed in the hands of militaries sent during certain periods by the central government, which held both the highest political position in the region and the supreme command of the armed forces.
[9] According to the 1842 regulation, those enlisted in the militia but not in active service had to attend military training in their hometowns each Sunday (Reglamento de la milicia local, August 6, 1842, APP 2:200). It is doubtful, however, that all of the men complied and the quality of the exercises remains questionable given the lack of officers with military education.

Government Forces

soldiers, who for the most part spoke Maya only and therefore needed local officers. According to Mexican observers the professional abilities of the latter left much to be desired, at least from the perspective of seasoned military personnel such as General Castillo, who even deemed them worthless and "not susceptible to instruction."[10] He recommended discharging most of the National Guard officers for reasons of "no utility," since they lacked all knowledge of military tactics, order and accountability. In view of his strong doubts about the local combatants' military capacities, the general considered it his "imperative duty" to inform the minister of defense that any attempt to conduct a campaign against Caste War rebels with these men "is to incur expenses entirely futile for the good of the Peninsula." Unless Mexican troops could be sent, operations should be limited to defensive action.[11] In the event, a successful operation against the kruso'b had to be deferred until additional Mexican regular forces arrived in Yucatán in 1899.

INDIANS AGAINST THE CASTE WAR REBELS

The role of Indians in the struggle against Caste War rebels has been consistently neglected or played down in much of the literature, possibly for its potential to question interpretations of the conflict as a racial or ethnic struggle. In fact, as mentioned in Chapter 6, many legal Indians fought against the rebels. The Indian caciques in Calkiní, Becal, Dzitbalché, Sahcabchén, Nunkiní, Tepakán and Halachó in the western part of the peninsula, for example, signed a declaration of loyalty to the government in June 1848, pledging to guard their towns against rebels, to form armed units in defense of the Yucatecan government and to render any other services the authorities might require. According to General del Castillo, Indians living in towns between Campeche and Mérida even became the "most terrible and fierce enemies" of the rebels.[12] They acted independently or joined government units on specific excursions.[13]

---

[10] S. Castillo to MGM, Mérida, May 2, 1865, AHM, XI/481.4/9976. Other contemporary observers had a more benign opinion of the militia's military virtues (Aldherre and Mendiolea 1869:77 notas).

[11] The quotes are taken from two letters from Severo Castillo to MGM, Mérida, July 4, 1865, AHM, XI/481.4/9987.

[12] GCY:70; see also J. Cadenas, Campeche, June 13, 1848, EHRY 3:274–275; see also T. Vazquez to Gobernador, Abalá, May 20, 1848, AGEY, PE, M, box 164, file 34.

[13] See, for example, R. Díaz de la Vega to MGM, Mérida, August 13, 1853, AHM, XI/481.3/3696.

96   *Part IV: Violence and the Government Forces*

Several authors consider Yucatán Indians an ethnic community and thus assume a natural inclination to act in solidarity. To account for the hostile attitude of Indians toward Caste War rebels, whom they erroneously depict as Maya in their entirety,[14] these authors attribute an "ambiguous and alienated identity" to western Indians, one they see as the result of long exposure to hacienda rule. In another publication I argue instead that Indians in colonial and post-colonial Yucatán were not a self-conscious community but belonged to an administrative or status category and that their loyalty lay primarily with their localities (towns, villages or haciendas).[15] While Indians in the west shared some grievances with their eastern peers, such as tax burdens, religious fees and the scarcity of land for cultivation due to privatization policies, in key aspects their situation differed. State capacity to control the population was greater in the west and northwest due to a more dense road network and stronger presence of government institutions and military units. Given local power relations and drawn by material incentives (poll tax exemption, debt cancellation and land allotments), numerous Indians decided to fight on the side of the government.[16] In later years, when the kruso'b had been pushed back to the extreme southeast of the peninsula, Indians in eastern Yucatán were also committed "to going on expeditions against the rebels of their race," and not without success.[17] The longer the conflict endured, the more revenge for past assaults became the motive to fight, beyond material incentives.

Once they had made peace with the government (1853 in the south and 1859 in the north) following their loss of faith in the success of the rebellion, the so-called pacíficos began to fight against the kruso'b.[18] Naturally, they too became the target of rebel raids.[19] According to

---

[14] See Chapter 13 for a discussion of vecino presence among the rebels.

[15] The role of the local community (*cah*) as the most important entity for Indian self-identification in the colonial period has been argued convincingly by Restall (1997).

[16] For the alienation hypothesis, see Bartolomé and Barabas 1977:22, 27; Barabas 1979:118, 127; Lapointe 1983:18–19, 28–29, 40, 47; Bartolomé 1988:117. A critique of this interpretation and further details on material incentives can be found in Gabbert (1997:211–220; 2004b:100–104). For Indians as a status category, see Gabbert 2004c:28–36, 60–79.

[17] M.F. Peraza to CGE, Valladolid, September 2, 1856, AGEY, PE, M, box 193, file 75.

[18] See, for example, P. Acereto to Gobernador, Valladolid, March 9, 1860, *EC*, March 12, 1860, 1; Itinerario de la marcha de las tropas sobre los indios bárbaros, D. Peniche, pueblo de Dolores, Isla Mujeres, August 19, 1872, *RP*, August 26, 1–2 and 28, 1872, 1–2; Correspondencia, J.A. Aguilar, Valladolid, January 18, 1873, *RM*, January 22, 1873, 3.

[19] J.M. Novelo to General en Jefe, Peto, March 31, 1855, AGEY, PE, M, box 186, file 93; J. M. Novelo to Mayor General de la division, Peto, September 24, 1855, and J.M. Novelo

Government Forces

Article 2 of the 1853 peace treaty, the pacíficos del sur were obliged to provide 400 armed men to fight alongside government troops against "Indians who refused to accept peace."[20] The treaty with the pacíficos del norte from 1859 required them to "repel and reduce any rebels in their direction" and if necessary to support the government with their forces.[21]

Besides volunteers and pacíficos, Indians were also recruited into regular military units at certain periods. Provisions for Indian conscription were diverse, however, and partly contradictory, at times permitting it, at others prohibiting it explicitly or not distinguishing between Indians and non-Indians at all, as was the case in the regulations of September 1846, January 1856 and February 1868.[22] Beyond this, while regulations

to Gobernador, Peto, December 29, 1855, both in AGEY, PE, G, box 103; J.M. de Vargas to MGM, Mérida, January 13, 1859, AHM, XI/481.3/7504; Itinerario de la marcha de las tropas sobre los indios bárbaros, D. Peniche, pueblo de Dolores, Isla Mujeres, August 19, 1872, *RP*, August 26, 1–2 and 28, 1872, 1–2; Letter by J. de la Cruz Pomol, Santa Cruz, July 1, 1872, *RP*, September 1, 1872, 1; Lista de los individuos cuyas casas fueron quemadas por los indios bárbaros en el mes de Julio, *RP*, November 22, 1872, 1. Lochhá, for example, was attacked and burned four times between 1853 and 1867 (see Appendix 3).

[20] Gobernador to MGO, Mérida, November 19, 1853, AGN, G, sin sección, box 416, file 10; GCY:99.

[21] Tratado de paz, October 2, 1859, *EC*, October 10, 1859, 3.

[22] Reglamento para la organización de la guardia nacional ..., Mérida, February 1856, CAIHDY, F, XI.1856/28; Ley que reforma la orgánica y reglamentaria de la guardia nacional, February 12, 1868, *EP*, March 20, 1868, 1. The law passed in August 1847 re-establishing the special administration of Indians, in contrast, prohibited Indian enlistment in the regular armed forces and local militia units, and their military instruction. Tantamount to a sign of distrust, Article 23 of the 1850 law for village administration pursued a similar objective with regard to military training and service in the National Guard (Restableciendo y reglamentando las antiguas leyes ..., August 27, 1847 and Ley para el régimen interior de los pueblos, October 7, 1850, APP 3:151, 479). Other relevant decrees merely exempted Indians "of pure race" (1858) or "of pure race matriculated in their Republics or who were servants on rural properties" (1866) from *compulsory* enlistment in the National Guard, leaving the possibility of voluntary service. Beyond this, decrees in 1849 and 1851 saw exemption restricted to "Indians not enrolled at the present time," while those in active service were to continue up to the end of the war (Nueva organización de la milicia local ..., November 8, 1849, and Suspediendo varios artículos ..., all in APP 3:284, 287; Reglamento provisional guardia nacional de Yucatán, Mérida, November 8, 1849, CAIHDY, F, VI.1847/24; Decreto, Guardia Nacional, *SDN*, February 28, 1851, 1; Decreto, M.F. Peraza, Mérida, April 3, 1858, *GS*, April 5, 1858, 1; Proyecto presentado por los Sres. Rejon y Rosado para emprender la nueva campaña contra los bárbaros alzados, Mérida, November 9, 1858, *EC*, November 15, 1858, 2–3; Decreto expedido por el Comisario Imperial llamando á las armas á los ciudadanos para la guerra contra los indios reveldes, Mérida, August 17, 1866, AGN, G, dossier 2001, box 2497, file2). Indians also enjoyed dispensation from service in the auxiliary companies for the defense of "towns of their vicinity" organized in 1855 (Parte Oficial, *EO*, June 22, 1855, 1).

98   *Part IV: Violence and the Government Forces*

granted Indians exemption from compulsory National Guard service in certain periods, it is not clear whether these stipulations were put into practice and, if so, for how long. Voluntary service was almost always possible. In fact, scores of documents prove that Indians performed military service in regular military units during the entire period under discussion.[23] Contrary to views held by several

---

[23] The following exemplary list of documents confirms that Indians served in army and National Guard units in all phases of the Caste War and in all parts of the peninsula. See R. Serrano to SGG, Mérida, May 5, 1848, box 67; M.F. Peraza to SGG, Mérida, August 17, 1848, box 68; Relación de los individous del batallon ligero permanente que existen en esta plaza, Campeche, March 20, 1849, box 67; J.E. Rosado to Comandante de Muna, Mérida, August 16, 1849, box 74 all in AGEY, PE, G; Relación de los muertos y heridos ... canton de Iturbide, Felipe Pren, Macanché, May 9, 1850, AHM, XI/481.3/2914; Decreto, Guardia Nacional, *SDN*, February 28, 1851, 1; M.F. Peraza to General en Jefe, Valladolid, April 3, 1855, *EO*, April 20, 1855, 1–3; Deserciones, batallon nacional del sur, Mérida, May 26, 1856, AGEY, PE, G, box 103; Decreto ..., Mérida, February 26, 1851, Orden ..., Mérida, November 2, 1852, and Bando ..., Mérida, March 27, 1855, all in GG:30–31, 36, 270–272, 398; J.M. Novelo to Gobernador, Peto, December 9, 1856, AGEY, PE, M, box 194, file 55; Lista de los Sres. jefes, oficiales y tropa ..., A. Duarte, J. Escalante, Tekax, October 31, 1857, *GS*, February 2, 1858, 1–2; J. Manrique to Gobernador, Peto, October 16, 1858, AGEY, PE, G, box 115; Relacion circunstanciada de los individuos de la tropa que han desertado del cuartel de Tijosuco, F. Pren, Peto, November 20, 1858, *EC*, November 24, 1858, 1; J. de la Cruz Salazar to General en Jefe, Yaxcabá, July 15, 1859, *EC*, July 20, 1859, 3; J.D. Romero to Gobernador, Bolonchén, December 28, 1860, AGEC, AH, G, AM, box 1; J.C. Contreras to Prefecto, Izamal, December 21, 1864, AGEY, PE, M, box 230, file 38; A. Barrera to Prefecto, Ticul, April 9, 1865, AGEY, PE, M, box 235, file 48; Relacion, J.T. Muñoz, Iturbide, August 4,1867, *EP*, August 9, 1867, 2; Relacion de los CC. Jefes, oficiales y tropas muertos y heridos ..., August 3, 1868, *EP*, August 11, 1868, 1; J. Pino Muñoz, Tenabo, February 1, 1869, AGEC, AH, G, AM, box 2; Relacion de los dispersos ..., Peto, February 16, 1869, *RP*, February 19, 1869, 1; J.A. Cepeda Peraza to Gobernador, Tekax, December 19, 1870, *RP*, December 26, 1870, 2; Relacion nominal de los CC rebajados del servicio de GN ..., Mérida, March 7, 1871, *RP*, March 8 and 10, 1871, 2; F. Coronado, to Gobernador, Valladolid, April 30, 1871, *RP*, May 5, 1871, 1; Relacion de los CC. Jefes y Oficiales del 5°, 6° y 7° Batallones G.N. del Estado ..., Valladolid, July 13, 1871, *RP*, July 20, 1871, 2; J. Vazquez to Gobernador, Peto, February 10, 1872, AGEY, PE, C, box 297, file 6; Comandancia Militar de Motul, L.G. Jaime, July 17, 1873, *RP*, July 21, 1873, 2; Matriculas GN, 1876, AGEY, PE, GN, box 195, vol. 2; Matricula de los CC de que se compone el Bat. GN No. 16 de Hunucmá, June 1, 1877, AGEY, PE, M, box 197; Relación de los soldados que prestan el servicio en la GN, Uman, November 28, 1877, AGEY, PE, SM, box 199; Batallon del partido de Sotuta, March 1878, AGEY, PE, SM, box 202; JP, Motul, Lista de la tropa, April 1878; Relacion de las individuos de tropa, Izamal, June 2, 1878, and Relacion de las individuos de tropa en las Colonias militares, Maxcanu, July 28, 1878, all in AGEY, PE, SM, box 204A; Colonia militar del Sur. Relacion de los individuos que ingresaron á esta colonia, J. Gomez, Tekax, July, 30, 1878, and Lista nominal de los individuos del batallon de este partido, Espita, September 30, 1878, both in AGEY, PE, box 202A; Relacion de los individuos de tropa que marchan a la colonia del centro, Acanceh, June 29, 1879, AGEY,

Government Forces

authors,[24] duties performed by Indians were not confined to auxiliary services (e.g., building trenches) but frequently included combat. The soldier Bonifacio Uh, for example, was commended for his participation in capture of an influential rebel caudillo in October 1850.[25] A few months earlier, rebel captain Pedro Naa was killed by Jacinto Canché, a soldier of the Tihosuco company, "who pursued and vanquished him alone."[26] According to a pension list, 87 of the 196 women who lost their fathers, husbands or sons in the 1864 campaign against the rebels bore Maya surnames.[27] Indians not only fought against the kruso'b but were also recruited to fight in the other insurrections and civil wars that haunted the peninsula even at the height of the Caste War.[28] Table 10.1 shows the

PE, M, box 206; Lista nomin . . ., H. Zapata, Motul, November 3, 1880, AGEY, PE, box 213; Relacion de los individuos de tropa, Sotuta, March 1, 1881, AGEY, PE, box 217; Lista de los individuos de tropa, Batallon Izamal, J. Fuentes to Gobernador, Tekax, March 2, 1881 and Relacion de los CC GGNN que componen el cupo de este partido, Hunucmá, June 28, 1881, both in AGEY, PE, box 217; Lista de tropa, Izamal, August 2, 1881, AGEY, PE, box 216; Lista batallon Acanceh, October 29, 1881, AGEY, PE, box 219; Relación de los CC. de la Guardia Nacional, Hunucmá, February 27, 1882, and Lista de tropa GN, Maxcanú, November 3, 1882, both in AGEY, PE, box 220; V. Salcedo to Gobernador, February 27, 1883, AGEY, PE, CI, box 367, file 48; Lista Nominal GN, Cozumel, July 1, 1883, AGEY, PE, SM, box 227A; Relación de los CC GGNN que pasan a la colonia del sur, Hunucmá, August 27, 1883, AGEY, PE, box 222-II; Listas de tropa GN, 1885, AGEY, PE, box 235; Lista . . . de tropa que componen la expresada, batallon 9 GN de Izamal, March 2, 1885, AGEY, PE, M, box 232; Relacion de los CC que tocó el servicio en la guarnicion, Muna, May 20, 1886, AGEY, PE, C, box 236.

[24] Cf., for example, Molina Solís 1927, 2:118.

[25] M. Micheltorena to MGM, Mérida, October 10, 1850, AHM, XI/481.3/2914.

[26] M. Micheltorena to MGM, Mérida, July 16, 1850, AHM, XI/481.3/2914. See also F. Martínez de Arredondo to Consejo de Estado, Mérida, April 11, 1848, AGEY, PE, G, box 67; Decree by Miguel Barbachano, Mérida, April 27, 1848, AGEY, PE, G, box 68; Decreto . . . guardia nacional, Mérida, February 26, 1851, GG:30–31, 36; M. Martin to Gobernador, Valladolid, September 1, 1856, AGEY, PE, G, box 103; M.F. Peraza to Comandante General, Valladolid, October 28, 1857, GS, November 4, 1857, 1; J.M. Covian to General en jefe, Valladolid, December 11, 1857, GS, December 18, 1857, 1–2; M. Cepeda Peraza to Gobernador, Valladolid, June 29, 1858, GS, July 2, 1858, 1; P. Acereto to Gobernador, Valladolid, May 17, 1859, EC, May 20, 1859, 1; P. Acereto to Gobernador, Valladolid, March 9, 1860, EC, March 12, 1860, 1; Lista de los . . . que marcharon . . ., Cansahcab, February 17, 1866, AGN, G, box 29, file 6; T. Correa to Gobernador, Valladolid, August 15, 1867, RP, August 18, 1867, 1.

[27] Relacion de las pensionistas de la guerra de indios . . ., Mérida, December 16, 1864, LNE, December 23, 1864, 3–4. See also several letters from Francisco Martínez de Arredondo to Subinspector de la milicia local, Mérida, May-June, 1849, AGEY, PE, G, box 111, file 50.

[28] See, for instance, Lista nominal de los soldados que marcharon en las filas de D. Pedro Acereto, Sucopo, November 4, 1862, AGEY, PE, M, box 208, file 17; F.M. Cossa to Gobernador, Valladolid, July 24, 1873, RP, August 1, 1873, 1.

Part IV: Violence and the Government Forces

TABLE 10.1 *Soldiers with Maya surnames in National Guard and army units*

Place	Year	Total	Maya Surnames Total	Percent	Source
Yovain	1850	36	3	8.33	Matrícula ... contribución religiosa ... con espresión de los q. no la verificaron por allarse en campaña, September 31, 1851, AHAY, G, O, box 436, file 1
Motul	1850	316	243	76.90	Matrícula del pueblo de Motul, Motul, October 1, 1850, AHAY, G, O, box 436, file 15
Peto	1857	81	7	8.64	Escuadron Activo de Lanceros, Peto, October 31, 1857, AGEY, PE, G, box 115
Tekax	1857	141	12	8.51	Lista de los Sres. jefes, oficiales y tropa ..., Tekax, October 31, 1857, GS, February 2, 1858, 1–2
Campeche	1859	100	6	6	Documentos del batallon Libre de Campeche ..., October 1, 1859, AGEC, AH, G, AM, box 1
Tenabo	1869	174	116	66.67	J. Pino Muñoz, batallon de G.N. Independiente to Gobernador, Tenabo, February 1, 1869, AGEC, AH, G, AM, box 2
Iturbide	1869	49	15	30.61	P.A. Lara to Gobernador, Hopelchén, March 14, 1869, AGEC, AH, G, AM, box 2
Chenes	1871	50	26	52.00	Lista de los integrantes del batallon Unión primera compañía de los Chenes, Bolonchenticul, February 8, 1871, AGEC, AH, G, box 16, file 22
Acanceh	1872	177	130	73.45	Batallon 1° número 9° G.N. del partido de Acanceh, February 27, 1872, RP, March 6, 1872, 2
Bolonchén	1873	301	168	55.81	Lista ... G.N., batallon Unión, Bolonchén, May 31, 1873, AGEC, AH, G, AM, box 6
Peto	1874	106	34	32.08	J. Corcó to Gobernador, Peto, January 6, 1874, RP, January 12, 1874, 2
Yaxcabá	1875	315	185	58.73	Lista para la rebista ..., Yaxcabá, February 2, 1875, AGEY, PE, CLM, box 202a

(continued)

Government Forces

TABLE 10.1 *(continued)*

Place	Year	Total	Maya Surnames Total	Percent	Source
Motul	1876	51	39	76.47	Lista de los individuos de la compañía de Muxupip..., Motul, September 18, 1876, AGEY, PE, box 195, vol. 1
Sotuta	1876	79	56	70.89	Colonias de centro, lista de revista..., 1a compañía, Sotuta, June 2, 1876, AGEY, PE, CLM, box 195, vol. 4
Sotuta	1878	45	28	62.22	Batallon G.N. no. 11, partido de Sotuta, March 15, 1878, AGEY, PE, SM, box 202
Mérida	1879	92	40	43.48	Relación de los individuos que... marcharán á las Colonias del Centro..., March 1, 1879, *RP*, March 5, 1879, 2–3
Acanceh	1879	60	46	76.67	Relación de los individuos de tropa..., Acanceh, April 29, 1879, AGEY, PE, JP, box 207bis
Cozumel	1883	54	9	16.67	Lista nominal de la fuerza alistada para el servicio, Cozumel, July 1, 1883, AGEY, PE, M, box 227
Sahcabchén	1883	62	16	25.81	Lista de los ciudadanos útiles para el servicio de Guardia Nacional, Sahcabchén, February 16, 1883, AGEC, AH, G, AM, box 14
Pocboc	1883	16	12	75.00	Lista de los ciudadanos útiles para el servicio de Guardia Nacional, Pocboc, February 15, 1883, AGEC, AH, G, AM, box 14
Hecelchakán	1883	156	105	67.31	Lista de los ciudadanos útiles para el servicio de Guardia Nacional, Hecelchakán, March, 1883, AGEC, AH, G, AM, box 14
Hunucmá	1884	41	32	78.05	Personal militar, Hunucmá, June 27, 1884, AGEY, PE, JP, box 227
Hunucmá	1885	41	31	75.61	Relación de los CC GGNN que marchan á la colonia del Sur..., Hunucmá, August 28, 1885, AGEY, PE, box 234

(continued)

102   *Part IV: Violence and the Government Forces*

TABLE 10.1 *(continued)*

Place	Year	Total	Maya Surnames Total	Percent	Source
Motul	1886	70	56	80.00	Lista nominal de los individuos ..., Motul, October 28, 1886, AGEY, PE, M, box 241
Mérida	1886	68	17	25.00	Lista ... oficiales é individuos de tropa del batallon 1° G.N., 1a compañía, Mérida, October 2, 1886, AGEY, PE, M, box 241
Muna	1886	92	39	42.39	Relación de los CC que tocó el servicio en la guarnicion, Muna, May 20, 1886, AGEY, PE, C, box 236
Chenes (district)	1888	396	185	46.72	Lista de los Ciudadanos inscritos en la Guardia Nacional ..., Hopelchén, March 31, 1888, AGEC, AH, G, AM, box 15
Total		3,169	1,656	52.26	

composition of several army and National Guard units from different towns between 1850 and 1888.

This data is not derived from a representative sample but provides examples from different time periods and regions. It shows, at least, that Indians, identified by their Maya surname, made up a substantial part of the army and National Guard units. Furthermore, although people with Maya surnames served as enlisted men, in some cases they even became sergeants or officers.[29] Indian participation in the war was not limited to

---

[29] See, for example, M. Micheltorena to MGM, Mérida, December 31, 1850, AHM, XI/481.3/2914; Comandancia accidental del batallon de Inf. GN "Independiente" de Tenabo, Campeche, September 30, 1869, AGEC, AH, G, AM, box 3; D. Traconis to Gobernador, Xocen, February 6,1871, AGEY, PE, M, box 293, file 40; Diario de la columna de operaciones ..., Valladolid, February 16, 1871, *RP*, February 22, 1871, 2–3; Relación de los CC. jefes y oficiales del 5°, 6° y 7° Batallones G.N. del Estado ..., Valladolid, July 13, 1871, *RP*, July 20, 1871, 2; D. Espinosa to Secretario de Guerra, Campeche, May 20, 1875, AGEC, AH, G, AM, box 8; Lista ..., batallon 9° GN de Izamal, Izamal, March 2, 1885, AGEY, PE, M, box 232; J.M. Tuyub to Gobernador, Sahcabchén, March 22, 1869, AGEC, AH, G, AM, box 2; Escuadron Activo de Lanceros, Peto, October 31, 1857, AGEY, PE, G, box 115.

individual regions or a specific point in time. Variations in the percentage of Indians serving in the different units are more than simply a reflection of their share in the total population of the respective locations and suggest that other factors, as yet unknown, must have been at play.

11

Violence and Suffering within the Government Forces

Soldiers are trained to exert force on others, a practice reinforced and legitimized by a value system that emphasizes manliness and courage, and by ideologies that define certain groups as enemies and therefore as rightful targets of violence. These traits foster the violent encroachment of situations that go beyond attacking or defending the enemy. In contrast to most warrior bands, armies in all societies are characterized by a marked internal hierarchy and a clear-cut chain of command. The threat or use of force against subordinates, for example, is vital to maintaining authority. Strict hierarchies also facilitate the abuse of inferiors by superiors.

RECRUITMENT

Violence for many men in the armed forces began with their enlistment. As mentioned earlier, each Mexican state was obliged to deliver a contingent of soldiers to the federal army. Since recruitment practices were never precisely regulated, some soldiers were enlisted by bounty, while others were forced to serve for several years, as in the case of wrongdoers or the allegedly vicious, such as vagabonds or men in poor condition (*vagos y mal entretenidos*).[1] The levy proved to be the principal means of swelling army ranks and by using such coercive measures the military began to resemble a "large penal institution."[2] The same holds true for soldiers sent

---

[1] See for Yucatán, for example, Sobre reemplazos del ejército y cupo asignado á Yucatán, March 1, 1825 and Aclaración al decreto de reemplazos, March 31, 1825, PG 1:207, 259; and for Mexico in general, Lozoya 1968:556; Escalante Gonzalbo 1993:176–177; Depalo 1997:159.

[2] Depalo 1997:31.

104

Violence and Suffering within the Government Forces 105

from central Mexico by the government and sentenced to military service in Yucatán for four to ten years.[3] Governor Barrera complained in 1856, for example, that Yucatán had been chosen as a "receptacle for the most infamous scum of the Republic, making successive referrals of bandits and criminals."[4] In 1866 alone, at least 1,000 "vagabonds" were sent to the peninsula to serve in the army.[5]

Recruiting practices differed, at least in theory, with respect to Yucatán's militia or National Guard. According to the relevant Yucatecan decrees, men between sixteen and fifty or fifty-five years of age were liable to serve in these military units.[6] There were, however, numerous dispensations. Article 6 of the 1856 decree included the exemption of ordained priests, civil servants, judges, physicians, surgeons, druggists, rectors, college professors and students, primary school teachers, active or retired military personnel, domestic servants, seamen, mine workers and people with physical impediments.[7] Exemption from service called for compensation in the form of a monthly sum paid to the state treasury. The amount to be paid differed greatly in the different groups, such as clerics, bureaucrats, judges, physicians, professors, teachers and college students, as well as in the respective regulations.[8]

---

[3] Lista de los reos sentenciados á Yucatán por el Gobierno del Distrito de Méjico como vagos, viciosos y nocivos á la sociedad . . ., Veracruz, June 9, 1856 and similar lists in AGN, G, dossier 1039, box 1, file 1; see also Traslado de presidarios al departamento de Yucatán, 1856, AHM, XI/481.3/5316; Propuesta relativa á que los reos sentenciados á la deportación sufran la pena de reclusión en Yucatán, México, February 22, 1866, AGN, G, SI, vol. 54, file 5.

[4] Gobernador P. Barrera to Ministro de Estado, Mérida, July 31, 1856, AGN, G, dossier 1039, box 1, file 1.

[5] J. de Dios Peza to Emperador, México, January 19, 1866, AGN, SI, vol. 50, exp. 57. The Yucatecan government occasionally resorted to enlisting men sentenced to National Guard service for "vagrancy or other crimes that were not shameful or degrading to the honorable institution of the militia" in order to increase the number of combatants in certain campaigns against the Caste War rebels (Proclamación, L. Irigoyen, Mérida, February 14, 1859, EC, February 16, 1859, 1).

[6] For age qualifications from sixteen to fifty years of age, see Reglamento de la milicia local, 1832, APP 1:54; Reglamento de la milicia local, August 6, 1842, APP 2:197; Reglamento provisional guardia nacional de Yucatán, Mérida, November 8, 1849, CAIHDY, F, VI.1847/24; Reglamento para la organización de la guardia nacional . . ., Mérida, February 1856, CAIHDY, F, XI.1856/28. For the age qualification from sixteen to fifty-five years of age, see Decreto, Guardia Nacional, SDN, February 28, 1851, 1.

[7] Reglamento para la organización de la guardia nacional, Mérida, February 1856, CAIHDY, F, XI.1856/28.

[8] Reglamento para la organización de la guardia nacional, Mérida, February 1856, CAIHDY, F, XI.1856/28; F. Pren to Gobernador, Teabo, September 10, 1858, AGEY, PE, G, box 115; Circular, Irigoyen, Mérida, December 27, 1858, EC, January 3, 1859, 1.

106   Part IV: Violence and the Government Forces

In reality, however, recruiting practices were chaotic and wide open to favoritism and abuse. Records of those obliged to serve or in possession of exemption rights were non-existent.[9] At first, eligibility for service was determined by local boards (*juntas calificadoras*). The latter's composition reflected the town's power structure and included the local elite or their relatives, friends and clients. They exempted kith and kin and tried their best to minimize the drain on the local labor force to military service. In six months the boards had led to "more casualties in the National Guard than the enemy in all of the daily encounters," remarked General Micheltorena somewhat ironically: "Each board exempts their relatives, friends, the relatives of friends and the friends and relatives of the latter, each time broadening the circle, so that it's a wonder anyone is left who is not exempt."[10] Even those who were unfortunate enough to be refused dispensation according to the legal provisions or favoritism did not necessarily have to serve. In 1842, anyone who paid 100 pesos was exempted from service in the local militia.[11] The regulation of 1846, which was reaffirmed in January 1856, allowed for dispensation of up to 50 percent of the conscripts. Those exempted were then obliged to pay up to four reales per month.[12] At other times, legislation permitted men eligible for service to pay a certain amount for a replacement. Patricio Novelo paid three pesos [8 reales=1 peso] a month in 1856, which was the regular quota in the late 1850s.[13] Prices rose to four pesos in 1880.[14] In addition, a certificate from a physician sufficed for dispensation, at least up to the late 1870s. This, of course, was not free of charge. While personal reasons may have led some people to act as a substitute, material incentives or an immediate cash payment were probably the main attraction. Hence, active military service fell disproportionately to the poor and the powerless, who

---

[9] J. Garcia Morales to MGO, Mérida, July 3, 1866, AGN, G, SI, vol. 34, box 12.

[10] M. Micheltorena to MGM, Mérida, August 5, 1850, AHM, XI/481.3/2914. See also Opinion presentada por el que suscribe al Gobernador Dn Agustin Acereto ..., P.A. González, Mérida, [November], 1865, AGN, G, SI, vol. 44, file 69. For the board composition, see articles 15 to 17 in Nueva organización de la milicia local, November 8, 1849, APP 3:284.

[11] Reglamento de la milicia local, Mérida, August 6, 1842, APP 2:197. The article was abolished in 1847 (Nueva organización de la milicia local, March 27, 1847, APP 3:111).

[12] Reglamento para la organización de la guardia nacional ..., Mérida, February 20, 1856, CAIHDY, F, XXVII.1874/07–2/2.

[13] P. Novelo to Gobernador, Tekax, July 8, 1856, AGEY, PE, G, box 121, file 87; F. Pren to Gobernador, Teabo, September 10, 1858, AGEY, PE, G, box 115. Most hacienda stewards earned no more than 12 pesos and received an allowance of three *cargas* (some 540 liters) of maize per month in the late 1850s (Bracamonte 1993:143).

[14] J. Cabañas to Gobernador, Mérida, November 8, 1880, AGEY, PE, SM, box 214.

Violence and Suffering within the Government Forces   107

had few, if any, links to local elites in the exemption boards and were more likely to accept offers to act as a substitute.[15]

Yucatecan governments recognized the injustice of these recruitment practices and pursued an alternative course. In the brief imperial interlude, soldiers were conscripted by casting lots (*sorteo*). The respective law, however, saw the number of men obliged to participate reduced to the extreme so that drawing a lot almost certainly meant entering active service. Hence sorteo, originally devised as a more just means of military service enlistment, proved "utterly inefficient" in this regard.[16] Only in the late 1870s did state governments begin to exert stronger control over eligibility for service exemption in order to mitigate the gross inequities of National Guard recruitment. They confined examination board competence to decisions on the conscripts' physical impediments and established jefes políticos as the men in charge.[17] All in all, however, there can be no doubt that the lower classes bore the brunt of active service in the National Guard up to the end of the Caste War.

Most men had a profound dislike for military service, which put their health and lives at risk, deprived their families of male protection and their fields of labor. In addition to miserable living conditions in the cantonments and on campaigns, discussed in the next section, National Guard soldiers were obliged to leave their families and occupations for extended periods of time, which was in turn highly detrimental to the upkeep of their households. National Guard service interfered with subsistence activities, a particularly irksome aspect for poorer people.[18] Hence, soldiers were eager to ensure that their households be given corn allowances during their absence.[19] More often than not, however, the grain failed to materialize, so that families were left "weeping from hunger and begging

---

[15] See, for example, Junta popular para trata sobre la guerra de castas, Mérida, *EC*, November 26, 1858, 2–4; Relacion de los CC que tocó el servicio en la guarnicion, Muna, May 20, 1886, AGEY, PE, C, box 236.

[16] P. Regil y Peón to Emperador, Mérida, November 10, 1865, AGN, G, SI, vol. 46, file 14. For the casting of lots as a means to decide who was to continue military service in Bacalar in 1851, see Cuaderno copiador de comunicaciones dirigidos por el comandante de Bacalar, Don Isidro González, al Comandante General del Estado, Bacalar, February 28 to August 4, 1851, CAIHDY, M, XLIV.1850–1859/22.

[17] Prevenciones para la organización de la guardia nacional, Mérida, March 27, 1878, EA:301–302; Guardia Nacional, *RP*, October 22, 1877, 4.

[18] See, for example, M. Medrano et al. to Gobernador, Cozumel, October 30, 1882, AGEY, PE, ODG, box 220.

[19] Three *almudes* per week in the case of the rank and file and five for officer families. According to Suárez Molina (1977, 1:100–101), the almud varied considerably in value. One almud could be equivalent to 3.5 or 5.5 kilos.

108 *Part IV: Violence and the Government Forces*

for corn." When the soldiers returned home to heal the wounds and diseases they had acquired in the course of service, they received neither salaries nor allowances, aggravating the problem of feeding their families.[20] The situation failed to improve in subsequent years. In 1855, the soldiers' families had to content themselves with the "paltry and dismal relief" of two pesos a month.[21]

Due to chaotic and unfair recruitment practices, which were frequently compromised by favoritism, military service risks and the ensuing difficulties for the families of recruits, many of those liable for service attempted to evade conscription by hiding or leaving their community. In addition to the numerous exemptions, this led to a permanent lack of soldiers. Force was therefore exerted time and again to catch recruits.[22] Petrona Dominguez, for example, complained to the jefe político that her adult son had been whipped during recruitment in Seybaplaya in 1849.[23] The inhabitants of the towns and villages decried the frequent abuse by officers who came to draft replacements for National Guard units in the cantonments. In 1879, the residents of Halachó declared that each time they had to deliver their district force for service on the southern frontier, the captains of the companies "surprised them in their homes at odd times during the night" and imprisoned them.[24]

Although the regulations put the minimum age at sixteen, once in a while younger youth or even children were coerced into military service. This was the fate of Andrés Obregón in 1848, for instance, who was twelve years old at the time.[25] In 1877, the government deemed it necessary to introduce a decree that prohibited the enlisting of minors under the age of sixteen in the National Guard, in the hope that this would put an end to the "repeated complaints of so many citizens, whose children had been snatched from the bosom of their family."[26] Clearly Obregón's fate was far from unique. Leaders of the numerous pronunciamientos and rebellions often resorted to violent means to recruit combatants for their

---

[20] M. Micheltorena to MGM, Mérida, August 5, 1850, AHM, XI/481.3/2914.
[21] CGE to MG, Mérida, [February 9] 1855, AGEY, PE, G, box 100.
[22] See, for example, P. Regil y Peón to Emperador, Mérida, November 10, 1865, AGN, G, SI, vol. 46, file 14.
[23] M. Contreras to Jefe Superior Político del Distrito, Seybaplaya, May 19, 1849, AGEC, PY, G, box 10, file 776. See also P. Regil y Peón to Emperador, Mérida, November 10, 1865, AGN, G, SI, vol. 46, file 14.
[24] C. Solís to Gobernador, Maxcanú, July 4, 1879, AGEY, PE, box 206A.
[25] Excepción del servico de armas, A. Obregón, Santa Elena, July 29, 1882, AGEY, PE, ODG, box 218.
[26] Guardia Nacional, *RP*, October 22, 1877, 4.

Violence and Suffering within the Government Forces 109

campaigns. Hence, conservative actors used canings and "other iniquities" to pressure Indian and vecino peons into joining the 1863 rebellion of Felipe Navarrete against the liberal government.[27]

To summarize, while some government forces fought voluntarily against the Caste War rebels, most men – both Yucatecans and soldiers of the Mexican army sent to the peninsula – were compelled to do so, either as compulsory service in the militia or National Guard or due to a sentence to serve in the army. The recruiting process was often fraught with arbitrariness and favoritism, and replenished by the ruthless use of force that deprived families of their providers or hijacked minors. In view of these facts, patriotic motives could hardly be expected either from Mexican soldiers, who considered Yucatán a foreign country or a penal colony, or Yucatecans forced into the armed service. Given these conditions, the relatively high level of internal violence in military units in the interests of discipline comes as no surprise.

HUNGER, MISERY AND ABUSE

Soldiers not only experienced ill-treatment during recruitment but were also subjected to various forms of hardship and abuse as members of military units. Uncertainty about their length of service was a serious annoyance for the National Guard. Theoretically, regulations limited the term of active service in the cantonments to a few months, after which the men were allowed to resume their civil occupations. Military service lasted six months in 1855 and was later reduced to two months. Although draftees were entitled to at least eight months leave before returning to active duty, this stipulation was frequently ignored. Many of the men were almost constantly on guard, especially in the frontier towns, and could be called upon to serve shortly after having been relieved. Only on request were they granted a month to order their private affairs.[28] In addition, officers and the rank and file were stressed by the risks common to any military activity, such as injury or death, but also suffered from lack of provisions, resulting in increased rates of illness, unrest and desertion. Supply transport was another major problem. In

---

[27] L. Irigoyen to MGM, Habana, February 22, 1864, AHM, XI/481.4/9373.
[28] J. Castillo Peraza to Gobernador, Tekax, April 9, 1855, AGEY, PE, G, box 101; A. Uitz and G. Dzul to Gobernador, Mérida, May 16, 1882, and P. Poot to Gobernador, Valladolid, November 13, 1882, both in AGEY, PE, ODG, box 220; E. Sosa, V. Pech et al. to Gobernador, Merida, November 24, 1884, AGEY, PE, ODG, box 227A.

110   *Part IV: Violence and the Government Forces*

1865, for example, the war commissioner (*comisario de guerra*) decried the shortage of pack animals. Although he required at least 331, he disposed of only forty-six mules and six horses, making it impossible to guarantee regular provisioning for the troops.[29] As a result, the cantonments were poorly supplied and soldiers left "without pay, without a uniform, forced to take corn from the enemy for a scanty meal."[30] General Micheltorena reported that soldiers rarely received two proper meals and had to be content with one dry tortilla [a cornmeal flatbread] and "poorly seasoned vegetables to complete their daily sustenance" in 1851.[31] In February 1866, the commanding general complained that the detachment in Dzonotchel had received no supplies for fifteen days. Due to lack of military funds he had used his own money and any belongings of value to buy provisions for his soldiers.[32] His successor, the Mexican General Francisco G. Casanova, stressed a few months later that supplying soldiers with good quality provisions was an "urgent need" since they had been "forced to eat rotten meat and pitted hardtack [*galleta picada*], which caused dysentery and other ills."[33]

Soldiers not only suffered from lack of food but also adequate clothing. In 1850, for example, the federal and state governments argued about who was to cover the expense. The commander of the frontier garrisons deplored the increased nakedness of the "defenders of the fatherland" and assured "without exaggeration that there are men who with great effort keep the patched remains of ragged drawers to cover their private parts."[34] The "unhappy soldier," who "attacks the barbarians through stony and thorny areas that render his footwear useless," lacked even the leather sole and the henequen to replace his sandals.[35] The rainy season was particularly harrowing. "It moves you to compassion," General Micheltorena reported on seeing squads returning from the enemy camp

---

[29] L. Gutierrez to Comisario Imperial, Peto, March 23, 1865, AGEY, PE, M, box 235, file 28.

[30] M. Micheltorena to MGM, Mérida, August 5, 1850, AHM, XI/481.3/2914. See also Cámara Zavala 1928, part 11; N. Remires to CGE, Yaxcabá, May 21, 1849, AGEY, PE, M, box 167, file 11; Causa seguida contra varios desertores . . ., Hunucmá, Febrero 12 – March 19,1852, AGEY, PE, J, box 145, file 27; GCY:45, 64.

[31] M. Micheltorena to MGM, March 28, 1851, AHM, XI/481.3/3257.

[32] S. Castillo to Comisario Imperial, Mérida, February 5, 1866, AGEY, PE, M, box 245, file 44.

[33] F.G. Casanova to Comisario Imperial, Mérida, May 19, 1866, AGEY, PE, M, box 254, file 19. See also M. Micheltorena to MGM, Mérida, January 10, 1851, AHM, XI/481.3/3255.

[34] M. Micheltorena to MGM, Mérida, August 28, 1850, AHM, XI/481.3/2914.

[35] J.E. Rosado to M. Micheltorena, Peto, April 1, 1850, AHM, XI/481.3/2914.

Violence and Suffering within the Government Forces   111

"in clothes soaked by persistent rain with no other garments to cover their damp flesh. This evil causes seasonal diseases."[36] The wet climate favored colds and fevers, and hospitals in the cantonments were crowded with invalids. Beyond this, constant rain made the landscape waterlogged and impassable so that soldiers occasionally found themselves up to their knees in mud.[37] Frugality became a "humiliating plight" with troops poorly armed and clothed, and surgeons, medicine or other items crucial to the campaign non-existent.[38] The years that followed brought little improvement in provisioning.

As if all this was not enough to demoralize the soldiers, they were often paid late or not at all. The commander-in-chief complained in 1855, for example, that he frequently had no funds to disburse his officers and soldiers, even at reduced rates, so that he owed them a month's pay or more.[39] On top of this, officers tended to abuse their power by coercing soldiers into working on their farms without compensation. Soldiers were also rented out as servants to suppliers or as field hands to private farmers "like parties of slaves." Flogging was one of the methods used to force soldiers to comply with these illegal orders.[40]

Given these conditions, it comes as no surprise that maintaining discipline constituted a major challenge. Punishment beatings were officially forbidden in government forces. In fact, several officers were sanctioned for disregarding this proscription.[41] Canings and whippings, on the other hand, remained a common punishment for insubordination. In more serious cases, soldiers were shot. On September 10, 1850, for instance, lack of supplies induced an entire company to rebel in the cantonment of Yaxcabá. They left the trenches, occupied the town's main square and in protest destroyed what the inhabitants had sown, and even broke into the jefe político's house. The citizens felt that their lives and interests had been

---

[36] M. Micheltorena to MGM, Mérida, August 28, 1850, AHM, XI/481.3/2914.
[37] M. Micheltorena to MGM, Mérida, October 10, 1850, AHM, XI/481.3/2914.
[38] CGE to MG, Mérida, February 11, 1855, AGEY, PE, G, box 100. See also P.A. Gonzalez to Gobernador, Yokdzonot, January 25, 1855, *EO*, February 16, 1855, 1–3.
[39] CGE to MG, Mérida, [February 9] 1855, AGEY, PE, G, box 100. See also F.G. Casanova to Comisario Imperial, Mérida, May 19, 1866, AGEY, PE, M, box 254, file 19.
[40] M. Ancona to Gobernador, Hunucmá, March 17, 1881, AGEY, PE, JP, box 217. See also P. Ortega Polanco to Gobernador, Acanceh, October 19, 1878, AGEY, PE, box 202A; P.M. Ruz to Gobernador, Sotuta, September 6, 1879, AGEY, PE, SM, box 206A; Declaration, n.p., [1882], AGEC, AH, G, AM, box 13; E. Sosa, V. Pech et al. to Gobernador, Mérida, November 24, 1884, AGEY, PE, ODG, box 227A; Cámara Zavala 1928, part 2.
[41] See, for example, J. Cadenas to CGE, Mérida, January 30, 1856, AGEY, PE, G, box 103.

Part IV: Violence and the Government Forces

threatened and that these rioters had allegedly committed "violent crimes." When reinforcements arrived, the supposed ringleaders, two privates, were executed and the rest of the protesters condemned to 100 canings.[42] A soldier serving in the canton of Tihosuco in 1851 refused to eat what was served up because of its moldy quality. The commanding officer, Colonel Eulogio Rosado, ordered him to be flogged. The soldier's screams attracted the attention of his comrades, who began to rebel against their officers. Rosado calmed the protesters by promising to attend to the soldiers' demands. Once reinforcements from other garrisons had arrived, however, the six ringleaders were arrested and shot.[43]

DESERTION AND ITS PUNISHMENT

The multiplicity of troubles sketched in the previous sections, including anarchic and unfair recruiting practices, lack of pay, grim living conditions, abuse by officers in the cantonments, and the risk of illness and death were reasons for mutiny, indiscipline and desertion, particularly in the case of soldiers about to march on campaign.[44] General Micheltorena summarized the critical situation in the frontier garrisons in 1850: "The canton forces are weakening every day with disease, the wounded, the dead, deserters and, in a word, because they are tired."[45] In fact, complaints by officials about desertion are legion.[46] General Díaz de la Vega

---

[42] M. Micheltorena to MGM, Mérida, September 14, 1850, AHM, XI/481.3/2914; Baqueiro 1990, 4:141–142.

[43] Baqueiro 1990, 4:157–159. Rosado defended his draconian sanctions by claiming the soldiers had planned to kill the officers and steal 1,000 pesos from the battalion cash box (R. Díaz de la Vega to MGM, Peto, August 25, 1851, AHM, XI/481.3/3259; Correspondencia del Siglo, Peto, August 26, 1851, SDN, September 1, 1851, 2).

[44] See, for example, GCY:45.

[45] M. Micheltorena to MGM, Mérida, January 10, 1851, AHM, XI/481.3/3255.

[46] See, for example, Circular, F.M. de Arredondo, Mérida, June 9, 1849, AGEC, PY, G, box 11, file 821; R. Díaz de la Vega to MGM, Mérida, November 16, 1852, AHM, XI/481.3/3300; M.F. Peraza to General en Jefe, Valladolid, [April?] 1855, AGEY, PE, G, box 100; M. Peraza to CGE, Valladolid, January 12, 1856, AGEY, PE, G, box 103; J.M. de Vargas to MGM, Mérida, January 13, 1859, AHM, XI/481.3/7504; numerous documents in Folder 1856, AGEY, PE, G, box 103; L. Irigoyen to MGM, Mérida, April 18, 1859, AHM, XI/481.3/7504; Prefecto J. García Morales, Mérida, June 7, 1866, AGN, G, dossier 2001, box 2497, file 3; J.D. Sosa to Comisario Imperial, Mérida, October 17, 1866, AGN, G, SI, vol. 33, file 27; F.G. Casanova to Comisario Imperial, Mérida, May 19, 1866, AGEY, PE, M, box 254, file 19; Itinerario de la marcha de las tropas sobre los indios bárbaros, D. Peniche, pueblo de Dolores, Isla Mujeres, August 19, 1872, RP, August 26 and 28, 1872, 1; P. Pérez Miranda to Gobernador, Motul, January 10, 1885, AGEY, PE, M, box 232; GCY:171.

Violence and Suffering within the Government Forces 113

found his forces reduced by desertion or illness to less than half their scheduled strength during preparation for his campaign against the kruso'b in 1851. Fifty percent of the reinforcements he had requested from Mérida as compensation deserted on their way to Díaz's headquarters in Tihosuco.[47] When soldiers were drafted en masse by force to replenish the line of defense following the defeat at Dzonot in 1865, a fifth of the able-bodied men deserted to the forests "remote from obedience to authority."[48] On occasion, entire companies failed to show up after they were called to report for duty.[49] Soldiers destined for military posts far from home were most likely to act in this way or later escape from service. Thus, members of the Campeche battalion deserted their posts on the frontier three times as often as their peers from Peto.[50] Inhabitants of the peninsula's western areas considered the frontier remote and did not see Caste War rebels as an immediate threat to their homes after mid-1848. Army units brought to Yucatán from other parts of Mexico had even less reason to feel enthusiastic about fighting and possibly dying in Yucatán and consequently fled in scores from the hated military service.[51]

Desertion clearly weakened the Yucatecan defense and represented a threat to public security. Every so often deserters ambushed and killed their persecutors.[52] As mentioned earlier, bands of deserters roamed the rural areas, committing robbery and assault or extorting money by force.[53] At times they went so far as to confront the military.[54] Rather than hide in the government-controlled areas of Yucatán or return to other parts of Mexico, many of the deserters fled to the pacíficos of the south or, worse still, to the kruso'b.[55] In at least one documented case, deserters were treated well when they incidentally came across a group of

---

[47] Cámara Zavala 1928, parts 2 and 3.
[48] P. Regil y Peón to Emperador, Mérida, November 10, 1865, AGN, G, SI, vol. 46, file 14.
[49] Letter to CGE, Campeche, January 8, 1856, AGEY, PE, G, box 103.
[50] Reed 1997a:6.
[51] J. García Morales to MGO, Mérida, June 1, 1866, AGN, G, SI, vol. 33, file 27.
[52] J. García Morales to Comisario Imperial, Mérida, October 1, 1866, AGN, G, SI, vol. 33, file 27.
[53] J. García Morales to Comisario Imperial, Mérida, June 7 and August 16, 1866 and D. Bureau to MGO, Mérida, August 19, 1866, all in AGN, G, dossier 2001, box 2497, files 2 and 3; D. Bureau to MGO, Mérida, August 7, 1866, AGN, G, SI, vol. 33, file 27.
[54] See, for example, N. Rendón to MGO, Mérida, June 17, 1866, AGN, G, SI, vol. 34, file 12; J.M. Morales to Comisario Imperial, Mérida, August 16, 1866, AGN, G, dossier 2001, box 2497, file 2.
[55] See, for example, M. Micheltorena to MGM, March 25, 1851, AHM, XI/481.3/3257; J. M. de Vargas to MGM, Mérida, January 13, 1859, AHM, XI/481.3/7504.

Part IV: Violence and the Government Forces

Caste War rebels and even given the choice of joining the kruso'b or availing of a permit to return home. While some accepted the latter option, two soldiers remained, one as a secretary and the other as a servant to the kruso'b leader José María Lira.[56] The frequent defection of soldiers and occasionally officials to the rebels gave the authorities a serious headache, since renegades could provide the kruso'b with information and military training.[57] The kruso'b attackers of Valladolid on April 1, 1858, for example, were led by several soldiers who had defected.[58] A number of deserters even became rebel leaders.[59] On the other hand, not all deserters survived their encounter with the kruso'b. The rebels killed some of the soldiers who had defected from Tunkas in 1848, although it is not clear whether they wanted to join the kruso'b or were merely weary of army service. In the event, the military command made an effort to draw advantage from their deaths by reading a description of the incident to his soldiers on three consecutive days as a deterrent to further defection.[60]

Understandably, the sanctions for desertion were harsh. A decree in January 1848 established six months imprisonment as punishment for first time desertion and six years if it occurred at an outpost, on guard, or under enemy fire.[61] The law on desertion from September 26, 1853, and the army general ordinance (*ordenanza general del ejército*) from 1855 dictated the death sentence for desertion in general and desertion on campaign.[62] In cases where deserters were caught, this was no idle threat.

---

[56] Causa seguida contra varios desertores ..., Hunucmá, February 12 – March 19, 1852, AGEY, PE, J, box 145, file 27.

[57] Cuaderno copiador de comunicaciones dirigidos por el comandante de Bacalar, Don Isidro González al CGE, R. Díaz de la Vega, Bacalar, February 28 to August 4, 1851, CAIHDY, M, XLIV.1850–1859/22; M. Barbachano: Sobre la última correria de los bárbaros, *EC*, September 11, 1861, 3–4; M.F. Rosado to Gobernador, Valladolid, June 18, 1881, AGEY, PE, box 217; GCY:96.

[58] Comandancia accidental de la línea del oriente to Gobernador, n.p., April 1858, AGEY, PE, G, box 115. A dozen deserters from the National Guard, among them two Mexicans, are mentioned in a kruso'b source from the same month (Declaracion del indígena José Cen, Valladolid, April 5, 1858, *GS*, April 7, 1858, 2–3).

[59] See, for example, R. Díaz de la Vega to MGM, Mérida, July 29, 1851, AHM, XI/481.3/3257.

[60] Gobernador to Comandante Principal del Distrito de Valladolid, January 11, 1848, AGEY, PE, G, box 67.

[61] Pena de los desertores, January 23, 1848, APP 3:180.

[62] Circular, Mayor General de la division, September 26, 1855, AGEY, PE, G, box 100; M. Peraza to CGE, Valladolid, January 12, 1856, AGEY, PE, G, box 103. The penal law of 1857 also provided for severe sanctions (L. Irigoyen to MGM, Mérida, April 18, 1859, AHM, XI/481.3/7504). A decree in 1857 ordered the same sanction for

Violence and Suffering within the Government Forces 115

Marcelino Martínez, who had defected to the rebels from the Tihosuco garrison in 1849, was decapitated in 1851 following his capture by government troops.[63] Other deserters were shot.[64] José Pech, who had joined the kruso'b after escaping from the army, was apprehended by government troops during an expedition to Puerto Ascención. Unlike other prisoners, he was not summarily executed because the commanding officer felt Pech's execution before the eyes of his former squad in Valladolid would be more effective.[65] Martial law during the empire of Maximilian applied to all areas where the combined French-Mexican army was on campaign. It saw numerous offender categories as liable for the ultimate penalty, including deserters on campaign, spies and prisoners of war caught a second time with a weapon in their hands.[66] Defectors not condemned to death faced severe sanctions such as corporal punishment or years of forced service in the army far from home. In 1858, for example, one soldier received 200 canings for desertion.[67] In 1866, a high-ranking military commander seriously considered employing the *banco de palos* as an exemplary punishment for desertion, whereby the delinquent was beaten with a stick while stretched out on a bench.[68]

The apprehension of deserters was often hindered by the protective attitude of their families, relatives, friends and employers, and the "criminal indolence of the local authorities," as one contemporary claimed.[69] In fact, the authorities showed little interest in capturing deserters, instead protecting their clients or the interests of local landlords, who in turn were

---

those who deserted "on campaign" or while carrying their weapons (Decreto, *GS*, April 20, 1857, 1–2). The Mexican Deserters' Law from 1859 was less strict and content to condemn those who deserted a second time to ten years of service in one of the regiments stationed on the northern or southern coasts (Ley penal para los desertores, Mérida, April 17, 1859, *EC*, April 17, 1859, 1–2). Deserters from military units destined to fight in the campaign against the rebels were threatened with the ultimate penalty in a decree from 1865 (Decreto, J. Salazar Ilarregui, Mérida, March 21, 1865, AHM, XI/481.4/9987).

[63] M. Micheltorena to MGM, Mérida, May 17, 1851, AHM, XI/481.3/3257. For the execution of a deserter, see also M. Micheltorena to MGM, March 25, 1851, AHM, XI/481.3/3257.

[64] See, for example, Baqueiro 1990, 3:168–169, 5:117.

[65] M.F. Peraza to General en Jefe, Valladolid, April 3, 1855, *EO*, April 20, 1855, 1–3.

[66] Aviso al publico, *LNE*, June 10, 1864, 3.

[67] M. Brito to Gobernador, Mérida, June 8, 1858, AGEY, PE, G, box 115.

[68] He was reminded by his superiors, however, that this sanction was prohibited (J.M. Segura to Comisario Imperial, Mérida, May 3, 1866, AGEY, PE, M, box 252, file 41).

[69] J. Zetina to MGM, Mérida, September 10, 1859, AHM, XI/481.3/7440. See also J. Puerto to Gobernador, Mérida, August 22, 1859, AGEY, PE, M, box 202, file 107; J. Oxtoll to Gobernador, Tekax, October 9, 1858, AGEY, PE, G, box 115.

Part IV: Violence and the Government Forces

concerned in the case of death or desertion that they might have to forfeit their meagre labor force to military service as well as the money they had advanced to their servants.[70] The General Secretary of the Government, Francisco Martínez de Arredondo, deemed it "scandalous" that armed deserters could walk around the towns with impunity in 1849.[71] The military commander in Espita lamented in 1856 that thirty-two of the thirty-eight men sent from the towns of Cenotillo and Chuilá had deserted within two days, and blamed the "cover" and "constant impunity" deserters enjoyed in the district.[72] In the same year, the local judge in Maní complained that most citizens deserted when they were destined to serve in a campaign, thus "scoffing at the orders of the authorities." He found himself isolated and without the power to enforce superior orders. In response, the jefe político in Ticul took serious measures to induce the deserters from Maní to present themselves to the authorities. He seized their wives as hostages, considered taking their fathers, brothers or sons as substitutes and pressed for confiscation of their goods to compensate for clothes taken.[73] Likewise in that year, the jefe político of Espita authorized the military commander to apprehend the families of defectors and to seize assets equivalent to the value of stops, weapons, belting and other equipment taken as "the only way to ensure their presence or capture."[74] In 1865, the Imperial commissary felt urged by the dimensions of the problem to threaten anyone with the death sentence who might "induce, assist in any way, or conceal" the crime of desertion if it actually occurred and with six years of military service if it did not.[75]

As we have seen, violence was widely used within the government forces in various contexts ranging from recruitment and efforts to enforce military discipline to the sanctioning of desertion. The bulk of violent acts committed by soldiers affected outsiders, however, such as non-combatants and, of course, Caste War rebels.

---

[70] P. Regil y Peón to Emperador, Mérida, November 10, 1865, AGN, G, SI, vol. 46, file 14.

[71] Circular, F.M. de Arredondo, Mérida, June 9, 1849, AGEC, PY, G, box 11, file 821.

[72] M. Peraza to CGE, Valladolid, January 12, 1856, AGEY, PE, G, box 103.

[73] Letters from J.M. Avila to Gobernador, Ticul, January 23 and 26, 1856, both in AGEY, PE, G, box 104.

[74] M. Peraza to CGE, Valladolid, February 11, 1856, AGEY, PE, G, box 103.

[75] Decreto, J. Salazar Ilarregui, Mérida, March 21, 1865, AHM, XI/481.4/9987.

12

Violence by Government Forces against Others

Offensive and defensive army action responded to multiple, partly contradictory logics. The supreme commander and his staff designed the official strategy to defeat the rebels, which officers at the lower levels were called upon to implement. The motives of officers and soldiers on the spot, such as personal gain, were frequently at odds with the official strategy, however, and shaped military activities and the use of force to suit their own needs. Finally, situational factors such as the immediate threats soldiers faced on duty, i.e., attacks, hunger and illness, impeded the pursuit of long-term goals.

ARMY VIOLENCE AND SPACE

The overview of the Caste War course in Part III has shown that the rebels were forced to learn a painful lesson in its early stages. When government forces recovered in 1848 as a result of reinforcements in the form of rifles, ammunition and regular army units from the central government, the rebel position in open battle was inferior as a rule. This led the latter to develop a hit-and-run guerilla strategy of surprise attacks, assaults and ambushes, as well as attacks on isolated outposts or frontier settlements. As a result, and given the lack of support from Yucatecan elites mentioned, government forces had little opportunity to end the war with a decisive battle and were obliged to combine counter-insurgency tactics with defensive measures such as establishing a front line of military posts. Both guerilla warfare and counter-insurgency, however, typically affect not only the contending armed groups but also countless non-combatants, not least since distinguishing insurgents from civilians was nigh to impossible and the latter

118   *Part IV: Violence and the Government Forces*

were themselves targeted in their capacity as moral and material supporters of either of the armed groups.[1] The Caste War was no exception to this rule.

In terms of warfare dynamics, the Yucatán peninsula can roughly be divided into three major areas following the first phase of the war: the west and northwest dominated by government forces and protected by the line of cantonments; the southeast held by the kruso'b; and a buffer zone about 80 kilometers wide in-between, where neither Yucatecans nor rebels had a permanent presence.[2] These areas were, of course, not separated by well-defined borders but merged into each other.

Inhabitants of the government-controlled area likewise suffered army infringements. Military commanders showed little respect for political and legal decisions or "even the person of the judge," particularly in frontier regions far from Mérida, where they were confident that "protected by distance" their arbitrariness would go unpunished. Hence, the civil authorities in frontier towns were entirely subordinate to military commanders.[3] The comportment of government troops in the frontier villages earned the following description:

> Based merely on carrying a sword they made themselves owners and masters of all things created, with sufficient titles to dispose of the lives and property of their fellow citizens, superior to all authority, because the judges were the sole of a shoe to them, and the caciques and Indians workhorses, whose backs they loaded inhumanely with heavy boxes of ammunition and anclotes [a cask of two demijohns] of brandy to be carried over long distances.[4]

The abuse of town residents by government troops was widespread. In April 1849, for example, a squad from Tixcacaltuyú cantonment forced Indians from Nenelá and Sabacché to work in the surrounding corn fields at harvest time to feed the soldiers.[5] The citizens resented the seizure of their possessions by officers to provide for the troops, accusing the soldiers of theft. One town official described the local military cantonment, where

---

[1] In their comparative study of casualties in warfare Valentino, Huth and Balch-Lindsay (2004) found that mass killing of civilians was particularly frequent in anti-guerilla wars.

[2] See, for example, Aldherre and Mendiolea 1869:73 and the map in Sapper 1895. This corresponds to the "division of sovereignty" between "zones of incumbent control, zones of insurgent control, and zones in which control is contested" suggested by Kalyvas (2006:88) as typical for civil wars in general. The territories settled by the pacíficos del sur in the south constituted another area beyond the domination of the government or the kruso'b.

[3] P. Regil y Peón to Emperador, Mérida, November 10, 1865, AGN, G, SI, vol. 46, file 14.

[4] García y García 1865:xlv.

[5] F. Pren to CGE, Tekax, April 24, 1849 and N. Remises to CGE, Yaxcabá, May 1, 1849, both in AGEY, PE, G, box 74.

Violence by Government Forces against Others

stealing any kind of foodstuffs from the villagers became the order of the day, as "even more atrocious than the Indian barbarians."[6] The military commander of Tizimín faced accusations of iniquities, among them covering the "outrages, sackings and robberies" his second son had allegedly committed in 1851.[7] One army officer even reported Yucatecan settlements were "being burned and people put to the sword" by military units on the frontier during their depredations.[8] Lacking the means to fend off such infringements, the lower classes in the towns and peasants scattered across small hamlets were the groups most affected. Military units often advanced with nothing other than *totoposte*, a crisp tortilla, as provisions, forcing the soldiers to live off the land and seize additional food in the settlements they passed.[9] General Díaz de la Vega's instructions to Colonel Rosado in 1851 could be read as a response to these problems. He advised troops to carry sufficient supplies on their campaigns in order to prevent an untimely retreat and avoid "molesting the citizens of the places they pass through" for food or pack animals:

Colonel Rosado will constantly see that the forces under his command cause no vexation, seizure, plundering or harm of any kind to the residents of their points of transit or residence. They will ask the authorities for whatever they need, pay fair prices or deliver a document endorsed by the paymaster of the battalion to ensure credit.[10]

Díaz de la Vega's orders had little effect, however, at least in the long term. Even in later years, military expeditions frequently failed to carry supplies, "always relying on spoils" instead.[11] Complaints of other transgressions continued. In 1879, for instance, married women in Halachó spoke out about soldiers who had violently offended them, having broken into their houses in their husbands' absence under the pretext of hunting down deserters. In addition, there were abundant complaints in the town about theft committed by soldiers and junior officers.[12]

---

[6] M. Palma to CGE, Dzidzantun, May 29, 1849, AGEY, PE, C, box 77, file 13.

[7] Cámara Zavala 1928, part 2.   [8] Cámara Zavala 1928, part 11.

[9] See, for example, M. Micheltorena to MGM, Mérida, July 30, 1850, AHM, XI/481.3/2914.

[10] Instrucciones á que debe sugetarse el Sr. Coronel Don José Eulogio Rosado, Mérida, July 4, 1851, AHM, XI/481.3/3256. See also the instructions Díaz de la Vega had received from the government (Instrucciones al general Rómulo Díaz de la Vega, Robles, México, April 16, 1851, AHM, XI/481.3/3255).

[11] Anonymous 1878:93.

[12] C. Solís to Gobernador, Maxcanú, July 4, 1879, AGEY, PE, box 206A.

Part IV: Violence and the Government Forces

This stealing of food and other useful items by soldiers and the lawlessness of the frontier area prompted particularly members of the "proletarian class" to flee to the Caste War rebels, where according to a Mexican officer they were "well received."[13] Others established independent settlements in the buffer zone in-between the contending forces.[14] The latter course of action offered certain benefits. Firstly, it presented a greater opportunity to escape military conflict and avoid being drafted to the National Guard or serving in kruso'b units. Secondly, it meant freedom from taxation and other obligations, unlike in the government-controlled area. Thirdly, land suitable for milpa cultivation was available in the buffer zone. Living dispersed in the forest "beyond the limits of civilization," that is, beyond the reach of the administration, was less a novelty than an ancient settlement form used by Yucatán's peasantry and deplored by colonial and republican institutions alike. There were, however, significant disadvantages. While people in the frontier area controlled by the government suffered abuse by the military, they could at least complain to political or legal institutions. Inhabitants of the buffer zone, in contrast, lacked these options and were fair game for infringements. Their sole protection was the remoteness of their hideouts. If detected, peasants in the buffer zone were threatened by both sides with confiscation of their possessions, physical assault and capture.[15]

The army and the National Guard combined attacks on known kruso'b hideouts, such as Chan Santa Cruz, with explorations into the forests of the buffer zone. The resident civilians were regarded with suspicion for living beyond the government-controlled area, or worse still, seen as rebel supporters. In fact, anyone residing beyond the Yucatecan line of defense became an army unit target. This corresponded to strategic calculations and, as a further asset, allowed soldiers to plunder. The aim of seizing several thousand peasants and their families in the buffer zone and bringing them back under the sway of the government was to make a greater distinction between friend and foe, and reduce the endemic uncertainty among the soldiers that arose from a sense of being surrounded by potential enemies.[16]

---

[13] Cámara Zavala 1928, part 11.

[14] See, for example, M.F. Peraza to General en Jefe, Valladolid, March 30, 1855, AGEY, PE, G, box 100.

[15] See, for example, J. Martinez Baca to Gobernador, Valladolid, June 9, 1858, AGEY, PE, M, box 201, file 9.

[16] Cf. Kalyvas's (2006:69) theoretical argument.

Violence by Government Forces against Others

The government forces pursued, in fact, a scorched-earth policy that saw the looting and destruction of anything that might be useful to the rebels. This also affected settlements in the buffer zone. In army thrusts into the buffer zone or rebel territory, settlements were attacked, people injured or killed and booty taken, including corn, beans, chickens, pigs, mules, horses, cooking pots, comales (griddles to prepare tortillas), coffee pots and agricultural tools.[17] A district commander from Valladolid reported on an expedition beyond the Yucatecan line of defense during which a squad of ninety soldiers had "ransacked" the rebel hamlet of Akabchén and found "a rich booty of wax, some money and several effects of little value," all of which was divided among the soldiers. They then set fire to the houses.[18] Mexican generals deemed it necessary to traverse kruso'b territory "in all directions, destroying their houses and fields, taking as many families prisoner as possible, thus displaying the power of the government to force the rebels to surrender."[19]

FIGHTING FOR FOOD

Hunger had a twofold impact on army action: it posed a challenge to army provisions and was used as a weapon against Caste War rebels.[20] As already seen, soldiers stationed at military posts often experienced food scarcity during the frontier war that followed the rebels' withdrawal to eastern Yucatán in mid-1848. This not only affected military discipline in the sense of causing protest, insubordination and desertion, but became a decisive trigger for thrusts into the buffer zone and rebel territory. Indeed, physical survival depended on appropriating corn cultivated by individual peasants or rebels in the forest.[21] Soldiers were thus forced to

---

[17] See, for example, M. Micheltorena to MGM, Merída, December 31, 1850, AHM, XI/481.3/2914; P.A. Gonzalez to Gobernador, Yokdzonot, December 14, 1854, EO, January 5, 1855, 1–3; M.F. Peraza to CGE, Valladolid, February 22, 1856, AGEY, PE, G, box 103; P.A. González to Emperador, Mérida, November 27, 1865, AGN, G, SI, vol. 44, file 69.

[18] M.F. Peraza to General en Jefe, Valladolid, April 3, 1855, EO, April 20, 1855, 1–3.

[19] Solucion de las preguntas hechas pr. el Sr. Gral. Dn. José Lopez Uraga, J. García Zavala, Mérida, November 28, 1865, AGN, G, SI, vol. 44, file 69.

[20] Military specialists suggest that lack of food has a tremendous impact on soldiers' morale and a "devastating effect on combat effectiveness" (Grossman 1996:72). See also Keegan 2001:434.

[21] See, for example, Comandancia Militar del Distrito de Campeche, A. Marcin, to CGE, Campeche, March 19, 1849, AGEY, PE, G, box 67; J.E. Rosado to Comandante General Interino del Estado, Ichmul, August 29, 1849, AGEY, PE, G, box 74; M. Micheltorena to MGM, Mérida, May 18, 1850, Comandancia General de Yucatán to MGM, Mérida,

122   *Part IV: Violence and the Government Forces*

risk "their blood and their lives" for survival, as General López de Llergo put it.[22] If their endeavor to loot foodstuffs failed, they remained hungry or had to content themselves for days with palm hearts and fruits found in the forest.[23] In fact, most skirmishes resulted from excursions undertaken by government troops "in the quest for corn and other crops they would harvest from rebel plantations" as stated in a document of the ministry of defense.[24] Military squads constantly left the cantonments in search of food, mostly accompanied by an equal or larger number of civilians known as *botineros* (plunderers). They advanced many kilometers into the buffer zone and rebel territory. As Father Canuto Vela's vivid description shows, these excursions were seen as an occasion to assault and loot:

[W]hen they arrive at the hamlets and cornfields, soldiers and non-soldiers pounce on the inhabitants, attacking, bullying and abusing them: and woe betide the women they seize …! This done, they proceed to plunder everything in sight, and then get down to the harvest.[25]

The need to harvest the fields and the opportunity to plunder settlements in the buffer zone or in rebel territory contributed substantially to prolonging the war. Peace talks between an official commission of Yucatecan clerics and rebel leaders failed in 1850, for example, because the government was unable to feed the troops due to lack of funds and the military commanders therefore refused to comply with the ceasefire.[26] Rebel captains vented their indignation and mocked the inability of Yucatecans to feed themselves:

October 25, 1850 and M. Micheltorena to MGM, Mérida, November 15, 1850, all in AHM, XI/481.3/2914; J.E. Rosado to J. Canuto Vela, Valladolid, January 5, 1851, CAIHDY, M, XLIV.1850–1859/22; M. Micheltorena to MGM, Mérida, January 22, 1851, AHM, XI/481.3/3255; M. Micheltorena to MGM, Mérida, February 10, 1851, AHM, XI/481.3/3257; letters from M. Micheltorena to MGM, Mérida, March 4, 7 and 12, 1851, AHM, XI/481.3/3258; R. Díaz de la Vega to MGM, Mérida, June 5, 1851, AHM, XI/481.3/3256; R. Díaz de la Vega to MGM, Mérida, July 29, 1851, AHM, XI/481.3/3257; F. Pren to CGE, Tekax, January 16, 1856, AGEY, PE, G, box 103; M.F. Peraza to CGE, Valladolid, March 30, 1857, GS, April 6, 1857, 2–3; GCY:83; Baqueiro 1990, 3:231, 240; 4:137.

[22] S. López de Llergo to MGM, Mérida, October 12, 1849, AHM, XI/481.3/2914.
[23] M. Micheltorena to MGM, Mérida, January 18, 1851, AHM, XI/481.3/3255.
[24] MGM, México, n.d [1850], AHM, XI/481.3/2914. See also Cartas de capitancillos indígenas, December 1849–March 1850 and M. Micheltorena to MGM, Mérida, October 31, 1850, both in AHM, XI/481.3/2914.
[25] J. Canuto Vela to A.M. Peon, Tekax, November 9, 1849, in Baqueiro 1990, 3:240.
[26] J. Rejón to Comision de Yucatán, Méjico, January 24, 1850, AGN, G, SI, sin sección, vol. 381, file 6; Discurso … gobernador D. Miguel Barbachano, el 10 de enero de 1851, AHM, XI/481.3/2914; Baqueiro 1990, 3:231–232, 239–241.

Violence by Government Forces against Others

And I tell you, do not come stealing our ears of corn because you have no idea how much work it takes to produce them. If you manage to be quiet in your villages, you will be fine, this is what I say ... Poor you who come to reap our fields; but there are also those who do not eat the ears of corn, dying from a bullet [instead]: if you come, it would be good manners to ask for [the ears of corn] as alms, we will give you some, but no, you come to steal.[27]

While ongoing army excursions were crucial to the survival of the soldiers, they also constituted a key element of the military strategy to starve out the kruso'b.[28] During the occupation of Chan Santa Cruz in February 1852, for example, General Díaz de la Vega ordered the reaping of rebel corn fields.[29] The general was convinced that depriving the rebels of their crops was "the most fitting [means] to end the war."[30] Corn plantings or grain deposits in no-man's-land or the rebel zone were deliberately destroyed if soldiers were unable to carry them.[31] The commanding officer of one such campaign ordered that all corn supplies and ranches be burned, adding in his report: "More than ever I am chasing the enemy in all directions in order to seize the families, so that the hunger and hardships they suffer will produce the intended effect."[32] In fact, the insurgents were under the permanent threat of hunger and for the most part survived on fruits and roots well into the 1850s. Many failed to obtain even this meagre diet and starved to death.[33]

---

[27] Version al castellano de cuatro escritos que tomaron á los rebeldes, September 11, 1850, AHM, XI/481.3/2914.

[28] M. Micheltorena to MGM, Mérida, October 31, 1850, AHM, XI/481.3/2914; P. Regil y Peón to Emperador, Mérida, November 26, 1865, AGN, G, SI, vol. 44, file 69.

[29] GCY:89.

[30] R. Díaz de la Vega to Gobernador, Mérida, September 7, 1852, AGEY, PE, M, box 180, file 34.

[31] J. Cadenas to General en Gefe, Campeche, July 7, 1848, AGEY, PE, G, box 68; Letters from R. Díaz de la Vega to Gobernador, Mérida, September 9 and 11, 1852, AGEY, PE, M, box 180, file 34; R. Díaz de la Vega to MGM, Mérida, August 13, 1853, AHM, XI/481.3/3696; P.A. Gonzalez to Gobernador, Yokdzonot, January 25, 1855, EO, February 16, 1855, 1–3; M.F. Peraza to CGE, Valladolid, May 23, 1857, GS, May 29, 1857, 1; Junta popular para trata sobre la guerra de castas, Mérida, EC, November 26, 1858, 2–4; P. Regil y Peón to Emperador, Mérida, November 26, 1865, AGN, G, SI, vol. 44, file 69; Ancona 1879/80, 4:143, 144, 178.

[32] P.A. Gonzalez to Gobernador, Chunkulché, February 1, 1855, EO, March 6, 1855, 3–4. Similar scorched-earth strategies were employed by the British in their conflicts with the Chichanhá Indians in 1867, when they burned the villages of San Pedro, San José, Santa Teresa, Naranjal and Chorro along with their corn fields (Captain Delamere to Brigadier-General Harley, March 9, 1867 and Brigadier-General Harley to Lieutenant Governor, September 7, 1867, both R. 95, ABH:284, 295).

[33] M. Micheltorena to MGM, Mérida, June 2, 1851, and R. Díaz de la Vega to MGM, Mérida, June 26, 1851, both in AHM, XI/481.3/3257.

WAR AS BUSINESS

Most Yucatecans and Mexicans were averse to military service and sought to evade it. This notwithstanding, military service provided opportunities for personal gain. Since pay was meagre or non-existent, soldiers and officers tapped several other sources of revenue. Plundering became their chief source of income. Even silver objects taken from abandoned churches or those recaptured from the rebels were "continuously sold by the soldiers," since for them "everything was booty."[34] But looting was not simply an incidental feature of warfare. It became an integral part of the government system to compensate soldiers and volunteers for their efforts in the struggle against the rebels and to cover campaign expenses. Faced with a chronic financial deficit and thus unable to provide soldiers with regular pay, the government passed a decree as early as February 1848 that fostered plundering in order to "restore the general enthusiasm still missing in the state troops and provide an incentive." It did not address soldiers exclusively but applied to "anyone." Article 1 indicated:

Half of the food, furniture and any other items the troops or anyone else take from villages, rural properties or industrial establishments after their occupation by the barbarians [Caste War rebels] will be awarded to those who fetched them and the other half to the treasury to cover the cost of the campaign.[35]

General Díaz's instructions to Colonel Rosado in 1851 stipulated that mules, horses and other animals stolen from Yucatecans by the rebels should be returned to their previous owners if taken by soldiers. The original owner was to pay five pesos per head if he was not in active military service at the time and the resultant sum to be divided among the captors. If no previous owner was identified, the animals were to be auctioned and the proceeds distributed in the same manner. The proceeds from the sale of jewelry taken from the enemy was likewise to be shared among the captors.[36] Those who did not belong to the army or National

---

[34] P. Badillo to Obispo, Peto, December 25, 1848, AHAY, G, I, box 227, file 4.

[35] A. Ibarra de Leon to SGG, Maxcanú, February 28, 1848, AGEY, PE, G, box 67. See also Que se rematen en beneficio del erario de las tropas los bienes muebles de los sublevados, October 10, 1848, APP 3:235.

[36] Instrucciones á que debe sugetarse el Sr. Coronel Don José Eulogio Rosado, Mérida, July 4, 1851, AHM, XI/481.3/3256. See also Letters from M. Micheltorena to MGM, Mérida, April 12, May 1, May 20, July 30, November 18, November 22, December 11, December 31, 1850, AHM, XI/481.3/2914; R. Díaz de la Vega to MGM, Mérida, May 17, 1853, AHM, XI/481.3/3505. The sale of army booty and the

Violence by Government Forces against Others 125

Guard units but fought the kruso'b independently had a right to any loot obtained from the "enemy camp."[37] In addition, government decrees gave anyone who fought the rebels "at their own expense" the opportunity to make money by taking captives and promised them a third of the 50 pesos fine prisoners had to pay.[38]

Officers, of course, had the lion's share when it came to opportunities to convert war into business for personal enrichment. They set up private farms in the vicinity of the cantonments and became active in commercial ventures.[39] Inflating payrolls so that the government paid for "alleged places," tapping the labor of prisoners, employing soldiers for "services inappropriate to their duties," or appropriating their pay were other methods of supplementing an officer's income.[40] Officers also conscripted more men than officially required, obliging the supernumerary individuals to pay in cash or labor for their release.[41] Captain Herrera, for example, was accused of exempting people from military service for money or service on his ranch and of employing soldiers as peons on his property in 1882.[42] Other officers sold equipment or supplies at the market that were intended for the troops. Soldiers serving in Tixcacaltuyú complained in 1879 that their diet consisted merely of "chayas [a spinach-like vegetable] and calabashes" since the commanding officer had sold their rice

---

distribution of the proceeds among the participants of the excursion remained standard practice in later years. See P.A. Gonzalez to Gobernador, Yokdzonot, December 14, 1854, *EO*, January 5, 1855, 1–3; Juan Ma. Novelo to General en Jefe, Pachmul, January 2, 1855, *EO*, January 23, 1855, 3–4; P.A. Gonzalez to Gobernador, Yokdzonot, January 25, 1855, *EO*, February 16, 1856, 1–3; Proyecto presentado por los Sres. Rejon y Rosado para emprender la nueva campaña contra los bárbaros alzados, Mérida, November 9, 1858, *EC*, November 15, 1858, 2–3; Junta encargada del proyecto para la conclusion de la guerra de castas, Mérida, December 1, 1858, *EC*, December 8, 1858, 1–2; Cámara Zavala 1928, part 5.

[37] Proclamación, L. Irigoyen, Mérida, December 27, 1858, *EC*, December 31, 1858, 2.

[38] Articles 5 and 6, Decreto que establece que los indios sublevados que cooperen de diversas maneras con el gobierno gozarán de los derechos de todo ciudadano, Maxcanú, February 6,1848, AGEC, PY, G, box 7, file 527. A draft law guaranteed 50 pesos for prisoners given the death sentence and 100 pesos in the case of leaders (*cabecillas*). The money was to be distributed among the participants if the prisoners had been taken during a military operation (A la comision de puntos constitucionales, Mérida, December 26, 1847, AGEY, PE, G, box 65). It is not clear, however, whether these regulations were ever put into effect.

[39] Cámara Zavala 1928, part 6.

[40] P. González to Emperador, Mérida, November 27, 1865, AGN, G, SI, vol. 44, file 69; GCY:88.

[41] See the discussion in Colonias militares, *RP*, June 6, 1888, 1.

[42] Declaración, n.p., [1882], AGEC, AH, G, AM, box 13.

126 Part IV: Violence and the Government Forces

and sugar supplies.[43] Even excursions beyond the front line were exploited by officers for personal gain. As one critic, an officer himself, noted, it was customary "to let Indians work their fields peacefully" and then send government troops to reap them at harvest time for their own benefit. They left half the harvest so that the Indians "would survive and not migrate. They parody the beehive harvesters, who leave some globules of honey in them to keep the bees there."[44] Hence although corn harvested in the buffer zone or on rebel territory was not officially considered booty but intended to satisfy the soldiers' basic need for food, the grain was often sold on the quiet in larger towns.[45] The troops also ran a "scandalous business" with ammunition of such dimensions that the governor demanded the crime be expiated by capital punishment.[46]

Looting, the sale of corn, army supplies, weapons and equipment, fraud by inflated review lists, and the abuse of prisoners and soldiers as a work force for private entrepreneurs all became more or less lucrative methods of making money and created a material interest in prolonging the war. Military commanders and officers in the frontier region could not hope to dispose of the same amount of authority, power and control over men and resources in peacetime. As a contemporary observer stated: "Show me the cantonment commander who had one single real when he took over his position. Show me the cantonment commander who has not become a fairly big capitalist."[47]

In summary, the government's reward system established looting as a legitimate act for members of military units as well as for the vecino and Indian civilians who fought voluntarily and independently against alleged Caste War rebels. Since personal profit depended on the amount of booty and number of prisoners taken, there were strong incentives not to be too scrupulous in deciding who was or was not a rebel or a sympathizer. Thus large segments of the population in the buffer zone and kruso'b strongholds – combatants and non-combatants – were victims of looting or captivity, if not injury or violent death.

---

[43] P.M. Ruz to Gobernador, Sotuta, September 6, 1879, AGEY, PE, SM, box 206A. See also GCY:108.

[44] Cámara Zavala 1928, part 6.

[45] J. Pío Poot and J.M. Canul to Comandante capitán ... de Tixcacalcupul, Tekom, November 15, 1849 CAIHDY, M, XLI.1842–1849/26; Comandancia General de Yucatán to MGM, Mérida, August 17, 1850, AHM, XI/481.3/2914.

[46] Gobernador to Comandante principal del distrito de Valladolid, Maxcanú, January 14, 1848, AGEY, PE, G, box 67. Unfortunately, the document fails to mention those who bought the ammunition.

[47] Cámara Zavala 1928, part 6.

Violence by Government Forces against Others

THE TREATMENT OF CAPTIVES

The army and National Guard units that moved beyond the government-controlled area were confronted with a complex mix of people: Caste War rebels and their families, independent peasants avoiding taxes and military service, deserters from the army and the National Guard, and people displaced after kruso'b assaults. As in all violent conflict, distinguishing friend and foe was crucial. To this end, the government established several categories of people encountered in the zones beyond the line of defense, each to be treated differently: 1. prisoners (*prisioneros*), that is, those living with the rebels of their own accord or captured with arms in hand by government forces; 2. people seized in that area (*recogidos*), including independent peasant families and deserters; and 3. those who presented themselves voluntarily to the army or civil authorities (*presentados*).[48] While people assigned to the first category were to be treated as enemies and those of the second with caution, their loyalty to the government being at the least dubious, the presentados seemed to find most sympathy with the authorities. At times they were even provided with arms to fight the rebels and hence became hidalgos.[49] Legislation subdivided the rebel prisoner category, establishing a system of sanctions. Ringleaders and those found armed or guilty of "cruel acts" were seen as deserving of capital punishment, all other males over the age of sixteen were liable to six years of forced labor in private service as compensation for the 50 pesos fine and, in accordance with a decree from February 1848, a lifelong double poll tax payment.[50] In late 1858, the government granted an amnesty to those who were prepared to lay down their arms by January 20 of the following year, threatening the rest with persecution "as enemies of society." It confined the death penalty to rebel leaders and government force deserters found among the kruso'b.[51] It will become clear in a moment that the actual treatment of rebel captives did not always conform to the legal provisions.

---

[48] Orden, November 7, 1849, APP 3:281–282; Instrucciones á que debe sugetarse el Sr. Coronel Don José Eulogio Rosado, Mérida, July 4, 1851, AHM, XI/481.3/3256.

[49] M. Micheltorena to MGM, Mérida, August 31, 1850, AHM, XI/481.3/2914.

[50] Decreto que establece que los indios sublevados que cooperen de diversas maneras con el gobierno gozarán de los derechos de todo ciudadano, Maxcanú, February 6, 1848, AGEC, PY, G, box 7, file 527. For evidence that these stipulations came into effect see, for example, G. Castillo to Obispo, Mérida, November 6, 1848, AHAY, G, I, box 227, file 3; M. Micheltorena to MGM, Mérida, October 10, 1850, AHM, XI/481.3/2914.

[51] L. Irigoyen, Amnestía a sublevados, Mérida, December 18, 1858, *EC*, December 22, 1858, 1.

128   Part IV: Violence and the Government Forces

Abuse and Murder

While legally defining clearcut categories such as rebel prisoner, recogido and presentado was a relatively easy task, the reality on the ground transpired to be more fuzzy. Firstly, it would be naïve to think that all presentados backed the government. Turning themselves in to the authorities was often little more than an attempt to avoid capture by government forces and some presentados were quick to leave the government-controlled area. This group also included former rebels suspected of spying for the kruso'b.[52] Secondly, deciding whether those picked up beyond the Yucatecan line of defense were rebels, their relatives or at least sympathetic to their cause was not an easy task. This led government forces to generally regard armed insurgents and people captured in rebel strongholds or the buffer zone as enemies and to treat them accordingly. The category of prisoner was not confined to men found bearing arms but also applied to women and entire families caught during army and militia thrusts. On December 11, 1854, for example, Captain Ocampo brought "eight prisoners of both sexes and different ages" to his superior, who was camping in Yokdzonot.[53] In addition, government forces frequently ignored legal regulations, immediately shooting or hanging alleged enemies following their capture, with or without a summary trial.[54] Male rebels caught bearing arms and supposed leaders faced the highest risk of being killed.[55] This could also apply to captives

---

[52] See, for example, M. Micheltorena to MGM, Mérida, April 27, 1850, AHM, XI/481.3/2914; Rugeley 2009:90, 128.

[53] P.A. Gonzalez to Gobernador, Yokdzonot, December 14, 1854, EO, January 5, 1855, 1–3; see also M. Micheltorena to MGM, Mérida, May 18 and December 11, 1850, AHM, XI/481.3/2914; M. Micheltorena to MGM, Mérida, May 5, 1851, AHM, XI/481.3/3257; M.F. Peraza to General en Jefe, Valladolid, April 3, 1855, EO, April 20, 1855, 1–3; M.F. Peraza to CGE, Valladolid, February 22, 1856, AGEY, PE, G, box 103; M.F. Peraza to CGE, Valladolid, April 7, 1857, GS, April 13, 1857, 3; Baqueiro 1990, 4:51–52, 54.

[54] Suárez y Navarro ([1861] 1993:164) suggests that "thousands of prisoners" were killed in the initial years of the conflict. The death sentence was not inevitable, however, as shown in cases where army officials pleaded for capital punishment for a particular leader by highlighting the specific damage he had caused. This would have been superfluous had execution been mandatory. See, for example, M. Micheltorena to MGM, Mérida, November 18, 1850, AHM, XI/481.3/2914.

[55] Gobernador to Comandante principal del departamento Valladolid, Maxcanú, February 5, 1848, AGEY, PE, G, box 67; letters from M. Micheltorena to MGM, Mérida, July 3, July 31 and November 2, 1850, all in AHM, XI/481.3/2914; J. M. Novelo to Gobernador, Peto, April 27, 1852, AGEY, PE, M, box 179, file 23; Cámara Zavala 1928, part 11; Baqueiro 1990, 2:11; 3:203, 223.

Violence by Government Forces against Others

wounded in combat.[56] Beyond this, Caste War prisoners were frequently murdered by the guards who conducted them from one place to another on the pretext of their attempted escape.[57] The violent treatment of prisoners and recogidos is vividly described by Serapio Baqueiro, one of the most perceptive contemporary observers of the Caste War:

When the expedition troops undertook their return to the cantonments these unfortunates had to follow at a rapid pace between lines [of soldiers], loaded with loot and luggage that pressed down on their backs. On these forced marches they suffered hunger, thirst, fatigue and other penalties of consequence. The elderly and the sick who succumbed to fatigue were murdered in front of their families, and women, often at the critical moment of giving birth to the fruit of their womb during the fatal journey, were abandoned at the edge of the forest, while their husbands, children and other relatives were brought to captivity. ... Finally, when they made their entry into the cantonments the spectacle was even more moving. The prisoners, who had been herded like beasts of burden, were confined to the dungeons, dragged out to work on the commanders' farms or dispatched to personages in Mérida and Campeche, while their wives were assigned to grinding corn and making tortillas for the garrison in a large building called the *molienda* [mill].

Orphans were equally distributed in the most inhumane manner ... These hapless creatures were converted into a business affair ... and many an officer collected up to twenty orphans to serve him ... or to sell to the sutlers swarming around the cantonments.[58]

Although, according to official policy, children under the age of twelve were not to be separated from their parents or prisoners forced to work, both regulations were constantly violated and, similar to orphans, the children of rebel prisoners most probably sold as criados.[59]

The massive use of violence against captives (recogidos and prisoners alike), including abuse and murder, was the result of attempts to deter people from joining the insurrection and to demoralize the rebels and their supporters by introducing draconian laws and pursuing a scorched-earth

---

[56] See, for example, J.D. Zetina to Comandante General, Bacalar, June 24, 1849, *BOGY*, July 10, 1849, 3.

[57] Comunicación Oficial, Mérida, September 12, 1849, EHRY 3:327.

[58] Baqueiro 1990, 4:75–76, emphasis in the original. For captured women dying of thirst on the way to the cantonment, see M.F. Peraza to General en Jefe, Valladolid, April 3, 1855, *EO*, April 20, 1855, 1–3. For female captives assigned to preparing tortillas for the soldiers, see also M. Micheltorena to MGM, Mérida, November 18, 1850, AHM, XI/481.3/2914; R. Díaz de la Vega to MGM, Mérida, May 17, 1853, AHM, XI/481.3/3505.

[59] See, for example, F. M. de Arredondo to Gobernador, Mérida, May 10, 1849, AGEC, PY, G, box 10, file 762; Trato a prisioneros, SGG, Mérida, February 4, 1850, AGEY, PE, G, box 77, file 74.

130   *Part IV: Violence and the Government Forces*

strategy. Such an approach, however, ran the risk of producing counter-productive results. Leading army generals occasionally voiced their concern that relying solely on repression could lead to further radicalization of the war and strengthen rebels' resolve to fight to the death given that capitulation was not an option.[60] Hence, General Díaz de la Vega pleaded for the good treatment of prisoners, recogidos and presentados "so that this healthy example might serve as encouragement to others who keep their weapons in hand, to turn themselves in voluntarily."[61] The same objective is made clear to Colonel Rosado in his instructions on army organization in the east and the south. Díaz de la Vega ordered that "under no circumstances was an enemy to be killed or harmed beyond acts of war." "Extremely severe sanctions" threatened soldiers who failed to treat prisoners, recogidos and presentados with "the greatest consideration, assisting them as far as possible and treating them with the clemency that humanity demanded." None of them, including women, children and orphans, were to be "given as a present or sold."[62]

In certain cases, officers adhered to Díaz de la Vega's plea for more humane treatment of prisoners. Captain Montero, for example, released married and widowed captives taken during an excursion in January 1851, but not single men, whom he suspected were more prone to rejoining the rebels.[63] On another occasion, the commanding officer set his captives free once they had sworn not to take up arms again.[64] General Díaz de la Vega decided to expatriate the renowned rebel commander Matías Ve to Veracruz instead of shooting him "to see if this humane political measure would work to the benefit of these delinquents and make them return to peace, believing that expatriation as punishment was powerful enough for every man."[65] Attempts to "humanize" the war

[60] M. Micheltorena to MGM, Mérida, August 5, 1850, AHM, XI/481.3/2914.
[61] R. Díaz de la Vega to MGM, Mérida, June 30, 1851, AHM, XI/481.3/3256.
[62] Instrucciones á que debe sugetarse el Sr. Coronel Don José Eulogio Rosado, Mérida, July 4, 1851, AHM, XI/481.3/3256; see also Baqueiro 1990, 4:160.
[63] M. Micheltorena to MGM, Mérida, February 4, 1851, AHM, XI/481.3/3257.
[64] R. Díaz de la Vega to MGM, July 28, 1851, AHM, XI/481.3/3257.
[65] R. Díaz de la Vega to MGM, Mérida, June 24, 1851, AHM, XI/481.3/3256. Matias Uh, "general commander" of the rebels in the east, was captured in September 1850. Although considered "a ferocious, murderous and arrogant Indian" who should be executed on the spot, after his wounds were tended he was sent to Mérida for examination (M. Micheltorena to MGM, Mérida, October 10, 1850, AHM, XI/481.3/2914). Several other rebel leaders were brought to Fort San Juan de Ulúa in Veracruz to await the decision of the Mexican government on their destiny (Comandancia General de Veracruz to MGM, Jalapa, April 23, 1850, AHM, XI/481.3/2914). Sadly, we have no information on the fate of these rebel captains.

Violence by Government Forces against Others 131

remained the exception, however, and had few lasting effects, if any. Even Colonel Rosado's instructions cited above evidence the widespread abuse of prisoners and civilians by government forces. What other reason could Rosado have had for threatening severe punishment? The abuse and killing of captives does not appear to have been prosecuted by the military or legal authorities and persisted accordingly.[66]

The sources confirm that in subsequent years rebel prisoners and recogidos also received harsh treatment from military squads on their way back to the garrisons. Thirty-six captives died "from illness and exhaustion," for example, on Lieutenant Herrera's return from Aguada Sayabsin in January 1855.[67] Forty-five prisoners "of both sexes and different ages perished from lack of water" and a small child from "the hardship of the trip" during Colonel González's retreat from rancho Hon two months later.[68] Unfortunately, the sources do not indicate the total number of captives taken, rendering calculation of the percentage impossible. Various documents suggest that the rebels greatly dreaded falling into the hands of their enemies. Captain Suares reported the killing of four kruso'b on his excursion to Pachmul in 1855. They had attacked his squad with machetes and were distraught once they realized their capture was inevitable.[69] Even in 1874, a jefe político indicated that many of the kruso'b wanted to surrender but desisted because they feared "being murdered when they come to us."[70]

That often no distinction was made in practice between rebel prisoners and recogidos and that numerous captives were abused or even killed was due to several factors, not least the difficulty of discerning friend from foe, a common challenge in civil wars or anti-guerilla campaigns. In addition, the taking and holding of captives in the course of army expeditions implies practical and material consequences.[71] It binds soldiers to sentinelling them and hinders squad movement. Releasing captives is likewise problematic, since they could resume fighting and reinforce the enemy. Captives taken back to base have to be housed,

---

[66] J.M. Novelo to Gobernador, Peto, April 27, 1852, AGEY, PE, M, box 179, file 23; M.F. Peraza to General en Jefe, Valladolid, April 3, 1855, EO, April 20, 1855, 1–3; D. Peniche to Gobernador, Espita, September 29, 1862, EN, October 1, 1862, 1.

[67] J.M. Novelo to General en Jefe, Pachmul, January 27, 1855, EO, March 16, 1855, 2.

[68] P.A. Gonzalez to Gobernador, Ichmul, March 14, 1855, EO, March 27, 1855, 2.

[69] P.A. Gonzalez to Gobernador, Chunkulché, February 7, 1855, AGEY, PE, G, box 100.

[70] R.A. Perez to Gobernador, Peto, December 11, 1874, RP, December 16, 1874, 2.

[71] For a discussion of the factors influencing the treatment of captives among the kruso'b, see Chapter 17.

guarded, clothed and fed – a costly affair. This expense could be avoided by killing enemies on the spot or confining military action to merely displacing the enemy. The latter, however, would leave enemy strength untouched. In fact, a large number of structural and situational factors influenced how government forces treated their captives, including the legal framework, superior orders, combatant personalities, fierceness of the fighting, and the distance to the next safe point of delivery for captives, such as a cantonment or town. The existing sources are patchy, particularly on situational aspects, making it impossible to say why some of those captured beyond the line of defense were slain and others were not. Information on the fate of recogidos or prisoners taken to Yucatecan cantonments or towns is equally scant. There is no mention, for example, of detention centers in the documents consulted. The impression is one of a somewhat improvised and less regulated approach, giving local authorities, and particularly the military, ample margin to act in line with their immediate concerns and their own interests. This left the door wide open for arbitrariness. The attitude of the Yucatán government to the treatment of Caste War prisoners was also a response to financial exigencies, as will become clear in the next section.

Captives and the "Slave Trade"

Although killing Caste War prisoners saved the treasury the cost of their upkeep and confinement, it was not only morally problematic but furthermore a drain on the labor force. The Yucatecan government and the elites saw this as particularly unreasonable in a region already suffering from a shortage of field hands for the haciendas. As mentioned earlier, legislation condemned all Caste War captives not deserving of the death penalty to a fine of 50 pesos to be paid off with forced labor in private service for six years. This corresponded to the common pattern of debt bondage in Yucatán, whereby peons remained tied to an estate by their masters' advancements in cash or kind. An unknown but probably large number of Caste War prisoners was distributed to estate owners who advanced the fine. Hence, the latter received much sought-after workers and money flowed into the empty treasury. At the same time, this method of dealing with captives was not unproblematic. Prisoners could not be trusted, could cause disturbances among fellow workers or escape to the southeast and rejoin the kruso'b. Against this backdrop, the Yucatecan government looked for new methods of handling captives that would prevent them from disturbing public order and, at the same time, continue to generate

Violence by Government Forces against Others

an income for the treasury. Thus Governor Barbachano issued a decree in November 1848 allowing Indians captured with arms in hand and those who had taken sides with insurgents to be expelled from the state for at least ten years should the government consider it "convenient."[72] This paved the way for the sale of prisoners to employers abroad. The Yucatecans attempted to justify their proceedings as a "humanitarian act." The jefe político of Hecelchakán, for example, argued that the town council "imbued with humanitarian sentiments ... prefers the expulsion of the irreconcilable enemies of Yucatecan society to the infamous death those beasts hidden in the jungles of the east deserve for their barbarity." Their expulsion was "advantageous to the state and more consistent with sound reason ... because a race brutalized and nourished by so many crimes is no longer capable of regeneration in a place where it lost its original state." A new breeding and very different way of life was necessary if Christianity were to prevail "and dissipate these sanguinary ideas leading to the extreme of resembling beasts more than man in his natural state."[73] This position was backed by several town councils in the frontier regions (Espita, Tizimín, Valladolid, Peto, Motul and Ticul).[74]

In fact, 1849 saw the beginning of a lively trade through which prisoners were sold as farm hands to Cuba. This not only affected adult men but also women and youth of both sexes. While González Navarro estimates the number of Yucatecans brought to Cuba between 1849 and 1861 at around 2,000, Remmers sets it at 3,000 at least. The real number was probably higher since some of the paper work dealing with contracts was deliberately destroyed by government officials. In addition, part of the business was carried out covertly. Suárez y Navarro reported that 100 Yucatecans were sold every month during the Acereto administration alone (October 1859 to November 1860 and February to December 1861), suggesting that "thousands of Indians" were living in

---

[72] Decreto facultando al gobierno para confinar y expulsar a los indios prisioneros, November 6, 1848, APP 3:240. A year later, another decree was issued to prevent "abuses," clarifying that "Indians" captured unarmed in the forest and showing no opposition to government troops should not be considered prisoners in this sense (Orden, November 7, 1849, APP 3:281–282). A decade later, in yet another decree, those who refused to accept an amnesty were threatened with banishment from the peninsula "to a place indicated by the government" for ten years (L. Irigoyen, Amnestía a sublevados, Mérida, December 18, 1858, EC, December 22, 1858, 1).

[73] S. Gúzman to Gobernador, Jequelchakan, February 10, 1858, GS, February 17, 1858, 1; cf. also Sobre la guerra de castas, GS, January 29, 1858, 4; Más sobre la guerra de castas, GS, February 1, 1858, 4; Rodríguez Piña 1987/88:80–83.

[74] Cf. letters to the governor in several issues of GS, February and March, 1858.

134   *Part IV: Violence and the Government Forces*

Cuba on contracts. In 1858, at least 783 prisoners were handed over to one contractor (Gerardo Tizón).[75] Contractors received alleged rebel captives for a certain sum of money or in exchange for loans granted to the government.[76] Troops who seized and delivered prisoners to the port of disembarkment also received monetary gratifications.[77] In other words, the government, officers, soldiers, and private entrepreneurs turned the capture and treatment of prisoners into a business deal. A covenant between the Yucatecan government headed by Agustín Acereto and José Madrazo from September 3, 1859, established, for example, that the latter was to hand over 60,000 pesos "for expenses in the Caste War" in exchange for a monopoly on the contract and export of prisoners. The government committed itself to securing a steady flow of captives, organizing regular thrusts into rebel territory until a sufficient number of prisoners had been delivered to settle the loan. The contract stipulated:

The Government is obliged to make war incessantly on the indigenous rebels, sending whatever troops it can move with its resources to their camp, so that at least partial raids will be carried out continually, except during the nortes [cold fronts producing thundershowers], *when the obligation to pursue the said rebels ceases.*[78]

Prices varied considerably in the course of time. In 1849, alleged rebel prisoners were sold as farm hands to Cuba at a price of 40 pesos for males and 25 pesos for females.[79] In 1853, offers of 25 pesos were made for male youths from sixteen to twenty years, 17 pesos for those from twelve to sixteen years, 8 pesos for male children under twelve years and 8 pesos for girls under sixteen years.[80] Prices rose considerably in later years. A government commission calculated the potential income from the sale of captives to private businessmen abroad to work as "personal servants" for eight or ten years at 200 pesos per prisoner in 1858.[81]

---

[75] González Navarro 1970:148–150; Remmers 1981:402 n. 29; Suárez y Navarro [1861] 1993:167, 189, 307, 317. Unfortunately little is known about the fate of the Yucatecans deported to Cuba.

[76] A detailed discussion of the sale of Yucatecan Indians to Cuba can be found in Menéndez (1923 and 1932) and González Navarro (1970:108–150); see also Baqueiro (1990, 5:128–136), Suárez y Navarro ([1861] 1993:164–168, 189–191, 300–338), Rodríguez Piña (1987/88) and the useful overview in Álvarez Cuartero (2002).

[77] Suárez y Navarro [1861] 1993:307.

[78] Cited in Suárez y Navarro [1861] 1993:332–333, emphasis in original.

[79] GCY:75; Baqueiro 1990, 5:130; Suárez y Navarro [1861] 1993:301.

[80] Superintendent to Naval Commander in Chief, Bermuda, June 10, 1853, R. 40, ABH:167.

[81] Junta patriótica to Gobernador, Mérida, February 12, 1859, AGEY, PE, G, box 126, file 38. Madrazo's loan was to be compensated with male captives valued at 120 pesos and

Violence by Government Forces against Others

Once the government had no more prisoners to sell, attacks on the insurgents were launched or people imprisoned for minor offences, while other members of the lower classes taken captive were delivered to settle government debts. This was the case in 1860, for example, when a major campaign led by Colonel Pedro Acereto on Chan Santa Cruz failed to achieve the expected result so that not enough kruso'b prisoners were available.[82] Thus deportation not only affected prisoners caught in the buffer zone or in rebel strongholds but also the lower classes in the government-controlled area. Some were field hands who had dared to ask their masters for their carta cuenta, which recorded the peon's debts, while others were peasants who had failed to pay their contributions. Hence, estate owners also used deportation to sanction peons they considered insubordinate. Neither was this restricted to debt peons. Free peasants from Tizimín were forced by the town caciques to work in a quarry for several months as compensation for their contribution debts. They then suffered the same fate as the servants already mentioned.[83] Even Mexicans from other regions, who were mostly soldiers, were sold to Cuba.[84]

The evidence clearly shows the close cooperation between military and political officials, landlords and Indian caciques in the sale and deportation of captives. The commanders of military posts (*jefes de cantones*), for example, handed over prisoners to the jefes políticos, who in turn transferred them to the contractors.[85] General Juan Suárez y Navarro, sent to Yucatán as a special envoy by President Benito Júarez, reported in 1861 that sending Indians abroad had become "a form of public and private income because it is notorious that the biggest share of the traffic's proceeds has been appropriated by the many people involved."[86]

---

females between sixteen and forty years of age at 80 pesos, while 50 pesos was offered for both male and female youths between ten and fifteen years of age. Children under ten years of age were to be handed over to the contractor free of charge. A contract with Miguel Pou & Co. from January 13, 1860, stipulated as much as 160 pesos for males and 120 for females between sixteen and fifty years of age and 80 pesos for male and female youths between ten and fifteen years of age. Similar to Madrazo's agreement, children under the age of ten were gratis (Suárez y Navarro, [1861] 1993:323–324, 333; Baqueiro 1990, 5:136).

[82] GCY:120; Suárez y Navarro [1861] 1993:167; Suárez Molina 1977, 2:290.
[83] Comercio de indios pacíficos, *EP*, November 20, 1860, 3–4.
[84] Suárez y Navarro [1861] 1993:166, 325.
[85] Suárez y Navarro [1861] 1993:305–306, 309, 315; Peniche Rivero 1993:103–104.
[86] Suárez y Navarro [1861] 1993:166–167.

136   *Part IV: Violence and the Government Forces*

The sale and deportation of captives and other people to Cuba did not, however, go uncontested. Critics denounced the practice as slavery and thus as a violation of the country's constitution. Yucatecans endeavored to respond to these allegations by downplaying the use of force. They argued that the whole affair was a voluntary business deal between a contractor and the laborers who had agreed to work in Cuba for a number of years.[87] Thus, when questioned by a judge about an agreement granting the Spanish contractor Gerardo Tizón the right to export Indian prisoners in 1858, Governor Pantaleón Barrera declared that the permit to contract prisoners was given "not in writing but verbally." According to his statement, he had not consulted the government council because he simply saw it as "a legal contract between various people" and because Mr. Tizón was undoubtedly free "to make his proposals to the Indians, who could either agree to or reject them." In addition, the state was "by no means impaired by the benefit" rebel prisoners would enjoy from the intended contract.[88] Indeed, contracts were signed by a clerk on behalf of the prisoners, who could as a rule neither read nor write.[89] Even if they had been asked for their consent, the captives were not in a position to refuse the offer, given that they were confined to prison or private homes. Mateo Canché, for example, a servant from a village near Valladolid, was sold by his master, Nemesio Osorno, to Miguel Pou in 1860 after he had solicited his carta cuenta. He was tied up and, along with his wife and companions, brought from Izamal to Mérida by soldiers, where they were locked up for five weeks in a house belonging to Pou. At 11 p.m. on October 28, Mateo Canché and his wife were transported to the port of Sisal to be confined in the fort. Pou informed them that they were being sent to Havana where they would earn seven pesos a month. Canché resigned himself to the fact, "since [Pou] had locked him up with his wife and he was afraid someone might harm him." Without doubt rebel prisoners had less latitude for objection.[90]

The central government in Mexico City did not have a consistent position on the trade with Caste War prisoners. While Presidents Herrera and Santa Ana had allowed the exportation of Indians to Cuba in 1849 and 1853 respectively, other administrations made repeated

---

[87] See, for example, the basis of Juan Miguel Fusté's contracts (Suárez y Navarro [1861] 1993:320–322).

[88] Declaración de D. Pantaleon Barrera, in Suárez y Navarro [1861] 1993:311.

[89] Suárez y Navarro [1861] 1993:316.

[90] Comercio de indios pacíficos, *EP*, November 20, 1860, 3–4.

Violence by Government Forces against Others

attempts to stop it.[91] In 1855, the government declared the concessions granted to two trading firms in Havana null and void and ordered that the respective rebel prisoners be dispatched to Baja California and occupied "in public works for six years." Thereafter they were to be freed to settle there.[92] While it is debatable whether deportee living conditions were better there than in Cuba, their fate was not the object of a private business deal but remained in the realm of the Mexican judicial and political system. The liberal President Benito Juárez was one of the staunchest opponents of prisoners being sold as "slaves" to Cuba. A letter from his minister of the interior, Melchor Ocampo, to the governor of Yucatán stated, for example: "Choose other means to pacify the Peninsula, because as it is untrue, no one will believe that the only possibility is to kill and [sic] sell most of its population. Consider finally that a noble race preferring death to slavery certainly deserves more respect than has been shown by the whites of Yucatan." In 1861, President Júarez finally prohibited the deportation of rebel prisoners to Cuba.[93]

Banishment to Baja California or Veracruz affected only "the most criminal" of prisoners. The majority of male and female captives, in contrast, were distributed to Yucatecan property owners, "who offered to take care of them" – probably after payment of a commission to the local military or political officials, as in the case of deportees to Cuba.[94] Although landlords complained that prisoners often fled from their haciendas, rejoined the rebels and were recaptured several times, more effective measures were not taken. According to one army officer, the reason was "fear that the war would end" and the exploitation of an "inexhaustible mine" of captives for sale draw to an end.[95]

The introduction of prices for prisoners, their sale as field hands to Cuba or distribution to Yucatecan estate owners, and the forced labor sanction were all powerful incentives to increase the number of captives. This led to the rounding up and displacement of many who lived beyond the Yucatecan line of defense, men, women and children, irrespective of their affiliation to the Caste War rebels. The remoteness of the frontier

---

[91] Rodríguez Piña 1987/88:47–49.

[92] J.M. Blancache to Comandancia Prinicipal del territorio de Baja California, La Paz, February 4, 1855, AHM, XI/481.3/4616.

[93] Ocampo to Governor of Yucatán, Veracruz, August 30, 1859, in Suárez y Navarro [1861] 1993:337 (quote). See also Suárez y Navarro [1861] 1993:335–336; González Navarro 1976:146.

[94] Cámara Zavala 1928, part 6. See also part 11; Peniche Rivero 1993:103–104.

[95] Cámara Zavala 1928, part 5.

138   *Part IV: Violence and the Government Forces*

settlements and cantonments paved the way for all kinds of abuse and arbitrariness. The war was thus transformed into a lucrative business for a wide array of actors ranging from independent bounty hunters, soldiers, officers and bureaucrats to the state government itself and private entrepreneurs in Yucatán and Cuba. This undoubtedly contributed to the prolongation of the war and even triggered specific campaigns.

EXCESSES

All wars imply by definition high degrees of violence. The killing of enemy warriors or soldiers is expected. No violence, however, is without normative or ethical limits in terms of means (e.g., the method of killing) or targets (e.g., soldiers, civilians, men, women). Certain acts of violence will always appear problematic to one or both of the contending parties for their particular brutality, methods, cowardice or transgression of what is acceptable. Allegations of "excesses" committed by the enemy are a popular ingredient of war propaganda to mobilize a group, party or society against its foes. At the same time, internal criticism of atrocities perpetrated by one's own group and based on tactical deliberations (e.g., fear of unnecessary provocation through enemy retaliation) or moral qualms was also possible. The Caste War was no exception to these considerations and, as we have seen, witnessed a variety of violent deeds by soldiers and militia men against rebels and non-combatants (kruso'b violence will be discussed in detail in Chapters 16 and 17). Several particularly gruesome acts stand out in this dire picture. While denunciations by Yucatecans of indiscriminate kruso'b violence are legion, we know of only a few rebel statements accusing government forces of brutality, such as the killing of women and children.[96] While accusations of outrages perpetrated by the foe could be suspected of being enemy propaganda in both cases, similar reproaches from the Yucatecan side of government cruelties cannot easily be dismissed as false. In the midst of a bloody war, where critique of one's own military forces runs the risk of strengthening the enemy, it comes as no surprise that few such comments are known. One of these rare contemporary voices was that of journalist, lawyer and

---

[96] For rebel atrocities, see, for example, A. Duarte to P. Barrera, Tekax, September 16, 1857, *GS*, September 18, 1857, 2–3; F. Seymour to C.H. Darling, Belize, March 13, 1858, TNA, CO, 123/96; Fowler 1879:41–42, cited in Buhler 1975:4. For denunciations of army violence, see Chapter 17. This does not necessarily mean that rebels were more prone to killing women and children, but it is rather an indication of the comparatively few remaining sources authored by the kruso'b and the power of government propaganda.

Violence by Government Forces against Others 139

historian Serapio Baqueiro, who recognized atrocities committed on both sides and attested the National Guard both heroism and crimes "in flagrant violation of the laws of war and humanity."[97]

That many Yucatecans had no such moral qualms when it came to the treatment of Caste War rebels is evidenced, for example, by the horrendous sanctions proposed by a government commission in late 1847. According to the draft law, insurgents caught with arms in hand, ringleaders, and those who had committed "atrocious offenses" were to be hanged. All other male prisoners over the age of thirteen were to be branded with an "S" on their right cheek "with a white-hot iron" and sold into peonage by public auction.[98] Behavior of this kind would have violated the Mexican constitution and probably smacked of Spanish colonial punishment for rebellion. Thus branding never made it into enacted legislation and the sale of prisoners was, as we have seen, white-washed as an act of humanity.

In view of this ideological climate, it comes as no surprise that supposed rebel prisoners were often physically abused, as mentioned earlier. Captives taken by government forces beyond the Yucatecan line of defense constituted a vital source of information on the enemy. Rugeley has already suggested that the army abused prisoners to obtain such information.[99] A contemporary account of the rebels' military capacity provides at least indirect evidence of the mistreatment of captives, stressing that the rebels would "prefer to suffer the worst kind of torture rather than give information

---

[97] Baqueiro 1990, 4:4. Generally accepted international laws for the regulation of warfare were non-existent at that time. The views of Baqueiro and his contemporaries were probably influenced by the heated discussions between politicians and the military from a dozen European states and the US delegates, who had adopted a convention on the issue at a diplomatic conference in Geneva in 1864, which included the protection of wounded or sick combatants. Although delegates from fifteen European states had agreed to a declaration on the Laws and Customs of War in Brussels in 1874, their governments failed to ratify it. The declaration stipulated that civilians were to be protected and, in Article 13, prohibited certain methods of injuring the enemy, such as the use of poison or poisoned weapons; murder by treachery; murder of an enemy who had surrendered; the declaration that no quarter would be given; the use of "arms, projectiles or material calculated to cause unnecessary suffering." Article 38 determined that civilian family honor, rights, lives and property, as well as religious convictions and practices must be respected. Article 39 forbade pillaging (http://web.ics.purdue.edu/~wggray/Teaching/His300/Handouts/Brussels-1874.html, accessed January 20, 2017).

[98] A la comision de puntos constitucionales, Mérida, December 26, 1847, AGEY, PE, G, box 65.

[99] Rugeley 2009:75.

140   *Part IV: Violence and the Government Forces*

or declare something that might hurt their comrades."[100] The fact that prisoners compromised prominent leaders and even made self-incriminatory statements suggests that pressure and occasionally torture was employed to obtain information. One rebel caught during the assault on Chichimilá in 1857, for example, confessed to his participation in the particularly bloody attack on Tekax in the previous month.[101] Another prisoner captured in the rancho Palmar declared that a leading rebel caudillo, José María Vázquez, lived on a nearby ranch known as Chanhalak, information that led to the latter's capture an hour later.[102] It is also highly likely that massive pressure was needed to induce newly taken prisoners to guide army units in combat against their comrades.[103]

While some excesses were the outcome of superior orders, others emerged from the dynamics of warfare on the ground and were the result of soldiers' individual decisions. An example of the former was the indiscriminate execution of anyone suspected of being involved in the Caste War by the commander of the 5th division, Colonel José Cosgaya, in the spring of 1848, causing numerous deaths.[104] Another case is that of explicit ordinances by commanding officers that no quarter was to be given in combat. The order came from the commander-in-chief of the brigade on campaign, General Castillo, in the battle of Dzonot in 1865. Hence, no prisoners were taken and the rebels lost at least 200 dead.[105] Atrocities were also the outcome of superior orders during the pursuit of Cecilio Chi when government troops seized Tepich on 7 August 1847. Having entered the town, Captain Ongay divided his forces into squads that immediately began to "burn houses, fill up wells and destroy everything else." Women, children and the elderly were locked into one of the torched houses "perishing mercilessly in the flames," as Baqueiro put it. Even the church with its statues of saints and sacred vestments was set on fire.[106] The official press justified the total destruction of Tepich with the following statement, which suggests that the actions of Ongay and his

[100] Anonymous 1878:91.
[101] M.F. Peraza to CGE, Valladolid, October 16, 1857, *GS*, October 21, 1857, 3.
[102] M. Micheltorena to MGM, Mérida, July 30, 1850. For another example, see M. Micheltorena to MGM, Mérida, December 11, 1850, both in AHM, XI/481.3/2914.
[103] See, for example, R. Díaz de la Vega to MGM, Mérida, October 30, 1852, AHM, XI/481.3/3300.
[104] Baqueiro 1990, 2:196.
[105] J. Salazar Ilarrequi to MGM, Ticul, June 22, 1865, AHM, XI/481.4/9976.
[106] Baqueiro 1990, 2:11. He cites a member of Ongay's squad as his source.

Violence by Government Forces against Others 141

soldiers were not merely an expression of individual outrage but reflected a widespread disposition among the general public:

These terrible examples of severity ... that horrify the whole of humanity have become necessary and are indispensable in the war we are waging against those half-savage barbarians and their bloody deeds ... and because it would be impossible to destroy and contain them with less severe conduct.[107]

In a similar vein, Colonel Cetina set fire to several towns during operations against rebels in the summer of 1848. In Santa Elena, he ordered wells to be plugged and "a poor child of the Indian class thrown into one of them." An old man who had served the rebels as a scribe was hanged and "left on an elevated platform with a feather in his hand."[108] The same officer was responsible for another outrage committed by government troops during the recapture of Tekax shortly after this episode. Soldiers threw prisoners from a building while their peers waited on the ground to spear them with bayonets. Among the unfortunate captives was "a poor boy, shedding tears, clasping his arms around the knees of an official, pleading to be saved; but not even for this angel of innocence was there mercy," according to Baqueiro. He was thrown down and landed on the bayonet points as the other prisoners had done.[109] Yucatecans loyal to the government attacked the rebels in Bacalar in late 1848 and early 1849. In one of these raids, they "burned to death" at least one rebel.[110] At 8 a.m. on April 3, 1852, army units under the command of General Rómulo Díaz de la Vega arrived at Chichanhá, a strategically important location for its role in the powder trade between Belize and the Caste War rebels. The town had already been taken by a detachment under Lieutenant Colonel Romualdo Baqueiro. An eyewitness who arrived with the general indicated that "excesses had been committed" during the occupation, which was "obvious from the condition of the houses." Díaz de la Vega expressed "dissatisfaction and displeasure" and confronted Baqueiro with "the severest of charges." The latter's official report, however, stated, "that the town had been taken by force, that the Indians had offered vigorous resistance and that the place had suffered in the disorder of the assault." The eyewitness commented: "Be that as it may, the truth is always in its place. We ascertained that the town had been seized without a gunshot." The residents had obviously not been slain during combat but were victims of a massacre. "That's the way a lot of our victories are against

---

[107] *SDN*, cited in Baqueiro 1990, 2:12.   [108] Baqueiro 1990, 3:18–19.
[109] Baqueiro 1990, 3:22–23.   [110] Dumond 1997:455 n. 34.

Part IV: Violence and the Government Forces

the Indians," the eyewitness remarked dryly, suggesting that these army unit excesses were far from unique.[111] Lieutenant Colonel Baqueiro apparently faced no further investigation of the iniquities presumably committed under his command.

Juan Chi, the cacique of Hecelchakán, warred against the rebels, leading hundreds of Indians against them from his own town as well as from Calkiní, Becal, Dzitbalché, Tepakán, Halachó, Motul and Bokabá.[112] He became a particularly cruel enemy of the rebels, prompting even a seasoned army officer such as General Castillo to the following statement:

> The ferocity of this Indian was extreme. Not content with killing the enemies, he burned their corpses in a bonfire, reducing them to ashes. He tied the captured Indians to a tree and decapitated them with the blow of an axe, sparing neither women nor children. It was harrowing to see him bestially kill three or four young children of ten or twelve years of age, who were shot one by one in the most horrible cold blood.[113]

Another context that led to atrocities was treachery. The town of Tizimín, for example, was seized in late 1853 by a joint force of more than 200 rebels and 200 Yucatecans headed by Narciso Pérez Virgilio. Pérez, the leader of an uprising against the government, had formed an alliance with an Indian rebel leader. Following the town's occupation, he persuaded the Indian chief to assemble his troops at the plaza for their joint march against Valladolid. Pérez's soldiers formed a line vis-à-vis the Caste War rebels. As arranged secretly beforehand, the soldiers suddenly fired their guns killing most of the rebels and murdering the few survivors on the spot.[114] The Indian general, his deputy, 20 junior officers and more than 200 rank and file rebels lost their lives. When Pérez learned that the adjacent towns had refused to back his insurgency, he saw his situation as desperate. Only recently another insurgent (Sebastián Molas) had been executed in Mérida. Pérez decided not to pursue his original insurgency plan but to murder his Indian allies instead, hoping to regain the government's favor. He reported his deed to the commander in Valladolid and the government granted Pérez and his officers a pardon.[115] As we will see later, cheating was not the prerogative of government forces.

---

[111] Cámara Zavala 1928, part 10.

[112] Se notifica ... que se recompensa a Juan Chi con una legua de tierra para sus servicios prestados, Hecelchakán, June 4, 1848, AGEC, PY, G, box 7, file 551; GCY:70; Baqueiro 1990, 3:26.

[113] GCY:70.   [114] GCY:96–97.

[115] Crónica, ER, December 12, 1853, 4. See also the detailed account in Baqueiro (1990, 4:206–210) and Pérez Alcala (1880:75–82). The latter reports more than 300 dead and names Clemente Uch, commander of Xmabén, as the rebel leader.

Violence by Government Forces against Others   143

Sexual violence against women is a common corollary of armed conflict. Employed as a military strategy to demonstrate supremacy, it undermines the social fabric of the victim group, and terrorizes and humiliates civilians.[116] Victims often conceal what has been done to them and are ashamed of their horrific experiences. They are also afraid of being ostracized in their own group as "polluted." It is therefore hardly surprising that very few sources document the rape of captive women. As mentioned above, a young girl was abused in Tepich by a Yucatecan officer in 1847. Serapio Baqueiro complained later of "abuses" committed by chiefs and officers of government forces during military operations in the spring of 1850. Daughters were often gang-raped in front of their parents. "Modesty would rise against us, reason protest and language deny us its rich words, if we were to explain in detail what we collected from the tradition on this matter. For this reason we prefer to remain silent," he added.[117] Another case is that of Francisca Chac and Justa Chuc, who were seized in 1853 by an army squad at their milpa near Chemax and brought to Valladolid. From there they were to be distributed to residents of Mérida in debt peonage along with other prisoners. Both women were raped by soldiers on their way to their destination.[118]

Why this cruelty? Although we lack the detailed information that would permit definitive answers, some hypotheses are possible. The most probable intention of these atrocities was to weaken enemy resistance and deter supporters from joining the rebellion. Prisoner abuse can be seen, at least in some cases, as a rational but morally questionable strategy to obtain crucial information. Revenge for losses experienced by the perpetrators is another conceivable motive for brutality. This seems to have been the case with the troops of the infamous Colonel Cetina, who entered Tixmehuac in late 1848 having suffered several dead and a considerable number of wounded in various ambushes. Although the villagers of Tixmehuac and fugitives from other areas, mostly women and children, offered no resistance, the soldiers vented their fury by killing them with bayonets.[119] During combat in Xcekil und Nohtook in May 1855, Captain Estebán Rodriguez and his men captured six kruso'b. They were "executed on the spot" for their vigorous resistance and the officer's "indignation at having seen two defenders of the fatherland

---

[116] See, for example, the overview in Koos 2015.
[117] Baqueiro 1990, 4:75. See also J. Canuto Vela to A.M. Peón, Tekax, November 9, 1849, in Baqueiro 1990, 3:238–242.
[118] Peniche Rivero 1993:103–104.   [119] Baqueiro 1990, 3:96–97.

Part IV: Violence and the Government Forces

injured by the savages' machete."[120] Finally, sadistic leanings acted out in war could account for some of the barbarities committed and would seem to be an explanation for Cetina's frequent ruthlessness. Be that as it may, Baqueiro imputes him with "bloodthirstiness" (*instinto de sangre*).[121] Juan Chi's behavior suggests similar impulses. Hostilities frequently occurred in forests or other remote places, where there were no unwanted witnesses to testify to the rage and sadism played out with little or no control. Demoralized from years of civil strife between factions of the elite and the struggle against the Mexican invasion, soldiers and the general public had become accustomed to violence, which in turn probably lowered inhibitions to commit atrocities.

CONCLUSION

Reliable quantitative data on violent acts committed during the Caste War within and by government armed forces is almost non-existent, making it impossible to asses their statistical frequency. Qualitative reasoning, however, allows for some informed guesses. The use of force was pronounced within the army and the National Guard and seen as a means of maintaining discipline among the rank and file, who for the most part were draftees or convicted delinquents. While in theory soldiers were citizens, in practice they had few or no rights and were more or less at the mercy of their superiors. In addition, Yucatecan elites had little respect for the rank and file, most of whom belonged to the poor and illiterate lower classes. Several factors were responsible for the abuse of civilians by military units in the government-controlled area. The inability of the government to cater for a sufficient quantity of regular supplies to the cantonments led to requisitions and robbery. Since military personnel came under military jurisdiction (*fuero militar*) most of the time, the civil authorities had little opportunity to intervene.[122] This allowed soldiers and officers to act without fear of prosecution. Violence against civilians in the buffer zone and against Caste War rebels was fostered by the nature of the struggle as an irregular war since 1848, where rebels employed guerilla tactics and government forces orchestrated counter-insurgency operations, including scorched-earth campaigns. Violence as a deterrent is a standard feature of this kind of warfare. Likely contributing factors were stress arising from the uncertainty of distinguishing friend and foe and the impunity with

---

[120] M.F. Peraza to General en Jefe, Valladolid, May 9, 1855, *EO*, May 15, 1855, 2–3.
[121] Baqueiro 1990, 3:22. [122] Unzueta Reyes 2006 and 2009:9–16.

Violence by Government Forces against Others 145

which violent acts were carried out, facilitated by the remoteness of the scenes. As comparative studies of armed groups have shown, the massive use of force against non-combatants is more likely to occur in unfamiliar social contexts, where the necessary information to exert violence selectively is lacking. Similar may be the case in situations where the front line either moves quickly or is ill-defined. The possible presence of the enemy at one's back "causes frustration, 'endemic' uncertainty, fear, anxiety, even panic . . . [and] in an environment where it is impossible to tell civilian from enemy combatant apart, it pays to be violent," as Kalyvas puts it.[123] These conditions clearly prevailed in the Caste War. Dividing booty among the soldiers, awarding prizes for prisoners and selling captives to Cuba all served to encourage military thrusts and pillaging. The conflict gave officers in frontier towns and garrisons exceptional power over soldiers and inhabitants, and a variety of opportunities for personal enrichment, including access to the labor of prisoners and soldiers, an aspect that undoubtedly contributed to the prolongation of the war.

---

[123] Kalyvas 2006:69; see also Grossman 1996:196–199; Schlichte 2009:77–79.

PART V

VIOLENCE AND THE KRUSO'B

Violence played a crucial role in kruso'b life. It was directed against enemy combatants and civilians in the government-controlled area but likewise prevailed among the rebels themselves as a result of their precarious situation marked by army attacks, hunger and disease. It will be argued in the following that violence was furthermore a vital element in the political and religious organization of rebel society. Indispensable to the appropriation of resources and valuables, as evidenced by the raids on Yucatecan settlements in the first three decades of the war, physical force contributed to the establishing and upholding of kruso'b leadership. In the course of the Caste War, however, its frequency, forms, aims and meanings altered, not least due to shifts in the relative importance of the different income sources and other material factors. Prior to a detailed discussion on violence as practiced both internally and externally by the kruso'b, an overview is given of their social composition, political economy and religious organization as a necessary background to later sections.

13

The Social Composition of the Rebel Movement

While Yucatecan elites consistently characterized the Caste War as a racial conflict and labeled the rebels as Indians, the insurgents were in fact a fairly mixed population. Ample evidence from contemporary observers shows that many non-Indians were found in the rebel ranks.[1] This was not confined to the initial stages of the war, when many people were still under the impression the conflict was part of the struggle between Barbachanistas and Mendistas, but persisted until the war came to an end. In June 1848, for example, the Yucatecan government, under the leadership of Miguel Barbachano, established the death penalty for non-Indians found among the rebels.[2] Had vecino presence been negligible, a special decree would not have been necessary. Most of the 107 captives of both sexes taken by Captain O'Horan during a thrust into rebel territory in mid-1850 were "vecinos," as non-Indians were generally called.[3] Following their apprehension by government forces in early 1852, several deserters from the army cantonment at Bacalar declared that Caste War rebels amounted to between 3,000 and 5,000 men armed with guns and about the same number equipped with axes and machetes, "most of the former being white people."[4] Non-Indian presence among the rebels was still of such importance in 1853 that the peace treaty between the Yucatecan government and the pacíficos del sur dedicated

[1] Cf., for example, Baqueiro 1990, 2:17, 156, 163, 167, 283; 3:28, 65, 371–372; 4:31. See Gabbert (2004b:98–99) and the references below for more evidence on this. Although Nelson Reed (1997c) has dedicated a separate article to the non-Indian rebel leaders, he maintains an ethnic interpretation of the conflict.

[2] Decreto de 5 de Junio de 1848, APP 3:210–211.

[3] M. Micheltorena to MGM, Mérida, July 30, 1850, AHM, XI/481.3/2914.

[4] Causa seguida contra varios desertores ..., Hunucmá, February 12–March 19,1852, AGEY, PE, J, box 145, file 27.

149

150 *Part V: Violence and the Kruso'b*

a special paragraph to this group, granting them the same guarantees conceded to Indians.[5] Of the more or less 500 men who made up the "Indian force" that raided Pisté on July 28, 1862, an eyewitness estimated that "three-quarters were whites."[6] As already mentioned, Yucatecan and Mexican soldiers deserted to the rebels in substantial numbers even in later years. Accordingly, Bishop Carrillo y Ancona wrote in 1865 that "government troop deserters, runaway debt peons, evildoers and all kinds of bad and debauched people of different races, such as Indians, whites, negroes, and mulattos" had joined the rebels.[7] Moreover, many of the rebel leaders were non-Indians. A list of major leaders revealed that eighteen (23 percent) of the seventy-seven individuals mentioned did not have a Maya surname, the main indicator of distinction between Indians and vecinos.[8] One contemporary emphasized that "generally the chiefs are not pure Indians but mostly deserters from garrisons, mestizos, mulattos and sometimes whites in fear of the law."[9] Contemporary Yucatecans even regarded José María Barrera, the founder of the Cult of the Speaking Cross, as white or mestizo rather than Indian.[10] Bonifacio Novelo, another prominent rebel leader, was described as a mestizo peddler.[11] As mentioned earlier, the rebels employed terms of self-identification that reflect their mixed social and ethnic composition and religious affiliation, generally referring to themselves as cristiano'b (Christians), otsilo'b (poor), masewalo'b (commoners) or kruso'b (the crosses) and not as Indians or Maya.[12] It comes as no surprise that legally most rank and file rebels were Indians, as revealed by their Maya surnames. Legal Indians were overrepresented among the rural lower classes, the insurgents' main

---

[5] See the text in GCY:98–101.

[6] L. Irigoyen to MGM, Mérida, August 7, 1862, AHM, XI/481.4/8772.

[7] Carrillo y Ancona 1950:67. See also El indio Chablé en Mejico, *EE*, September 2, 1894, in Wilhelm 1997:35.

[8] The list is in Reina (1980:415–416). It mentions Jacinto Pat and must therefore refer to a time before his death in September 1849. Seven or eight (7–8 percent) of the 103 rebel captains listed in another table do not have a Maya surname (Lista de capitancillos indios, M. Micheltorena to MGM, Mérida, April 4, 1850, AHM, XI/481.3/2914). However, several more prominent vecino leaders, such as José María Barrera or Bonifacio Novelo, are not mentioned. For the presence of vecino leaders among the rebels, see also P. Balam to General J.F. Tun Cantón, Cauil Akal, May 13, 1855, CAIHDY, M, XLII.1850–1866/27; M.F. Peraza to CGE, Valladolid, May 26, 1857, *UL*, June 2, 1857, 1–2; Declaración de José Estevan Cen, Mérida, April 11, 1879, AGEY, PE, CLM, box 207bis.

[9] Aldherre and Mendiolea 1869:74.

[10] *RY*, 1849, II:70–71; Reed 1964:287; Bricker 1981:108.   [11] Rugeley 1997:482.

[12] See the evidence presented in Chapter 7.

The Social Composition of the Rebel Movement 151

social base. In addition, the preponderance of Indians simply mirrors Yucatán's demographic structure, since the bulk of the rebels came from areas where this group outnumbered vecinos by three or four to one.[13] Most Caste War rebels were peasants from the eastern and southeastern borderlands. Maya-speaking caciques, townspeople and peasants in the area around Valladolid triggered the uprising and were soon joined by others from the surroundings of Sotuta, the southern borderlands of Tekax and the Chenes region.[14] Dumond gives a concise account of the rebellion's spatial dimension:

The rebellion began, and in an important sense was to end, as an eastern movement. The only lasting leadership began and remained in eastern hands, while recruits from the newly risen regions to the west and south acted more or less independently for as long as they were in rebellion. Like most Yucatecans, the general run of the rebels showed a determination to stay close to whatever place they called home.[15]

Paul Sullivan has come to a similar conclusion with regard to the kruso'b who, for the most part, originated in frontier towns such as Peto, Ichmul, Sabán, Chikindzonot, Tihosuco and Tixualahtun, the settlements to the east, south and west of Valladolid and, to a certain extent, places along the major roads of invasion into Yucatecan territory. When the kruso'b began to assault frontier settlements "they marched through their hometowns, raiding, in a certain sense, their own communities, burning their own villages, killing or capturing the countrymen of their youth."[16]

These short remarks should make clear that a dichotomous interpretation of the Caste War as a conflict between Indians and non-Indians would not suffice for an understanding of the causes of violence and its dynamics in this struggle. The rebels and, as already seen, government forces had people of both categories in their ranks, and each of these contending parties raided and killed both Indians and vecinos. This issue will be resumed in Chapter 18.

---

[13] Cf. the data in Cline (1950, V:154–157) and Gabbert (2004c:50).
[14] Baqueiro, 1990, 1:224–225, 3:8; Ancona 1879/80, 4:18, 31, 36, 74–75, 77, 137; Reed 1964:48, 76.
[15] Dumond 1997:107.   [16] Sullivan 1997a, II:7.

14

Of Loot and Lumber: the Kruso'b Economy

As argued in Chapters 11 and 12, warfare is not only about exerting military force but also about logistics. Men need arms to fight efficiently and, above all, they have to eat. Thus, to a significant degree, the struggle for survival and foodstuffs determined the Caste War during its first two decades. Although government forces often suffered as a result of insufficient supplies, they could at least rely on existing structures of production, distribution and transport, such as haciendas, trades and roads. The Caste War rebels, on the other hand, had to create their own economic system from scratch. While insurgents were mostly in a position to live "off the country," commandeering or plundering the required resources in the areas under their control during the first year of the conflict, provisioning combatants and their families became more trying after their withdrawal to the eastern and southeastern parts of the peninsula. Firearms, powder, lead and other desired items had to be procured either by looting in the government-controlled area or purchasing them in Belize.[1] Arms and ammunition improved the kruso'b capacity for self-defense against government forces and, beyond that, served as a "means of appropriation" in

---

[1] When Colonel Maldonado ambushed a group of kruso'b returning from Belize in December 1854, he captured about 100 pounds of lead, 13 guns, 39 cargas of salt, and "various pieces of crude cotton cloth and other articles" (J.M. Novelo to General en Jefe, Pachmul, January 2, 1855, *EO*, January 23, 1855, 3–4). Over time, luxury goods were added to the shopping list. Thus, on a visit to British Honduras in January 1876, the kruso'b bought "large quantities of silks and other sorts of clothing" in addition to guns (R.M. Mundy dispatch No. 7, January 7, 1876, CO 123/129, cited in Dumond 1997:326).

152

Of Loot and Lumber: the Kruso'b Economy 153

raids on Yucatecan and pacífico settlements.[2] Since loot obtained from these assaults remained the principal revenue for quite some time,[3] the kruso'b made regular excursions into Yucatecan territory, sacking farms, villages and towns, and stealing money, valuables, breeding cattle, horses and rice.[4] The rebels seized handsome booty on some of their raids. In Tihosuco, for example, they captured 200,000 cargas of corn, jewels of considerable value, large quantities of other goods and articles, casks of rum, lead, gunpowder, guns and about 16,000 pesos in cash on November 10, 1847.[5] The loot obtained in Tunkas in 1861 amounted to 47,000 pesos – 25,000 in cash and the rest in valuables – as well as 100 mules and merchandise worth 4,000 pesos.[6] In addition to 159 prisoners taken from raids on ranchos and haciendas in the surroundings of Kaua and Uayma in January 1873, the kruso'b captured fifty horses and eighty-two hogs.[7] They planned their raiding expeditions carefully and selected targets according to specific criteria, among them the anticipated resistance and special opportunities such as the fiestas in Yucatecan towns, where numerous heads of cattle were rounded up to feed the scores of visitors at the festivities.[8] This demonstrates that the kruso'b were generally well informed about events in the government-controlled parts of

---

[2] For the arms trade with Belize, see, for example, Informacion contra capitan William Longworth et al., Bacalar, September 25, 1849, and P. Pech to J.P. Pech, San Antonio, October 26, 1849, both in AHM, XI/481.3/2914; Superintendent to H.B.M. Minister, November 10, 1849, R. 32b, ABH:126; M. Barbachano to Ministro de Relaciones, Mérida, December 31, 1849, AGN, PY, G, sin sección, vol. 381, file 6; M. Micheltorena to MGM, Mérida, April 27, 1850, AHM, XI/481.3/2914; Informe sobre el plan de campaña del Gral. Castillo, J.L. Uraya to Emperador, n.p., [November 27] 1865, AGN, G, SI, vol. 44, file 69; P. Regil y Peón to Emperador, Mérida, November 26, 1865, AGN, G, SI, vol. 44, file 69; Respuesta á las cuestiones hechas pr. el Exmo. Sr. Gral. Urago, M.F. Peraza, Mérida, November 28, 1865, AGN, G, SI, vol. 44, file 69; Cal 1983:118.

[3] See, for example, Baqueiro 1990, 3:150; Dumond 1997:172; Sullivan 1997a, I:5; Villalobos González 2006:76–79.

[4] J.M. Barrera and Manl. Ná, patron, to Comandante J.M. Torres, Chan Santa Cruz, March 22, 1851, letter 5 in Traduccion de once manuscritos de lengua maya, April 2, 1851, AHM, XI/481.3/3257; J.M. Novelo to General en Jefe, Pachmul, January 2, 1855, EO, January 23, 1855, 3–4; J.A. Cepeda to Gobernador, Tekax, March 11, 1868, RP, March 16, 1868, 1; El ex-coronel José Antonio Muñoz (a) el chelo, EP, October 1, 1869, 4; GCY:124.

[5] GCY:35.

[6] M. Barbachano: Sobre la última correria de los bárbaros, EC, September 11, 1861, 3–4.

[7] C. Moreno Navarrete to Gobernador, Valladolid, January 25, 1873, RP, January 29, 1873, 1.

[8] See, for example, E. Esquivel to General en Jefe, Sotuta, February 11, 1873, RP, February 14, 1873, 1; D. Vazquez to Gobernador, Peto, February 7, 1885, AGEY, PE, JP, box 232.

154 Part V: Violence and the Kruso'b

Yucatán. Occasionally kruso'b raided "on demand," that is, traders from Belize made it clear beforehand the sort of items the rebels were to look out for on their assaults, such as horses, mules or cattle.[9]

In addition to British residents, Yucatecan refugees in Belize and even some local dealers in Yucatán were involved in the arms trade with kruso'b.[10] In 1850, General Micheltorena accused the trading houses of Christie, Cox, and a Frenchman whose name he did not mention, of financing this "criminal traffic," which was frequently transacted by Yucatecan refugees like Florencio Vega, Pedro N. Rosado, Jose Orio and, "the most criminal of all," the presbyter Juan Trujillo, as well as many former residents of Bacalar.[11]

Income from looting was at first complemented and later gradually replaced by other revenues, including articles produced and animals bred by kruso'b. From late 1848 to the mid-1850s, the rebels were pushed to the edge of survival, since constant persecution by government forces seriously affected corn cultivation. In 1859, the kruso'b were still making incursions into the pacífico area to harvest the milpas the latter had prepared.[12] In the course of time, however, they extended their capacity to produce goods both for their own consumption and for exchange. Swidden agriculture provided most of the necessary foodstuffs, notably corn, beans, squashes, camotes (sweet potatoes), yuca and other crops. In addition, they raised chicken and hogs.[13] Since corn and chicken had been available in excess of kruso'b subsistence needs since the 1860s, they were

---

[9] See, for example, J. Escalante to Juez 1a Ins. de este Dept., Tekax, July 6, 1873, AGEY, PE, M, box 306, file 53; Villalobos González 2006:88–90.

[10] For Yucatecan refugees in Belize involved in the arms trade, see Gobernador to Comandante paylebot de guerra Sisaleña, Maxcanú, January 2, 1848, and Gobernador to Comandante principal del distrito de Valladolid, Maxcanú, January 5, 1848, both in AGEY, PE, G, box 67; J.M. Lanuza, México, November 22, 1850, AHM, XI/481.3/2914; CGE to MG, Mérida, February 24, 1855, AGEY, PE, G, box 100; Letter to Gobernador, n.p., 1856, AGEY, PE, G, box 103; Superintendent to Governor, Jamaica, December 17, 1857, R. 55, ABH:199; E. Ancona to Ministro de Relaciones Exteriores, Mérida, March 18, 1876, RP, May 3, 1876, 2. Yucatecan refugees held different opinions about the kruso'b. Some saw them as enemies, some sympathized with them and others "shifted their loyalties to suit the circumstances" (Cal 1983:107). For traders in Yucatán, see, for example, José Martínez Baca to Gobernador, Valladolid, May 21, 1858, GS, May 26, 1858, 2.

[11] M. Micheltorena to MGM, June 11,1850, AHM, XI/481.3/2914.

[12] G. Ruiz to Gobernador, Peto, March 12, 1859, EC, March 16, 1859, 1.

[13] See, for example, Respuesta á las cuestiones hechas pr. el Exmo. Sr. Gral. Uraga, M.F. Peraza, Mérida, November 28, 1865, AGN, G, SI, vol. 44, file 69.

Of Loot and Lumber: the Kruso'b Economy

155

exchanged for other goods.[14] Cattle were bred to be sold to Belize, where they were slaughtered to feed the logging gangs.[15] Some salt was manufactured on the beach.[16] An impressive variety of crafts developed in Chan Santa Cruz and probably other places, although to a lesser extent. A map of the town from 1860 shows the church, a number of stone buildings erected for the chiefs and houses for various artisans.[17] This information is confirmed by an escaped prisoner who reported having seen workshops for carpenters, blacksmiths, silversmiths, tinsmiths, shoemakers and tailors. In 1862, there were still no formal shops in Chan Santa Cruz and goods were sold regularly in the commanders' houses.[18] Well-stocked dry goods and grocery shops were located on the plaza and the surrounding area in the late 1860s.[19] By then, distilling plants for rum and facilities to process sugar and honey had also been established.[20] Chan Santa Cruz and Tulum had not only become political and religious hubs but also supply centers for surrounding settlements.[21]

In the 1880s, or possibly earlier, the kruso'b acquired the ability to produce their own machetes, using iron imported from Belize and embellishing them with handles made of horn. On seeing the small number of tools the rebels possessed, a contemporary observer praised them as "very well made."[22] In addition to the above-mentioned corn, chicken and cattle, the kruso'b traded a wide variety of other products with the British on the Río Hondo, New River, at Corozal and Belize, among them horses, mules, hogs, hides, hats (sombreros), hammocks, liquor, henequen, vanilla and other forest products, in exchange for powder,

---

[14] An abundance of corn was reported from Chan Santa Cruz in 1869, for example (N. Novelo to Gobernador, Tekax, December 12, 1869, *RP*, December 17, 1869, 1).

[15] Kruso'b rarely ate beef and the soles of their sandals were not made of leather but henequen, which was cultivated in minor quantities (Un indio de Santa Cruz capturado, *EE*, August 22, 1894, 4, in Wilhelm 1997:29). For cattle breeding, see also Villalobos González 2006:91, 110.

[16] M.F. Peraza to CGE, Valladolid, February 22, 1856, AGEY, PE, G, box 103.

[17] See Dumond 1985:298 and the map in Dumond 1997:246. Cf. Figure 14.1.

[18] Noticias que emite el C. Anastasio Durán ..., *LRP*, September 5, 1862, 1–3.

[19] R. Novelo to Gobernador, Valladolid, June 24, 1869, *EP*, July 2, 1869, 1–2.

[20] F. Gil to Gobernador, Tekax, May 20, 1868, *RP*, May 20, 1868, 1; Chan Santa Cruz Report, Mérida, June 2, 1882, TULAL, M-26, box 2, folder 14.

[21] N. Urcelay to General en Jefe, pueblo de Dolores, Isla Mujeres, August 19, 1872, *RP*, August 26, 1872, 1.

[22] Miller 1889:27. For the buying of iron, see, for example, M. Micheltorena to MGM, Mérida, April 13, 1850, AHM, XI/481.3/2914.

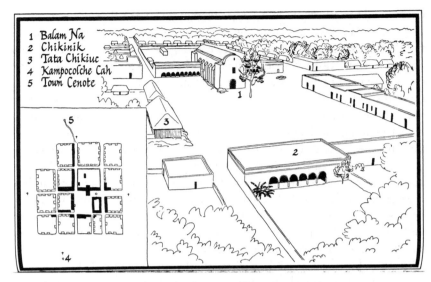

FIGURE 14.1 Chan Santa Cruz in the 1860s. Reed 1964:172.

lead and other articles.[23] Even captive children were occasionally sold to the British as servants.[24] The rebels also established commercial relations with the inhabitants of Isla Mujeres, exchanging corn and chicken for salt, among other things.[25] Some kruso'b even worked in fields the islanders had established on the mainland. They were paid half a real for each sack of harvested corn and obtained lead, flint, powder, clay pots (made in Lerma, close to the city of Campeche), and other essential goods.[26] The statement of a captured rebel in the 1890s indicates that, in contrast to the late 1860s, no shops existed in Chan Santa Cruz. Sugar was sold at the home of the producers and rum in the two factories. Clothing and other

---

[23] P. Pech to J.P. Pech, San Antonio, October 26, 1849, AHM, XI/481.3/2914; W. Anderson to F. Seymour, Belize, February 15, 1858, GBFO in Rugeley 2001b:66; S. Castillo to MGM, Mérida, June 1, 1865, AHM, XI/481.4/9976; Declaración de José Estevan Cen, Mérida, April 11, 1879, AGEY, PE, CLM, box 207bis; Informe de Demetrio Peraza, Isla Mujeres, November 14, 1882, AGEY, PE, ODG, box 220; Un indio de Santa Cruz capturado, EE, August 22, 1894, 4 in Wilhelm 1997:29. The Río Hondo, New River and the Espiritu Santo Bay were the main trading routes to Belize. See, for example, M. Micheltorena to MGM, June 11,1850, AHM, XI/481.3/2914.

[24] A. Espinosa to Gobernador, Valladolid, February 28, 1871, RP, March 3, 1871, 1.

[25] Informe de Demetrio Peraza, Isla Mujeres, November 14, 1882, AGEY, PE, ODG, box 220.

[26] Brigada Peraza. Comandancia militar de Tizimín, F. Ruíz, to Gobernador, Tizimín, April 2, 1858, GS, April 9, 1858, 1–2.

Of Loot and Lumber: the Kruso'b Economy   157

supplies were acquired from Chinese peddlers, "who constantly walk around the place laden with goods."[27]

The cutting of dyewood and mahogany and its sale to Belize, which probably began as early as 1848, represented the key revenue apart from loot.[28] Collecting rent for permission to cut mahogany and logwood or farming on the Mexican side of the Río Hondo by people residing in Belize commenced after the first rebel conquest of Bacalar in April 1848. This became increasingly important in the 1850s.[29] Rents for the exploitation of dyewoods and mahogany generated a substantial income for the kruso'b. The Belizian firm Young, Toledo & Co., for example, agreed to pay 300 pesos rent for the area around Blue Creek in 1857 and 900 pesos for terrains around Agua Blanca in 1860.[30] Two other entrepreneurs paid as much as 1,000 pesos each, while yet others paid minor sums totalling 3,064 pesos in 1863.[31] High-ranking kruso'b chiefs made annual visits to Belize City since 1880 in order to trade, draw up contracts and grant wood-cutting licenses. They even counted on the services of a regular agent there.[32] The mid-1880s saw a charge of twelve reales (1.5 pesos) per ton of dyewood and a decade later, one peso. Thus, the kruso'b

---

[27] Un indio de Santa Cruz capturado, *EE*, August 22, 1894, 4 in Wilhelm 1997:29. For cattle breeding, see also Villalobos González 2006:91, 110.

[28] M. Micheltorena to MGM, Mérida, April 13, 1850, AHM, XI/481.3/2914; M.F. Peraza to General en Jefe, Valladolid, April 3, 1855, *EO*, April 20, 1855, 1–3; Respuesta á las cuestiones hechas pr. el Exmo. Sr. Gral. Uraga, M.F. Peraza, Mérida, November 28, 1865 and Informe sobre el plan de campaña del Gral. Castillo, J.L. Uraya to Emperador, n.p., [November 27] 1865, both in AGN, G, SI, vol. 44, file 69. The British had already exploited mahogany and logwood on the Yucatecan side of the border before 1847. They resumed these activities after the first rebel occupation of Bacalar in early April 1848 (Cal 1983:46, 60). For an in-depth study of the importance of mahogany and dyewood exploitation for the kruso'b and their relations with Belize, see Villalobos González 2006.

[29] Commandant of Bacalar to Superintendent, October 5, 1848, R. 28, ABH:112; Superintendent to Governor, Jamaica, September 9, 1856, R. 55, ABH:192; J. Hodge, Manager, to British Honduras Co. Ltd., London, September 20, 1864, R. 86, ABH:258; F. Pren to Gobernador, Sotuta, February 14, 1862, *EN*, February 19, 1862, 2; Comisión del gobierno de Yucatán ..., June 13, 1864, *LNE*, June 24, 1864, 1–3; A.E. Morlan to J. D. Parker, Belize, April 27, 1886, TULAL, MIC 736, reel 5; Jones 1974:675; Cal 1983:79–80; Dumond 1997:208–209, 240–241, 252, 265, 274, 353, 362, 379; Villalobos González 2006:53–55. In 1872, Belizian authorities excluded Indians and mestizos from the right to hold landed property. As a result, they were forced to hire themselves out to sugar plantations or lumber camps, or to rent lands in Belize or on the Mexican side of the border from the kruso'b (Villalobos González 2006:182–182, 186–187).

[30] Cal 1983:80, 92–93.   [31] La Redacción, *LNE*, July 1, 1864, 3.

[32] A.E. Morlan to J.D. Parker, Belize, April 27, 1886, TULAL, MIC 736, reel 5; Causa seguida á Alonso Salazar y otros, October 9, 1886, *RP*, October 20, 1886, 2–3; Dumond 1997:353; For further details, see Villalobos González 2006:171–173.

158   *Part V: Violence and the Kruso'b*

received 10,500 pesos from Belizian loggers in 1895.[33] In fact, revenue obtained from rent replaced raids on Yucatecan settlements as the main source of rebel income in the 1870s. I agree with Villalobos González that this may explain why only two or three incursions into Yucatecan territory took place after 1875, as mentioned in Chapter 8.[34] Rent collection was a far more reliable and less dangerous means of acquiring money and goods than raiding, which entailed arduous journeys into enemy country with the inexorable risk of being captured, wounded or killed. In any case, the change in the source of revenue implied a reduction in the use of direct physical violence against Yucatecans, without which raiding was inconceivable. The kruso'b, however, were obliged to at least uphold the image of fierce warriors in order to deter those who might threaten their independence or attempt to access their rich forest resources without their consent. Beyond this, these new sources of wealth became a bone of contention among the kruso'b. Rivalry resulted time and again in bloodshed, as will be shown.

[33] Causa seguida á Alonso Salazar y otros, October 9, 1886, *RP*, October 20, 1886, 2–3; Villalobos González 2006:172.
[34] Cf. Villalobos González 2006:106.

15

Kruso'b Politics and Religion

The characterizations of Caste War rebels both by contemporaries and later commentators are diverse. Descriptions range from a disorderly bunch of barbarians attacking civilization and bloodthirsty criminals to ethnic freedom fighters struggling against the repression of national society. What the movement's goals were, in general and at particular time periods, and the extent to which they were achieved, is still open to debate.[1] The rebel movement was quite successful, however, in one respect at least, since it managed to survive for half a century and defend its autonomy against all odds. Without the development of a social and political organization capable of satisfying people's basic needs and providing a minimum of security, the long-term survival of kruso'b society would have been impossible.

In principle, several factors account for the durability of an insurgent organization: the advantage to its members (e.g., material assets, security, status), the charisma of its leaders and the legitimacy of its leaders and of the organization (both must be distinguished from each other), habitualization (increases with the length of its existence), and the limited exit options for its members. Any military organization demands some form of centralization and command, for example, the provisioning of combatants must be ensured and behavior in combat coordinated. These organizational needs increase in accordance with group size and the control of larger areas, and require a certain amount of coordinated administration.[2] In his comparative study of armed groups, Klaus Schlichte distinguishes between two ideal types of mechanisms to achieve these aims.

[1] See Chapter 18 for a discussion of this topic.   [2] Schlichte 2009:176.

160   *Part V: Violence and the Kruso'b*

While "patrimonialization" sees control of resources and chains of command centralized in the hands of one or a few individuals and power relations are highly personal, "formalization" is characterized by functional differentiation, formal rules and procedures, and the depersonalization of power (power attached to social positions is dissociated from the personal qualities of the respective incumbent).[3] As will be shown in the following, elements of both mechanisms can be discerned in kruso'b politics and religion.

While the previous Chapter addressed the rebel economy, the following pages concentrate on their political and religious organization. In fact, both aspects are closely related and should only be seen separately for analytical purposes. The Cult of the Speaking Cross became a cornerstone in the organization of politics and collective violence and served to legitimize the use of physical force, as witnessed in the sanctioning of wrongdoers, raids against Yucatán or the slaying of captives. My point of departure is a brief description of a model of kruso'b political and religious organization proposed by Nelson Reed (1964) in his now-classic book on the Caste War, which deeply influenced later scholars and the interested public. First, however, the origins of the cult will be presented.

THE CROSS CULT'S BEGINNINGS

As mentioned in Chapter 7, the origins of the Cult of the Speaking Cross reach back to early 1850, when the rebels were in a dire situation, fragmented into various bands and continually persecuted by government forces. Information on the origins of the cult is sketchy and contradictory in part, particularly regarding the number of crosses venerated, which ranged between one and three. The sources nonetheless agree that the cross or crosses communicated with their adherents with the aid of a medium and became a point of cohesion for the dispersed rebel population.

One of the earliest pieces of information on the cult is included in a letter from General Micheltorena to the minister of defense reporting the results of an army thrust into rebel territory. At the break of dawn on March 23, 1851, Colonel Juan María Novelo attacked José María Barrera's headquarters at Chan Santa Cruz with 170 men. Barrera managed to escape but the soldiers captured two crosses venerated by the rebels and killed their "patron," Manuel Nauat, a native of Kanxoc in the

---

[3] Schlichte 2009:167–168, 175–177.

Kruso'b Politics and Religion

partido of Valladolid. The crosses and their "tabernacles" were brought to the army camp at Kampocolché. From prisoners and from letters taken from the village, Novelo learned that Indians believed the crosses had appeared in a well at Chan Santa Cruz, "that they speak and, in the name of the Divinity, guaranteed the triumph of their cause" provided they managed to occupy Kampocolché, Barrera's farm and former headquarters. A great number of families had come there "with the sole purpose of getting to know and worshipping the crosses, lighting candles and donating money, corn and other articles." These items were received by the patron of the crosses, who delivered them to Barrera.[4]

The papers taken at Chan Santa Cruz contained purely secular military orders and several Maya texts written in a religious style, giving them the semblance of divine revelations. They were signed by Juan de la Cruz and stamped with two small crosses.[5] One of the letters included a critique of the murder of prisoners, which the rebels had committed in the early months of the war. The present sufferings "of hunger and thirst in the forest" were explained as divine sanctions for the "amount of harm the creatures had done to their fellow beings when the war began, as the other creatures, your fellow beings, were killed begging on their knees, invoking the name of my father [God]." "All grave wrongs" were forgiven, however, and final victory announced, "the enemy will never win, only the crosses will win."[6] In another letter, Juan de la Cruz promised that the enemy's rifle fire would do no harm to the rebels as "the time has come to give my blessing to the struggle."[7]

The account of one army officer in 1852 mentions three crosses confiscated by troops in Chan Santa Cruz and brought to Kampocolché and, although phrased with the typical elite contempt for folk religiosity, adds

---

[4] M. Micheltorena to MGM, Mérida, April 2, 1851, AHM, XI/481.3/3257. Another early report mentions only one speaking cross but confirms that apart from adorning it daily with flowers, the patron had the duty to receive "alms from the faithful to support the cult, which is to surround the log with lights that are ignited at night, while believers worship the symbol of redemption." In addition, it was he who "always spoke on behalf of the cross" (Correspondencia del Siglo, *SDN*, September 17, 1851, 2).

[5] Rebel leader Máximo Huchin had stamped a letter to one of his peers with three crosses in 1847 (M. Huchin to P. Chuc, n.p., September 15, 1847, CAIHDY, M, XLI.1847–1849/1).

[6] Juan de la Cruz, Balamna, December 11, 1850, letter 1 in Traduccion de once manuscritos de lengua maya, April 2, 1851, AHM, XI/481.3/3257; see also Proclama de Juan de la Cruz, Balamna, October 15, 1850, CAIHDY, M, XLII.1850–1866/12; Correspondencia del Siglo, *SDN*, September 17, 1851, 3.

[7] Juan de la Cruz, n.p., n.d., letter 3 in Traducción de once manuscritos de lengua maya, April 2, 1851, AHM, XI/481.3/3257; see also Proclama de Juan de la Cruz, Balamna, October 15, 1850, CAIHDY, M, XLII.1850–1866/12.

162   *Part V: Violence and the Kruso'b*

valuable information on the cult and its origins. The crosses were "dressed in a highly ridiculous manner with hipiles [a loose-fitting tunic] and fustanes [a lace petticoat] embroidered in the style of the mestizas" (a more elaborate form of the folk costume; see Figure 15.1). They had originally appeared "at the trunk of a mahogany tree at the very edge of the cenote in the middle of the square" of Chan Santa Cruz. The repeated capture of crosses by army units failed to put a stop to the cult. Whenever crosses were taken away others of the same size were placed at the bottom of the same tree, allegedly by Barrera, and "with feasts and rejoicing the crowds are made to believe they had returned." In the bark of the "miraculous mahogany tree" was a "small crudely carved cross of three or four inches, which is, as they say, the mother of the crosses, and therefore no ax or tool or human force can cut the tree."[8] A newspaper report added that after Manuel Nauat had been killed, he was

succeeded in his ministry of interpreter by a boy of seven years of age, who is covered in a long tunic and wears a necklace made of silver pesos around his neck in the manner of a rosary. The boy, like the Cumaean Sybil, speaks to the people as though inspired and writes down what he says the cross communicates to him.[9]

The following years saw consolidation of the religious cult centered on the veneration of miraculous crosses. Despite change and conflict, the cult became one of the most important elements of kruso'b religion and politics.

NELSON REED'S MODEL

The political and religious organization that emerged in the kruso'b-controlled area in the second half of the nineteenth century has been characterized quite differently. Whereas some scholars consider it a chiefdom or an aggregate of several chiefdoms,[10] others see it as a centralized state.[11] This notwithstanding, all of these interpretations agree on its comparatively high degree of formalization and centralization. Nelson Reed, following the lead of Alfonso Villa Rojas, developed a diagram of kruso'b religious and political organization that had a strong

---

[8] Cámara Zavala 1928, parts 4 and 5.

[9] Correspondencia del Siglo, *SDN*, September 17, 1851, 2–3. For contemporary descriptions of the ritual, see, for example, Buhler (1975:10), referring to the late 1850s, or Aldherre and Mendiolea (1869:74–75) and Rogers (1885:223–225) for the 1860s.

[10] Villa Rojas 1945; Dumond 1977.

[11] Sapper 1895; Jones 1974:659; Hostettler 1996:19; Rugeley 1997:495–496; Reed 1997b:523; Careaga Viliesid 1998:120; Robins 2005:62.

Kruso'b Politics and Religion 163

influence on later scholars and the interested public. Under the heading "Cruzob, 1850–1901," it shows a four-tiered hierarchy of offices above the common people. At the top is the "Patron of the Cross" or *tatich*, the second tier consists of the "Interpreter of the Cross" (*tata polin*), the "Oracle of the Divine Word," the "Secretary of the Cross," and the "General of the Plaza" (*tata chikiuc*), below which are the priests and company officers, followed by the lowest tier, subordinate to the priests, made up of medicine men (*h-meno'b*) and village secretaries (*ahdzib huuno'b*).[12]

Reed's view is largely accepted by Careaga Viliesid, who considers the kruso'b polity a military theocracy ruled by a "triumvirate" comprised of the Patron of the Cross, the Interpreter of the Cross and the Organ of the Divine Word.[13] These views essentially rely on information published in the renowned *Boletín de la Sociedad Mexicana de Geografía y Estadística* in 1869. Written by a Yucatecan author and a well-informed Austrian officer who had accompanied Maximilian to Mexico, the article described the functions of the principal actors in the cult as follows: "[T]he patron ... summoned the people to the temple grounds, and in the midst of obscurity interrogated the cross. The organ of the divine word was in charge of answering, and the tata Polin communicated divine will to the people."[14] From this description and some scattered information on the cult, Reed and others derived the schematic representation of kruso'b organization. Although such models have their merits, of necessity they stress structure rather than process and run the risk of suggesting too much stability, even during highly dynamic historical developments.[15] This seems to be the case with kruso'b society during the nineteenth century.

Reed and Careaga Viliesid's models suggest a number of things: 1. a stable authority structure existed; 2. the highest religious leader (Patron of the Cross) was the supreme authority over the kruso'b; 3. the relative significance of religious and political positions remained fairly constant; and 4. the kruso'b cult differed fundamentally from religious practices in the rest of the peninsula. A closer look at the sources leads me to doubt these assumptions. As I will

---

[12] Reed 1964:212. On page 161, however, he refers to the third position as "Organ of the Divine Word."

[13] Careaga Viliesid 1998:112, 122–123, 168–169.

[14] Aldherre and Mendiolea 1869:75.

[15] See Reed 1964:160–161, 209–220, Villa Rojas 1945:22–23 and, to a lesser extent, Bartolomé and Barabas 1977:33–35. The revised edition of Reed's book (2001) does not include the diagram but gives a more dynamic account. It does not, however, provide an alternative interpretation of rebel organization.

164   *Part V: Violence and the Kruso'b*

attempt to show in the following, no stable political hierarchy or theocracy governed the rebel population. Instead, almost constant competition for power and wealth prevailed among the leaders and often led to bloodshed. Beyond this, the Cult of the Speaking Cross was less unique than ordinarily assumed. It shared numerous facets of Yucatecan folk religiosity. Its persistence, however, and its close relationship to the military organization remain as special features. Before discussing the cult's development and the kruso'b organizational structure in more detail, some remarks are called for on the intellectual environment that allowed for its emergence and success.

A WORLD OF MIRACLES: KRUSO'B RELIGION AND FOLK CHRISTIANITY

Yucatecan, Mexican and British contemporary observers generally depicted the Cult of the Speaking Cross as proof of the Indian belief in superstition and lack of civilization, and as a deliberate trick employed by kruso'b leaders to deceive their henchmen. It was, of course, standard practice in ideological warfare to question the legitimacy of the rebel cause and its leadership. The following quote from a Yucatecan newspaper is a typical specimen of this delegitimizing discourse:

Some of the Indians' captains, knowing the nullity to which they were reduced and that they had lost their influence among the troops, made use of a ridiculous expedient to dazzle it with the most puerile superstition. They pretended that a cross planted close to their entrenchments could speak.[16]

An officer who had participated in an army attack on Chan Santa Cruz in early 1852 described and interpreted what they found in the church:

A barrel was placed in an excavation behind the altar and served as a soundboard to produce a hollow and cavernous sound. All this was well hidden from the view of those in the nave of the church. The person in charge of proclaiming what Barrera wanted to be said to the crowd, ignorant of this swindle, went into the excavation and thus achieved that the Indians brought him corn, chickens, wax, pigs, money and all he desired as an offering because the crosses spoke endlessly. They also gave orders concerning the war, which were listened to with great attention and as precautions emanating from above.[17]

---

[16] Correspondencia del Siglo, *SDN*, September 17, 1851, 2. See also M. Micheltorena to MGM, Mérida, April 2, 1851, AHM, XI/481.3/3257; Ancona 1879/80, 4:314–316 and Rogers (1885:224) for a British example.
[17] Cámara Zavala 1928, part 6.

Kruso'b Politics and Religion

Whether kruso'b leaders were true believers, as Paul Sullivan and Don Dumond suggest, or not, is hard to decide given the limitations of existing sources.[18] At least some rebel leaders referred to themselves as "soldiers of our Blessed Cross and of the Three persons [the Trinity], whom we respect and venerate" in a form of open letter to the Yucatecans, promising quarter to anyone who gave themselves up peacefully, while threatening those who continued fighting with death.[19] Suffice it to say here that the cult could only win adherents if what leaders said and did appeared plausible to their audience and addressed their psychological or spiritual needs. This assumption gains additional persuasiveness if we examine the argument of several scholars, who depict the kruso'b cult as a unique invention containing several pre-Christian elements.[20] Both views – the cult as a more or less arbitrary invention of the leaders and the cult as a resurgence of pre-Christian beliefs and practices – tend to set it apart from official Catholicism and folk religiosity in the government-controlled area. There are nonetheless several similarities to the latter. Bricker has rightly stressed that kruso'b religion had much more in common with the beliefs and ritual practices of Maya speakers in other parts of the Yucatán peninsula than with those of the ancient Maya. She affirms that "virtually the same syncretism of Maya and Christian elements exists in all parts of the peninsula, including areas not under Cruzob control, which suggests that this pattern *predated* the Caste War."[21] One might add that this syncretism was by no means restricted to Indians but encompassed the lower classes in general. Belief in wonders was widespread and apparitions were an integral part of folk Catholicism in Mexico and beyond. Images of saints, Jesus, Mary or the cross were held in high esteem and attributed certain powers. As Rugeley suggests, "this was a time and place where many – not only Maya peasants – believed that statues of Jesus and the saints rose up at night and walked

---

[18] In a comment on an earlier version of my thoughts on kruso'b political organization, Paul Sullivan (personal communication, June 27, 2002) rightly emphasized the relevance of ideational and spiritual components: "That is to say, people really believe, and belief inspires them and constrains them, and it's my impression Maya leaders were themselves among the true believers. They didn't use religion. Religion used them. True god was the top caudillo, and the leaders just his clients." See also Dumond 1997:420.

[19] J.C. Poot, J.A. Cobá, A. Ek, C. Novelo, T. Moreno, A. Chablé, J. Aguilar, Tibolon, July 1, 1869, *EP*, July 27, 1869, 3–4.

[20] See, for example, Reed 1964:209–220; Zimmerman 1965:139, 147; Careaga Viliesid 1998:109–111.

[21] Bricker 1981:113, emphasis in the original.

166   *Part V: Violence and the Kruso'b*

the land."[22] The sainted cross in Corozal, Belize, was credited with having "brought a dead child to life and withstood the fire of a burning house," where it was previously located.[23] A contemporary observer complained that Indians in Yucatán worshipped "Saint Anthony [of Padua] and the Cross in an idolatrous way, because they pray to him not as a mediator to God but believe he himself is a divinity and the Cross another."[24] Charlotte Zimmerman observes in this respect:

The Christian symbol of crucifixion, the cross, becomes a cosmological hierophany, it possesses the power and sacredness of the god or gods; this sacredness dwells within it and hence it becomes a "santo," a holy being no longer an object, for it is a hierophany, and as a hierophany it is no longer itself.[25]

The association of certain images of saints and crosses with particular localities was common practice in Latin America. In the colonial period, villages were assigned a particular saint, a form of the Virgin Mary or the Holy Cross as spiritual guardians of the community's wellbeing. Villagers assumed a distinct relationship of reciprocity with their saints.[26] A description of the feast of the Holy Cross in Peto, a town in the government-controlled area, confirms that veneration of patron saints and crosses for their supernatural powers was a widespread phenomenon in Yucatán. Most streets contained small palm-thatched oratories close to a family dwelling. "During the year and waiting for the festive season, pilgrimages or processions now to one chapel and then to the other are constant. People go there to give votive offerings and to pray." The person who tended the cross kept in the chapel was called a "patron." "He's a sort of priest who always has some miracle at hand to relate." Paying a visit to this cross or that cross "to satisfy the piety of the simple people" was by no means the same thing, as some crosses "enjoy a certain reputation for miracles." A reputation that was far from stable, however, since "general opinion would sometimes give one cross more credit, while that of another was on the wane."[27] Yucatecan folklore also ascribed spiritual properties to trees located in the vicinity of cenotes.[28] Thus, the first

---

[22] Rugeley 2001a:112; see also pp. 115, 120; Farriss 1984:315–316, 514–515 n. 61–63.

[23] Ch. Leas: "Belize or British Honduras," 1863, TULAL, MIC 736, reel 2.

[24] García y García 1865:xxiv. See also Supersticion de los indios Yucatecos por el padre Juan Pablo Ancona, Mérida, 1865, CAIHDY, M, XLVIII. 1865/2; Méndez 1870:380–382.

[25] Zimmerman 1965:146.

[26] See, for example, Farriss 1984:320–333; Rugeley 2001a:113.

[27] Correspondencia, Peto, Costumbres populares, *RM*, May 11, 1873, 2.

[28] Norman 1843:136; Rugeley 2001a:134.

Kruso'b Politics and Religion

appearance of kruso'b crosses close to a well is not surprising. Stories about kruso'b crosses returning to their original location after abduction by the army or the mahogany tree that resisted felling have a strong resemblance to the "validating stories" reported for many Yucatecan towns as to why a particular saint chose "his" village.[29] Neither were talking idols a unique kruso'b invention but had historical precedents in Yucatán and beyond, both before and after the Spanish conquest.[30] Rumors of a "speaking cross" at Chan Santa Cruz circulated even before the Caste War broke out.[31] Messages from idols had to be received, typically in a trance, by people endowed with this particular gift and transmitted or interpreted so that ordinary believers could understand them. The so-called "Interpreter of the Cross" in the kruso'b cult was therefore able to build on pre-existing role models.[32] While Reed considers the designations of ritual positions among the kruso'b to be unique titles in a theocracy, at least some were employed for religious specialists in the rest of the peninsula. As we have seen, the office of patron was clearly not a kruso'b invention. According to contemporary observer García y García, "tatich" and "tata polin" were also designations for ritual specialists among Maya speakers all over Yucatán. According to him, they "have as prophets the *Tatich*, the *Tata Polin* and the first Indian who tells them to have his *zaztun* [a piece of crystal used as an instrument for oracles], whom they call *hmen* with absolute confidence in all that he reveals."[33] "Tatich" was also used to denote caciques in Yucatec Maya. The meaning of "tata polin" is less clear. Reed translates it as "Father of the Wooden Object." Dumond argues instead that it was the nickname of Apolinar Sánchez, who acted as "Interpreter of the Cross" from 1863 to 1864.[34] While the quote from García y García backs Reed's interpretation of the terms as titles, it questions his assumption of their uniqueness.

---

[29] See for the term and an outline of these stories, Rugeley 2001a:119.

[30] Villa Rojas 1945:21. They also played a key role in the War of St. Rose in Chamula (1867–1870), where a local girl had seen "three stones drop from the sky while she was tending her sheep." The stones were attributed the power of speech and became the most important symbols of a religious cult the Ladino government repressed by force (Bricker 1981:119).

[31] Reed 1964:214.

[32] See, for example, Roys 1972:79; Reed 1964:161, 214–215. For descriptions of the prophetic functionaries in kruso'b ritual, see Aldherre and Mendiolea 1869:75; Rogers 1885:224–225; Buhler 1975:10.

[33] García y García 1865:xxiv, emphasis in the original.

[34] See Reed 1964:214–215; Dumond 1997:258–261, 481 n. 52 and CORDEMEX:779 for the meaning of *tatich*.

168   *Part V: Violence and the Kruso'b*

That the veneration of idols was more than a purely spiritual affair and implied important economic transactions was not a particularity of the kruso'b either. Goods and money had to be raised all over the country as offerings or to buy candles, clothes for the saint or other paraphernalia. A santo could expect donations from believers and amass material property. During the colonial era, organization of the saint cult in towns and villages, and the administration of its wealth, had mostly been in the hands of lay brotherhoods (*cofradías*) and the local priest.[35] As a result of the expropriation of cofradía property by church and state since 1780, individual patrons became more important as custodians of certain saints in the nineteenth century. Possession of a santo endowed its owner with prestige and potentially with access to some wealth, since he (or she) could expect a contribution from the devotees who were allowed entry to the holy figure.[36] The cacique of Stilpech, a town in the northwest of Yucatán close to Izamal, for example, had a cross "accredited as very miraculous," which he called San Victoriano and for whom he constantly obtained "offerings from his subjects of money, wax, chickens, pigs and other animals."[37] Although holy images were bought, sold and bequeathed, they did not constitute private property in the strict sense of the word. They were "at once owned and not owned," as Rugeley puts it, since there were customary restrictions on their use. Images had to be lent, for example, for the benefit of the community.[38]

These established traditions of devotion to santos, and particularly their potential to accumulate funds for the common good, provided a solution to one of the most pressing problems Caste War rebel leaders had to solve. While kruso'b were deeply suspicious of contributions, a grievance they had put forward to justify their struggle, some centralized form of organization and accumulation of wealth to procure weaponry, ammunition and other essential goods was vital. Although money to buy guns, powder and lead was occasionally collected, the kruso'b rank and file abhorred regular tax payments.[39] Religious fees and donations were

---

[35] See, for example, Farriss 1984:264–270; Rugeley 2001a:143–150.

[36] Farriss 1984:362–363, 371–374, 377; Rugeley 2001a:112, 117–119, 129. For Corozal, Belize, it was reported that "the cross is claimed as the private property of the Padre and it is alleged that from all who come to worship before it, he receives a contribution" (Ch. Leas: "Belize or British Honduras," 1863, TULAL, MIC 736, reel 2).

[37] García y García 1865:xxxii.   [38] Rugeley 2001a:119.

[39] For the collection of funds for ammunition, see, for example, J.M. Cocom to P. Pech, Nohayin, February 4, 1850, AHM, XI/481.3/2914. When cult leaders tried to impose a high tax "for the crosses" in Chan Santa Cruz, most of the inhabitants simply left the town (La guerra de casta, *RP*, March 29, 1871, 3).

Kruso'b Politics and Religion 169

more likely to be accepted than dues levied for secular purposes. In one of the earliest known proclamations to his "beloved Christian people" [the kruso'b], Juan de la Cruz expressed his identification with the poor, distinguished between generals and commanders, on one hand, and religious leaders (the patron of the cross) on the other, and justified cult fees as the sole path to personal success. Only the patron could be fully trusted:

I reside under my abode of palm leaf, I am located just in the shade of the tree for the small and the great and those so named to see that my father [God] did not place me with the rich, neither did he place me with [rebel] generals, nor with commanders or nobles, who have money or claim to have it; but my father put me with the poor, because I am poor; because only my patron feels affection for me and loves me, because only for him who gives me a medio [half a real] will my father turn it into a spring and make profitable all endeavors he takes up in his heart, because with that [medio] I buy drinking water when I cross all over Yucatán walking around, because this medio my family gives me for that, all you humans [todos los nacidos] do not think that my patron retains what you bestow on me.[40]

In fact, adherents of the Cult of the Speaking Cross were obliged to contribute to ritual expenses and other issues deemed necessary by the leaders. The cult received donations and a share of the booty obtained from raids on Yucatecan towns.[41] Beyond legitimizing the pooling of funds, the cult fulfilled several other functions. It provided rebels with a common point of identification, strengthened their stamina to resist persecution by government forces, promised supernatural protection, and imbued their struggle with religious meaning. Thus, fighting the enemy and guarding ritual sanctuaries were not merely secular necessities but also religious duties. Venerated crosses were taken along as spiritual guardians and as the source of advice on important issues. Such was the case in negotiations with a British officer about the fate of Yucatecan prisoners after rebels had conquered Bacalar in 1858. According to the officer's testimony, the kruso'b "brought their Santa Cruz with them, which they consulted on all occasions of importance."[42] A report in

---

[40] Juan de la Cruz, Balam Na, December 11, 1850, in Traduccion de once manuscritos de lengua maya, April 2, 1851, AHM, XI/481.3/3257. See also slightly different versions in Villa Rojas (1945:163) and Bricker (1981:202–203).

[41] See, for example, P.A. Gonzalez to Gobernador, Yokdzonot. January 25, 1855. EO, February 16, 1855, 1–3, for Chan Santa Cruz and Itinerario de la marcha de las tropas sobre los indios bárbaros, D. Peniche, pueblo de Dolores, Isla Mujeres, August 19, 1872, RP, August 28, 1872, 1, for Muyil.

[42] W. Anderson to F. Seymour, Belize, February 15, 1858, GBFO in Rugeley 2001b:66; see also F. Seymour to C.H. Darling, Belize, March 13, 1858, TNA, CO, 123/96; Jones 1974:671–672.

1872 suggests that at the center of their bivouacs the rebels constructed elevated shelters "with a palm roof in a triangular shape, where they place the cross they usually carry with them on their raids."[43] Beyond veneration of the Speaking Cross, religious motives were also instrumental when it came to inciting kruso'b to conduct particular raids. According to Anastasio Durán, who had been captured during a kruso'b assault on Tunkas in 1861 and escaped a year later, news of a miracle spread among the rebels, namely, that the Virgin of Tunkas was crying. A piece of cotton had been soaked with her tears, "which they distribute as a relic." The tears were interpreted as a sign that the Virgin wanted to have "her sister from Izamal at her side;" the kruso'b offered to bring her soon so the two could be reunited. While the rebels failed to reach Izamal, they advanced well beyond Valladolid in 1862, raiding Dzitas and defeating an army detachment at the crossroads to Sahcabá.[44]

The evidence presented so far indicates that the Cult of the Speaking Cross was less peculiar than has frequently been assumed. Most of its elements, including religious offices such as the patron of the cross and belief in the capacity of crosses or saints to act and communicate, were well-known features of Yucatecan folk Catholicism. This helps to understand why and how the cult emerged, why it quickly found numerous devotees and why deserters, criminals and many others who simply wanted to escape from landlord or government control integrated easily into kruso'b society and religion. What Yucatecan and British commentators dismissed as deliberate fraud by rebel leaders was most probably a typical example of a cult based on divine possession of media in trance. While the cult offered opportunities to muster adherents under a common cause and leadership, its structure contained the potential for fragmentation, as will be seen in the next section.

A FOREST OF CROSSES

The Cult of the Speaking Cross and the rebel organization have frequently been depicted as a unitary movement in the nineteenth century with a single ritual center at Chan Santa Cruz.[45] The cult at Chan Santa Cruz

---

[43] Itinerario de la marcha de las tropas sobre los indios bárbaros, D. Peniche, pueblo de Dolores, Isla Mujeres, August 19, 1872, *RP*, August 26 and 28, 1872, 1–2.

[44] Noticias que emite el C. Anastasio Durán . . ., *LRP*, September 5, 1862, 3. For the kruso'b raid on Dzitas and the army rout, see the letters from L. Irigoyen to MGM, Mérida, August 30 and September 10, 1862, both in AHM, XI/481.4/8772.

[45] See, for example, Villa Rojas 1945:22–25; Reed 1964; Bricker 1981.

Kruso'b Politics and Religion

was indeed the most persistent, functioning as it did from 1850 until the 1890s. Don Dumond, on the other hand, has convincingly argued that the cult had an inherent tendency toward "real and profound fission."[46] Several essentially independent religious centers emerged in the kruso'b area, each drawing on separate constituencies. In the 1850s, a ritual hub existed in Mabén, forty kilometers northeast of Valladolid. It was relocated to Kantunilkin in 1858 due to frequent army attacks. When most of the local rebel groups made peace with the government in 1859, the northern cult declined.[47] Other ritual centers were active in Tulum from 1864 (or earlier) to about 1892, in San Antonio Muyil between 1872 and the 1890s and in Chunpom from 1897 or earlier to the present.[48] A church with several crosses was found in all of these places, as were barracks where men from surrounding villages lived during periodic guard service (*guardia*) to protect the ritual center and venerated idols.[49] The fact that "patron of the cross" was not a unique position but a title held by individuals in the ritual centers mentioned above indicates the absence of a clear and durable hierarchy of religious offices among them.[50]

Numerous crosses existed with varying degrees of spiritual power, the most important of which were housed in ritual centers. The results of Alfonso Villa Rojas's ethnographic research among Caste War rebel

[46] Dumond 1985:291; see also 1997:421–422.

[47] Dumond 1985:296–297. On the attacks see, for example, M.F. Peraza to General en Jefe, Valladolid, March 30, 1855, AGEY, PE, G, box 100. More than sixty rebels, including the head chief (José Luciano Chan) and the patron of the crosses (Nicolás Batún), were killed during an army attack in 1857 (M.F. Peraza to CGE, Valladolid, May 26, 1857, *UL*, June 2, 1857, 1–2).

[48] Dumond 1985:300–302; 1997:370–371, 376. Tulum and San Antonio Muyil were deserted by most of the inhabitants in the late 1890s, probably as a result of factional conflicts between cult centers. New religious hubs emerged in the twentieth century at Chancah Veracruz and Tixcacal Guardia. See Hinz 2013:32–33, 38–39.

[49] We have no detailed information on the composition of guard units with reference to the age or locality of origin of their members. The sources show, however, that such rotational guard service of varying strength and duration existed at least from the late 1850s in Bacalar and Chan Santa Cruz, and later in a few other places (e.g., Comisión del gobierno de Yucatán . . ., Mérida, June 13, 1864, *LNE*, June 24, 1864, 1–3; N. Remirez to Sub Inspector de las colonias militares, Tekax, February 27, 1879, Suplemento al Num. 16 de la *Revista de Mérida*, 1879, in AHAY, G, O, box 445, file 6). For Muyil in 1872, see Itinerario de la marcha de las tropas sobre los indios bárbaros, D. Peniche, pueblo de Dolores, Isla Mujeres, August 19, 1872, *RP*, August 26 and 28, 1872. Guard service is discussed in more detail by Sullivan (1997a, II:3).

[50] See J.M. Iturralde to Gobernador, Valladolid, March 23, 1888, *RP*, April 6, 1888, 3; La guerra de casta, *RP*, March 29, 1871, 2–3; Correspondencia recojida á los indios bárbaros en el pueblo de Tulum, *RP*, March 1 and 3, 1871; Miller 1889:26; Dumond 1985:296–297, 300–301 and 1997:317–319, 371.

FIGURE 15.1 Clothed cross in Yucatán. Photograph by Wolfgang Gabbert.

descendants in the 1930s can help to understand the situation in the nineteenth century. He described the kruso'b religious system as including a multiplicity of crosses. Patron crosses (also called saints) appeared as intermediaries between God and man, while domestic crosses were kept to protect the elementary family. Some domestic crosses gained prestige by virtue of their exceptional powers and became the patron of families belonging to a patrilineage. The lineage cross, which was ascribed the greatest power, became the patron cross of the village and was kept in the village church. Finally, a village cross could acquire such regional importance that homage was widely paid and guard service performed.[51] Unfortunately, we do not know whether patrilineages existed in the nineteenth century. Evidence suggests, however, that many traits described by Villa Rojas, such as the multiplicity of crosses venerated by families and larger groups, already existed at that time. Thirty-nine crosses covered with shawls stood, for example, on the main altar of the church in Muyil in 1872.[52] William Miller, Assistant Surveyor-General of British Honduras, who visited the rebel area in the late 1880s, found that each village had a church with an altar on which twelve or fifteen crosses were

[51] Villa Rojas 1945:97–98.
[52] Itinerario de la marcha de las tropas sobre los indios bárbaros, D. Peniche, pueblo de Dolores, Isla Mujeres, August 19, 1872, *RP*, August 26 and 28, 1872.

Kruso'b Politics and Religion 173

placed. He also mentioned a cross near Tulum "from which the Indians say the voice of God issues."[53] Family crosses existed on the ranch and in the house of kruso'b General Leandro Santos.[54] Since crosses differed in the degree rather than the kind of supernatural power, of which there may be conflicting evaluations, rivalry for prominence and a potential for fragmentation are to be expected. As will be shown in the next section, similar proclivities for competition and division were inherent in the kruso'b political system. As Don Dumond puts it, "it is no surprise to find that the periodic fragmentation of political rule was accompanied inevitably by fragmentation of the religious organization, or that regional splinters within the religious cult became the separatist centers of diverging polities."[55]

KRUSO'B MILITARY AND POLITICAL ORGANIZATION

Apart from the religious models discussed, rebel society was influenced by the secular organizational paradigm of Yucatán's militia. At the beginning of the conflict, rebel fighting units were formed along the lines of the National Guard. Companies consisted of men from single towns led by elected officers – corporals (*cabos*) and sergeants (*sargentos*) under an elected captain. The local batabo'b often filled this role among the insurgents.[56] Nominally, companies were grouped into larger units under majors (*comandantes*) or generals. In reality, however, each company operated independently with no firm structure of command.[57] Coordination at a more inclusive level was merely the result of the more or less stable attachment of individual companies to a small number of influential chiefs capable of attracting followers from larger areas. In the initial months of the war, Jacinto Pat emerged as the most prominent leader in the south, Cecilio Chi dominated the east and Florentino Chan led the rebel forces in the center.[58] As mentioned in Chapter 7, these overarching command structures collapsed after the death of Pat and Chi in 1849. Moreover, many of the early batab leaders had also died in battle, companies were heavily decimated and survivors joined other units according to the fortunes of the war.[59] Despite numerous challenges and

---

[53] Miller 1889:26. [54] Buhler 1975:9–10. [55] Dumond 1985:303.
[56] Cartas de capitancillos indígenas, December 1849, AHM, XI/481.3/2914; Jones 1974:665–666; Rugeley 1995:486. For militia organization, see Chapter 5.
[57] Reed 1964:122–123; Dumond 1977:106–107 and 1985:292–293.
[58] Ancona 1879/80, 4:260. [59] Reed 1964:122–123; Rugeley 1995:486.

174   *Part V: Violence and the Kruso'b*

changes, these quasi-military companies endured for several decades as the skeleton of the kruso'b military and of their social and political organization. This is clearly shown in Villa Rojas's ethnographic account:

> All males who were married or over sixteen years of age were obliged to belong to one of these companies, each of which was directed by a group of chiefs, ranging from *cabo* (corporal) to *comandante* (major or higher). On the death of one of these chiefs, the lower officers were promoted to the next rank, thus leaving the lowest position of cabo vacant. The cabo was then elected by all the members of his company in assembly. An individual worthy of the post was nominated by the chiefs and if confirmed by the assembly, he became cabo; if not, nominations were continued until one met with the approval of the whole company. No ceremonies or rites accompanied the promotions, nor were any insignia of rank worn. . . .
>
> Upon the death of the main commander he was succeeded by one of the comandantes. Since there was a comandante at the head of each company, the one possessing the most dominant personality or the greatest influence usually succeeded to office.[60]

Beyond purely military and political functions, according to Villa Rojas, the companies constituted the "principal organizing force for all communal activities," including social control, and carried out ceremonies and feasts.[61] His account is based on information obtained in the early 1930s. It came from older kruso'b, whose personal memories may have reached back to the final decades of the nineteenth century, well before the occupation of Chan Santa Cruz by government troops in 1901. Although we have no other equally detailed first-hand account for the nineteenth century at our disposal, the sources confirm that crucial aspects of the social and political system were already in place at that time. Kruso'b military service was probably compulsory in the nineteenth century and deserters were sometimes persecuted. In late December 1868, for example, Ysidoro Aké, commander of Ramonal at the Río Hondo, entered Corozal in an attempt to bring back to rebel territory a number of men "enrolled among the forces of the Santa Cruz Indians" who had left for Belize.[62] A few months later, rumors circulated in Belize that Bernardino Cen was to cross the Río Hondo and bring back the Indians who had left rebel territory to avoid military service.[63] Their duty evidently referred to guard service only and to defensive actions in the case of army attacks. While many

---

[60] Villa Rojas 1945:24, emphasis in the original.   [61] Villa Rojas 1945:92.

[62] Address to Legislative Assembly by Lieutenant Governor, January 30, 1868, R. 101, ABH:298–299. Gann (1918:36) confirms that military service was compulsory among the kruso'b in the early twentieth century and adds that "many avoid such service by payment to the chief of a certain sum in money or its equivalent."

[63] Lieutenant Governor to Governor, Jamaica, November 13, 1869, R. 98, ABH:316.

Kruso'b Politics and Religion

peasants who lived independent of the government in the buffer zone were probably keen to stay clear of the conflict and any form of superior control, at least some of them settled fairly close to rebel strongholds, were pressured into accepting kruso'b authority and taking part in guard service at cult centers. This happened to the inhabitants of San Antonio, for example, who lived peacefully, "hidden and withdrawn from obedience to the government" until they were detected by kruso'b and obliged to perform guard service at Muyil.[64] As to raids on Yucatecan towns, however, men had the choice of participating or staying at home. When the principal chiefs intended to conduct a raid "they summon the men, telling them that whatever loot they can get is theirs. With this inducement they plunder the defenseless towns of the South and the East."[65] It seems that kruso'b rank and file had a say in whether or not to go on raids. Most rebels refused to take part in an assault on Valladolid in 1871, for example, having experienced several defeats in the past.[66] Rebel soldiers could also influence the course of events on the way. During an expedition in December of the same year, for instance, participants asked their commanders: "Why do you bring us to an old village that has nothing?" It would appear that the answer was not convincing, since the squad changed the course of the raid and attacked three towns not originally targeted. Commanders could not force soldiers to obey and were ignored when they ordered a withdrawal from the town of Xaya, their men preferring to rest and spend the night in the settlement.[67]

Relative continuity seems to have reigned in the military hierarchy. A report reflecting the situation in the 1870s describes a system of ranks divided into commanders, captains, lieutenants, sergeants and corporals, similar to what Villa Rojas found decades later. Each captain commanded thirty soldiers, two lieutenants, two sergeants and four corporals. A commander headed three or four companies "he had formed himself." The command was hereditary. Should the commander concerned be at fault, he was reduced to the rank of soldier. The highest position, that of "governor," was appointed by "direct election" and, as the source continues, "his appointment has no limits and he can only be dismissed in the case of abuse."[68] As will become clear in a moment, however, this system

---

[64] N. Urcelay to General en Jefe, pueblo de Dolores, Isla Mujeres, August 19, 1872, *RP*, August 26, 1872, 1.

[65] Chan Santa Cruz, *RM*, December 19, 1873, 2.

[66] Manuel Cicerol, Circular, Mérida, March 6, 1871, *RP*, March 6, 1871, 1.

[67] J.C. Poot to I. Chablé, Gran pueblo Santa Cruz, December 28, 1870, *RM*, March 1, 1871, 3.

[68] Chan Santa Cruz Report, Mérida, June 2, 1882, TULAL, M-26, box 2, folder 14.

176 *Part V: Violence and the Kruso'b*

of government led to more or less permanent power struggles for leadership, the accumulation of wealth in the name of the cross and privileged access to Belizian trading partners and captive labor rather than to a stable political hierarchy. Time and again these rivalries escalated into bloodshed. Mutual distrust between the rank and file and their superiors, and among the leaders themselves, seems to have been the order of the day.[69] As Miller remarked on Aniceto Dzul ("Don Anis"), who killed Crescencio Poot and twenty other chiefs in 1884 or 1885: "Don Anis now reigns in his stead and will continue to do so until some other chief contrives to get a party sufficiently strong to kill him in his turn."[70] Thomas Gann, a British archaeologist who visited the area in the 1910s and 1920s, described the situation as follows:

On the death of a head chief of the Santa Cruz Indians the oldest of the sub-chiefs is supposed to succeed him; as a matter of fact, there are always rival claimants for the chieftainship, and the sub-chief with the strongest personality or greatest popularity amongst the soldiers usually succeeds in grasping the office. There are nearly always rival factions endeavouring to oust the chief in power, and the latter rarely dies in bed.[71]

A look at Table 15.1 makes it clear that these dramatic statements were not mere sensationalism. Whereas numerous kruso'b chiefs died in battle, the majority fell victim to internal strife. Periods of relative stability alternated with times of upheaval and intense power struggles. This pattern strongly suggests that internal violence was not an aberration but an inherent feature of kruso'b politics in the nineteenth century. It was one of several resources potential chiefs could tap to gain and retain leadership positions.

Instead of assuming a consolidated governmental structure, I would therefore argue that kruso'b political organization might be better understood as a form of "caudillo politics" or caudillaje. This is an analytical framework proposed by Eric Wolf and Edward Hansen. They define caudillo politics as the "emergence of armed patron–client sets" based on "personal ties of dominance" and a "common desire to obtain wealth by force of arms." An institutionalized means of succession to office is lacking and violence a common feature of political competition. Finally, leaders repeatedly fail "to guarantee their tenures as chieftains."[72] Caudillo systems are particularly prone to leadership rivalry since there

---

[69] Aldherre and Mendiolea 1869:76. [70] Miller 1889:28.
[71] Gann 1924:49. See also Adrian 1924:237; Villa Rojas 1945:24.
[72] Wolf and Hansen 1967:169. See also Riekenberg 1998:201.

TABLE 15.1 *Causes of death of major rebel leaders*

Name	date	cause of death	sources/additional information
Marcelo Pat	26/11/1848	killed in battle	Baqueiro 1990, 3:92
Cecilio Chi	June 1849	killed by his secretary (Atanasio Flores)	GCY:79; Ancona 1978, 4:260–261
Jacinto Pat	September 1849	killed by rivals (Venancio Pec, Florentino Chan, Crescencio Poot)	M. Micheltorena to MGM, August 1, 1850, AHM, XI/481.3/2914; Declaracion de Pablo Encalada, Campeche, August 12, 1867, *EP*, September 24, 1867, 1; GCY:79 n. 17
Manuel Nahuat	23/3/1851	killed in battle	M. Micheltorena to Gobernador, Mérida, April 2, 1851, *SDN*, April 7, 1851, 1; Baqueiro, 1990, 4:122; Reed 2001:372 (3/5/1851)
Domingo Cahum	early June 1851	killed in battle	R. Díaz de la Vega to MGM, Mérida, 12/6/1851, AHM, XI/481.3/3256
Miguel Huchim	September 1851	killed in battle	R. Díaz de la Vega to MGM, September 17, 1851, AHM, XI/481.3/3259
Venancio Pec, Juan Bautista Yam	18/6/1852	killed in battle	R. Díaz de la Vega to MGM, Peto, June 26, 1852, AHM, XI/481.3/3300
Cosme Damian Pech	26/12/1852	killed in battle	Baqueiro 1990, 4:178
José María Barrera	31/12/1852	sickness	Baqueiro, 1990, 4:178, 215; [1887] 1989:25
	April 1853	killed by rivals (Isac Pat, Zacarias May)	R. Díaz de la Vega to MGM, Mérida, May 17, 1853, AHM, XI/481.3/3505
Paulino Pech	May 1853	killed in battle	Dumond 1997:192
Juan Chable, Pedro Dzul	August? 1856	killed by rival? (Claudio Novelo)	M.F. Peraza to CGE, Valladolid, October 17, 1856, *GS*, October 22, 1856, 1–2
José Dolores Tec	mid-1862	executed for putsch against Puc and Zapata	P. Rosado Lavalle to Comandante en Jefe, Valladolid, July 23, 1863, *LNE*, July 27, 1863, 2

(*continued*)

TABLE 15.1 (*continued*)

Name	date	cause of death	sources/additional information
Agustín Barrera	December 1863	killed by rivals (Venancio Puc?)	Reed 1964:287
Venancio Puc	late August or early September 1863	killed by rivals (Ti Lisch)	Ch. Leas to W.H. Seward, Belize, September 5, 1863, TULAL, Mic 736, reel 2
Venancio Puc, Apolinario Sánchez	23/12/1863	killed by rivals	Dumond 1997:254–255; Reed 2001:370, 372 (Dionisio Zapata, Leandro Santos); F.A. Canton to Prefecto, Valladolid, February 12, 1864, *LNE*, February 15, 1864, 1 (Dionisio Zapata, Crescencio Poot)
Leandro Santos	early 1864	killed by rivals	F.A. Canton to Prefecto, Valladolid, February 12, 1864, *LNE*, February 15, 1864, 1 (Dionisio Zapata, Crescencio Poot); Dumond 1997:256 (Dionisio Zapata or Crescencio Poot, Bonifacio Novelo, Bernardino Cen)
Dionisio Zapata	10/3/1864	killed by rivals (followers of Venancio Puc, indios from Chancaj or Derepente)	E. Burke to secretario colonial, Corosal, April 4, 1864, *LNE*, April 25, 1864, 3; A. Sandoval to General en Jefe, Peto, June 12, 1864, *LNE*, June 17, 1864, 1; Comisión del gobierno de Yucatán . . ., Mérida, June 13, 1864, *LNE*, June 24, 1864, 1–3
Bernardo Ueh	February 1864	killed in battle	F.A. Canton to Prefecto, Valladolid, February 12, 1864, *LNE*, February 15, 1864, 1
Bonifacio Novelo	1868	natural death	Reed 2001:267
Pedro Dzul	1871	killed in battle	Chan Santa Cruz Report, Mérida, June 2, 1882, TULAL, M-26, box 2, folder 14
Claudio Novelo	March 1873 or before	unclear	C. Moreno Navarrete to Gobernador, Valladolid, March 4, 1873, AGEY, PE, M, box 302, file 41
Alvino Aké	late 1873	killed by rival leaders	R.A. Perez to Gobernador, Peto, December 11, 1874, *RP*, December 16, 1874, 2

Bonifacio and Claudio Novelo	July 1874	death confirmed	F. Díaz to Gobernador, Valladolid, July 29, 1874, AGEY, PE, CLM, box 311, file 44
Bernardino Cen, Juan de la Cruz Pat	13/10/1875	killed in battle	B.M. Montilla to Gobernador, Puntachén, October 15, 1875, *RP*, October 20, 1875, 1
Crescencio Poot	August 1885	killed by rival (Aniceto Dzul)	Informacion practicada con Saturnino Fernandez . . ., September 1886, AGEY, PE, M, box 241; Miller 1889:28; Baqueiro [1887] 1989:27
Juan Bautista Chuc	before October 23, 1884	killed by rivals	Secetaria de Guerra y Marina to Gobernador, México, November 17, 1884, AGEY, PE, ODG, box 230
	22/8/1885	killed by rival leaders	Noticias verídicas . . ., P. Roca, Hopelchén, January 19, 1886, AGEC, AH, G, AM, box 14
Luciano Canul (patron), Luciano Pech (gobernador), Generales Aguilar and Sixto Pa (all in Tulum)	mid-1887	killed by rival leader (Aniceto Dzul)	Los indios de Chan Santa Cruz, *RM*, June 30, 1887, 3; J.M. Iturralde to Gobernador, Valladolid, March 23, 1888, *RP*, April 6, 1888, 3
Aniceto Dzul,	January 1890	sickness	Dumond 1997:372 [source: *RM*, February 20 and August 12, 1890]
	1888	killed by rival leaders	Villalobos González 2006:259 [source: *RM*, August 12, 1888; *SDN*, September 30, 1894]
	unclear	killed by Román Pec	Los sublevados de Chan Santa Cruz, *EE*, March 9, 1897, 3, in Wilhelm 1997:80
Crescencio Puc	October? 1894	killed by rival leaders	S. di Pietro to C. Carrillo y Ancona, Belize, October 30, 1894, AHAY, G, O, box 438, file 2; Dumond 1997:372
Román Pec	September 1896	sickness	Dumond 1997:380 [source: *RM*, August 12, 1897, 2]; Reed 2001:371

(continued)

TABLE 15.1 (*continued*)

Name	date	cause of death	sources/additional information
	September 5, 1896	sickness	Indios sublevados de Chan Santa Cruz en Mérida, *EE*, August 22, 1897, 1, in Wilhelm 1997:85
	1897?	killed by Felipe Aké	Los sublevados de Chan Santa Cruz, *EE*, March 9, 1897, 3, in Wilhelm 1997:80–81.
José María Canul, José María Aké	early 1897	killed by rival leader (Felipe Yama)	Villalobos González 2006:265
José María Aké, Hilario Cab, José María Canul	early 1897	killed by rival leaders (León Pat by direction of Felipe Yama)	Dumond 1997:380–382
José María Aguilar	late April 1897	killed by rival leaders	Dumond 1997:381
Felipe Yama	April 1901	killed by rival leaders (León Pat, Teres Cob, Prudencio May)	Dumond 1997:395 [source *RM*, April 13 and 19, 1901]; Reed 2001:371
Leon Pat	Feb 1903	killed in combat	Dumond 1997:398

Kruso'b Politics and Religion   181

are "always more men qualified to become *caudillos,* or aspiring to demonstrate their capabilities as potential chieftains, than there are *caudillos.*"[73] Violence against both enemies and competitors for leadership was thus indispensable to achieving their position and maintaining it. As Wolf and Hansen pointed out:

> The claimants to victory must be prepared to kill their rivals and to demonstrate this willingness publicly. For the loser there is no middle ground; he must submit to the winner, or be killed. ... Leadership can be achieved only through violence; resources claimed only through violence.[74]

Caudillo politics can be described as a form of charismatic rule based on the leader's personal qualities rather than on tradition or legal rules. The polity was pulled together by his capacity to provide for essential goods such as wealth and security and by his personality and performance. This urged the caudillo to continually seek new sources of wealth for distribution among his adherents or tap into self-replenishing resources.[75] However, the caudillaje was "a true political system" as Wolf and Hansen perceptively argued. While the use of force against enemies and group members was a "predictable aspect of the system" and internal violence permanently lurked beneath the surface, stability alternated with periods of upheaval.

The particular importance of internal and external violence in kruso'b politics arose to a certain extent from a shift in the character of the competitors for dominance. As already mentioned, many of the first rebel chiefs were batabo'b, that is, men who could count on "traditional legitimacy," to adopt a term from Max Weber, and some wealth to attract adherents and provide supplies and arms. Hence, they appeared to be "natural leaders," qualified by high birth and even before the Caste War were in possession of more or less extended networks of dependents, clients, political relations and business connections. Jacinto Pat, for example, was a personal acquaintance of Miguel Barbachano and an educated man. He owned sizable landed property and had "a fortune of between fifteen and twenty thousand pesos."[76] The next generation of leaders, in contrast, consisted of "men of obscure origins" who succeeded with

---

[73] Wolf and Hansen 1967:176, emphasis in the original.
[74] Wolf and Hansen 1967:174, 177; see also Riekenberg 1998:210–211.
[75] Wolf and Hansen 1967:175.
[76] M. Micheltorena to MGM, August 1, 1850, AHM, XI/481.3/2914; Baqueiro 1990, 2:140; Bricker 1981:98. Pat, Chi and Chan were all batabo'b (Ancona 1879/80, 4:17; Rugeley 1995:486).

Part V: Violence and the Kruso'b

"luck, audacity, military skill, and sheer personal charisma," as Rugeley has aptly characterized them.[77] Some tried to back their claim to leadership by alleging a special relationship to supernatural forces, as has already been shown.[78] At first, successful pillaging was the only option for them when it came to acquiring wealth to secure their followers' loyalty. Since raids were a risky affair, however, and success far from guaranteed, kruso'b leaders attempted to back their position by gaining a more solid economic footing. They made efforts to monopolize trade, notably the liquor trade, and established private commercial farms, planting sugar cane, distilling rum and raising cattle on their own behalf.[79] Rebel leaders also displayed personality traits typical for caudillos, such as masculinity and the readiness to use violence.[80] This is aptly illustrated by the following description of Bernardino Cen, a rebel chief in the 1860s and 1870s. While the statement is colored by the Yucatecan elite perspective on rebel leaders, its tenor is confirmed by additional sources:

Although he is of advanced age, his strength of character, his eminent services and sanguinary instincts make him dreaded, not only among his followers but even by [the renowned chief Crescencio] Poot himself, who is also respected and feared as

---

[77] Rugeley 1995:486. José María Barrera, for example, played little role in the organization of the rebel forces before 1850. His name does not appear in the correspondence of the time (Jones 1974:669). Before the war, Bonifacio Novelo was a "peddler, agitator, and general riffraff" (Rugeley 1995:492–493 n. 34).

[78] This was common among caudillos of lower-class background in Latin America (Riekenberg 1998:204–205).

[79] Crescencio Poot, for example, maintained a sugar farm in San Isidro and one or two others elsewhere (N. Novelo to Gobernador, Peto, February 26, 1879, RP, March 3, 1879, 2–3). For farming activities, see L. Espinosa to Gobernador, Tekax, August 24, 1862, EN, August 27, 1862, 1–2; La guerra de casta, RP, March 29, 1871, 2–3; for the distillation and sale of rum, see S. di Pietro to C. Carrillo y Ancona, Belize, October 30, 1894, AHAY, G, O, box 438, file 2; Comisión del gobierno de Yucatán ..., Mérida, June 13, 1864, LNE, June 24, 1864, 3. Even early rebel leaders like Jacinto Pat produced sugar and liquor (Rugeley 1997:488). For a detailed discussion of the evidence on kruso'b leaders' farms, see Sullivan (1997a, I:9 n. 3); Villalobos González (2006:239 table 5). Villalobos González suggests that cattle and objects of great value, such as jewelry, were controlled by the chiefs and reserved for exchange with the British. Access to prisoners was also the prerogative of generals and commanders (Villalobos González 2006:110, 233–236). However, very little information exists on property rights, production relations or the distribution of goods among the rebels. While it is clear that participants on their return from a raiding expedition had to present the booty, part of which was taken as payment for ammunition (Chan Santa Cruz Report, Mérida, June 2, 1882, TULAL, M-26, box 2, folder 14), we do not know how distribution took place in reality. The particular bases according to which access to objects of value, prisoners, cattle or private farms was granted are also unknown.

[80] Wolf and Hansen 1967:173–174.

Kruso'b Politics and Religion

a leader of major rank. In his bacchanals Cen even takes the liberty of killing anyone who gets in his way.[81]

The excessive consumption of alcohol has frequently been interpreted as a pathological trait and Yucatecan sources in particular depict rebel leaders as bloodthirsty drunkards.[82] Heavy drinking, however, may have been a key component of the social assertion of masculinity in a male-dominated context such as nineteenth-century Mexico in general and rebel communities in particular.[83]

The organization of successful raids on Yucatecan territory was a key secular function of the leadership, with armament control as a vital means of attracting followers. According to a report by John Carmichael, a British merchant from Belize involved in the gunpowder trade, the kruso'b received no pay for guard service performance or participation in raiding expeditions. They had to provide their own rations, "which consist of a few hard, dry corn-cakes and red pepper" but were allowed to keep the spoils. At the same time, they were expected to make "an offering of some portion to the Church" on their return, as mentioned earlier. Carmichael suggests that leaders provided "their rifles, accouterments, and ammunition."[84] Dumond argues that the leaders controlled the ownership of firearms and that this factor worked against fragmentation of the movement.[85] Carmichael's report from the 1860s could support this assumption. Another source from that time, however, indicates that all kruso'b were armed, "each has his rifle stored at home, in the town or in the woods." In the case of alarm they were summoned by signal rockets or bombs. Once these exploded, armed men from neighboring hamlets flocked together.[86] This statement is confirmed by a report from the 1870s asserting that each man went on raids "armed and well provisioned at his own expense," receiving "from the common fund only the ammunition that they consider necessary for each one, taking as well some boxes of reserve ammunition."[87] The contradiction between the sources is

---

[81] La guerra de casta, *RP*, March 29, 1871, p. 2; see also A. Espinosa to Governor, Valladolid, February 28, 1871, *RP*, March 1, 1871, 1.

[82] See, for example, Comisión del gobierno de Yucatán ..., Mérida, June 13, 1864, *LNE*, June 24, 1864, 2; Rogers 1885:225.

[83] Wolf and Hansen made this point for caudillo politics in general (1967:174).

[84] J. Carmichael to Longdon, Corozal, November 15, 1867, Archives of Belize, Record 96, in Rugeley 2001b:85–86.

[85] Dumond 1997:418. Unfortunately, he fails to give a source to back up his claim.

[86] Comisión del gobierno de Yucatán ..., Mérida, June 13, 1864, *LNE*, June 24, 1864, 2.

[87] Anonymous 1878:92.

184 *Part V: Violence and the Kruso'b*

possibly apparent rather than real. It seems plausible that male kruso'b kept their own guns for both raiding and hunting, captured in Yucatán or bought, and that a certain number of more modern rifles were acquired from the central fund of the cross and controlled by kruso'b leaders.

POLITICS AND RELIGION

Wolf and Hansen (1967) did not discuss the role of religion in their ground-breaking article on caudillo political systems. Nevertheless, the significance of this issue in kruso'b politics and society is obvious. There seems to have been no clear distinction between military, political and religious leadership roles. The alleged cult founder, José María Barrera, for example, was not only a military chief but also fulfilled religious duties such as baptizing children.[88] Other leaders likewise combined secular and religious functions. The relationship between religious and secular power was not stable[89], nor were ordinances of the Speaking Cross necessarily observed. While José María Barrera attracted numerous followers by founding the cult, he did not possess unchallenged political authority among the rebels. An early sermon of the Speaking Cross that has survived in written form laments the disobedience of many military leaders and can be interpreted as an indication of factional conflict: "[T]here are very few generals that come because none of the generals believe in any of my ordinances and the generals say that there is no truth whatever in my orders."[90] In fact, rebels under the command of Florentino Chan neither respected nor complied with the orders of the cross to attack Tihosuco a few months later.[91] Barrera was apparently not the only rebel leader who endeavored to bolster his position with supernatural support in late 1850. According to a Yucatecan source, Bonifacio Novelo allegedly made the "barbarians" believe that "an image of the Blessed Virgin had appeared to him announcing rebel victory." The

---

[88] See, for example, J.T. Kau to J.M. Barrera, Chan Santa Cruz, March 22, 1851, letter 11 in Traduccion de once manuscritos de lengua maya, April 2, 1851, AHM, XI/481.3/3257.

[89] This point was emphasized by Jones (1974) and Dumond (1977, notably p. 126).

[90] Juan de la Cruz, X-Balam Nah, Xocen, Xcenil, Xocen, December 11, 1850, in Villa Rojas 1945:162. See also a Maya version in Proclama de Juan de la Cruz, Balamna, October 15, 1850, CAIHDY, M, XLII.1850–1866/12. While Jones already made this point, he otherwise accredits Barrera with "strict control over the military hierarchy" (1974:676; see also pp. 668–669).

[91] B. Novelo to Sr. Tres Personas, Xcopoil, February 24, 1851, letter 2 in Traduccion de once manuscritos de lengua maya, April 2, 1851, AHM, XI/481.3/3257.

Kruso'b Politics and Religion

image was then conducted in a procession to various rebel camps.[92] It is not clear whether Barrera agreed to this or Novelo attempted to found his own cult. In any case, neither a clash between the two nor the spread of a rival cult led by Novelo are reported in the sources.

Barrera died in December 1852 or spring 1853 and we have only scant and partly conflicting information on rebel politics in the years that followed. The sources employ a variety of terms to refer to rebel chiefs of some importance and no clear-cut stable hierarchy of offices can be discerned. Various leaders are addressed as first or head chief, for example, and the same individual may be referred to with different ranks during a certain period. There seems to have been no centralized decision-making and at certain times major rebel factions acted more or less independently.[93] The existence of a division of labor among the leaders and the relative significance of particular rebel chiefs is difficult to trace in the sources. It is certain, however, that not all major secular leaders also discharged religious tasks. One report suggests, for example, that Zacarías May was the "first chief" after Barrera's death and held this position up to 1856 at least.[94] He is not reported to have administered the cult. Another source, in contrast, designates Juan Chablé as "head chief" (*caudillo principal*) in 1854 and refers to Bonifacio Pué (probably Venancio Puc) as "patron of the crosses."[95] What seems clear is that in 1857 or earlier, Venancio Puc became the most influential religious and probably secular leader, as he participated in military expeditions. He appears in the sources as "patron" in 1857, "tatich" and "generalissimo"

---

[92] J.E. Rosado to J. Canuto Vela, Valladolid, January 5, 1851, CAIHDY, M, XLIV.1850–1859/19.

[93] R. Díaz de la Vega to MGM, Mérida, May 17, 1853, AHM, XI/481.3/3505.

[94] Captivity narrative of José Maria Echeverría, Izamal, November 8, 1856, AGEY, PE, G, box 65, in Rugeley 2001b:63.

[95] P.A. Gonzalez to Gobernador, Yokdzonot. December 12, 1854, *EO*, January 2, 1855, 1–2. "Pué" is probably a misspelling of the last name Puc and the source possibly errs on the first name. As the names Bonifacio Pué or Bonifacio Puc do not appear to my knowledge in any other source of the period, it may in fact refer to Venancio Puc. A report from 1858, mentions him at least as "patron or headman, also the padre, [who] had charge of the Santa Cruz," refers to [Zacarías?] May as "commander" and to Dionisio Zapata and Leandro Santos as "fighting chiefs" (W. Anderson to F. Seymour, Belize, February 15, 1858, GBFO, in Rugeley 2001b:67; Rogers 1885:226). Claudio Novelo is entitled "main leader" (*jefe principal*), Juan Chablé "governor" (*gobernador*) and Pedro Dzul "general commander of the rebels" (*comandante general de los sublevados*) in 1856 (M.F. Peraza to CGE, Valladolid, October 17, 1856, *GS*, October 22, 1856, 1–2), all of which demonstrates the diversity of designations for the same leader in contemporaneous sources and through time.

186   *Part V: Violence and the Kruso'b*

in 1858, "general" and "patron" in 1861, and "patron of the cross," "interpreter of the divine will" and "principal caudillo" in 1863.[96] As Reed puts it, Puc "had taken the role of Patron, and turned it into a position of power far beyond that held by the generals, or the village chiefs before the war, based on his control of the Cross."[97] Reed may have slightly overstated Puc's position. One Yucatecan, who had been a rebel captive at Chan Santa Cruz for some time, declared that there were ten or twelve commanders "of the same rank" [*de una misma categoría*] and that orders had to be "authorized by all."[98] Serious issues were resolved at meetings of the chiefs. This assembly decided, for example, on the fate of the prisoners taken during the assault on Bacalar in 1858. In the same year, the assignment of tasks among the generals for an attack on Valladolid was arranged at a meeting of officers and soldiers. In addition, major decisions, such as the release of prisoners, had to be legitimized in general assemblies as rulings of the cross.[99] Thus, Puc may be better conceived as a caudillo who backed his claim to political supremacy with religious authority rather than as an autocrat. It appears that not even Puc was above the orders of the cross, as the following statement of the US commercial agent in Belize indicates:

Old Pook [Puc] pretends to govern his orders by the dictates of a Sainted Cross which is located in a church at Santa Cruz and which is represented to have the power of speech, or rather Pooks followers allege that God converses with the Old chief through the Cross – Hence all questions are submitted to the Cross for adjudication, and whatever answer it makes is executed. – If the Cross cries for blood and Old Pook has a few hundred prisoners, they [word illegible] satisfy the demand and, if General Pook has done wrong, the Cross orders him twenty lashes, which he himself directs to be administered.[100]

---

[96] W. Anderson to F. Seymour, Belize February 15, 1858, GBFO in Rugeley 2001b:67; Rogers 1885:223; F.A. Canton to Prefecto del Departamento, Valladolid, February 12, 1864, and J.L. Montalvo to Prefecto Político, Peto, February 12, 1864, both in *LNE*, February 15, 1864, 1, 4; Comisión del gobierno de Yucatán . . ., Mérida, June 13, 1864, *LNE*, June 24, 1864, 1–3; Buhler 1975:11; Jones 1974:673; Dumond 1985:297 and 1997:221, 252, 259.

[97] Reed 1997b:519.

[98] Noticias que emite el C. Anastasio Durán . . ., *LRP*, September 5, 1862, 1–3.

[99] Buhler 1975:7–8, 11, 13–14; W. Anderson to F. Seymour, Belize, February 15, 1858, GBFO, in Rugeley 2001b:66. This form of decision-making is also reported for the early 1870s (J.M. Muñoz to Secretario de Estado, México, June 2, 1882, TULAL, MIC 736, reel 5).

[100] Ch. Leas: "Belize or British Honduras," 1863, TULAL, MIC 736, reel 2.

Kruso'b Politics and Religion   187

There is no way for us to know if Puc was a true believer who received orders from the cross in dreams or in a trance or if his submission to its decisions was a political maneuver to convince the audience of the cult's veracity and his own deep devotion. Beyond this, ostentatiously acknowledging the rulings of the cross, albeit painful to himself, allowed Puc to deflect from his responsibility in the case of critical or unpopular decisions. Be that as it may, Puc's predominance ended abruptly in late 1863, when he was killed in a coup by Generals Santos and Zapata.[101] Following another coup only four months later, Bonifacio Novelo, Crescencio Poot and Bernardino Cen are mentioned in the sources as the new principal leaders.[102] Again, this saw a division between military and religious roles. Novelo, who was about sixty years of age at the time, seems to have been weary of the troubles of warfare and confined his activities to acting as "head of the Church" and administering "civil justice" in Chan Santa Cruz. Crescencio Poot and Bernardino Cen assumed responsibility for military affairs. Poot became the supreme leader around 1868, probably as a result of Bonifacio Novelo's death in that year.[103] In his correspondence, he referred to himself with the secular titles of governor and commander-in-chief.[104] Not unlike several of his predecessors, however, he attempted to tap supernatural sources of legitimacy to bolster his claim to power. A source reflecting the situation in the

---

[101] See the details in Chapter 16.

[102] J.E. Tejero to Prefecto, Peto, March 26, 1864, AGEY, PE, M, box 225, file 91; E. Burke to secretario colonial, Corosal, April 4, 1864, *LNE*, April 25, 1864, 3; Comisión del gobierno de Yucatán ..., Mérida, June 13, 1864, *LNE*, June 24, 1864, 1–3; J. Carmichael to Longdon, Corozal, November 15, 1867, Archives of Belize, Record 96, in Rugeley 2001b:85; Jones 1974:676–677. An anonymous report presents a slightly different picture, however, claiming that Novelo was the head chief of the rebels and "had his government relatively well organized, and the obedience and submission that they [the rebels] showed him was absolute. His influence reached, without exception, from one end to the other of the territory they occupied, passively and blindly obeying his orders" (Anonymous 1878:88).

[103] J. Carmichael to Longdon, Corozal, November 15, 1867, Archives of Belize, Record 96, in Rugeley 2001b:84–85. Novelo is mentioned as having assumed the position of "interpreter of the cross" in late 1863, after his predecessor José Ná had been killed along with Venancio Puc and the priest Tata Polin during the coup carried out by Zapata and Santos (J.L. Montalvo to Prefecto Político, Peto, February 12, 1864, *LNE*, February 15, 1864, 4; Supersticion de los indios Yucatecos por el padre Juan Pablo Ancona, Mérida, 1865, CAIHDY, M, XLVIII. 1865/2). According to Reed (2001:267), Bonifacio Novelo died of natural causes in 1868. See also F. Díaz to Gobernador, Valladolid, July 29, 1874, AGEY, PE, CLM, box 311, file 44.

[104] J.C. Poot, J.A. Cobá, A. Ek, C. Novelo, T. Moreno, A. Chablé, J. Aguilar, Tibolon, July 1, 1869, *EP*, July 27, 1869, 3–4.

188   *Part V: Violence and the Kruso'b*

early 1870s ascribes not only the positions of governor and first general to him but adds that it was he who communicated directly with the cross in Chan Santa Cruz.[105]

Chan Santa Cruz nonetheless lost some of its importance in the 1870s for a number of reasons. Most inhabitants left the town in disgust at the "high tax" imposed by the cross in 1871.[106] Only "a small number of families and their more outstanding military *caudillos*" remained, recognizing Crescencio Poot as the "main chief."[107] Bonifacio Novelo's son, Claudio, also an important leader, died before March 1873 under nebulous circumstances and Bernardino Cen left after a quarrel with Poot (as we shall discuss).[108]

Parallel to the political turmoil of coups and counter-coups in Chan Santa Cruz in the mid-1860s and the gradual decline of that place as the main religious, political and commercial center in the years that followed, Tulum rose to hitherto unknown prominence.[109] Tulum was the center of a series of emerging settlements "all well combined with each other and with a particular organization of their customs and ends." The place owed its relevance to its proximity to a place on the coast where rebels supplied themselves with arms, powder and other valuable goods from ships arriving from Belize and to the fame of local idols.[110] Tulum is first mentioned as a cult center in a report stating that officials from Chan Santa Cruz consulted an oracle at "Santa Cruz Xtulmul" in June 1864.[111] The local cult was headed by an Indian woman, "the mother of the cross."[112] Her name was María Uicab, as letters from 1867 to 1870 addressing her husband as "patron" and herself as "patroness" indicate.[113] According

---

[105] Chan Santa Cruz Report, Mérida, June 2, 1882, TULAL, M-26, box 2, folder 14. The author, José María Muñoz, had been a rebel captive for almost three years up to 1873 (J. M. Muñoz to Secretario de Estado, México, June 2, 1882, TULAL, MIC 736, reel 5).

[106] La guerra de casta, *RP*, March 29, 1871, 2–3.

[107] Anonymous 1878:90, emphasis in the original.

[108] For the death of Claudio Novelo, see C. Moreno Navarrete to Gobernador, Valladolid, March 4, 1873, AGEY, PE, M, box 302, file 41; F. Díaz to Gobernador, Valladolid, July 29, 1874, AGEY, PE, CLM, box 311, file 44.

[109] Here, the supremacy of relegous leaders seems to have persisted until the town was evacuated in 1892 (Dumond 1985:301–302, 369).

[110] D. Traconis to Gobernador, Valladolid, February 17, 1871, *RP*, February 22, 1871, 1–2.

[111] A. Sandoval to Comandante militar de Mérida, Peto, July 2, 1864, *LNE*, July 8, 1864, 1; Dumond 1985:299.

[112] Informe sobre el plan de campaña del Gral. Castillo, J.L. Uraya to Emperador, n.p., [November 27,] 1865, AGN, G, SI, vol. 44, file 69.

[113] B. Novelo to Sr. Santo Patron, Sr. Juan Bautista Pat y la Patrona Sra. Da. Maria Vicab, Gran pueblo Santa Cruz, [no month given] 8, 1867, and Juan Casmichael to Santo

Kruso'b Politics and Religion

to an anonymous report from the 1870s, María Uicab, also referred to as "queen" in the sources, acted as the interpreter of three crosses she kept on an altar in the "grand temple of palms" in Tulum. The rebels attributed to her "the ability to understand or interpret their [the crosses'] language":

> If one of the raids she orders turns out badly or whatever order is not carried out exactly, the punishment of lashes is irremediably applied. They inform her of the result of the raids, as well as of whatever other news that might occur, and they faithfully hand over to her part of the booty.[114]

This is confirmed by evidence Daniel Traconis collected during an expedition into rebel territory in 1871. María Uicab's prestige and influence were immense, reaching beyond the confines of Tulum. Traconis reported that the "patroness or queen" was even honored in Chan Santa Cruz at the time.[115] Villalobos González goes so far as to suggest that Tulum replaced Chan Santa Cruz as the cross cult center after Bonifacio Novelo's death in 1868. She further argues that the cult and its priests in Chan Santa Cruz lost much of their political influence, the patron of the cross no longer gave secular orders, and the administration became more secularized in the years that followed. According to her, military and religious activities were conducted separately, with "the principal priestess or patroness, María Uicab, residing in Tulum, maintaining a strong moral influence, while the military command was concentrated in the hands of the

---

Patron D. Inocente Chablé y Sra. Santa Patrona Da. Maria Vicab, San Andrés, August 10, 1870, both in Correspondencia recojida á los indios bárbaros en el pueblo de Tulum, *RP*, March 1, 1871, 3–4.

[114] Anonymous 1878:90. Rosado Rosado and Santana Rivas (2008) suggest that some women played a major political and religious role among the kruso'b, one of whom was María Uicab. Another "patroness" is mentioned in addition to the patron of the cross at Chan Santa Cruz as early as 1855 (P.A. Gonzalez to Gobernador, Yokdzonot, January 25, 1855, *EO*, February 16, 1855, 1–3). A prisoner who had escaped from Chan Santa Cruz mentioned a "queen" ("la titulada *reina*") at that place in 1861. She died probably in August of that year while giving birth. According to the same source, "the crosses declared that her child would lead the rebels and end the war by taking the capital [Mérida]" (Noticias que emite el C. Anastasio Durán..., *LRP*, September 5, 1862, 1–3). No further information is given on the part these women played. Their reputation may have stemmed from their personal charisma and from being the daughter or spouse of important leaders. This seems to have rendered their social and political role exceptional but did not reflect female status in general. Women most probably held subordinate positions in kruso'b society, whose independence relied to a large extent on the prowess of male warriors. The description by Villa Rojas (1945:71) suggests at least that women had secondary status in the 1930s. To my knowledge, no in-depth study has been carried out on gender relations among the kruso'b in the nineteenth century.

[115] D. Traconis to Gobernador, Valladolid, February 17, 1871, *RP*, February 22, 1871, 1–2.

190   *Part V: Violence and the Kruso'b*

generals."[116] In fact, a report from the 1880s proves the persisting religious importance of Tulum and suggests that Chan Santa Cruz was still key to political issues as the "centre of the Indian country and their capital," where the chiefs meet "for consultation and for settling the affairs of the nation."[117] However, there was no clear-cut division between secular and spiritual tasks or formal hierarchy between the two centers. This is indicated in a statement by the general of Tulum, who underlined in his conversation with a trader from Isla Mujeres "that Tulum is one State and Chan Santa Cruz is another; and each one is ruled by its own government."[118] Thus, relations between Tulum and Chan Santa Cruz during the 1870s and 1880s oscillated between competition and cooperation, and reflected their shifting military strength, economic significance and ritual standing. They seem to have been independent of one another but people from both centers occasionally carried out joint activities such as raiding expeditions.[119] Crosses were venerated at both places as well as at San Antonio Muyil and probably other sites. The fact that Crescencio Poot, as mentioned earlier, communicated directly with the local cross, which "issued orders to go on a [raiding] party or not," confirms that the religious cult remained active in Chan Santa Cruz.[120] Kruso'b continued to receive communications from the cross (or Juan de la Cruz) in Chan Santa Cruz in 1887.[121] Hence, Paul Sullivan rightly stresses that the cult did not lose its political significance in every respect and that military leaders remained true believers. "The simplest interpretation," according to Sullivan, "is that there was continuity in the cult, its forms, its role in rebel Maya society."[122] Villa Rojas's description of the kruso'b in the 1930s distinguishes between the roles of ritual and of political offices, but makes clear, on the other hand, that this picture was far from complete since ritual leaders continued to a certain extent to play a role in secular matters.[123]

[116] Villalobos González 2006:204, 207, 223 (quote); see also Jones 1974:677–678.
[117] Miller 1889:25–27.
[118] Informe de Demetrio Peraza, Isla Mujeres, November 14, 1882, AGEY, PE, ODG, box 220; see also Dumond 1985:300–301.
[119] See, for example, J.C. Poot to I. Chablé, Gran pueblo Santa Cruz, December 28, 1870, *RM*, March 1, 1871, 3. Sullivan (2004:93) suggests that Poot borrowed fighters from Tulum for a raid on the frontier. This would prove that there was military cooperation but not submission.
[120] Chan Santa Cruz Report, Mérida, June 2, 1882, TULAL, M-26, box 2, folder 14.
[121] See the text of a proclamation in Villa Rojas 1945:164.
[122] Paul Sullivan (personal communication, June 27, 2002).
[123] Villa Rojas 1945:72, 92–93.

Kruso'b Politics and Religion

I would argue, then, that there was no continuous trend toward the secularization of kruso'b politics and no strict division of centers as religious or political hubs. Although religion and politics remained intertwined there are clear indications that, in pace with Reed, the relation between and relative importance of religious and political positions changed over time. Whereas some leaders held top ritual and political positions simultaneously (e.g., Venancio Puc), these were held in other periods by different people (e.g., Novelo and Poot between 1864 and 1868). Not all ambitious kruso'b chiefs had this inclination or they simply lacked the necessary qualities to convince followers of their special relationship to the cross. The multiplicity of crosses implied the potential for fragmentation in cult and politics; instead of a stable political or religious hierarchy to govern the rebel population, there was heavy rivalry among the leaders (in the same as well as in other places) for influence, power and wealth. From time to time these dynamics led to bloody confrontations and murder. Violence was a constitutive feature of this type of caudillo rule and used in assaults to procure resources for distribution to adherents and to deter or eliminate contenders for positions of leadership. The pattern of temporary stability and violent upheaval in kruso'b politics derives from the personalized nature of caudillo rule. Similar to any charismatic form of domination, it is intrinsically volatile and depends on the subordinates' belief in the exceptional qualities of the leader. Changes to his person, such as illness, or in the group situation, for example, loss of access to specific sources of income, could shake this conviction. Since institutionalized mechanisms to regulate succession were non-existent or ineffective, the political order was jeopardized by a leader's death, his failure to provide his followers with the desired goods or any sign of weakness that might prompt competitors to challenge his rule.[124] For all its real or alleged deficiencies, the caudillo political system proved capable of defending kruso'b strongholds and supplying the population with essential goods by means of raids or trade. Caudillo rule could indeed offer a measure of security for followers, at least for some time, and should not be confused with a constant state of anarchy, a permanent Hobbesian "war of all against all."

---

[124] See also Wolf and Hansen 1967:175.

16

Violence among the Kruso'b

Kruso'b military organization was apparently less formalized and hierarchical than that of the Federal Mexican Army or of Yucatecan militia units. Nevertheless, a certain amount of discipline was called for during combat and on raiding expeditions. In addition, fundamental norms had to be guaranteed to maintain order in kruso'b settlements or to settle personal disputes. The threat or use of force was key in achieving these aims. Beyond this, as argued in the previous Chapter, the particular nature of the kruso'b political system as a form of caudillaje made violence a recurrent part of the system. While the scarcity of sources does preclude a full understanding of rebel politics, some of the factors that led to internal violence emerge from better-documented instances of conflict between leaders. These will be discussed in more detail in the following section.

INFIGHTING

Several major periods of political infighting can be traced in the rebel historical record. The first culminated in the death of the most prominent rebel leaders in 1849. Since insurgent forces had been in retreat for more than a year, opportunities to finance the war by plundering conquered towns dwindled. This notwithstanding, substantial sums of money were required to buy arms, ammunition and other items. Having run out of funds, Jacinto Pat attempted to introduce a contribution of one real per head, a scheme that earned him the hatred of countless rebels, whose main motivation for joining the struggle was tax liberation. Pat's rivals, Venancio Pec and Florentino Chan, saw an opportunity to strengthen

Violence among the Kruso'b

their own position and slew the principal leader and at least six of his henchmen on their way to Bacalar. Pec, Chan and other leaders made efforts to legitimize the killings in a circular letter, accusing Pat of imposing a war contribution, the sanction of whipping, and forced labor (*servicio de semaneros*), thus "robbing his subordinates." There was to be "no money collected from the poor" and the troops were to keep the spoils from acts of war.[1]

A couple of years later, in mid-1862, a major putsch against the kruso'b principal chiefs, Dionisio Zapata and Venancio Puc, failed and culminated in the death of putsch ringleader José Dolores Tec and 250 of his followers. Differences about the course to be taken against the Yucatecans were the alleged background to this episode. Two refugees reported that a significant number of rebels were no longer in favor of the continuous raiding of Yucatecan towns, ostensibly due to "the damage they usually suffer," suggesting the existence of a pro-peace party that sought to take over command.[2] Other hitherto unknown causes may, however, have been responsible for the conflict. In fact, the rebels had little reason to seek peace at that time or to abandon raiding. No major casualties are reported for the various raids after their last major setback during assaults on Yaxcabá, Tiholop and Ichmul in July 1859.[3] The last significant government attack occurred in January 1860 and ended in complete disaster for the aggressors.[4] In addition, Yucatán struggled with the autonomy movement of Campeche and had to face countless pronunciamientos and counter-coups, which led to no less than eight changes of government between 1859 and 1862.[5] Thus, no major Yucatecan

---

[1] F. Chan, V. Pec et al., San Antonio, September 3, 1849, cited in Baqueiro 1990, 3:197–198. See also D. Pasos to Comandante general interino, Peto, September 14, 1849, AGEY, PE, M, box 169, file 42. Other sources mention the introduction of a head tax among the rebels (M. Micheltorena to MGM, August 1, 1850, AHM, XI/481.3/2914) and Pat's alleged inclination to surrender to the government with 300 followers and 12,000 pesos (GCY:79) as motives for the killings. See also Declaración de Pablo Encalada, Campeche (part 1), August 12, 1867, *EP*, September 24, 1867, 1; Ancona 1879/80, 4:262–264; Baqueiro 1990, 3:197–199. Crescencio Poot was involved in Pat's killing. At that time, however, he was still a second rank commander (*capitancillo*) (S. López de Llergo to MGM, Mérida, November 23, 1850, AHM, XI/481.3/2914; see also Baqueiro [1887] 1989:21–22).

[2] P. Rosado Lavalle to Comandante en Jefe, Valladolid, July 23, 1863, *LNE*, July 27, 1863, 2.

[3] See Appendix 1.   [4] See Chapter 8.

[5] See, for example, Baqueiro 1990, 5:92, 105, 111–113; Negrín Muñoz 1991:87, 90; Rugeley 2009:183–184, 189–190.

194   *Part V: Violence and the Kruso'b*

offensive was to be feared for the foreseeable future and little outer pressure for the kruso'b to end the struggle.

Some time later, a deep rift developed between Zapata and Puc, leading to a period of serious turmoil among the kruso'b. As mentioned earlier, Venancio Puc, the principal caudillo and patron of the cross, his secretary, tata Polin, "who executed the priestly tasks," and José Ná, the interpreter of the cross, fell victim to a coup led by Generals Zapata and Santos on December 23, 1863.[6] Although information on these events is confusing and partly contradictory, it can at least help to detect critical sources of internal strain, one of which was Puc's imperilment of the commercial and political relationship with the British so essential to maintaining kruso'b autonomy.[7] Attempting to pressure people from Belize to pay rent for their cultivation of food crops on rebel territory, Puc had in fact approved cattle stealing in northern Belize and humiliating a delegation of British officers who had come to complain about these abuses. Hence, news of his death was met with "no little satisfaction and comfort of the Authorities at Belize, and the inhabitants that reside in the northern portion of this colony, who have for years lived in almost continued dread, fearing that General Pook [Puc] with his warriors would make a sudden descent upon them, making them all prisoners."[8] Another bone of contention, possibly related to the aforementioned, seems to have been his treatment of prisoners. Puc had gained a reputation for being particularly bloodthirsty and Reed credits him with a "policy of slaughter" during the years he controlled the Cult of the Speaking Cross.[9] In a letter addressed to the British superintendent of Belize in 1864 justifying the putsch, Zapata and Santos claimed that "certainly not less than 6,000 souls" had been killed over the

---

[6] J.L. Montalvo to Prefecto Político, Peto, February 12, 1864, *LNE*, February 15, 1864, 4; see also F.A. Canton to Prefecto, Valladolid, February 12, 1864, *LNE*, February 15, 1864, 1; D. Zapata, L. Santos, G. del Castillo to the superintendent of Belize, January 1, 1864, Archives of Belize, R. 84, cited in Dumond 1997:254–255.

[7] One source claims, however, that Puc had already been killed in late August or early September on order of the Speaking Cross and that his successor was a certain Ti Lisch, "a ventriloquist, supposed to communicate with the Cross" (Ch. Leas to W.H. Seward, Belize, September 5, 1863, TULAL, MIC 736, reel 2).

[8] Ch. Leas to W.H. Seward, Belize, September 5, 1863, TULAL, MIC 736, reel 2. Relations with Belize had indeed been strained by several incidents since 1860. See, for example, Cal 1983:92–110 and 1991:345–346; Dumond 1997:240–245, 252–253; several documents in ABH:251–253; José de los Angeles Loesa, Archives of Belize, Record 74, August 26, 1861, 174–175, in Rugeley 2001b:80.

[9] Reed 2001:238.

Violence among the Kruso'b

past sixteen years.[10] While this figure seems exaggerated, there can be no doubt that rebels killed numerous Yucatecan prisoners and that these atrocities were disapproved by British officials.

Be that as it may, growing social tension among the kruso'b seems to have been a major reason for the coup against Puc. As mentioned earlier, follower loyalty at that time depended much on the capacity of leaders to organize lucrative raids. Since the success of such ventures could never be guaranteed, numerous leaders set about gaining additional revenue with the promise of more reliable returns. The wealth generated by these activities allowed them to draw on their own resources to prefinance raids or weather periods of scarcity when looting was impossible. Hence, farming or commercial activities such as the sale of rum would have rendered the authority structure more stable. The accumulation of wealth, however, was a double-edged sword. Kruso'b were not only suspicious of taxation but also of individual wealth (unlike that for the cult).[11] The open display of wealth could trigger the covetousness of competitors for leadership and the envy of the population in general so that, in most cases, "anyone who happens to have a peso buries it, so that everyone seems poor," as one contemporary observer remarked. Competition for sources of wealth and the tension between egalitarian pretensions and trends toward individual enrichment occasionally resulted in bloodshed among the kruso'b, as will be seen in the following.

Several documents indicate that kruso'b leaders accumulated wealth and exploited the rank and file by selling them overpriced goods. One prisoner reported in 1858, for example, that traders from Corozal sold salt, gunpowder, shot and other goods to rebel leaders. The soldiers, for their part, "were not allowed to buy anything direct [sic] but only through the chiefs."[12] A British officer reported that Puc and the other chiefs "had their fingers 'entirely covered with [gold] rings', while the soldiers were

---

[10] D. Zapata, L. Santos, G. del Castillo to the superintendent of Belize, January 1, 1864, Archives of Belize, R. 84, cited in Dumond 1997:254–255; see also Sullivan 2004:87.

[11] Chan Santa Cruz Report, Mérida, June 2, 1882, TULAL, M-26, box 2, folder 14. As Villa Rojas's statement for X-Cacal indicates, this pattern seems to have continued into the early twentieth century: "Nothing one observes in their ordinary, daily behavior suggests the existence of differences in accumulated wealth. They all dress alike, have the same diet, live in the same type of houses, and engage in the same type of activities." The possession of money was "not so much a matter of general knowledge as of conjecture, for the possessor keeps such holdings a secret" (1945:65; see also Gann 1924:40).

[12] Buhler 1975:12; see also Noticias que emite el C. Anastasio Durán . . ., *LRP*, September 5, 1862, 2.

196   *Part V: Violence and the Kruso'b*

not allowed to keep more than half a dollar."[13] Both the distillation and the sale of rum were lucrative ventures and therefore contested among the leaders. In mid-1862, only General Santos disposed of the necessary distillation equipment, offering a bottle of rum at one peso. Venancio Puc, on the other hand, set up a distillery with facilities captured during the assault on Tunkas.[14] Reed suggests that Puc monopolized the distillation of liquor, which he sold to the rank and file at elevated prices.[15] It remains unclear whether Puc indeed drove Santos out of business. In any case, the sale of rum constituted a point at issue.[16]

Some sources indicate that Santos and Zapata's putsch was motivated by disbelief in the cult. Whether religion was genuinely at the core of the conflict is difficult to discern. Santos, at least, had already shown disdain for the cult some time before the putsch against Puc. On one occasion in the late 1850s, when he was drunk and the cross was talking, he shouted, "Stop talking Braulio (Tata Naz's son, probably called José Braulio, who acted for the cross) we have enough of sorcery." He was immediately sanctioned with whippings, arrested the next day, taken before the tatich Venancio Puc and three important generals (Zapata, Poot and Bonifacio Novelo), made to pay two bags of corn and cautioned that "if such an offence was committed again immediate death would follow."[17] On the other hand, it may have been Puc's amassing of wealth in the name of the cross rather than religious belief that sparked the putsch against him. Whatever the case, the anti-Puc rebels argued that the Speaking Cross was a hoax and that the capital built in its name should therefore be divided among the soldiers.[18]

---

[13] Jones 1974:672, quoting Anderson to Seymour, March 4, 1858, Archives of Belize 61.

[14] Noticias que emite el C. Anastasio Durán ..., *LRP*, September 5, 1862, 1–3; see also Buhler 1975:12.

[15] Reed 2001:239.

[16] Following the putsch against Puc the new leaders came to a Solomonic solution. The chiefs ran a still jointly and distributed the rum among themselves or, "extremely expensive at six *reales* a bottle," sold it to rebel soldiers. Although this meant a price reduction of 25 percent compared to Zapata's rate, it did not entirely satisfy the rebel masses (Comisión del gobierno de Yucatán ..., Mérida, June 13, 1864, *LNE*, June 24, 1864, 1–3).

[17] Buhler 1975:11. Another source suggests that disbelief in the cult was also widespread among Zapata's followers in 1864 (A. Dugall to P. Barrera, Corosal, n.d. [the document has "15 del pasado," the year is missing, the content suggests that it was written in 1864], CAIHDY, M, XLIV.1850–1859/4).

[18] F.A. Canton to Prefecto, Valladolid, February 12, 1864, *LNE*, February 15, 1864, 1; see also Dumond 1997:255 based on E. Burke to G. Berkeley, January 25, 1864, Archive of British Honduras, R 84. While Jones (1974:676) and Dumond (1997:254–255) assume

Peace failed to be restored after Puc's death. On the contrary, various leaders attempted to exploit the fragile situation to further their own ambitions. Again there are conflicting versions of subsequent events. According to Reed, Bonifacio Novelo convinced Zapata that General Santos "was preparing treachery of an unexplained nature." Santos was arrested and supposedly murdered by Bernardino Cen.[19] Another source suggests that Zapata killed Santos only a few weeks after Puc's death, suspecting that his former co-conspirator was about to make peace with the government.[20] That this was the reason for the killing is debatable, since both generals had informed the British confidentially of their readiness to enter into peace negotiations with Yucatán in the letter that justified their killing of Puc. In addition, a Yucatecan commission destined to enter into negotiations with rebel leaders had instructions to specifically contact Zapata, who was obviously seen as the least intransigent of the kruso'b chiefs.[21] In reality, Zapata had contacted the Mexican consul in Belize, José María Martínez, to offer subordination to the government in exchange for autonomy. His secret negotiations were discovered, however, and he was killed with an unknown number of followers during an attempt to flee to Belize on March 10, 1864.[22] The Yucatecan commission blamed former Puc henchmen for the murder of both Santos and Zapata.[23] The new strongmen, Crescencio Poot, Bonifacio Novelo and

---

that Santos and Zapata actually distributed the wealth amassed by Puc in the name of the cross as they had promised, I have my doubts about this. Bonifacio Novelo reported a mere three years later that the cult possessed "over $200,000 – in specie, irrespective of jewels and gold ornament" (J. Carmichael to Longdon, Corozal, November 15, 1867, Archives of Belize, Record 96, in Rugeley 2001b:85).

[19] Reed 2001:241.

[20] J.L. Montalvo to Prefecto Político, Peto, February 12, 1864, LNE, February 15, 1864, 4.

[21] Comisión del gobierno de Yucatán . . ., Mérida, June 13, 1864, LNE, June 24, 1864, 1.

[22] A. Sandoval to General en Jefe, Peto, June 12, 1864, LNE, June 17, 1864, 1; Reed 2001:241. Discrepancies between rebel leaders may also have been related to economic competition for profitable revenues, such as rum sales or the control of trade with Belize. This may also have been the motive behind the death of several traders from Corozal (Gregorio Trejo, José Castillo, Feliciano Pérez y Victoriano Alcocer), who were killed with Zapata (E. Burke to secretario colonial, Corosal, April 4, 1864, LNE, April 25, 1864, 3).

[23] Comisión del gobierno de Yucatán . . ., Mérida, June 13, 1864, LNE, June 24, 1864, 1. Another document imputes the killing of Puc, Sánchez, Ná and Santos to Dionisio Zapata and Crescencio Poot (F.A. Canton to Prefecto, Valladolid, February 12, 1864, LNE, February 15, 1864, 1). This account seems to merge two phases of infighting, since Santos had appeared with Zapata as the co-author of a letter dated January 1, 1864, justifying the killing of Puc and his associates (D. Zapata, L. Santos, G. del Castillo to the superintendent of Belize, January 1, 1864, Archives of Belize, R. 84, cited in Dumond 1997:254–255; Sullivan 2004:87–88).

198   *Part V: Violence and the Kruso'b*

Bernardino Cen, denied responsibility for the killings and even executed eight men from the party that had massacred Zapata and his companions. This did little to appease the anger of Zapata's followers and heavy fighting ensued, claiming possibly more than 500 victims but failing to effect a change in leadership.[24]

After the death of Bonifacio Novelo in 1868, Poot and Cen remained the most influential chiefs for some time. A conflict over the fate of a female prisoner and the ransom of 2,000 pesos paid to Poot for her release led to a definitive rupture with Cen. The woman was set free despite the latter's fierce opposition. The dispute may have been as much about Cen's fear of losing face as an influential chief as it was about money. According to one source, the fighting that ensued between the parties supporting the adversaries claimed the lives of 600 kruso'b in April 1875.[25] Poot's party finally prevailed, while Cen and his henchmen were forced to flee to Tulum. In a raid on the hacienda Xuxub in mid-October of the same year, Cen was killed.[26] His death left Poot the unrivaled leader for several years.[27]

As mentioned before, rents paid by Belizian entrepreneurs for the exploitation of mahogany, dyewoods and logwood replaced raiding in the 1870s as the principal source of kruso'b revenue. In addition, leaders generated income from growing sugar cane and breeding cattle on their farms. The need for offensive military action declined as a result and some found the prospect of enjoying the fruits of these commercial activities in peace attractive. Negotiations between Yucatecan representatives and Poot and several other chiefs failed to bring agreement in 1878, however, and again in 1884.[28] In the spring of 1885, General Aniceto Dzul attempted to overthrow Crescencio Poot, still the most significant leader in Chan Santa Cruz. The putsch came to nothing, at least for the moment, and Dzul withdrew with some of his followers to Tulum or Chunpom. Several authors attribute Dzul's putsch to his disapproval of Poot's alleged

---

[24] J.E. Tejero to Prefecto, Peto, March 26, 1864, AGEY, PE, M, box 225, file 91; E. Burke to secretario colonial, Corosal, April 4, 1864, *LNE*, April 25, 1864, 3; Comisión del gobierno de Yucatán . . ., Mérida, June 13, 1864, *LNE*, June 24, 1864, 1–3.

[25] C. Moreno Navarrete to Gobernador, Valladolid, March 6, 1875, *RP*, March 8, 1875, 1; Yucatan y los Ingleses, *RP*, November 26, 1875, 3; Sullivan 2004:111–117, 236–237 n. 38 and 39.

[26] B.M. Montilla to Gobernador, Puntachén, October 15, 1875, *RP*, October 20, 1875, 1. See Sullivan (2004) for a meticulous analysis of the raid and its context.

[27] J.E. Tejero to Gobernador, Peto, August 6, 1880, *RP*, August 13, 1880, 1–2.

[28] A detailed analysis of the peace efforts is provided by Sullivan (1997b); see also Jones (1978).

Violence among the Kruso'b

inclination to cede kruso'b autonomy to the government.[29] This interpretation is questioned by the fact that rebels in Tulum traded with and worked in agriculture for Yucatecans, casting doubts on assumptions of a general aversion to peaceful relations. According to Sullivan, Dzul may have been even more inclined toward peace than Poot.[30] The break between the two was probably not about war or peace but an attempt to oust Poot from the top position and gain control of the income generated by logging rents. The time seemed ripe for change. Poot was already sixty-eight years of age and his strength was fading. Trips to Belize for rent collection or other matters had become burdensome and he preferred instead to send his second-in-command, Juan Chuc.[31] According to Serapio Baqueiro, Poot began to drink heavily in the years before the putsch, something he had never done before.[32] Typical for caudillo systems, signs of weakness induced competitors to challenge the rule of the dominant leader.[33] On August 22 or 23, 1885, Dzul returned to Chan Santa Cuz, killed commander Juan Chuc and shortly afterwards Crescencio Poot along with about seventy of his followers. Infighting was not yet over, however, since the remaining leaders began to compete for the control of forest resources.[34]

The late 1880s witnessed the intensification of dyewood extraction in the kruso'b area, while chicle (a natural gum) became an additional and much sought after forest product, increasing social tension and rivalry among the leaders "for distribution of the proceeds from rents paid by the Belizians."[35] German traveler Karl Sapper, who visited the region in early 1894, reported that rents were employed to cover "public expenses" (such as the buying of weapons and ammunition, payment of the scribe) and

---

[29] Jones 1978:8; Dumond 1997:330; Villalobos González 2006:246.

[30] Sullivan 1997b:28, 30, 43 n.55.

[31] Sullivan 1997b:17; La guerra contra los mayas . . ., *EE*, August 20, 1899, 1–2, in Wilhelm 1997:116.

[32] Baqueiro [1887] 1989:26.

[33] Cf. Wolf and Hansen 1967:175. For Dzul's aspirations to replace Poot, see Baqueiro [1887] 1989:27.

[34] Noticias verídicas sobre la cuestion de los indios rebeldes, P. Roca, Hopelchén, January 19, 1886, AGEC, AH, G, AM, box 14; Informacion practicada con Saturnino Fernandez . . ., September 1886, AGEY, PE, M, box 241; La guerra contra los mayas . . ., *EE*, August 20, 1899, 1–2, in Wilhelm 1997:115–116; Villalobos González 2006: 246–248; Sullivan 1997b:25–26. Pacíficos in Xkanhá had already falsely reported the killing of Chuc and Poot's family before October 23, 1884 (Secretaria de Guerra y Marina to Gobernador, México, November 17, 1884, AGEY, PE, ODG, box 230).

[35] Un indio de Santa Cruz capturado, *EE*, August 22, 1894, 4 in Wilhelm 1997:29.

200   *Part V: Violence and the Kruso'b*

added "eventual surplus seems to belong to the general."[36] As the high exportation levels of dyewood and mahogany from Belize – mostly from the kruso'b area – in the 1880s and 1890s suggest, these profits must have grown considerably.[37] Wealth differences further increased and, contrary to the past, it seems that the kruso'b rank and file began to toil on farms belonging to commanders and generals, to cut dyewood or work in Belize.[38] From the outset, inequalities had resulted in violence among the rebels and, as we have seen, leaders suspected of appropriating rents paid by the British for lumber or chicle exploitation ran a high risk of being slain after a brief period in their privileged position. Growing wealth produced a surge in the number of homicides. At the end of the nineteenth century, "the chiefs enriched themselves with the rents the English paid and were frequently killed after a short period in office by their envious inferiors," according to an eyewitness.[39]

Since the beginning of the Caste War, negotiations with the Yucatecans had been observed by many of the rebels with suspicion, with some considering them outright treason. True or false, blaming a competitor for selling out to the hereditary Yucatecan enemy was a recurrent and effective tool when it came to mobilizing rank and file support in the struggle for leadership and revenue from the exploitation of forest products. Confronted with the growing threat of a Mexican invasion, divided opinions on peace negotiations were a serious bone of contention in addition to wealth differentiation and competition for rents. This led to the eruption of violent conflict among the kruso'b chiefs again in 1887 in relation to a pacification attempt by archaeologist Juan Peón Contreras, who convinced the leader of Tulum, Luciano Pech, of his good intentions. Peón Contreras presented himself as Juan Xiu, a messiah who had come to save the kruso'b.[40] He was even granted the military title of general and married Isabel Xuluc, the widow of former rebel leader Juan Pech. According to one version, Aniceto Dzul attacked Tulum in mid-1887 when he learned that the supposed messiah was a Yucatecan from Mérida. Peón Conteras was not there at the time und thus survived. Others were less lucky. Dzul had Luciano Pech executed. He then decapitated him and placed his head on a spear, allegedly as a sanction for

[36] Sapper 1895:199.
[37] For export data, see Lapointe 1983:94; Villalobos González 2006:75 tabla 1.
[38] Captura de un espía maya en Yucatán, *EE*, August 19, 1894, 4, in Wilhelm 1997:27; Lapointe 1983:86; Villalobos González 2006: 110–111, 260–263; see also S. di Pietro to C. Carrillo y Ancona, Belize, October 30, 1894, AHAY, G, O, box 438, file 2.
[39] Adrian 1924:237.   [40] Dumond 1997:356–358.

treason and granting Contreras the title of general. Other alleged traitors were also slain. At the same time, another version holds that Dzul accepted the arrangement with Peón Contreras and blamed the leaders of Chunpom, Muyil, Xulhás, San Francisco and Chunyuy for the attack on Tulum and the killing of Pech and the local patron of the cross, Luciano Canul. When Dzul was informed of these events he assailed the invaders, killing some of them.[41] In any case, the slaughter established Dzul's hegemony and control over kruso'b external commercial relations. When he traveled to Belize in December 1887 to renew wood-cutting contracts, for example, the leaders of Tulum and Bacalar were absent in contrast to earlier occasions.[42]

New attempts to end the war led to further turmoil a couple of months later. Possibly with the intention of preventing a major offensive by the Mexican forces, Dzul had a meeting with Enrique Sardanetta, a representative of President Porfirio Díaz, on July 6, 1888, and agreed to enter into negotiations to establish formal peace with Mexico, to the explicit exclusion of any interference by the government of Yucatán.[43] Back in kruso'b territory, Dzul was heavily criticized by General José María Puc for negotiating with the government and, as some reports have it, ultimately killed. Another version, however, sees embezzlement of the rent Dzul collected in Belize as the reason for his murder.[44] The latter version is supported by the fate of other kruso'b chiefs. José María Puc, for example, was killed by other leaders because he failed to account for money received as payment for renting the forests in late 1894.[45] General José María Canul, Commander José María Aké and Hilario Cab met a similar fate. They were slain with more than fifty others on order of Felipe Yama, having been accused of defrauding part of the money collected in Belize in 1896.[46] Yama himself was murdered by

---

[41] Los indios de Chan Santa Cruz, MR, June 30, 1887, 3; J.M. Iturralde to Gobernador, Valladolid, March 23, 1888, RP, April 6, 1888, 3; Villalobos González 2006:251–254.

[42] Attempts by Chan Santa Cruz leaders to bring Tulum under their control in 1892 and 1896 resulted in numerous deaths, the emigration of most of Tulum's surviving inhabitants to Belize and the final destruction of the place (Villalobos González 2006:254; Los sublevados de Chan Santa Cruz, EE, March 9, 1897, 3, in Wilhelm 1997:80).

[43] La pacificación de los bárbaros, MR, Augsut 7, 1888, 3. According to Dumond (1997:360–361), Dzul soon changed his mind about peace, declaring that Sardanetta had threatened to send in troops and destroy Chan Santa Cruz.

[44] Villalobos González 2006:259. Dumond (1997:372), in contrast, sees no indication that Dzul died violently.

[45] Villalobos González 2006:265; Dumond 1997:372–373.

[46] Indios sublevados de Chan Santa Cruz en Mérida, EE, August 22, 1897, 1, in Wilhelm 1997:85.

202   *Part V: Violence and the Kruso'b*

rival leaders in April 1901. While some see the reason for this in his willingness to make peace with the government in view of the advancing Mexican army, Villalobos González suggests he was killed as a result of his alleged responsibility for the loss of rent resources.[47]

To conclude: As mentioned earlier, rents paid by Belizian entrepreneurs for the exploitation of mahogany, dyewoods or logwood had replaced raiding as the main source of revenue since the 1870s. This meant a decline in violence against Yucatecans, on the one hand, but fueled rebel infighting, on the other, due to personal ambition, competition for resources, mistrust of the just spending of income from loot and logging rents, and envy. Between 1887 and 1901 alone, half a dozen or more major kruso'b chiefs were killed in the ensuing conflicts.[48] Beyond this, increasing pressure from the Yucatecan and Mexican governments exacerbated internal tensions among the kruso'b and challenged the hope of remaining unmolested in the future. Hence, staying in the rebel territory seemed less attractive and since the mid-1880s a growing number of kruso'b had taken flight to Belize or the frontier with Yucatán. Apprehended fugitives were shot or slain by machete blows "irrespective of age or sex."[49] These radical measures, however, failed to stall the attrition of the rebel forces.

The pattern of kruso'b internal violence fits quite well into what is expected from a caudillo political system as described by Wolf and Hansen. Leadership was charismatic and thus depended on the capacity of the incumbents to attract enough henchmen to back their claim with military skill, a special relationship to supernatural forces, accented masculinity or other personal traits. Any sign of weakness in the prominent could mean loss of followers to a rival and, if things went badly, loss of life. With few institutionalized alternatives, violence remained the sole means to settle competition and conflict. Nevertheless, a cautionary note seems appropriate at the end of this section, which might well appear to be a story of constant intrigue, murder and turmoil. It is true to say that many rebel leaders were killed by rivals in the struggle for power. At the same time, internal upheaval was concentrated in certain periods: 1849, 1862 to 1864, 1875 and the final fifteen years of the nineteenth century stand

---

[47] Villalobos González 2006:267. See also La guerra contra los mayas..., *EE*, December 19, 1899, 1, in Wilhelm 1997:153–154; Dumond 1997:395; Reed 2001:371.

[48] J.M. Iturralde to Gobernador, Valladolid, September 28, 1886, AGEY, PE, C, box 236; Indios sublevados de Chan Santa Cruz en Mérida, *EE*, August 22, 1897, 1, in Wilhelm 1997:87; Dumond 1997:372; Villalobos González 2006:264–265.

[49] Un indio de Santa Cruz capturado, *EE*, August 22, 1894, 4 in Wilhelm 1997:29; see also J. M. Iturralde to Gobernador, Valladolid, September 28, 1886, AGEY, PE, C, box 236.

Violence among the Kruso'b 203

out in this respect. The rest of the five decades that followed the uprising in 1847 were devoted for the most part to consolidating kruso'b society and evinced a relative degree of stability.

SANCTIONS

The Caste War rebels had to provide for a certain amount of order in two major spheres, namely, military discipline during combat or raiding expeditions and the regulation of day-to-day affairs in their settlements. Since neither law codes nor sentences from regular courts existed in kruso'b society, particulars on norms and their control are few and far between. We consequently rely on a few general statements in the sources and a number of individual cases mentioned in the records for a glimpse of the rebel normative system.

The cult played a major role in legitimizing decisions, at least during the 1850s and 1860s. Generals, commanders and even the "head of the army" (*tata chikiuic*) were subject to the oracle's verdict and castigated when found delinquent or guilty of some fault.[50] A trader from Belize reported in 1861: "Whenever the Cross speaks ... every person in Santa Cruz must be present. The Cross alone orders people to be punished. . . . Without the orders of the Cross, Puc could not chastise anyone, although he is patron of the Cross."[51] A report from an ex-prisoner describes the legal situation in the 1870s in some detail. All officers from general to corporal administered justice "according to the exigencies of the case."[52] According to Gann, fines, flogging and execution were the usual sanctions. Only the principal chief could impose the death sentence.[53] These sources do not mention legitimation of the verdict by the cross. It can thus be assumed that it was merely required for severe cases.

Flogging was the habitual punishment for a variety of wrongdoings. Theft was chastised with between 25 and 100 canings "depending on the circumstances" and compensation paid for the stolen object.[54] The most common sanction for disobedience by soldiers in the military units was whipping. On occasion this also applied to corporals, sergeants and

---

[50] Aldherre and Mendiolea 1869:75.
[51] J. de los Angeles Loesa, Archives of Belize, Record 74, August 26, 1861, 174–175, in Rugeley 2001b:80.
[52] Chan Santa Cruz Report, Mérida, June 2, 1882, TULAL, M-26, box 2, folder 14. See also J.M. Muñoz to Secretario de Estado, México, June 2, 1882, TULAL, MIC 736, reel 5.
[53] Gann 1918:35.
[54] Chan Santa Cruz Report, Mérida, June 2, 1882, TULAL, M-26, box 2, folder 14.

204   *Part V: Violence and the Kruso'b*

officers.[55] Commander Juan Tomás Tzuc, for example, received 200 lashes for cowardice in late 1848 after his squad was defeated in combat and dispersed. Tzuc in turn ordered fifty lashes to be given to a number of his soldiers who had left the front.[56] Ten years later, Venancio Puc, allegedly on orders of the cross, enforced discipline with similar methods, sanctioning soldiers and generals on their return from a raiding expedition to Valladolid that ended in complete disaster. The rebels had indulged in the liquor stocks of a farm they passed, allowing the army to attack and kill many of them.[57] An unnamed chief, probably Bonifacio Novelo, was given fifty lashes for insubordination in 1861.[58] As mentioned above, General Santos was whipped for questioning the authenticity of the cult and a prisoner killed for doubting the divine nature of the cross.[59]

Capital punishment constituted the second most common sanction for misdeeds such as desertion to the enemy or sorcery.[60] Aniceto Dzul, for example, killed a man and his wife whom he suspected of bewitching him in the 1880s.[61] A kruso'b soldier was executed by his commander for slaying a Yucatecan refugee on Belizian soil after the British superintendent had denounced the murder.[62]

Moral lapses could also become the object of sanction. The common sentence for adultery consisted of public flogging of the individuals involved.[63] In some cases, however, chastisement of marital infidelity was left in some measure to the aggrieved party. A kruso'b who had run away with another man's wife was shot by the husband in pursuit. The wife was punished in public with fifty lashes.[64] The action of the cheated

---

[55] B. Pec to J.T. Cocom, Tihosuco, August 30, 1848, Version al castellano de varias comunicaciones que tuvieron entre si los indios sublevados del oriente de Yucatán, 1848, CAIHDY, M, XLIII.1847–1849/39; Magistrate, Northern District to Superintendent, April 26, 1861, R. 71, ABH:240.

[56] Baqueiro 1990, 3:82.

[57] Buhler 1975:11. He estimates rebel losses at 200 men. This was probably an exaggeration. Yucatecan sources reported more than a dozen dead and numerous wounded kruso'b (M.F. Peraza to MGM, Mérida, April 3, 1858, AHM, XI/481.3/6444; Declaracion del indígena José Cen, J. Martínez Vaca, Valladolid, April 5, 1858, GS, April 7, 1858, 2–3).

[58] Rogers 1885:224. Dumond (1997:241) gives Novelo as having suffered the punishment.

[59] Buhler 1975:11.

[60] Chan Santa Cruz Report, Mérida, June 2, 1882, TULAL, M-26, box 2, folder 14; Gann 1918:36.

[61] Miller 1889:27.   [62] Dumond 1997:151.

[63] Chan Santa Cruz Report, Mérida, June 2, 1882, TULAL, M-26, box 2, folder 14; According to Yucatecan law, adultery was punishable with imprisonment from six months to three years (Gobierno del Estado 1871b:127–128, Art. 650).

[64] Adrian 1924:243.

Violence among the Kruso'b

husband corresponded to judicial practices in the rest of Yucatán, where, as we have seen, the killing of an adulterer by the offended male was also free of sanction. One captain was condemned to death for running away with another man's wife in the early 1860s.[65] This severe punishment could be explained by his elevated position, which rendered his misdeed not only an infraction of moral standards but also affected the reputation of leaders in general. It may also have been perceived as a form of desertion.

Delinquents among the kruso'b and the pacíficos were normally put to death by machete.[66] An eyewitness reported that prisoners in Chan Santa Cruz were executed under the Sapodilla tree at the center of the plaza, where they were "cut to pieces by machetes or cutlasses."[67] The eyewitness description of one man's execution suggests that the executioners addressed the victims in Maya with words that delegated responsibility for the deed to the supernatural sphere: "You must die. It is not our doing, it is the will of God." According to the same source, the killing was carried out as follows: "The Indian's macheat then cleft the back of the unfortunate man's head, across. When he fell a second cut was then made diagonally to the first and the body was then run through with the macheat which was vigorously twisted round and round in the wound."[68] Wrongdoers were often hacked to death by several men, dividing liability for the act.[69]

The evidence on jailing is contradictory. One source explicitly denies the existence of "any kind of jail."[70] An earlier source, however, mentions a "square block surrounded by a high wall with thatched houses in the center" that served as a "site of reclusion," at least for Yucatecan prisoners.[71] The latter were locked up in bullpens (*calabozos*) according to another eyewitness.[72] A further description of Chan Santa Cruz mentions not only a schoolhouse where children were "taught the early

---

[65] Buhler 1975:11.

[66] See, for example, F. Medina to Gobernador, Ticul, July 14, 1867, *RP*, July 23, 1867, 1; Declaracion de Pablo Encalada, Campeche (part 2), August 12, 1867, *EP*, September 27, 1867, 1; García y García 1865:xxiv, n. 6.

[67] J. Carmichael to Longdon, Corozal, November 15, 1867, Archives of Belize, Record 96, in Rugeley 2001b:86.

[68] R.W. Pickwoad to Colonial Secretary, April 18,1892, enclosed with A. Maloney dispatch No. 146, May 12, 1892, CO 123/198 cited in Dumond 1997:475 n. 9.

[69] Correspondencia, P. Bolio, Izamal, *RM*, May 2, 1873, 3; Gann 1918:35.

[70] Chan Santa Cruz Report, Mérida, June 2, 1882, TULAL, M-26, box 2, folder 14. See also Gann 1918:35.

[71] Noticias que emite el C. Anastasio Durán . . ., August 26, 1862, *LRP*, September 5, 1862, 3.

[72] J.M. Díaz to Gobernador, Sotuta, December 1,1871, *RP*, December 6, 1871, 1.

rudiments of Spanish and Maya" but also a "prison."[73] The case of Andrés Canul shows that confinement served as a sanction. His father had joined the rebels when Andrés was seven. When his father died, he was to take his father's place. Andrés refused and was jailed until he finally escaped to government territory.[74]

Although lacking in written laws, specialized courts and police forces, kruso'b society was not anarchic. The scant evidence rather confirms the existence of a normative system that followed particular rules to maintain, for example, military discipline, public order and fundamental social norms such as marital fidelity. Jailing was negligible, since guarding and feeding inmates would have been a heavy burden on the relatively small communities. Physical punishment was therefore the most common sanction.

[73] J. Carmichael to Longdon, Corozal, November 15, 1867, Archives of Belize, Record 96, in Rugeley 2001b:86.

[74] P. Rosado Lavalle to Comandante en Jefe, Division del Estado, Valladolid, July 23, 1863, *LNE*, July 27, 1863, 2.

17

Kruso'b Violence against Outsiders

While the use of physical force played a key role in kruso'b political organization and was instrumental in dealing with deviant behavior, the bulk of violence was directed at outsiders, such as government soldiers in battle, civilians during rebel assaults or captives. As will be seen in the following, the reasons for using force were manifold and its forms and intensity varied through time and according to context. The capacity of the rebels to defend themselves against attack and procure loot from assaults on Yucatán was largely contingent on their equipment. Hence, a few words on weaponry at this point are justified.

ARMAMENT

Notably at the beginning of the war, the rebels had a comparatively small number of guns and did not manage them well. Their gunfire caused "very little damage," as Mexican General Castillo remarked. No more than 3,000 of the 25,000 to 30,000 men were in possession of firearms, mostly shotguns effective only at short range. Most of them fought with pointed sticks and clubs.[1] Beyond this, the few firearms they had were often in bad condition. General Micheltorena deemed them "unusable for us," adding

---

[1] GCY:38, 71 (quote), 174. After the rebel attack on Bacalar in the spring of 1851, government troops found arrows on the battle field (I. Gonzales to CGE, Bacalar, May 12, 1851, *SDN*, June 16, 1851, 1). For the lack of firearms, see also Lista de capitancillos indios, M. Micheltorena to MGM, Mérida, April 4, 1850, and M. Micheltorena to MGM, Mérida, May 18, 1850, both in AHM, XI/481.3/2914; Magistrate, Santa Helena, to Superintendent, April 12, 1850, R. 33, ABH:132; M. Micheltorena to MGM, Mérida, January 31, 1851, AHM, XI/481.3/3257; J. Orihuela to General en Jefe,

208 *Part V: Violence and the Kruso'b*

that only rebels could fire a gun "tied together with crude strings of henequen fiber" that lacked essential parts, compromising "the existence of the stupid warrior."[2] Of the 800 men who attacked Yaxcabá in 1854, mostly army deserters who had joined the rebels, forty at most carried guns, while the rest of them were armed with sticks, axes and machetes.[3] Only six of the twenty-five rebels who assaulted Chan Hunuku in 1859 were equipped with a firearm.[4] The insurgents were repeatedly short of powder and lead for bullets and thus forced to employ projectiles made of other materials such as "crudely worked copper from pan sheets," round pebble stones gathered on the coast, old nails or pieces of hardwood.[5]

During the reconquest of large parts of Yucatecan territory by government forces, rebel inferiority in terms of armament and military training was conspicuous, not least because time and again "more than nine or ten thousand Indians were attacked by numerically minor detachments of Yucatecan troops without losing more than four or five killed and a similar number injured, while the Indians left a good number [of dead]" behind.[6] Although the author of that quote, General Castillo, may have overstated the case somewhat, analysis of army attacks in the first half of 1850 confirms that in comparison with government forces, the rebels suffered much heavier casualties.[7] The report by Captain Ongay of an incursion into rebel territory in April 1850 is a telling example of the insurgents' military inferiority at that time. Although Ongay's detachment ran into an ambush, was fired on from all sides for an hour and obliged to fight from a seriously disadvantaged position, the encounter culminated in the attackers' dispersion, at least six rebels slain and an unknown number injured, while only two government soldiers were killed and three wounded.[8] In many instances, army sections attacked numerically superior rebel groups. In 1852, for example, 125 soldiers assaulted Chan Santa Cruz, which was defended by 300 rebel warriors, 200 of them armed.[9] At

---

Valladolid, August 30, 1855, *EO*, September 18, 1855, 1–3; Reed 1997a:4–5 and the evidence presented in the rest of this section.

[2] M. Micheltorena to MGM, Mérida, September 5, 1850, AHM, XI/481.3/2914.

[3] José D. Castro to Gobernador, Izamal, September 12, 1854, *EO*, September 22, 1854, 2.

[4] J.M. Iturralde to General en Jefe, Valladolid, August 9, 1859, *EC*, August 12, 1859, 1–2; L. Irigoyen to MGM, Mérida, August 17, 1859, AHM, XI/481.3/7504.

[5] M.F. Peraza to General en Jefe, Valladolid, April 3, 1855, *EO*, April 20, 1855, 1–3; M.F. Peraza to CGE, Valladolid, October 17, 1856, *GS*, October 22, 1856, 1–2; J.M. Echeverría, Izamal, November 8, 1856, AGEY, PE, G, box 65, in Rugeley 2001b:63.

[6] GCY:71.   [7] See Appendix 2.

[8] M. Micheltorena to MGM, Mérida, April 12, 1850, AHM, XI/481.3/2914.

[9] R. Díaz de la Vega to MGM, Mérida, August 18, 1852, AHM, XI/481.3/3300.

rancho Hacch in the same year, sixteen soldiers struck and dispersed ninety rebels.[10] In 1855, forty soldiers attacked and defeated between 200 and 300 rebels in Pacchén, who were about to assault Dzitas. While the rebels left twenty-eight dead, the army lost only one soldier through dispersion, rued one corporal slightly wounded by a bayonet and two corporals and five soldiers "mistreated by the savages' club."[11] More often than not, water shortage and disease turned out to be more dangerous to the soldiers than rebel assaults. When Colonel Pren marched back to his cantonment from an incursion on Macanché in May 1850, his soldiers were repeatedly ambushed but suffered no damage. One soldier died of thirst, however, as did thirty of those "gathered and seized," most of whom were women and small children.[12]

The mid-1850s saw a shift in the military situation when Mexican soldiers who had deserted from General Vega's expedition began to instruct the rebels and lead them in military operations. In the 1860s, the then 3,000 to 5,000 kruso'b fighters were better armed than before and, according to contemporary observers, also well trained.[13] They obtained muskets from Belize, which were later replaced by percussion rifles.[14]

While firearms were crucial to the kruso'b defense, the machete remained the rebels' most valuable weapon for several reasons. Machetes were cheaper than guns, available with relative ease and the kruso'b, like any peasant, knew very well how to use them. In addition, machetes were quite efficient in hand-to-hand combat and, as mentioned, in many instances were the only weapon apart from the bayonet that functioned in the rain. The rebels captured cannons on various occasions.

---

[10] R. Díaz de la Vega to MGM, Peto, July 5, 1852, AHM, XI/481.3/3300.
[11] J. Orihuela to General en Jefe, Valladolid, August 30, 1855, *EO*, September 18, 1855, 1–3.
[12] M. Micheltorena to MGM, Mérida, May 18, 1850, AHM, XI/481.3/2914.
[13] P. Regil y Peón to Emperador, Mérida, November 26, 1865, AGN, G, SI, vol. 44, file 69; GCY:102, 146, 148, 175. However, not all observers were convinced of the good quality of kruso'b firearms. At least one former prisoner held their arms to be "generally poor" in the early 1870s (Chan Santa Cruz Report, Mérida, June 2, 1882, TULAL, M-26, box 2, folder 14).
[14] N. Novelo to Gobernador, Peto, February 26, 1879, *RP*, March 3, 1879, 2–3; Reed 1997a:4. The kruso'b bought several hundred Enfield rifles in the mid-1870s. A visitor reported that they were still the customary firearm in 1888 (R.M. Mundy dispatch No. 7, January 7, 1876, CO 123/129, cited in Dumond 1997:326; Miller 1889:27). According to another source, rebels acquired 500 Remington rifles and 100 arrobas (ca. 2,500 pounds) of powder from a Mr. Tamps in Corozal in 1877. See V. Hernandez to Gobernador, Tekax, December 12, 1877, AGN, G, 2a 877 (11) 2 (51).

210   *Part V: Violence and the Kruso'b*

Difficult to handle, however, and ill-suited to the hit-and-run tactics that prevailed after the initial years of the war, they were mostly used at festivities as a form of firework.[15]

Kruso'b military equipment improved in the course of the war, but so did that of the Yucatecan and Mexican soldiers. Hence, kruso'b weaponry tended to be inferior in quality and smaller in number than that of government forces, particularly of regular army units. As will be seen in the next section, this had a strong impact on their military tactics.

TACTICS: THE BOON OF THE FOREST

As mentioned earlier, engagements between large combat units occurred only in the first phase of the war. Given their inferior firing power, the rebels subsequently avoided open battle and the Caste War was fought for the most part in raids and ambushes. The kruso'b pursued three major strategies in confrontation with Yucatecans. Their attacks on the frontier served to secure booty and finance the purchase of supplies in Belize rather than territorial conquest. Raids also sought to force the Yucatecans to withdraw their line of defense to the west and the north, expanding the buffer zone between government and rebel territories. Finally, permanent occupation of their settlements by government forces had to be prevented.

Whereas the rebels had simply been fighting for survival since 1849 and were primarily confined to defensive action, the mid-1850s saw them on the offensive. This was due to several factors. The kruso'b gained reinforcements from southern rebels who had rejected the peace treaty of 1853. The removal of Yucatecan troops to the west and northwest of the peninsula, where infighting among the political elites rose to new heights, weakened the defense of the frontier. The Yucatecan government was unable or unwilling to muster sufficient funds for a decisive offensive against the rebels. In addition, time abetted the kruso'b, they acquired military experience and armaments, and their defense positions gained security from natural vegetation growth. One Mexican general clearly recognized that the "extremely forested territory closed by lianes and branches" provided the kruso'b with their "real and positive force." Old paths were overgrown and the rebels "take good care not to clear them, leaving only a narrow path for transit, so close that no two men could pass

---

[15] C. Moreno Navarrete to Gobernador, Valladolid, March 6, 1875, *RP*, March 8, 1875, 1; Chan Santa Cruz Report, Mérida, June 2, 1882, TULAL, M-26, box 2, folder 14.

Kruso'b Violence against Outsiders

abreast."[16] When army squads penetrated into rebel territory, a rare occurrence after the mid-1850s, the kruso'b did nothing to defend their towns and villages. Instead they allowed the attackers to enter and withdrew into the forest to besiege the invaders.[17] Dense vegetation also helped rebels in other engagements. The kruso'b ambushed military units, shielding themselves where possible with walls of rough stone and retreating into the bush after firing their guns.[18] Thick underwood protected their flanks from enemy attack.[19] Striking where least expected, they would withdraw quickly and reappear to the rear of the persecutors, disturbing their operations or firing at them from positions where "nothing but the stones and trees of the forest could be seen."[20] While most kruso'b offensive military action consisted of raiding expeditions, some of the most exposed Yucatecan frontier towns and military posts were besieged. Rebels blocked roads and advanced a line of wooden and stone trenches, awaiting evacuation by the garrison in order to attack the soldiers in retreat.[21]

According to Paul Sullivan, rebel bands were large, well organized and well commanded. There was "no private initiative or independent action" against the Yucatecan frontier. A small group of leaders headed the assaults.[22] Kruso'b raiding parties varied in size from 50 to 2,000 men. In most cases, however, they consisted of several hundred participants. Units of more than 1,000 fighters attacked Yucatecan towns on several occasions in the 1860s.[23] Such groups often split up into smaller squads, attacking several targets and reuniting before returning to kruso'b

---

[16] Informe sobre el plan de campaña del Gral. Castillo, J.L. Uraya to Emperador, n.p., [November 27] 1865, AGN, G, SI, vol. 44, file 69.

[17] Chan Santa Cruz Report, Mérida, June 2, 1882, TULAL, M-26, box 2, folder 14.

[18] R. Díaz de la Vega to MGM, Peto, May 11, 1852, AHM, XI/481.3/3300; P.A. Gonzalez to Gobernador, Yokdzonot, December 14, 1854, *EO*, January 5, 1855, 1–3; S. Castillo to MGM, Mérida, September 15, 1865, AHM, XI/481.4/9987; Cámara Zavala 1928, part 11; Anonymous 1878:92.

[19] J. Salazar Ilarrequi to MGM, Ticul, June 22, 1865, AHM, XI/481.4/9976.

[20] Baqueiro 1990, 2:14. See also CGE to MG, Mérida, [February 9] 1855, AGEY, PE, G, box 100.

[21] GCY:38–39, 149; J. Salazar Ilarrequi to MGM, Ticul, June 22, 1865, AHM, XI/481.4/9976.

[22] Sullivan 1997a, I:4. See further evidence for the organization and coordination of the assaults on Yucatecan towns in J.M. Novelo to CGE, Peto, October 28, 1856, *GS*, October 31, 1856, 1.

[23] Sullivan 1997a, I:4; II:4–5; Anonymous 1878:89–90. For the figure 2,000 see, for example, N. Novelo to Gobernador, Peto, November 25, 1862, *EN*, November 28, 1862, 1–2; J. Salazar Ilarrequi to MGM, Ticul, June 22, 1865, AHM, XI/481.4/9976; A. Sandoval to General en Jefe, 7a division territorial, Fuerte de Carolina, December 6, 1865, AGEY,

Part V: Violence and the Kruso'b

territory.[24] Travelling to distant targets was safer in large groups; dispersion in small raiding parties made it easier to rob a greater number of settlements and eased the dilemma of provisioning. Combat units were comprised of men armed with guns and others merely equipped with a machete. The latter, known as *ligeros* (light ones), had to clear paths through the forest, build trenches, set up barricades, and carry ammunition, supplies and loot or wounded comrades. Several youths accompanied raiding parties as dispatch runners or spies.[25]

Raids on Yucatecan towns, villages and haciendas were scheduled to fit the agricultural cycle and the phases of the moon. Most assaults were realized after the planting period of kruso'b milpas (from early March to mid-June), when men had spare time to engage in forays or commercial activities. By night, the moonlight facilitated raiding party movements.[26] The duration of these expeditions varied depending on the distance they had to walk to reach their targets. Sullivan analyzed ten cases where sufficient information was available to calculate the distances and trajectories. The kruso'b spent between thirteen and forty-three days on their forays. Raiding parties covered distances from twenty to twenty-five kilometers a day, approximately a six-hour walk.[27] Yucatecan settlements were generally assaulted with surprise attacks at night or dawn.[28] Every so often the rebels took advantage of Yucatecan expectations by varying their tactics. Peto, for example, was assaulted at noon on February 11,

---

PE, M, box 242, file 5; Informe sobre el plan de campaña del Gral. Castillo, J.L. Uraya to Emperador, n.p., [November 27] 1865, AGN, G, SI, vol. 44, file 69.

[24] See, for example, F. Canton to Gobernador, Valladolid, January 18, 1873, *RP*, January 24, 1873, 1.

[25] Anonymous 1878:91–92; GCY:148; Informe sobre el plan de campaña del Gral. Castillo, J.L. Uraya to Emperador, n.p., [November 27] 1865, AGN, G, SI, vol. 44, file 69.

[26] J.M. Iturralde to Gobernador, Valladolid, April 12, 1859, *EC*, April 15, 1859, 1; F. Pren to Gobernador, Sotuta, February 14, 1862, *EN*, February 19, 1862, 2; V. Rios to Gobernador, Izamal, February 15, 1862, AGEY, PE, M, box 206, file 45; R. Novelo to Gobernador, Valladolid, June 24, 1869, *EP*, July 2, 1869, 1–2; Sullivan 1997a, II:4; Villalobos González 2006:108.

[27] Sullivan 1997a, II:4.

[28] Kaua at 5 a.m. (Baqueiro 1990, 4:89); Tekax in 1850 at 4 a.m. (M. Micheltorena to MGM, Mérida, November 8, 1850, AHM, XI/481.3/2914); Kancabdzonot at 10 p.m. on April 21, 1856; Yaxcabá at dawn and hacienda Xul at 3 a.m. on April 22, 1856; Tihosuco at 6 a.m. a day later (J.M. Esquivel to Gobernador, Sotuta, April 25, 1856, *GS*, April 30, 1856, 2–3; J.M. Novelo to Gobernador, Peto, April 24, 1856, *GS*, April 30, 1856, 2). Hacienda Kancabchén was raided at 9 p.m. (Declaracion de Mónica May, Sabino Piña, Peto, August 1, 1874, AGEY, PE, C, box 310, file 86); Chan-Huku was assaulted at 10 p.m. (L. Irigoyen to MGM, Mérida, August 17, 1859, AHM, XI/481.3/7504; Anonymous 1878:91).

Kruso'b Violence against Outsiders

1855, "when it was least expected."[29] Kruso'b hit-and-run tactics made the defense of settlements along the front line, which stretched fifty leagues (about 200 kilometers), almost impossible. General Castillo complained:

Indian raids are fast as lightning. They appear unperceived from the vast unpopulated terrain covered by forest and attack the defenseless or weakly protected locality and when one attempts to help and beat them, they have already disappeared after committing iniquities.[30]

While many raids were primarily motivated by the quest for loot, other assaults on haciendas, ranches and even small hamlets along the frontier were aimed at cutting off larger Yucatecan settlements such as Peto or Valladolid from supply lines. The more advanced towns and cantonments were clearly among the most sought after targets. Tihosuco in the far southeast, for example, suffered at least twelve assaults (1847, besieged from December 1848 to April 1849, 1851, 1853, July and October 1854, April 1856, besieged from October to November of the same year, 1857, 1861, 1865, besieged from August to September 1866). The plan was to terrorize the inhabitants of smaller settlements and drive them away.[31] The kruso'b murdered people of all ages and both sexes indiscriminately, burned houses and destroyed everything they could not take with them.[32] Tihosuco, Ichmul, Chikindzonot, Saban, Sacalaca, Dzonotchel, Tahdzibichén, Tixcacaltuyú, Yaxcabá and Santa María, for example, sustained severe inroads and destruction in late 1853.[33] Frightened by the attacks, peasants dreaded harvesting the mature corn in outlying fields. Yucatecan officials feared that small settlements in the area, seen as "the vanguard of the other villages in the interior" could be abandoned as a result of starvation.[34] Assaults on Tunkas and its surroundings in September 1861 are another case in point. The town's inhabitants were abducted and their houses burned. In the aftermath, most of the outlying

[29] G. Ruiz to SGG, Tekax, February 18, 1855, AGEY, PE, G, box 101.
[30] S. Castillo to MGM, Mérida, July 4, 1865, AHM, XI/481.4/9987; see also J.A. Cepeda Peraza to Gobernador, Tekax, December 23, 1870, *RP*, December 26, 1870, 1.
[31] See, for example, L. Espinosa to Gobernador, Tekax, July 3, 1867, *RP*, July 12, 1867, 2; J. Vasquez to Gobernador, Peto, January 16, 1872, AGEY, PE, CO, box 297, file 6; N. Novelo to Gobernador, Peto, April 19, 1879, AGEY, PE, JP Peto, box 207bis.
[32] See, for example, the raids on Peto and its surroundings in 1855 (G. Ruiz to SGG, Tekax, February 18, 1855, AGEY, PE, G, box 101) and on the area around Yaxcabá and Kancabdzonot in 1856 (J.M. Esquivel to Gobernador, Sotuta, April 25, 1856, *GS*, April 30, 1856, 2–3).
[33] Baqueiro 1990, 4:199–200; Ancona 1879/80, 4:350.
[34] G. Ruiz to SGG, Tekax, February 18, 1855, AGEY, PE, G, box 101.

hamlets and haciendas remained deserted.[35] Eleven months later the kruso'b slew all of the prisoners taken in the farms around Dzitas at the start of their retreat.[36] Heavy attacks also led to the temporary or permanent abandonment of several frontier settlements in 1865 and 1866.[37] In 1867, the inhabitants of Tixmeuac complained that with the exception of Peto, Tekax, and Ticul, "everything else is an immense desert because the barbarians destroyed numerous towns, ranches and haciendas, to the extent that even places only a few leagues from the capital have been converted into enemy country."[38] To counteract and if possible reverse the attrition of frontier settlements, the government went so far as to decree that citizens who had abandoned their homes and interests on the southern and eastern frontier and moved to other places without the necessary legal requirements were to return to their former abode.[39]

In addition to Yucatecan settlements, kruso'b repeatedly raided pacífico villages. As mentioned above, pacíficos were the decided enemies of the kruso'b, who regarded them as traitors. In addition, strategic considerations influenced the course of kruso'b advances. The Icaiché, for example, threatened the kruso'b southern flank. Beyond this, they disputed kruso'b control of the area adjacent to the Río Hondo, which was coveted as a source of land rent for agriculture and wood-cutting, and as a strategically important transit area for arms and other supplies.[40] The kruso'b also terrorized other pacífico groups to frighten them off or compel them to change sides. In Chanchumpich, for instance, they burned all the houses with the exception of two churches and killed all the animals, which they "cut to pieces and littered all over the village."[41] Occasionally, people in no-man's-land were forced to resettle in rebel territory by the use of threats and by burning their huts.[42] This might have been an attempt to create a "fire-free zone" that would encumber the advance of government forces by depriving them of the supply of foodstuffs they usually took from scattered hamlets on their way to rebel strongholds. In their zone of influence, the kruso'b practiced "strategic

---

[35] GCY:117–118.

[36] S. Pérez Virgilio to Gobernador, Espita, August 29, 1862, *EN*, September 9, 1862, 1.

[37] S. Castillo to MGM, Mérida, July 4, 1865, AHM, XI/481.4/9987; Editorial, *RP*, September 4, 1867, 3–4.

[38] J.A. Hernández y otros to Gobernador, Tixmeuac, August 26, 1867, *RP*, August 28, 1867, 1.

[39] Circular, Agustin O'Horan, Mérida, August 27, 1867, *RP*, August 28, 1867, 1.

[40] Cal 1983:237; Sweeney 2006: 90–95, 109, 112–114, 116, 122–124, 150–151.

[41] J.L. Santini to Gobernador, Noh-Ayin, July 26, 1867, *RP*, August 9, 1867, 2–3.

[42] M. Micheltorena to MGM, Mérida, May 18, 1850, AHM, XI/481.3/2914.

Kruso'b Violence against Outsiders

resettlement" in at least one case. A group of pacíficos del sur that had defected to the rebels was sent with an escort to take up residence at Polyuc in 1867, probably to safeguard the path to Bacalar.[43]

The guerilla war the kruso'b forced on their enemies and the atrocities they committed also undermined the morale of government forces. The soldiers suffered from the unpredictability of confronting a frequently invisible enemy hidden in the dense forest, an aspect that was intensified by surprise kruso'b attacks and hit-and-run tactics. This put extreme pressure on their moral strength. More often than not their grit yielded to terror once they presumed themselves to be in enemy territory "because of the forest, where the savage lurks and, unseen, waylays our soldiers to deliver their deadly blow at an advantageous moment" as one contemporary observer recognized.[44] To further demoralize their enemies, the rebels would shout at the soldiers and, as Nelson Reed puts it, throw "the heads of their comrades at their feet."[45] Understandably, many of the soldiers were not equipped with the nerves of steel this type of warfare required. Mexican commanders in particular criticized the poor fighting spirit of Yucatecan troops. The imperial commissary, for example, rated a single soldier from central Mexico "worth a thousand Yucatecans," who only had to see "just one Indian to make them run."[46] In the same vein, the Mexican imperialist General Severo del Castillo asserted the Yucatecan troops' "true terror" of the kruso'b, which drove them to abandon their chiefs and officers when it came to combat and made it impossible to hold them back.[47] He added in other correspondence that Yucatecan soldiers were "of such a scared nature that they even fail to resist the Indians in their own terrain." In his view, Yucatecans were terrorized to such a degree that when attacked by a "savage," armed soldiers bowed their heads and accepted the machete blow without any attempt to defend themselves. "Almost all dispersed soldiers are slaughtered by Indians in this sad way without offering the slightest resistance to the enemy, dominated by the idea of their own inferiority and futility of defense."[48]

---

[43] F. Medina to Gobernador, Ticul, August 2, 1867, *RP*, August 9, 1867, 1.

[44] J.M. Gutierrez to Gobernador, Espita, July 22, 1867, *RP*, August 7, 1867, 1.

[45] Unfortunately, Reed (1997a:6) does not mention a source for this statement. On shouting, see GCY:148, for example.

[46] S. Ilarregui to J. de Dios Peza, Mérida, June 24, 1865, CAIHDY, M, XLVII.1864/21.

[47] Informe, S. Castillo, F. Navarrete to MGG, Mérida, March 23, 1866, AGEY, PE, M, box 249, file 62; see also P. Regil y Peón to Emperador, Mérida, November 10, 1865, AGN, G, SI, vol. 46, file 14.

[48] GCY:149.

216 Part V: Violence and the Kruso'b

While complaints about the Yucatecans' lack of morale were exaggerated and reflected the viewpoint of battle-tested professional soldiers such as General Castillo, they probably contain a kernel of truth. As shown in the Chapter 10, National Guard units, which built the bulk of the forces that fought against the kruso'b, consisted of drafted men, many of whom lacked military training and combat experience.[49] As part-time soldiers they were filled with terror when confronting the enemy. In cases where the relief system worked, replacing draftees after a comparatively short term of active service simply magnified the problem. The jefe político of Tekax, at least, traced the "lack of discipline" to the system that replaced soldiers with new recruits when the former were still "getting to know how to grasp a gun," making military formation impracticable. Thus, the units often disbanded "at the first shot" and the militia officers did no better.[50] The kruso'b, in contrast, accumulated combat experience so that government forces were faced with seasoned warriors after the first years of the conflict.

THE VICTIMS

Cross cultural studies show a wide variation of ways in which societies deal with their foes; some kill them all, some spare only women and children, others spare men, at times even enemy warriors. As Keith Otterbein argues, prisoners could be taken for slave labor or, in the case of females, as wives. Children could be appropriated as slaves but also as future group members. Killing outside of battle was motivated by revenge or to instill fear in the enemy. Societies that use terror as their principal means of confronting external enemies and upholding internal order are the most likely to kill enemy combatants and non-combatants indiscriminately. These patterns are linked to the respective society's political and economic organization – the ability to use additional labor profitably, for example – as well as to their social structure and the presence of such traits as feuding or polygyny.[51] Studies like Otterbein's provide valuable ideas on the possible factors that lead to killing or sparing enemies and some clues to understanding kruso'b behavior. They cannot account for specific cases, however, or behavioral changes through time. The following

---

[49] S. Castillo to MGM, Mérida, July 4, 1865, AHM, XI/481.4/9987.
[50] M. Galera to Gobernador, Tekax, January 18, 1870, *RP*, January 21, 1870, 1–2.
[51] Otterbein 2000.

Kruso'b Violence against Outsiders 217

elucidates how kruso'b treatment of the enemy differed from one case to another and changed in the course of the war.

As mentioned earlier, kruso'b assaulted settlements in Yucatán ranging from small, entirely Indian hamlets to haciendas, villages and larger towns, such as Peto or Tekax. Obvious targets were army soldiers, National Guard members, those involved in the self-defense of settlements, and Indians in positions of authority.[52] The kruso'b killed or captured Indians, vecinos, men and women, children and the elderly indiscriminately.[53] The offensive against Peto and its surroundings in 1855 is a case in point. The kruso'b slew more than sixty people of both sexes and all age groups, took numerous prisoners and burned several villages and hamlets.[54] Women often represented the majority of the slain or abducted victims, notably in the 1850s, when the rebels themselves suffered heavy losses as a result of army thrusts on their strongholds. During the assault on Kancabdzonot on April 21, 1856, for example, eighty-two people were killed, among them sixty-five women. Twenty-six people were put to death in Yaxcabá the next day: one soldier, four boys and old men and twenty-one women.[55]

Kruso'b behavior during and after raids on Yucatecan or pacífico settlements did not follow a uniform pattern. While members of a certain age, gender or administrative category were slain in some cases, they were spared in others. Several examples illustrate the complexity of their behavior and the unpredictability of killing or sparing people without obvious reason, at least none that appear in the sources. At 10 p.m. on August 5, 1859, twenty-five rebels invaded rancho Chan Hunuku, one and a half leagues to the northeast of Valladolid, where they killed three Indians and two vecinas, and seriously injured two youths. The attackers abducted five women, three small children, and two criados. One day later the kruso'b raided hacienda Kampepén, a quarter of a league southeast of Valladolid, killing an Indian man and a woman, and kidnapping three other women and two small children.[56] At other times, the kruso'b evinced signs of humanity. After raiding Kantunilkin on July 5, 1872, one resident was left behind unharmed and his wife was allowed to stay and take care of him because he suffered from a bad leg.

---

[52] See, for example, Rugeley 2009:173.   [53] For numbers, see Chapter 20.

[54] G. Ruiz to Gobernador, Tekax, February 14, 1855, AGEY, PE, G, box 101; Relacion de las personas que machetearon los indios sublevados ..., February 13, 1855, AGEY, PE, G, box 120, exp. 14.

[55] J.M. Esquivel to Gobernador, Sotuta, April 25, 1856, GS, April 30, 1856, 2–3.

[56] L. Irigoyen to MGM, Mérida, August 17, 1859, AHM, XI/481.3/7504.

The couple's two sons, in contrast, were forced to accompany the rebels.[57] The kruso'b probably intended to integrate the youths into their ranks and were anxious not to arouse their anger by killing their parents. On the other hand, this might not have been the reason, since "useless" inhabitants of raided settlements were also spared, as in the case of an elderly couple, a lame man and a certain Florentino Calderón who suffered tremors during the raid on rancho Ayin in 1875.[58] Kruso'b leaders occasionally attempted to prevent outrage. When Pisté was assaulted on July 28, 1862, for example, Bonifacio Novelo is reported to have forbidden "any disorder and offense to anyone." It was only when Novelo was absent that seven people of different sexes and ages were slain.[59] Even leaders like Crescencio Poot, who was renowned among the Yucatecans for his particular brand of bloodthirstiness, showed mercy every now and then. During the raid on rancho Xkuil on December 31, 1862, he let two Indian women and their two children go and returned their belongings. When kruso'b assaulted Lochhá on January 3, 1863, they killed several people, took numerous prisoners and captured livestock and goods worth 10,000 pesos. The lives of six Yucatecan traders from Tekax, however, were spared.[60]

In many cases we simply lack the relevant information to deduce the motivation for specific acts of violence, the killing of some and the sparing of others. There are, on the other hand, tendencies that suggest possible underlying causes. Demographic and economic factors can, to a certain extent at least, explain this patterning and the fate of the slain and captives concerned.

The Capture of Prisoners

Not unlike government forces, the kruso'b had three options once they seized their enemies – release them immediately after combat, kill them on the spot or take them prisoner. Freeing captives seen as adversaries was

---

[57] Itinerario de la marcha de las tropas sobre los indios bárbaros, D. Peniche, pueblo de Dolores, Isla Mujeres, August 19, 1872, *RP*, August 26 and 28, 1872, 1–2.

[58] Letters from R.A. Perez to Gobernador, Peto, October 12 and 16, 1875, *RP*, October 15, 1875, 1 and October 20, 1875, 1.

[59] L. Irigoyen to MGM, Mérida, August 7, 1862, AHM, XI/481.4/8772; see also Baqueiro [1887] 1989:17, 21 and, for Bacalar in 1858, Buhler 1975:7.

[60] C. Montes de Oca to Gobernador, Tekax, January 4, 1863, R. Lopez to General en Jefe, Peto, January 4, 1863 and C. Montes de Oca to Gobernador, Tekax, January 7, 1863, all in *EN*, January 9, 1863, 1; M. Barbosa to Gobernador de Campeche, Mesapich, January 4, 1863, *EP*, January 20, 1863, 1.

Kruso'b Violence against Outsiders

problematic, since they could return to combat or support the enemy economically or emotionally, for example, as wives and family members. Taking prisoners also posed a dilemma. They had to be guarded, which reduced the number of warriors available for combat, and they hindered retreat, which could be awkward if government forces were in pursuit of rebel squads. Captives taken to kruso'b strongholds had to be fed or organized in such a way that they produced their own food. From this sinister vantage point, giving no quarter was often the best option. Thus, as mentioned earlier, the kruso'b sometimes slaughtered soldiers injured in combat and killed the inhabitants of raided settlements on the spot or dispersed them.[61] In other instances, however, they took captives. While some were murdered on retreat to or arrival in the rebel area, others remained rebel captives for extended periods. A last group of prisoners was integrated into the kruso'b population after some time.

It seemed logical to take at least some captives into rebel territory and refrain from killing all of the enemies on the spot when forays were successful and large amounts of loot (money, goods and livestock) or injured kruso'b had to be transported on retreat from raiding expeditions.[62] This meant that fewer ligeros were required for raids and a smaller number of people shared the booty. For several reasons, however, many captured Yucatecans never made it to rebel strongholds. If they failed to keep pace on the brisk hikes back to rebel territory, if they were too weak to carry loot and the wounded or hampered the retreat in any other way, they were slain.[63] A particularly cruel example is the Tunkas raid on September 7, 1861. From the outskirts of the town, the kruso'b "began to kill the old and the feeble, who could not make their way and who in the twelve-day passage from Tunkas to Santa Cruz suffered the effects of hunger, thirst and inclement weather. Many of those who fainted on the way were exterminated." Little more than half the prisoners, mostly men, made it to Chan Santa Cruz. The rebels had seized rich loot, which the male captives were obliged to carry.[64] When the raiding

---

[61] Anonymous 1878:92; Aldherre and Mendiolea 1869:79.

[62] R. Díaz de la Vega to MGM, Mérida, September 24, 1852, AHM, XI/481.3/3300; Noticias que emite el C. Anastasio Durán ..., *LRP*, September 5, 1862, 1–3; J.M. Díaz to Gobernador, Sotuta, December 1, 1871, *RP*, December 6, 1871, 1; Declaración de José Estevan Cen, Mérida, April 11, 1879, AGEY, PE, CLM, box 207bis.

[63] See, for example, E. Rosado to Gobernador, Peto, May 17, 1853, AGEY, PE, G, box 94; M. Barbachano: Sobre la última correria de los bárbaros, *EC*, September 11, 1861, 3–4; F. Canton to Gobernador, Valladolid, January 18, 1873, *RP*, January 24, 1873, 1; Crown Surveyor to Superintendent, July 6, 1860, R. 71, ABH:230.

[64] Noticias que emite el C. Anastasio Durán ..., *LRP*, September 5, 1862, 2.

party that assaulted Xuxub in 1875 learned that their leader, Bernardino Cen, had been killed by Yucatecans who came to rescue the plantation and that they themselves might be persecuted by the army, they slew some of their prisoners in flight.[65]

The arrival in kruso'b territory was another critical moment for captives. No longer needed as porters, many of them were instantly slain. During assaults on Sacalaca, Sabán, Uaymex, Tituc, Polyuc and other places, for example, the kruso'b took numerous prisoners and seized "immense booty" in the final months of 1853. They killed almost all captives on their way to Chan Santa Cruz or upon arrival. A few of the abducted who had relatives among the rebels were spared.[66] The return of raiding bands to Chan Santa Cruz was an occasion for feasting. Again, this could culminate in the death of the captives, as an anonymous account suggests:

When they return with their prisoners and their booty, they invariably go to Chan Santa Cruz and there deposit their prisoners and spoils, which are distributed proportionally, leaving a part, which they sell in Belize, by which method they keep their war chest stocked. They withdraw to rest and a few days later get together once more to celebrate their victory with a religious festival, a bullfight, drunken sprees, and as a direct consequence, the slaughter by machete blows of some of the unfortunate lovers of civilization who had the bad luck of falling into their hands.[67]

Captives not considered "useful" were not always killed on arrival at Chan Santa Cruz but slain every now and then on order of the cross.[68]

Changing Patterns: Demography and Exploitation

While rebels may have had comprehensible – if inhumane – reasons to kill those they encountered in Yucatecan settlements on the spot or to slay them after exploiting the strongest as porters, why were some men kept alive and what can account for the capture of women and children? In fact,

---

[65] B.M. Montilla to Gobernador, Puntachén, October 15, 1875, *RP*, October 20, 1875, 1; Causa contra Encarnacion Cahum ..., Mérida, May 29, 1876, *RP*, June 2, 1876, 1. Cen died from a heavy machete or saber blow on the head, probably from behind, according to the forensic examination of his skull by Tiesler (2001).

[66] P.A. Gonzalez to Gobernador, Yokdzonot, December 12, 1854, *EO*, January 2, 1855, 1–2; GCY:94.

[67] Anonymous 1878:92.

[68] Ch. Leas: "Belize or British Honduras," 1863, TULAL, MIC 736, reel 2; GCY:119, 127; Buhler 1975:8; Dumond 1997:224.

Kruso'b Violence against Outsiders

kruso'b systematically abducted people of both sexes and different ages in particular periods. While on the offensive during the initial months of the war, they frequently took prisoners. Jacinto Pat had ordered that no one be killed. Occasionally, captives were forced to work in cornfields to feed the insurgents.[69] Political reasons were probably decisive for this policy, too, since the rebels aimed at conquering the entire peninsula. Alienating the population with indiscriminate massacres would have been unwise.

The situation changed, however, when the rebels were almost constantly on the defensive, driven more and more to the so-called *despoblado* (wilderness) in the east of the peninsula from mid-1848 to the early 1850s. According to General Castillo, the great mass of insurgents "roamed in the thick forests from Bacalar to the Bahía de la Asención, unable to establish themselves anywhere." Their temporary camps consisted of nothing more than tents or huts and had to be relocated time and again to escape pursuers.[70] Under these circumstances, holding a larger number of captives was nigh to impossible. They would have posed an obstacle in the case of an attack by government forces and constituted unnecessary food rivals. After all, the rebels themselves were often starving.[71] Significant gender differences did, however, exist. During their raids on ranchos along the southern frontier in the early 1850s, rebels killed "a multitude of unfortunate workers and their small children, taking all of the women prisoner."[72] Infants would not have endured the extreme hardships of life in temporary rebel settlements. Male captives represented a liability and a possible danger rather than a benefit. Women, on the other hand, were coveted as potential spouses to satisfy the sexual needs of male insurgents and guarantee the physical reproduction of rebel society, which was jeopardized by high mortality rates due to epidemics and all manner of deprivation. In addition, female labor was highly welcome when it came to preparing food, since this was an arduous task. Grinding corn and kneading *masa* (dough) was particularly time-consuming. The exploitation of female prisoners was described by a contemporary in the 1860s as follows: "They work without cease; prepare food, not only for the master of the house but for all the Indian servants, make clothes, water the fields, look after the pens, clean the hens and the pigs, and ultimately perform the hardest chores."[73]

---

[69] J. Cadenas to General en Gefe, Campeche, July 22, 1848, AGEY, PE, G, box 68; see also Declaracion de Pablo Encalada, Campeche (part 1), August 12, 1867, *EP*, September 24, 1867, 1.

[70] GCY:123; see also pp. 101–102.   [71] See, for example, Cámara Zavala 1928, part 5.

[72] Cámara Zavala 1928, part 11.   [73] Aldherre and Mendiolea 1869:75.

Part V: Violence and the Kruso'b

A marked shift had become apparent in the mid-1850s with regard to male captives when Yucatecan offensive actions abated and the kruso'b gradually began to establish more formal and more permanent settlements. Besides Chan Santa Cruz, which became the "capital of the insurgents," Pachmul, Xunantunich and countless hamlets emerged.[74] Chan Santa Cruz began to take on the appearance of a typical Yucatecan town. It was described in late 1854 as a settlement of "numerous private houses," several barracks and a wooden church about twenty-five meters in length and ten meters wide, "built of excellent wood and thatched with chosen huano [palm leaves]."[75] Despite its repeated destruction by government forces, it was rebuilt time and again. The most important buildings had been erected since 1858 in stone rather than the wood of older constructions (see Figure 17.1). In 1860, Pedro Acereto expressed his admiration for the robust "beautiful church under completion, two handsome houses with portals inside and outside, twenty-nine houses made of rubble and much straw," seven open wells and "very well delineated streets."[76] Chan Santa Cruz was described in the late 1860s as "a solid and neat [formal y arreglada] town with shops, liquor distilleries, all sorts of workshops and several houses in lime and stone."[77] This did not happen out of the blue. Male captives now constituted a welcome labor force for public works and the growth of commercially based agricultural products on private farms for the personal enrichment of the rebel leaders who owned them. Explicit orders were given to bring prisoners back alive to Chan Santa Cruz to conduct public works, that is, to clear forests, collect wild honey, break stones, sweep streets, construct buildings or work in artisan shops.[78] They were then distributed to rebel leaders to work on their private ranches as their personal servants.[79]

[74] GCY:102, 123
[75] P.A. Gonzalez to Gobernador, Yokdzonot, December 12, 1854, *EO*, January 2, 1855, 1–2.
[76] P. Acereto to Gobernador, Chan Santa Cruz, January 23, 1860, *EC*, February 3, 1860, 3; see also GCY:127.
[77] F. Gil to Gobernador, Tekax, May 20, 1868, *RP*, May 20, 1868, 1; see also Declaraciones de indígenas sospechosos . . ., May 1, 1866, AGEY, PE, J, box 252, file 6; R. Novelo to Gobernador, Valladolid, June 24, 1869, *EP*, July 2, 1869, 1–2.
[78] Informes proporcionados por los indios de Oxuas Akal, Peto, March 11, 1868, AGEY, PE, M, box 273, file 15; J.A. Cepeda to Gobernador, Tekax, March 11, 1868, RP, March 16, 1868, 1; N. Novelo, to Gobernador, Tekax, May 17, 1868, *EP*, May 29, 1868, 4; F. Gil to Gobernador, Tekax, May 20, 1868, *RP*, May 20, 1868, 1; N. Novelo to Gobernador, Tekax, December 12, 1869, *RP*, December 17, 1869, 1; GCY:126.
[79] F. Pren to Gobernador, Sotuta, February 14, 1862, *EN*, February 19, 1862, 2; L. Espinosa to Gobernador, Tekax, August 24, 1862, *EN*, August 27, 1862, 1–2; Aldherre and Mendiolea 1869:75–76.

FIGURE 17.1 Church in Chan Santa Cruz, 1901. By permission of the Secretaría de la Cultura y las Artes del Estado de Yucatán, Biblioteca Yucatanense, Fondo Audiovisual.

Hence, Yucatecans repeatedly observed a shift in the rebel treatment of captives. When kruso'b raided Ekpedz on June 22, 1860, for example, they abducted all of the families. More than 250 people were taken prisoner in Tunkas in September 1861, 83 in Pisté on July 28, 1862, and "countless families" during assaults on various settlements in autumn of that year.[80] General Castillo remarked that kruso'b expeditions now had the intention of taking captives, "killing only those who were unable to follow them on their march."[81] Table 17.1 shows the duration of captive employment in public works before entering into the private service of kruso'b leaders, where they generally stayed until they managed to escape.

As Table 17.1 shows, the amount of time captives were occupied in public works decreased, while the amount spent in personal service on the leaders' farms increased. This may be a reflection of the comparative

---

[80] J.A. Esquivel to Gobernador, Sotuta, June 24, 1861, EC, July 1, 1861, 2; Noticias que emite el C. Anastasio Durán ..., LRP, September 5, 1862, 1–3; GCY:117–118; L. Irigoyen to MGM, Mérida, August 7, 1862, AHM, XI/481.4/8772; D. Peniche to Gobernador, Espita, November 1, 1862, EN, November 5, 1862, 1.

[81] GCY:119; see also La Redaccion: Indios Rebeldes, EN, January 12, 1863, 4.

224 Part V: Violence and the Kruso'b

TABLE 17.1 *Captive employment*

Year	Name	Public works (duration)	Personal service (ranch, owner)	Source
1861–2	Anastasio Durán and other captives from Tunkas	5 months	ranches of various kruso'b leaders	Noticias que emite el C. Anastasio Durán..., *LRP*, September 5, 1862, 1–3
1867–8	José Can	11 months	–	N. Novelo to Gobernador, Tekax, May 17, 1868, *EP*, May 29, 1868, 4
1869–9	Luciano Cahum	n.d.	San Isidro (C. Poot)	N. Novelo to Gobernador, Peto, February 26, 1879, *RP*, March 3, 1879, 2–3.
1871	Bernardino Cauich	3 months	n.p. (C. Poot)	J.M. Díaz to Gobernador, Sotuta, December 1,1871, *RP*, December 6, 1871, 1
1873	Vicente Uc, Leandro Camal, Gregorio Dzul, Dionisio Dzul	3 weeks	supposed to work on hacienda Chunllá (C. Poot); fled on the way	E. Esquivel to General en Jefe, Sotuta, February 11, 1873, *RP*, February 14, 1873, 1
1873	Andres May, Lazaro Uc, Pedro Ku	–	ranches of various kruso'b leaders	Declaration of Andres May, Lazaro Uc and Pedro Ku in C. Moreno Navarrete to Gobernador, Valladolid, March 4, 1873, AGEY, PE, M, box 302, file 41
1873	Juan Nah, Cayetana Un	2 weeks	n.p. (V. Vitorín)	E. Esquivel to Comandante Militar del Estado, Sotuta, April 4, 1873, *RP*, April 7, 1873, 1

(continued)

Kruso'b Violence against Outsiders

TABLE 17.1 *(continued)*

Year	Name	Public works (duration)	Personal service (ranch, owner)	Source
1875	Nazario Cutis and 29 others	–	San Pedro (B. Cen)	F. Piña to Gobernador, Sotuta, February 19, 1875, AGEY, PE, M, box 314, file 94
1875	Marcus Balam	–	Derepente (B. Cen)	C. Moreno Navarrete, to Gobernador, Valladolid, March 6, 1875, *RP*, March 8, 1875, 1
1875	Santos Escamilla	3 weeks	San Felipe (C. Poot)	S. Piña to Gobernador, Peto, March 11, 1876, *RP*, March 17, 1876, 1
1879	Apolinario Gorocia	2 weeks	Tzol Yaxché (Don Justo)	N. Novelo to Gobernador, Peto, May 13, 1879, *RP*, May 13, 1879, 1
1879	José Cen	2 weeks	Sahcabchén (V. Vitorín)	Declaración de José Estevan Cen, Mérida, April 11, 1879, AGEY, PE, CLM, box 207bis
late 1870s -1888	José M. Ay	–	Chunyah, San Isidro and Nohcah (C. Poot)	J.M. Iturralde to Gobernador, Valladolid, March 23, 1888, *RP*, April 6, 1888, 3

decline of Chan Santa Cruz as a town and the growing significance of agricultural production on ranches owned by rebel leaders. While captives taken in Tunkas in 1861 had to work in a quarry for several months to garner construction material for Chan Santa Cruz prior to being distributed to the chiefs, prisoners in the 1870s were assigned to personal service straightaway or two or three weeks after their arrival in the town.[82]

---

[82] Sullivan (1997a, I:6; 2004:107, 229–230) drew attention to the increase in captives and their importance as workers for kruso'b leaders.

FIGURE 17.2 Northeastern corner of the central plaza in Chan Santa Cruz, 1901. By permission of the Secretaría de la Cultura y las Artes del Estado de Yucatán, Biblioteca Yucatanense, Fondo Audiovisual.

The capture of children was also quite common following the consolidation of rebel society.[83] There are several possible reasons for this. Kruso'b raised some of the captive children as members of the group to compensate for losses suffered as a result of war, famine or disease.[84] Pablo Encalada's son, for example, was separated from his father when both were caught by rebels in the early months of the Caste War. He grew up as a kruso'b. After many years of separation, he attempted to convince his father, now a pacífico leader, to enter into an alliance with the kruso'b.[85] As mentioned earlier, other children were sold as criados to tradesmen in Belize.[86]

The Fate of Captives among the Kruso'b

Prisoners with special skills such as a particular craft, the ability to play an instrument or to read and write had the best chance of being spared by the

---

[83] See, for example, Declaracion de Mónica May, Sabino Piña, Peto, August 1, 1874, AGEY, PE, C, box 310, file 86.

[84] See also Gann 1918:32–33.

[85] Declaracion de Pablo Encalada, Campeche, August 12, 1867, *EP*, September 24 (part 1) and 27 (part 2) 1867, 1.

[86] A. Espinosa to Gobernador, Valladolid, February 28, 1871, *RP*, March 3, 1871, 1.

Kruso'b Violence against Outsiders

kruso'b and surviving captivity.[87] José María Matos, captured in Tiholop in 1853, for example, was a blacksmith and thus of vital importance to the rebels as a maker of arms. This was his salvation and allowed him to survive.[88] José Loesa, a Yucatecan who had fled to Belize from the Caste War, and his companions fell into captivity as they made their way from Bolonchén to X-Noh Akal to buy hogs on December 8, 1860. Loesa managed to escape initially, wandering in the bush for five days before finally being recaptured by the rebels. During their eight-day march to Chan Santa Cruz, the kruso'b took 360 other prisoners. According to Loesa, they killed all of the male and female captives when they reached (Chan Cah) Derepente, Bernardino Cen's farm, eight leagues away from Santa Cruz. Only he and the fifty children were spared. Loesa's knowledge of writing had possibly saved his life and he became Venancio Puc's servant.[89]

The fate of prisoners who survived among the kruso'b for longer periods was quite grim, notably during the early months of captivity. According to Yucatecan sources and accounts by captives who managed to escape, they were treated for the most part with great cruelty.[90] Men captured in Tunkas in 1861 received fifty lashes the day after their arrival at Chan Santa Cruz before being seconded to break stones for the great town plaza (see Figure 17.2). This continued for eight days. As mentioned earlier, female captives were distributed as domestics, although it is not clear in whose households they worked. Prisoners seem to have moved quite freely around the settlement, since they were obliged to beg for food in the streets in their spare time. One description of Chan Santa Cruz suggests that at least some female captives lived in huts surrounded by

---

[87] F. Seymour to C.H. Darling, Belize, March 13, 1858, TNA, CO, 123/96; J.M. Iturralde to Gobernador, Valladolid, April 12, 1859, EC, April 15, 1859, 1; F. Pren to Gobernador, Sotuta, February 14, 1862, EN, February 19, 1862, 2; Aldherre and Mendiolea 1869:75; Declaracion de Mónica May, Sabino Piña, Peto, August 1, 1874, AGEY, PE, C, box 310, file 86.

[88] P.A. Gonzalez to Gobernador, Yokdzonot, December 12, 1854, EO, January 2, 1855, 1–2.

[89] J. de los Angeles Loesa, Archives of Belize, Record 74, August 26, 1861, 174–175, in Rugeley 2001b:79–80. See La guerra de casta, RP, March 29, 1871, 2–3 for Cen as the owner of Chan Cah De Repente.

[90] See, for example, GCY:126; L. Espinosa to Gobernador, Tekax, August 24, 1862, EN, August 27, 1862, 1–2; Correspondencia, Pablo Bolio, Izamal, RM, May 2, 1873, 3. In early 1848, the cacique of Sabán, Felipe Cahuich, complained that he had been arrested during the uprising in his town and conducted to the rebel stronghold in Tihosuco, where he was "cruelly mauled" (Gobernador to Comandante en Gefe, división en operaciones, Maxcanú, January 7, 1848, AGEY, PE, G, box 67).

228   *Part V: Violence and the Kruso'b*

a high wall.[91] But this was not a permanent abode since, similar to their male peers, they were distributed to prominent rebels to work on their farms.

Captive women were not only held as domestics in kruso'b households. Some were wedded to rebel leaders. Josefa Rodríguez Solís, abducted from Tunkas, was married to "one of the most prominent chiefs" of Chan Santa Cruz.[92] Crescencio Poot took Pastora Rean as his wife, another captive from the said town. Three sons resulted from this union.[93] Other abducted women became the "concubine" or consort of kruso'b men.[94] Male captives were sometimes forced to marry local women and establish social relations that would prevent them from fleeing. José María Gonzales was caught by kruso'b during an army thrust on Chan Santa Cruz, probably in 1860. He remained a prisoner for two years and was subsequently obliged to marry Manuela Chac. Later he served as a kruso'b spy in the pacífico area.[95] The rebel strategy of holding captives was not always successful, as illustrated by the case of Luciano Cahum, a kruso'b prisoner for fourteen years. Cahum experienced harsh treatment at the hands of Crescencio Poot while working as his servant following the former's arrival in Chan Santa Cruz. After four years, he was married to Laureana Balam, a native of the kruso'b capital. As Cahum declared at the Yucatecan institutions, the wedding took place in the "style of the Indians" to eliminate "any notion of escape" he might have had. The couple were assigned to work on Poot's sugar farm, San Isidro. Laureana willingly joined her husband to escape "the mistreatment Poot incurs when he is drunk."[96]

Pablo Encalada's report is a vivid example of the tragic fate of rebel prisoners and demonstrates the complex and often ambivalent relationship between captives and captors. Encalada was born in Tekax around 1807. According to his account, rebels led by Jacinto Pat killed Encalada's

---

[91] Noticias que emite el C. Anastasio Durán ..., *LRP*, September 5, 1862, 1–3.

[92] Yucatán y los Ingleses, *RP*, November 26, 1875, 3.

[93] Relacion de los vecinos que existen prisioneros en el campo de Chan Santa Cruz, Peto, August 22, 1862, *EN*, August 27, 1862, 2; F. Díaz to Comandante General, Valladolid, June 29, 1874, AGEY, PE, M, box 311, file 44; N. Novelo to Gobernador, Peto, February 26, 1879, *RP*, March 3, 1879, 2–3; J.M. Iturralde to Gobernador, Valladolid, March 23, 1888, *RP*, April 6, 1888, 3.

[94] It is difficult to discern the appropriateness of such terms as "wedding." Captive women probably had little or no choice in most cases. In some instances, however, the sources report that formal ceremonies were held to establish the union.

[95] Informe, November 24, 1880, AGEY, PE, JP Ticul, box 211A.

[96] N. Novelo to Gobernador, Peto, February 26, 1879, *RP*, March 3, 1879, 2–3.

Kruso'b Violence against Outsiders 229

first wife and their eighteen-month-old daughter in rancho Pisté in 1847, where he lived and worked. Along with numerous others, Encalada himself was brought to Peto for two months and subsequently held prisoner for eight months in Tihosuco, after which time Pat freed him for some unknown reason. He spent about two years in Pat's service and became foreman at his ranch, Hotomoop. He accompanied Pat on a trip to Bacalar to buy gunpowder. As previously mentioned, Pat and his companions were attacked at hacienda Holchén by a rebel group headed by Venancio Pec. Pat and six of his followers were killed. Encalada was taken captive along with twenty others and forced to return with the gunpowder to ranch San Antonio, where he worked for about two years. He then spent six months in Mahas where Pec had taken him. Fearing an attack by government forces, Pec fled with his followers and workers to rancho Xyaxley. At this point Encalada was once again set free. After six months he moved on to settle at the aguada Lochhá, where he became a renowned pacífico leader.[97] While not reliable in every detail, Encalada's account seems fairly plausible.[98]

The behavior of prisoners taken during rebel raids varied. Some took the first opportunity to escape, others stayed and were integrated into kruso'b society for some time, as in the case of Encalada, or for the rest of their lives.[99] José María Ay, a prisoner who worked for a while on various farms owned by Crescencio Poot, was liberated by his master and settled in rebel territory.[100] José Solís served in the government forces of Pedro Acereto during the expedition to kruso'b strongholds in 1860. He deserted or was dispersed and went to the pacífico village of Lochhá (he did not specify the circumstances). He came to Chan Santa Cruz when a pacífico faction joined the kruso'b two months later. At that point he was working as a carpenter and learned how to build sugar mills. Solís was married to Clemencia Aguilar, a young captive from Tunkas, in a ceremony held by Agustín Barrera, who acted as a priest with the rebels.[101]

---

[97] Declaracion de Pablo Encalada, Campeche, August 12, 1867, *EP*, September 24 (part 1) and 27 (part 2) 1867, 1.

[98] Encalada obviously played down his active role in combat as a rebel leader. His name is mentioned in that position as early as July 1848. He was also party to the attack on Sabán on January 17, 1849 (Baqueiro 1990, 3:20, 116).

[99] See, for example, Comandancia accidental de la línea del oriente to Gobernador, n.p., April 1858, AGEY, PE, G, (complemento), box 115.

[100] J.M. Iturralde to Gobernador, Valladolid, March 23, 1888, *RP*, April 6, 1888, 3.

[101] Declaration of José Maria Eduardo Solís in R. Cisneros to Gobernador, Izamal, February 20, 1885, AGEY, PE, M, box 232.

230   *Part V: Violence and the Kruso'b*

Several captives grew so accustomed to life amidst the kruso'b that they participated in or even led rebel raids. A case in point is the long-term prisoner Juan Ontiveros, who ultimately became a kruso'b corporal (*cabo*).[102] Antonio Espadas, juez de paz of Sahcabá, was seized by rebels during an attack on his town in the summer of 1848. He became a rebel leader, led the force that killed the murderer of Cecilio Chi and headed raids on several Yucatecan towns.[103] Secundino Manzanilla, caught during the assault on Tekax in 1857, commanded the raid on Xkuil on December 31, 1862.[104] Sixto Chacon, abducted by the rebels in the early 1860s, participated as a guide (*práctico*) in kruso'b assaults in early 1873.[105] Mónica May recognized various figures in the force that attacked hacienda Kancabchén in 1874. One of them was Florentino Tox, whose father and brother had been killed during the assault on Dzonotchel in October of the previous year and he himself taken captive. Tox accompanied the group that raided Kancabchén as a guide, "armed and entirely free."[106]

As these examples indicate, many of those caught by kruso'b in the course of raids on Yucatecan settlements endeavored to make the best of their vulnerable position by showing submission. Some even began to bond with their captors. Similar phenomena are known from other violent contexts, such as hostage taking or wars, and identified in the literature as the "Stockholm syndrome" or "capture bonding."[107] They are interpreted as a survival strategy of those entirely at the mercy of others in life-threatening situations.

We have no detailed information on the living conditions of captives among the kruso'b but it is highly probable that their situation resembled in many aspects that of prisoners of North American Indians. In both cases it was impossible to uphold their permanent surveillance for any length of time. After a short period of strict control captives were permitted to move freely around the camp but not allowed to leave. This restriction was lessened after a while if the captives behaved well. While many captives were formally adopted into the North American Indian kin

---

[102] A. Medina to Gobernador, Tekax, August 27, 1884, AGEY, PE, M, box 227A.

[103] Baqueiro 1990, 3:24, 100–101, 116, 180.

[104] C. Montes de Oca to Gobernador, Tekax, January 4, 1863 and R. Lopez to General en Jefe, Peto, January 4, 1863, both in *EN*, January 9, 1863, 1.

[105] F. Canton to Gobernador, Valladolid, January 18, 1873, *RP*, January 24, 1873, 1.

[106] Declaracion de Mónica May, Sabino Piña, Peto, August 1, 1874, AGEY, PE, C, box 310, file 86; J. Carbó to Gobernador, Peto, August 1, 1874, *RP*, August 5, 1874, 2.

[107] See, for example, Adorjan et al. 2012.

Kruso'b Violence against Outsiders

groups, integration into kruso'b society seems to have been more gradual and often took place via concubinage or marriage.[108] A considerable number had subordinate positions as personal servants of rebel chiefs, others apparently became full members of the group, with some even rising to leadership positions.

FRATERNIZATION

As mentioned above, rebels raided hamlets, farms and towns in the frontier zone, killing not only the rich but many poor Maya-speaking people. Relations between kruso'b and inhabitants of the government-controlled area, however, were not always as hostile as a first glance might suggest. Many rebels were born and raised before the struggle began. Hence, local and kin ties between people on both sides of the frontier still existed in the initial decades of the Caste War. Juan Pio Iuit and Juan P. Yam, seized in rebel territory by government forces in 1869, declared, for example:

They saw that indigenous inhabitants of the town of Tiholop known as Facundo Chuc and the cacique May ... brought cattle to the insurgents [in Chan Santa Cruz] to sell; and the intimacy they observed between them and the chief leaders made them believe that this was a long-standing relationship. There was even the distinction that they were accommodated in the house of the main ringleader, Crescencio Poot.[109]

Furthermore, kruso'b and pacífico areas were an attractive refuge for those who were discontent with their current situation or faced legal problems, such as deserters, fugitive peons and criminals. As mentioned in the Chapter 11, many of the soldiers preferred to desert to the kruso'b than to stay in the army. Desertion to the rebels was not confined to soldiers but included the inhabitants of frontier settlements from all "castes," who were drawn to the liberties of life beyond government control. As early as 1855, this situation alarmed Governor Santiago Méndez, who wrote to the minister of defense that the war had acquired a "more fearful and dangerous" aspect with a "well-known advantage for the enemy." What troubled him was "the fatal case of many of our troops, needy from all sorts of miseries, deprivation and suffering, deserting and joining them, swelling their ranks" and the behavior of inhabitants in the frontier towns who did the same "without

---

[108] See for the Iroquois, Richter 1992:65–69.
[109] R. Novelo to Gobernador, Valladolid, June 24, 1869, *EP*, July 2, 1869, 1–2.

232   *Part V: Violence and the Kruso'b*

distinction of caste … attracted to absolute independence, they enjoy living remote from authority of any kind and not being subjected to any form of personal contribution or service."[110] While Méndez's description of life beyond government territory was obviously somewhat idyllic, the pros outweighed the cons for a sufficient number of people.[111]

Beyond this, fugitive peons informed kruso'b about the military situation in their former haciendas or hometowns or served as guides.[112] In other instances, local supporters helped the rebels when it came to raiding their towns.[113] Kruso'b assaults were sometimes led by former inhabitants of the towns, villages or haciendas to be raided, perhaps with the aim of settling old scores.[114] Consequently, kruso'b became embroiled in local conflicts and power struggles. Former inhabitants of towns or fugitive peons went so far as to instigate rebel groups to assault the locality or hacienda in which they had once lived and worked.[115] One example is Cosme Cob, a fugitive peon from the sugar plantation Xuxub, who abetted rebel leaders Bernardino Cen and Juan de la Cruz Pat to raid his former workplace, promising they would find "magnificent booty." As attested by his behavior during the raid, he sought revenge on his former master, Robert Stephens, for a grievance unknown to us. The kruso'b force surprised Stephens and his companion, Mr. Byrne, while they were reading their correspondence from Mérida. They were then tied to coconut palms and Stephens died "cruelly murdered in the presence of his

---

[110] S. Mendez to Ministro de Estado, Mérida, December 15, 1855, AHM, XI/481.3/4820.

[111] For further examples, see J. García Morales to Comisario Imperial, Mérida, October 1, 1866, AGN, G, SI, vol. 33, file 27; J.L. Solís to Secretario de Gobernacion y Hacienda, Bolonchén, April 20, 1875, AGEC, AH, G, AM, box 8; N. Novelo to Gobernador, Peto, May 13, 1879, *RP*, May 13, 1879, 1.

[112] See, for example, M. Micheltorena to MGM, Mérida, November 22, 1850, AHM, XI/481.3/2914; D. Traconis to Gobernador, Valladolid, September 6, 1870, *RP*, September 9, 1870, 1; F. Canton to Gobernador, Valladolid, January 18, 1873, *RP*, January 24, 1873, 1; F. Canton to General en Jefe, Valladolid, January 25, 1873, and C. Moreno Navarrete to Gobernador, Valladolid, March 4, 1873, both in AGEY, PE, M, box 302, file 41; Declaracion de Mónica May, Sabino Piña, Peto, August 1, 1874, AGEY, PE, C, box 310, file 86.

[113] M. Micheltorena to MGM, Mérida, December 11, 1850, AHM, XI/481.3/2914; Redacción: Lo de Chichimilá, *RP*, September 2, 1870, 4; F. Canton to Gobernador, Valladolid, January 18, 1873, *RM*, January 26, 1873, 2.

[114] See, for example, P. Acereto to Gobernador, Valladolid, February 13, 1859, *EC*, February 21, 1859, 2.

[115] M. Galera to Gobernador, Tekax, January 18, 1870, *RP*, January 21, 1870, 1–2; Redacción: Lo de Chichimilá, *RP*, September 5, 1870, 3–4; N. Urcelay to General en Jefe, pueblo de Dolores, Isla Mujeres, August 19, 1872, *RP*, August 26, 1872, 1; J. Gutuna to Gobernador, Tekax, October 20, 1883, AGEY, PE, JP, box 226.

servant [Cob], who enjoyed flinging bloody insults at him in his agony."[116] There are indications that Stephens had not been a kind master (in fact he was the owner's administrator). One eyewitness commented that "servants of the unfortunate Xuxub were constantly on the lookout for an opportunity to flee the despotism of the administration."[117] This statement may well be exaggerated since it stems from the local National Guard commander, Baltazar Montilla, a person who had quarreled with Stephens. The fact that six of the latter's peons had launched a revolt but failed to kill him some time before his ultimate death indicates that Stephens had problems with at least part of his work force.[118]

From this it clearly emerges that relations between people in the Yucatecan frontier region and the kruso'b were far more complex than any neat distinction into friend and foe would allow. While some frontier inhabitants sought economic benefits from commercial relations with kruso'b, others took advantage of their military skills for personal revenge. Yet others considered living with the rebels a more promising option than their present situation of subordination to hacienda owners, government officials or military officers. The above-mentioned cases notwithstanding, the kruso'b meant suffering and death for the majority of Yucatecan frontier settlements.

RAPE, ATROCITIES AND MODES OF KILLING

Very few reports give details of violent acts committed by kruso'b. Those we have stem from Yucatecan, pacífico or British sources and are therefore almost certainly biased. Some may be pure propaganda. Eligio Ancona's description of atrocities committed by Caste War rebels during a raid on a rancho in 1847 is a possible case in point. According to Ancona's account, rebels killed the female owner's son "throwing themselves on the young man, who was still shaking [se agitaba] on the ground with the final convulsions of agony, they stabbed his chest open the way a Mayan priest does with a sacrificial victim, plucked his heart out and drank with savage joy the blood that flowed in abundance from his wounds."[119] There are, however, a number of eyewitness accounts from

---

[116] B. Montilla to Gobernador, Puntachén, October 15, 1875, *RP*, October 20, 1875, 1.

[117] B. Montilla to Redactor, Puntachén, October 8, 1875, *RP*, October 15, 1875, 4.

[118] See Sullivan (2004, especially pp. 146–148) for a meticulous discussion of the Xuxub raid and the revolt against Stephens in particular.

[119] Ancona 1879/80, 4:43. His source is *Siglo XIX*, September 9, 1847. See also Baqueiro 1990, 2:14–15. The followers of the Yucatecan socialist movement faced similar

234   *Part V: Violence and the Kruso'b*

surviving prisoners that cannot be entirely discarded. From this essentially fragmented picture, several patterns of violence emerge.

As mentioned earlier, the machete was the rebels' most important weapon and they usually killed their victims with one or several machete blows. Since many members of the raiding parties did not carry guns, the machete was their only weapon. In addition, it saved ammunition, a scarce and expensive commodity. On their retreat from the previously mentioned assault on rancho Chan Hunuku in 1859, for example, the kruso'b inflicted seven cuts on one of the criados they had taken and then left him behind, "deeming him dead."[120] In March 1869, an army detachment reached a spot on the road to Xul where their comrades had been in a confrontation with rebels. They found "five bodies of our people, who were so badly mutilated we could not recognize them."[121] As already mentioned, from time to time the kruso'b slew prisoners they considered "useless" in their strongholds. Their bodies were "horribly mangled" and "thrown into the forest to feed beasts and birds of prey." The execution of Manuel Castellanos, the priest in Tunkas, saw him cut to pieces with machete blows, for example.[122]

There are several reports of sexual violence against victims of rebel assaults. During their forays on Yucatecan settlements in 1865 close to the military line of defense, rebels allegedly "burned the men and nailed the women to stakes, cut off their bosom, and condemned them to horrible martyrdom."[123] The sexual nature of the abuses, however, was bashfully paraphrased in most cases. In August 1847, shortly after government troops confined women, children and the elderly to a house they then burned with the rest of Tepich, rebels raided rancho Yaxché, eight leagues

---

allegations of blood drinking and cannibalistic acts by their liberal rivals in the 1920s (Gabbert 2004c:93). As the civil wars in Sierra Leone and Liberia have shown, however, appalling atrocities and acts such as blood drinking or the consumption of body parts did genuinely take place in the twentieth century. See, for example, Ellis 1995:192–193.

[120] L. Irigoyen to MGM, Mérida, August 17, 1859, AHM, XI/481.3/7504; for the infliction of several machete blows, see also C. Baqueiro to CGE, Hopelchén, October 20, 1856, AGEY, PE, G, box 103; Baqueiro 1990, 4:223; Sullivan 1997a, II:5. The machete was also employed in combat by government forces and as an execution tool. See, for example, R. Díaz de la Vega to MGM, Peto, May 11, 1852, AHM, XI/481.3/3300; Baqueiro 1990, 5:173. Killing with several machete blows was likewise common in acts of violence unrelated to the war. See, for example, Asesinato en el Partido de los Chenes, *EP*, May 25, 1869, 4.

[121] J.A. Cepeda Peraza to Gobernador, Tekax, March 11, 1869, *RP*, March 15, 1869, 2.

[122] GCY:127; see also Ch. Leas: "Belize or British Honduras," 1863, TULAL, MIC 736, reel 2; Buhler 1975:8.

[123] Aldherre and Mendiolea 1869:80.

Kruso'b Violence against Outsiders   235

away from Tihosuco. There they encountered Dolores Padron, the female owner of the farm, and one of her daughters. The rebels stole their jewelry and their money, stripped and bound them up, and committed "all types of excesses."[124] García y García describes the entry into Mérida of refugee families from the interior in the early phase of the conflict: "An old man was heard to refer to his escape, having seen his young wife and daughters subjected to the most brutal compliancies [complacencias] before suffering the most shameful death."[125] When the juez de paz de Tiholop tried to investigate the outcome of a kruso'b attack in 1856, he found the square of the town "strewn with the dead bodies" of both sexes and different ages "torn apart, others naked, and a thousand follies committed, the telling of which prudency prevents."[126] In the wake of a kruso'b attack on Tekax on September 14, 1857, an inhabitant of the town, Anselmo Duarte, found people "raising their heads pleading for water and others of the female sex, for clothing to cover themselves."[127]

The following accounts give an insight into the fate of female captives among the rebels. A Mexican officer reported in relation to rebel assaults on several Yucatecan frontier settlements in the early 1850s that the newly married Manuela Escamilla was captured by a kruso'b party who raided Chumvec. Her husband was "hacked to pieces" in her presence and she was dedicated "as a concubine to the son of the captain who commanded the [kruso'b] force." In the afternoon of the same day she found herself at the center of a skirmish and was recovered by an army detachment.[128] Mónica May fell into kruso'b hands during a raid on hacienda Kancabtun in the summer of 1874 along with three of her younger brothers and two nephews aged between two and fourteen. Although she witnessed the rebels inflicting numerous wounds on her father, they did not harm her or the boys. Mónica was "married" to an individual named Gonzalez, as the Yucatecan official put it in his version of her declaration.[129] She managed to escape after a day or two during the retreat of the rebel force. Given her short time among the rebels, the verb "marry" could either mean that she was promised as a future concubine or wife or be read as a euphemism for violation. This notwithstanding, she did not complain of abuses to herself. One of the rare explicit references to the violation of

---

[124] Ancona 1879/80, 4:43.   [125] García y García 1865:ix.
[126] Cited in J.M. Esquivel to Gobernador, Sotuta, April 25, 1856, GS, April 30, 1856, 3.
[127] A. Duarte to P. Barrera, Tekax, September 16, 1857, GS, September 18, 1857, 2.
[128] Cámara Zavala 1928, part 11.
[129] Declaracion de Mónica May, Sabino Piña, Peto, August 1, 1874, AGEY, PE, C, box 310, file 86.

FIGURE 17.3 Caste War fortifications in Bacalar. Photograph by Wolfgang Gabbert.

women comes from the trial in 1875 of the raiders of Xuxub, who were convicted of murder, robbery and rape.[130]

On some occasions, people were not just killed but tortured. One of the most detailed accounts of atrocities allegedly carried out by kruso'b relates to the assault on Bacalar in 1858 (see Figure 17.3). The town, close to the border with Belize, was an annoyance to the rebels as it obstructed their trade with the British. After several months of siege, the kruso'b managed to overcome Yucatecan resistance in a surprise attack on the night of February 21. All of the inhabitants were taken prisoner the next day:

A number of the men who were obnoxious were murdered in various ways – some being shot, others had their brains beat out with the butt end of a musket, others again were cut to pieces with machetes, while others were tied by their feet to the jails of horses and mules, and then dragged through the town until torn to pieces. The number who perished in these ways is supposed to be something over one hundred, leaving about two hundred women and children.

As soon as the news reached Corozal, Mr. Blake, the principal magistrate of that town, and two others, immediately went up there in order to secure the release of the remainder of the inhabitants. When they reached the town a ransom of $4,000 was demanded for their lives by the Indians. Two of the messengers of mercy agreed to remain there as hostage for the others return, who immediately returned to Corozal for the amount to ransom them. Corozal being a long distance

[130] Causa contra Encarnacion Cahum..., Mérida, May 29, 1876, RP, June 2, 1876, 1–2.

Kruso'b Violence against Outsiders

from this town and money not plenty, the whole sum could not be raised, but a courier was sent to Belize with the news for the balance of money, while the messenger, with $2,500, immediately went back to pay the ransom and to secure the lives of the prisoners. Meanwhile the Indian priests had so worked up the minds of the Indians that they gladly seized the plea of the time for which they agreed to spare their lives having expired, and that the cross (which they worshipped) did not want money but blood; they rejected the money offered, and decreed that they all should die. This decree they subsequently carried into effect. An eyewitness describes the scene as one of the most disgusting things he ever saw. Many of the children who cried for their mothers were taken by the heels and had their brains knocked against the wall, floor or ground, while, if their mothers made any noise or evinced any signs of affection for their offspring, their children were beaten to death over their heads and shoulders. Subsequently these poor creatures were taken outside the walls of the town, their clothes entirely taken off, their persons violated, and then they were bound back to back to a stake, exposed to the sun, and left in that state until near night, when the Indians went out and commenced their work of torture. They were all armed with machetes, and with these they cut slices of flesh from off the arms, thighs, legs and breasts of their victims; at times they would take the flesh so cut off and and [sic] strike them on the mouth; others would thrust the flesh so cut off their bodies into their mouths, using their machetes to thrust it down their throats, while others would cut off an arm, and again others thrust their machetes into their bodies, and in the most horrible and indecent manner end their sufferings and their lives together. The particulars, still more horrible, disgusting and indecent, I cannot write.[131]

Although the author of this disturbing account claimed that his description was based on an eyewitness account, its reliability is debatable, notably with respect to some of the more gruesome details of the massacre. Other sources, however, confirm the general account. There were indeed several episodes to the massacre. The first occurred shortly after the kruso'b conquest of Bacalar. The disturbing account suggests that in this phase of the butchery, torture and killing specifically affected a number of men whom the kruso'b detested for reasons unknown to us. Several days later, most of the remaining prisoners were slain by machete blows after negotiations for their release had failed and the cross ordered their death. The execution itself seems to have lasted only a few minutes. Atrocities against some of the prisoners left were resumed at night. Anderson, the British officer who witnessed the second phase of the massacre, described the scene as follows:

---

[131] This account first appeared in the *New York Herald* (June 2, 1858, 3), was then translated into Spanish and published in Yucatán, *GS* (June 23, 1858, 1). Dumond (1997:474–475 n. 9) suggests that it was not written by an eyewitness and considers it "almost certainly unreliable" but does not provide arguments for this claim.

238   *Part V: Violence and the Kruso'b*

The prisoners were stripped, bound up by bush-rope to separate trees, and literally hacked to pieces with machetes. It being a festival, most of the Indians were so incapable from the effects of drink that the blows fell sometimes without sufficient force to amputate a limb or penetrate a vital spot; so the task of the butchery was transferred to boy and girls, who amused themselves for hours by chopping the faces and bodies of the shrieking Spaniards.[132]

The kruso'b spared the lives of a number of women and children, and several male artisans from Bacalar. Sources differ widely on the number of victims.[133] The dispatch of another British official from Belize adds a further detail, suggesting that "the Indians always strip themselves and victims of all clothes during these massacres so there was no appearance of blood on their shirts next morning."[134] That heavy drinking preceded the executions is confirmed by the account of a child who was spared. Alcohol has also been mentioned in association with atrocities in other cases. Venancio Puc, for example, was ascribed a particular inclination to whip up cruelties when he was drunk.[135] Strong drink also played a role in another example of rebel outrage. In the afternoon of Saturday, January 3, 1863, a kruso'b party headed by Crescencio Poot raided the pacífico village of Lochhá at a time when the inhabitants were celebrating their fiesta. The 300 invaders stayed the night in the town and all of the next day, probably feasting on whatever provisions they found, which undoubtedly included liquor. When the rebels left, the villagers found the bodies of ten people who had been "sacrificed in the square, one of them butchered like a bull in a corrida [toreada en el circo de ella], and five women murdered along the road" they had taken.[136]

---

[132] Cited in Rogers 1885:221. The veracity of this description is debatable since the details provided were not included in Anderson's earlier statements (Paul Sullivan, personal communication, February 18, 2018).

[133] Captain Anderson to Superintendent (March 4, 1858, R. 61, ABH:202) reported thirty women, eleven men and about twelve children killed and seven women "reserved" for kruso'b chiefs. According to Superintendent Seymour, thirty-five females and ten to twelve males were butchered with machetes. The lives of four or five women and eight young children were spared (F. Seymour to C.H. Darling, Belize, March 13, 1858, TNA, CO, 123/96; see also Fowler 1879:41–42, cited in Buhler 1975:3–4). A Yucatecan source provides the names of 125 victims, men, women and children, and estimates the total number of slain at 250 (Impreso "Sucesos de Bacalar," Mérida, March 29, 1858, AHM, XI/481.3/6288). Differences in numbers may partly be explained by the fact that Seymour's and Anderson's reports do not include victims of the assault on Bacalar and the massacre that immediately followed.

[134] F. Seymour to C.H. Darling, Belize, March 13, 1858, TNA, CO, 123/96; Buhler 1975:4.

[135] See Buhler 1975:8 for Bacalar and GCY:127 for Venancio Puc.

[136] Nazario Novelo to Gobernador, Dzonotchel, January 12, 1863, *EN*, January 23, 1863, 1.

Kruso'b Violence against Outsiders

MOTIVATIONS FOR THE USE OF LETHAL VIOLENCE

Several strategic and practical reasons for the kruso'b to kill Yucatecans have already been mentioned. Weakening the enemy directly by slaying combatants or indirectly by eroding their morale with the slaughter of non-combatants are obvious motives. Massacres may have also been perpetrated to demonstrate the fierceness of the group (to deter enemies) or of individuals (to impress other group members deemed peers or competitors for positions of rank). This reasoning may account for a number of brutal cases of violence perpetrated in the Caste War that would otherwise be incomprehensible examples of cruelty or bloodlust, such as the killing of the Bacalar prisoners in 1858 described in the previous section. In fact, Reed has suggested that Venancio Puc pursued a political aim with the conscious brutality of the massacre, precluding a compromise with the Yucatecan government. The idea may have been to thwart any attempt to arrive at a peace treaty as rebel groups in the south had achieved in 1853.[137] Yucatecan sources were indeed worried about the possible impact of the massacre on pacífico morale. It was feared that the pacíficos might reconsider their relations with Yucatán after the kruso'b strategic success and show of force.[138] Another interpretation is to see the carnage as a demonstration of kruso'b strength and firmness vis-à-vis the British. In the aftermath of crushing rebel defeats and Bacalar's recapture by the army in 1851, the Yucatecan government and the Belize mahogany logging firm Young, Toledo & Co. signed a contract that allowed the enterprise to cut wood on the Mexican side of the border along the Río Hondo. The intention was to reduce rent payments to the rebels. When kruso'b re-established control of the border area, they launched an assault on the logging camps there in June 1857. As a result, the company was obliged to resume rent payments to the rebels and settle the debt accumulated in the past.[139] The reconquest of Bacalar in 1858 completed kruso'b control over the border area and the massacre sent the unequivocal message that it was wiser to comply with their requests than to string them along. The kruso'b might have had yet another reason for making the carnage an example. Captain Anderson, dispatched to Venancio Puc with a letter from the British superintendent, declined the demand to hand over the former commander of Bacalar, who

---

[137] Reed 1997b:520.
[138] J.M. Novelo to M.F. Peraza, Tekax, March 10, 1858, GS, March 15, 1858, 4.
[139] Villalobos González 2006:59–61; Dumond 1997:208–209; Cal 1983:79–81 and 1991:340.

240   *Part V: Violence and the Kruso'b*

had fled to the British possession when his town was assaulted, in exchange for the lives of the prisoners. Beyond this, the British intention to pay a ransom may not have been sincere, as evidenced by the following note from the Mexican Consulate in Belize:

> A commission made up of two government officials leaves today for Bacalar to see if they can liberate them [the Yucatecan captives], despite the fact that they [the kruso'b] have requested the enormous sum of 8,000 pesos from several Englishmen who passed by that place at the request of some Yucatecans. [The kruso'b] were finally content with receiving 4,000 pesos: I eagerly await the [return of the] commission, *which had strict orders not to give them a penny* [llevó órdenes estrechas para no darles ni un centavon].[140]

Practical reason, however, cannot account for all acts of violence or the particular brutality with which some of these were allegedly executed. Hatred and revenge come to mind as additional motives. The idea of retribution, notably of "taking a life for a life," is present in most societies.[141] Kruso'b are no exception to this.

Borrowing Frantz Fanon's ideas on the role of violence in anti-colonial movements, Terry Rugeley has suggested for the kruso'b that "the murder of people belonging to the overlord race glued rebels to a common cause and strengthened the leadership of those who directed it. Violence may well be a liberating act for the oppressed."[142] Indeed, violence against people considered oppressors may have had a cathartic dimension in some cases. In the Yucatán case, however, it was not based on racial hatred but on class antagonism toward members of the Yucatecan elite, such as Spanish-speaking landlords or prosperous town dwellers. At the same time, as mentioned earlier, kruso'b violence not only affected the comfortable classes but often poor Maya-speaking families. Paul Sullivan has therefore rightly characterized the Caste War as civil strife.[143]

While only certain members of kruso'b raiding parties actually killed or injured their enemies during assaults, Sullivan assumes that this was "not for lack of desire but for lack of opportunity." He considers the killing and physical abuse of prisoners, vecinos and Indians, both men and women, as a "sign of the assailants' hate and not merely as a tactical element."[144] It resulted from the rancor against those who had stayed behind when the rebels fled to the forests in 1848: "They made to pay those countrymen

---

[140] J.M. Martínez to Gobernador, Belice, February 26, 1858, *GS*, March 31, 1858, 1, my emphasis.
[141] Daly and Wilson 1988:226.   [142] Rugeley 2009:64.   [143] Sullivan 1997a, II:7.
[144] Sullivan 1997a, II:6.

Kruso'b Violence against Outsiders

who chose not to share the sufferings of the exile in the oriental forests, and who helped, and perhaps continued helping, directly or by passivity, the efforts of the common enemy to destroy them."[145] The war itself fueled hatred on both sides. Yucatecan attacks led to heavy rebel losses in the first half of the 1850s. Many others probably died of hunger.[146] Indeed, the rebels were often entirely devoid of corn and depended on fruit and roots for subsistence.[147] The harsh living conditions in rebel hideouts claimed numerous victims, particularly in the early years of the struggle. A member of the expedition to Chan Santa Cruz led by General Rómulo Díaz de la Vega in 1851 describes the rebel capital at the time as "nothing more than a vast cemetery":

[T]ombs are found everywhere, at the foot of tree trunks, and even in the middle of the paths, graves are scattered without order or care, and unburied parts of corpses emerge from many of them. Combined with the unhealthy climate, this makes it an immensely deadly place and the annual number of deaths is estimated to equal that of a settlement of one hundred and fifty thousand inhabitants.[148]

Beyond the hatred provoked by the countless dead as a result of army thrusts, hunger and disease, the atrocities ascribed to army and militia units aroused the rebels' anger and stimulated their desire for retaliation. While downplaying the excesses committed by government forces in Tepich in the summer of 1847, General Severo del Castillo's remarks are evidence of their lasting impact on the rebels:

All these little incidents recognized and astutely exaggerated by Indians were the source of and pretext for the horrible attacks the rebels committed later; for their setting on fire and sacking [of towns] and the butchering of women and children, saying that whites had burned and plundered [their houses] and raped their women in Tepich.[149]

Venancio Puc explicitly mentioned revenge as a motive for slaughtering the captives from Bacalar in 1858. According to a British source, he sent

---

[145] Sullivan 1997a, II:7.

[146] For numbers, see Chapter 20; Appendix 1 and 2; Sullivan 1997a, II:5 cuadro 2. For hunger used as a weapon by the army, see Chapter 12. For concrete evidence that kruso'b starved to death, see R. Díaz de la Vega to MGM, Mérida, June 26, 1851, AHM, XI/481.3/3257.

[147] Letters from M. Micheltorena to MGM, Mérida, April 24 and June 2, 1851, both in AHM, XI/481.3/3257; J.E. Rosado to CGE, Cruzchén, May 6, 1851, AHM, XI/481.3/3258; R. Díaz de la Vega to MGM, Mérida, June 12, 1851, AHM, XI/481.3/3256; M.F. Peraza to Comandante General, Valladolid, October 28, 1857, GS, November 4, 1857, 1.

[148] Cámara Zavala 1928, part 5.   [149] GCY:30.

242   *Part V: Violence and the Kruso'b*

word "he hoped the Superintendent would not be offended by what had happened. The Spaniards always treated their prisoners in that way. The Indians merely followed a lesson which had been taught them."[150] In addition to such general grudges, specific causes for revenge can be inferred from the historical record. Indeed, the war offered countless motives for enragement. The killing or capture of relatives by government forces was not a rare occurrence, particularly in the first two decades of the war. Nor did the families of rebel leaders escape this sad fate.[151] The army, for example, captured a daughter of Venancio Pec in 1850.[152] When government forces conquered Chan Santa Cruz on December 2, 1854, they found the remains of more than 200 soldiers and scores of captives taken during recent kruso'b incursions into Yucatecan frontier settlements.[153] It is conceivable that these massacres were revenge for the five or more attacks Chan Santa Cruz suffered in 1853 and 1854, as well as for the treachery of Narciso Pérez Virgilio in Tizimín in 1853, which cost more than 200 rebels their lives.[154]

In the mid-1860s, the nature of the Caste War changed, shifting from a civil war to a conflict between two polities. Neither side had a realistic chance of conquering enemy territory in the foreseeable future and a new cohort of kruso'b born and raised in rebel territory had reached maturity. To them, the Yucatecan frontier was "an unknown land, a foreign country, and the resentment they would keep towards the neighbors of that strange terrain could not be as intense and concrete as it was for their parents," as Sullivan puts it.[155] Although most of the younger kruso'b were unfamiliar with life in Yucatecan towns from their own experience, this did not of necessity favor a more benign attitude toward Yucatecans, who became something of a hereditary enemy, as contemporary Yucatecan commentators noted:

[150] F. Seymour to C.H. Darling, Belize, March 13, 1858, TNA, CO, 123/96; see also Fowler 1879:41–42, cited in Buhler 1975:4.
[151] See, for example, Ancona 1879/80, 4:303; M. Micheltorena to MGM, Mérida, July 16 and 31, 1850, both in AHM, XI/481.3/2914; R. Díaz de la Vega to MGM, Mérida, June 5, 1851, AHM, XI/481.3/3256; J.D. Pasos to CGE, Peto, July 8, 1851, AGEY, PE, M, box 175, file 80.
[152] M. Micheltorena to MGM, Mérida, April 13, 1850, AHM, XI/481.3/2914.
[153] P.A. Gonzalez to Gobernador, Yokdzonot, December 12, 1854, *EO*, January 2, 1855, 1–2.
[154] See Chapter 12.
[155] Sullivan 1997a, II:7. He dates the maturity of the new kruso'b generation around the late 1870s, arguing that probably few children born in the rebel territory before the 1850s had survived. Although there is not enough information to decide the issue, the reports discussed in the following suggest an earlier date.

The children of the first rebels were born and raised as savages and these are now the true rebels who make war on us. Born into it [savagery], they have inherited nothing from their parents but viciousness, an abhorrence of a society they did not know; they know only its bad traditions, they have no idea of the good ones, of that tincture of civilization of their ancestors.[156]

In the course of the conflict, the social and cultural gap between government-controlled and kruso'b territories broadened, at least from the perspective of the Yucatecan elite. A newspaper commentary remarked in 1868, for example, on the separation of the kruso'b from "the rest of the Indians, and especially from the whites" in terms of religion and other customs, "for they have their prophets, and although their sign is the cross, they worship it in their own way,"[157] As General Castillo recognized, submission was not to be expected from "a race that already has to rely on young men who have no knowledge of those of their own blood who exist here but only of their bloody struggles with those who for the same reason cannot harbor any other feeling than hatred, from infancy."[158] He described the new generation in the 1860s as follows:

[T]here is already a new generation in that population [Chan Santa Cruz] that only know Yucatecans from the battlefield to drink their blood; who have been suckled with that hatred, not only infused by their parents but that [also] evolved in bloody encounters. .... This new generation consists of a robust youth full of that ardor, of that courage, and of that desire for adventure and the dangers peculiar to the youthful and bellicose age, and that multitude of young Indians now in existence constitute a good part and the best of their troops.[159]

A former captive reported on the rebel enthusiasm to continue the war, "even the smallest [children] cry when they are not led to the incursion [into Yucatecan settlements] to wet their machete, as they say."[160] In 1865, one Mexican general recognized that the long-lasting frontier war had shaped kruso'b men into "trained and intelligent warriors and both youngsters and children have this school that strengthens them every day."[161] In fact, there are some hints that youngsters were socialized as warriors and participated in forays as messengers and spies or by

---

[156] La cuestion de colonias militares en Yucatán, *EP*, May 29, 1868, 3–4.
[157] Informe sobre el plan de campaña del Gral. Castillo, J.L. Uraya to Emperador, n.p., [November 27] 1865, AGN, G, SI, vol. 44, file 69.
[158] S. Castillo to MGM, Mérida, June 1, 1865, AHM, XI/481.4/9976.
[159] GCY:147.
[160] Noticias que emite el C. Anastasio Durán ..., *LRP*, September 5, 1862, 1–3.
[161] Informe sobre el plan de campaña del Gral. Castillo, J.L. Uraya to Emperador, n.p., [November 27] 1865, AGN, G, SI, vol. 44, file 69.

244 *Part V: Violence and the Kruso'b*

shouting to make raiding groups appear larger than they were in reality. José Chan, for example, taken along by Bernardino Cen on the raid on Xuxub on October 12, 1875, was no more than twelve years of age.[162] The active role of youth in warfare is further confirmed by a report on Chan Santa Cruz reflecting the situation in the early 1870s, which states that everyone there was a soldier "as of ten years of age."[163] Interestingly, the source does not specify gender, although male and female children may well have been accustomed to participation in violence and cruelties. This is suggested by Captain Anderson's description of male and female children's involvement in the slaughtering of the Bacalar captives in 1858.[164] To my knowledge, however, female kruso'b did not participate in raids on Yucatecan settlements.

While data on socializing rebel youths to violence is limited and debatable, such practices are well-known from other cases. The involvement of children in collective atrocities has been identified for other warrior societies and is standard practice in most of the current irregular wars in Third World countries.[165] Children of both sexes took part in the torture of captives of the North American Iroquois and the South American Chiriguano, for example.[166] This can be interpreted as an attempt to desensitize the young and condition them to use other forms of violence in the future, such as killing in the course of raids.[167]

In addition to the hatred caused by the experience of Yucatecan attacks or socialization in rancor against one's enemy, several structural features of kruso'b society may have favored the recourse to violence. Societies entrapped in almost constant warfare are highly likely to develop a warrior cult of honor, emphasize prowess and socialize male children in particular for aggression.[168] Specialized institutions such as men's houses may also foster violence.[169] While these were unknown among

---

[162] Causa contra Encarnacion Cahum ..., Mérida, May 29, 1876, *RP*, June 2, 1876, 1. See also J.M. Muñoz to Secretario de Estado, México, June 2, 1882, TULAL, MIC 736, reel 5.

[163] Chan Santa Cruz Report, Mérida, June 2, 1882, TULAL, M-26, box 2, folder 14.

[164] Cited in Rogers 1885:221.

[165] See, for example, Murphy (2003) for the civil wars in Liberia and Sierra Leone.

[166] See, for example, Wallace 1972:33; Métraux 1949:402.

[167] For the importance of desensitization and conditioning in modern armies, see Grossman 1996:250–261.

[168] Ember and Ember 1994.   [169] Riches 1986:24; Hallpike 1977:230.

the rebels, men living together in barracks during guard service annually for about two months would have played a similar role in kruso'b society.[170]

The new kruso'b generations saw Yucatecans as alien foes and were raised to defend their autonomy by force, which probably lowered their inhibitions to kill them. Army thrusts into rebel territory had already ended in 1872, however, and raiding lost its economic importance after 1875, as has been shown. Thus, the descendants of the first rebel generation had no concrete scores to settle with Yucatecans and external violence declined. Internal violence, on the other hand, was fostered by increasing competition for the revenues from logging and chicle exploitation and, at the end of the century, by attempts to prevent defection in view of renewed pressure from Yucatecans.

CONCLUSION

The use of physical force was a common experience among the kruso'b in the second half of the nineteenth century. Up to the 1870s, they suffered repeated assaults by government forces. In turn, they exerted violence for practical and expressive purposes against Yucatecan soldiers and civilians, as well as against various pacífico groups, searching for loot, scaring Yucatecans away from their frontier settlements, demoralizing soldiers etc. Internal violence was stimulated by the particularities of rebel political organization (caudillo rule), the ingrained rejection of contributions and suspicion of anyone who displayed wealth not dedicated to the acquisition of armament and ammunition or the religious cult. Despite its charismatic and thus inherently unstable political organization, kruso'b society evinced a remarkable capacity for survival. The religious order contained the potential for division, manifested in the emergence of several religious centers in the course of time, but basic rituals and creeds associated with the Cult of the Speaking Cross acted as a major cohesive force. In addition, rebel organization combined features of both patrimonialization, which tied access to key resources to a few leaders competing among themselves for followers, status and wealth, on the one hand, and formalization, on the other. The system of companies and military ranks, at least at the

---

[170] For a calculation of the length of guard service, see Sullivan 1997a, II:3.

lower levels, seems to have provided a relatively stable organizational structure for kruso'b society to lean on in the course of surviving major upheavals caused by external pressure or infighting among leaders. Beyond this, the common enmity toward Yucatecans and the collective acts of violence committed against them certainly helped to sustain rebel society.

PART VI

INTRICACIES OF CASTE WAR VIOLENCE

As shown in the preceding chapters, the Caste War was a bloody and enduring conflict that claimed countless victims on both sides, particularly among non-combatants. This was due to the guerilla character of the war for most of its duration. Distinguishing civilians from fighters in this type of conflict can be challenging. Insurgents primarily attacked small or unprotected settlements in the government-controlled area, while the military employed scorched-earth strategies in rebel strongholds and the buffer zone to deprive the guerillas of support from the populace. Violence was not, however, confined to Caste War contentions but also permeated other contexts in nineteenth-century Yucatán. It was common in the domestic sphere and in hacienda labor relations, and was furthermore a key feature of the politics that prevailed after Independence, a period marked by frequent coups and the mobilization of conflict groups by local or regional strongmen. Whether as a threat or a reality, violence was a familiar experience notably among the lower classes, who bore the brunt of military service and were forced to work on the haciendas. For soldiers and hacienda peons, freedom of movement was restricted and corporal punishment commonplace. Hence, contrary to what a first glance might suggest, the fate of the many captives working for kruso'b leaders did not differ radically from that of the lower classes in the government-controlled area. Physical force was likewise prominent during the quest for kruso'b leadership.

While the Caste War involved great suffering and constituted a deadly threat to participants and civilians alike, it also provided kruso'b, government soldiers and officers, and private entrepreneurs active in the trade with war prisoners, for example, with opportunities for personal gain that would have been threatened by the conclusion of peace – a factor that contributed to prolonging the war. The strength of its impact is hard to assess. It is obvious, however, that perpetuation of the war was only possible as long as the rebels were in a position to procure arms, ammunition and other indispensable goods from Belize. This in turn depended largely on the state of diplomatic relations between Mexico and Great Britain, which, as already mentioned, only began to improve in the mid-1880s. In addition, the war could only linger on for so long because the commercial pull of the rebel area for Yucatecans dwindled as a result of the shift to henequen cultivation in the northwest of the peninsula. Thus, from the mid-1850s, the existence of rebels did not constitute a real threat to the Yucatecan economy and motivate the government to bear the brunt of a decisive blow against them. What is more, almost constant political unrest and civil wars kept the Yucatecans busy with infighting for decades.

Not unlike other civil wars and insurrections, the Caste War was a highly dynamic process that generated its own momentum. Acts of violence triggered chains of counter-violence and retaliation. Symbolic aspects and emotions such as revenge likewise played a significant role. As argued in the introduction, violence is particularly suited to expressing the author's power and ferocity. It can be used to demonstrate to the enemy the combat readiness of a group or, within a group, to express an individual's fierceness, thereby intimidating competitors for positions of rank. Hence, violent actions are not always motivated by confrontation with the foe but can spring from internal group dynamics such as competition for leadership or the preservation of discipline. The mistreatment and killing of prisoners by kruso'b, for example, was sometimes prompted by the desire of rebel leaders to send a symbolic message of fierceness to their rivals rather than by practical calculations such as lack of food or shortage of manpower to supervise prisoners. As the discussion of caudillo politics suggests and given the lack of institutionalized succession procedures, kruso'b leadership called for a particularly aggressive personality with the ability to maintain the strongman image and willing to resort to violence in order to rise to power and defend their interests.

The chapters that follow discuss the role ideology played in the Caste War, compare the behavior and motivations of soldiers and kruso'b, present an overview of the magnitude of the casualties suffered in the conflict, and consider which general conclusions can be drawn from the empirical material presented so far.

18

Civil War, Ideology and Motivation

With Kalyvas, I am skeptical of approaches that rely exclusively on macrolevel motivations and dynamics, and emphasize overarching and pre-existing cleavages such as class or ethnic distinctions to account for violence in civil wars.[1] Violence at the local level cannot be deduced from what he calls the "master cleavage" that drives the war at the national or (in our case) regional level. Instead, civil wars should be understood as "concatenations of multiple and often disparate local cleavages, more or less loosely arrayed around the master cleavage." Beyond this, violence is often "jointly produced" by actors at all levels.[2] While national and regional elites or rebel leaders need local actors to realize violence on the ground, the latter attempt to tap superior power sources to foster their idiosyncratic interests, as in the case of the soldiers in our example who used the war as a pretext for pillaging in the buffer zone. According to Kalyvas:

Civil war fosters a process of interaction between actors with distinct identities and interests. It is the convergence between local motives and supralocal imperatives that endows civil war with its intimate character and leads to joint violence that straddles the divide between the political and the private, the collective and the individual.[3]

Civil wars like the Caste War transform "the political actors' quest for victory and power and the local or individual actors' quest for personal and local advantage into a joint process of violence." Instead of assuming that supralocal and local actors necessarily share the same ideology and

[1] Kalyvas 2006:6.   [2] Kalyvas 2006:365, 384 (quote).   [3] Kalyvas 2006:387.

250   *Part VI: Intricacies of Caste War Violence*

aims or despising the latter as puppets of the former, their relationship should be seen as an alliance, as Kalyvas suggests, whereby "the former supply the latter with external muscle, thus allowing them to win decisive local advantage; in exchange, supralocal actors recruit and motivate supporters at the local level."[4] This is exemplified in the Caste War by Yucatecan peons or villagers who instigate rebel raids on their (former or current) residence (hacienda or town) to settle old feuds or retaliate for wrongs suffered. Consequently, the decision of local actors to support one side or another in a civil war often fails to conform to macro-cleavages such as race, ethnicity or class. Furthermore, allegiance may not be stable and can shift according to developments at the national, regional and local level.

By emphasizing the multiple motivations and diverse needs of participants at different levels, Kalyvas's approach gives a more realistic view of the volatile dynamics of civil wars than other accounts. On the whole, however, he seems to ascribe political motives to actors at the center while imputing personal reasons for violence and fighting to local actors. I would argue instead that private interests such as the quest for personal power or economic gain among the former may be equally important in shaping the war at the center. Think of the rivalries and side-changing of leading Yucatecan politicians and officers before and during the Caste War. What divided Santiago Méndez, Miguel Barbachano and their elite followers can hardly be described as profound ideological differences. Personal interests and practical necessities frequently determined their use of violence in the conflict.

As recent social psychological research shows, worldviews and ideologies – as held by individuals – are not necessarily stable, consistent and logically coherent belief structures. Depending on the "demands of both ongoing and temporary social relationships," they can change radically and are "influenced by the individuals and groups that surround us."[5] As the following examples show, many people in the Caste War were in fact driven by their circumstances and short-term interest in surviving a precarious or life-threatening situation rather than by political ideology or deep-rooted convictions. Thus, as mentioned in the previous chapter, Antonio Espadas, juez de paz of Sahcabá, began as a captive of the rebels and became a leader after a relatively short time in 1848. In Tekom in the 1880s, Serapio Baqueiro met several "Indians from the town" who were former prisoners of Crescencio Poot and later his friends. "They made us

---

[4] Kalyvas 2006:365.   [5] Jost, Ledgerwood and Hardin 2008:181.

Civil War, Ideology and Motivation

laugh," Baqueiro wrote, "for the frankness with which they told us that, once subject to his orders, they also had to wage war on us; but restored to their homes, they had bravely defended the town every time Poot invaded it."[6]

Kalyvas is certainly right in arguing that local actors in civil wars are rarely motivated by explicit political ideologies as formulated by elites. Local individual and collective actors, however, can be moved by their own understandings of the world, their ideas about right and wrong or their standards of justice, such as equal rights. It is therefore crucial for elites to discover points of contact where local and elite views seem compatible (or can at least be represented as such). Promises by Barbachanistas to reduce taxes and end land privatization, for example, took up key lower-class problems. Thus, worldviews and ideologies as systems of belief and morality cannot be dismissed as irrelevant. They define the boundaries of contending parties and frame the objectives pursued, at least to a certain extent. In addition, they facilitate the recourse to violence by representing one's own struggle as legitimate and that of the enemy as illegitimate, and produce schemes and scripts for dehumanization of the foe, as in the Yucatecan elite's depiction of rebels as barbarous savages. Worldviews and ideology also allow for the dispersion of individual responsibility by alluding to the orders of superiors or God's will.

Despite its ambiguity and malleability, ideology can become a strong motivational force, mobilizing both rational and emotional energy for a specific cause. This can only happen, however, if its content addresses at least some of the actors' needs and fears. Consequently Yucatecan politicians cultivated the deep-rooted fright of a mass Indian uprising to attract followers to fight against the Caste War rebels. In their desperate situation during the first years of the war, the latter found moral support in the Cult of the Speaking Cross.

While as a rule it is extremely difficult to ascertain the specific contribution of ideology to motivation for action – not least since actors may refer to ideology to legitimize acts of self-interest in hindsight or be unaware of the underlying reasons for particular deeds – a discussion of the contending parties' worldview or ideology remains important. At the same time, the lack of sources precludes a detailed reconstruction of the belief systems of Caste War participants and their modification through time. We can only discuss certain aspects of the "official" discourse inferred from written statements by Yucatán's elite, on the one hand,

---

[6] Baqueiro [1887] 1989:29.

252   Part VI: Intricacies of Caste War Violence

and the utterances of rebel leaders and the Speaking Cross, on the other, and confront them with what soldiers, rank and file rebels and civilians actually did on the ground.

ELITE RACISM AND ITS REFLECTIONS

Thanks to numerous unpublished and published sources, we have the clearest notion of the Yucatecan and Mexican elites' view of the conflict. As mentioned earlier, newspapers, official documents and contemporary historical works, such as those of Serapio Baqueiro and the later State Governor, Eligio Ancona, coincide in their interpretation of the Caste War as a racial or ethnic conflict, a struggle between civilization and barbarism. This official discourse tied in with established images of Indians as savages, created at the time of the conquest to legitimize colonialism. Elites regarded Indians and the lower classes in general as child-like, brutish beings driven solely by their instincts and passions. The later bishop Crescencio Carrillo y Ancona, for example, considered contemporary Indians "indolent, indifferent, cunning, cruel ... and increasingly stupid."[7] Education and, if necessary, force were required to control them and elevate them to a state of civilization, making them "useful" to themselves and to society.[8] Rebels were habitually identified as Indians and depicted as ferocious savages or even man-eaters (see Figure 18.1).[9] Blaming peasant insurgents for their alleged aim to "exterminate the white race" was a common delegitimization discourse of the elite in Mexico.[10] Yucatán was no exception. Ancona, for instance, suggested that the "descendants of the Maya had a traditional hatred of anyone with a drop of white blood in their veins."[11] The profound Indian hatred of whites has been accepted by many contemporary and several later authors as the main reason for rebellion and violence.[12] Hence, the use of violence

---

[7] Carrillo y Ancona 1950:62.

[8] See Gabbert (2004c:64–70 and 2015) for extended discussions of the elite view on Indians.

[9] See, for example, J.E. Rosado to Gobernador, September 26, 1849, AGEY, PE, G, box 66.

[10] The rebels denied this allegation in Yucatán, as mentioned above, as did insurgents in other regions. See, for example, for the Huasteca, Ducey (2001:543) and for Guerrero, Guardino (2005:211).

[11] Ancona 1879/80, 3:486.

[12] See for the racial war thesis, for example, Dictamen de las comisiones primera de guerra y defensa contra los bárbaros sobre la pacificacion de Yucatán, Mexico, 1873, CAIHDY, F, XXV.1873/5; Sierra O'Reilly [1848–51] 1994, 1:17; GCY:13, 48, 49, 128; Baqueiro 1990, 2:209; 3:81; García y García 1865:vii-viii. For references to later scholars, see the Introduction.

Civil War, Ideology and Motivation 253

was presented as a legitimate and appropriate means of engaging with an enemy allegedly driven by animosity and bloodthirstiness, and intent on wiping out the civilized part of the population. Removing this "cancer" (the rebels) from the social body of Yucatecan society clearly called for radical measures. Annihilation or banishment seemed the only realistic alternatives. "The Indians of the east must be exterminated, finished off," a Yucatecan informed Emperor Maximilian in 1865, and "removed from the peninsula so that not a single insurgent remains."[13]

While the elite perspective on the kruso'b can easily be inferred from the sources, it is far more difficult to reconstruct the outlook of Indians and the lower classes in the government-controlled area. Given the power relations in that area and the documents' objectives, it comes as no surprise that Maya speakers in the northern and western parts of Yucatán joined the hegemonic discourse on the rebels in their loyal addresses to the government. Homún's community officials (*república*) sent a letter to the governor that included the following:

Your Excellency – Julian Pisté, Isidoro Huchim, Florentino Pech, José Marcelino Couoh and Santiago Ché, all residents of Homun and members of the indigenous republic, declare before you with the most submissive respect: that the scandalous and criminal conduct of the rebellious Indians of the east, who come fiercely and impudently, bring about our misfortune by destroying the towns of our beloved Yucatecan soil and assassinate with an insidious hand and not the least pity the whites from whom we derive infinite benefits and which we acknowledge in our humble heart, is quite repugnant in our opinion and to our good sense. Consideration of these circumstances, worthy of the highest attention, moves us to offer Your Excellency our services where they are deemed most necessary, and if possible we shall pounce on the infamous, who have reciprocated so badly and therefore dishonored our Indian race. We therefore consider it appropriate to give Your Excellency proof of the sentiments that encourage us in favor of the just cause, a cause that will undoubtedly be protected by Divine Providence, and we hope to share in the glory of triumph united with the defense of the rest of this peninsula.[14]

Besides such instances of ostentatious patriotism and loyalty to the government, there is at least some evidence of present-day Maya speakers' retrospect views on Indians and kruso'b. During my fieldwork in the 1990s in the Chenes region in the state of Campeche, for example, I asked local Maya speakers what they associated with the term Indian

---

[13] Informe sobre el plan de campaña del Gral. Castillo, J.L. Uraya to Emperador, n.p., [November 27] 1865, AGN, G, SI, vol. 44, file 69. For the rebels designated as a "cancer," see R.J. Piña: "Revista de los Chenes" (part 1), *LD*, March 17, 1871, 3.

[14] *BOGY*, July 6, 1848, AGEC, PY, G, box 8, file 588.

FIGURE 18.1 Captives in Chan Santa Cruz and Tekax massacre, Sociedad Patriótica Yucateca, 1878. Courtesy of Tozzer Library, Harvard University. Left: "The barbarians leading the captives to kill them like beasts." Right: "The barbarians surprise the city of Tekax, leaving all over it, more than two thousand corpses quartered."

Civil War, Ideology and Motivation

(indio). Some of my interviewees replied that they were "those who burned down the villages, those who had no compassion."[15] Considering that numerous Maya speakers in the west and north of the peninsula became victims of kruso'b assaults and many others fought them as members of army or militia units, these negative evaluations of Caste War rebels cannot be dismissed entirely as reflections of an elite ideology. What is more, official views on the Caste War changed utterly after the Mexican Revolution. The struggle has since then been interpreted as a precursor to the revolution and considered a heroic liberation movement of the Maya Indians.[16] Thus, present-day critical opinions on the rebels run against decades of government discourse.

REBEL PERSPECTIVES: THE QUEST FOR EQUALITY AND THE ORDERS OF THE CROSS

Contemporary kruso'b views on the conflict have come to us mainly through letters from the Speaking Cross (or Juan de la Cruz), other written rebel statements, and a few reports by Yucatecans or Britons on what rebels allegedly said at certain moments in time. While the insurgents did not have an elaborated political program, their major concerns emerged from the sources, the most prominent of which were reduction of taxes and religious fees, free access to land for cultivation and equal rights. The principal leaders summarized their demands in a letter to a mediation commission in 1850 as follows:

You know perfectly well what was established in the agreement [of Tzucacab 1848] with us. We are fighting so that nobody has to pay poll tax, neither the ts'ul, nor the box [black], nor the masewal. Three reales is to be the fee for baptism, for the ts'ul, the box, and the masewal. Ten reales is to be the fee for a wedding, for the ts'ul, the box, and the masewal. As for the old debts, no one will have to pay, neither the ts'ul, nor the box, nor the masewal. No one will have to pay for land [k'ax]. Each person can till their field [kol] wherever they want, the ts'ul, the box, and the masewal.[17]

---

[15] Interview with the author, Xcupil, May 7, 1995; see also interview with the author, Campeche, August 29, 1998.

[16] Cf. for example, Cárdenas 1972:154, 170–171. This point is discussed by Bustillos Carrillo (1957:111, 175–179), Joseph (1980:158) and Fallaw (1995:446–473; 1997:560, 561–569).

[17] J.M. Barrera et al. to J. Canuto Vela, Tehaz [Haas], April 7, 1850, CAIHDY, M, XLII. 1850–1866/7. See also C. Chi to Don Il. Ma. Díaz, Expec, November 21, 1847 and E. Rosado to Secretario de Guerra y Marina, December 13, 1847, both in AGEY, PE, G, box 66, file Programa de indios sublevados; Jose Benito Bitorin Capitan, Anast.o Puc,

256 Part VI: Intricacies of Caste War Violence

Statements by army deserters captured by the kruso'b bear witness to rebel persistence on these demands several years later. On their return to the government-controlled area, they reported that the kruso'b wanted to "abolish all kinds of contributions and seek restitution of lands [baldíos] sold by the superior government to several private individuals."[18] These claims by far exceeded the existing economic order and, for the time, had a genuine revolutionary character. Granting free access to land endangered the labor supply of hacienda owners eager to expand their production of export crops, such as henequen. Demanding equal rights for all (male and adult) members of Yucatecan society reflected the spirit of the liberal constitution of the Spanish national assembly (cortes), in effect between 1812 and 1814.[19] Its main content was widely publicized even among the peasantry through proclamations read by officials in each town.[20] In fact, the administrative distinction between Indians and vecinos had been reintroduced in the final period of the colony and survived Independence in practice and, with the exception of the years 1820 to 1824 and 1841 to 1847, also in the law. Civil and religious taxes had been hotly debated in Yucatán, at least since the late eighteenth century. Special religious contributions for Indians (obvenciones) were abolished and re-established several times since the adoption of the liberal constitution in 1812.[21] In contrast to the interpretation of the war as a racial conflict that pervaded official Yucatecan discourse, rebel statements demanded equality for all groups and were generally phrased in economic and political terms.[22] As mentioned earlier, they repeatedly denied the extermination of non-Indians as their objective and we will see later on how they conceptualized their enemies.

Jose Ramon Carrillo to padre Manuel Sanchez, Tacchivichén, February 16, 1848, AHAY, G, I, box 227, file 3; several letters in EHRY 2:298–302. Interestingly, the earlier documents do not mention the box.

[18] Causa seguida contra varios desertores ..., Hunucmá, Febrero 12 – March 19, 1852, AGEY, PE, J, box 145, file 27.

[19] Including people of African descent, which even went beyond the constitution of 1812 that debarred this group from citizenship in Art. 22 (www2.uca.es/grup-invest/lapepa/pdf/constituciones/cons_1812.pdf; accessed August 1, 2017).

[20] Rugeley 1996:39.

[21] See, for example, Rugeley 1996:39–44, 48, 132–141; Dumond 1997:52–54, 72, 76.

[22] In a comment on a draft of this book, Paul Sullivan argued that "[a] demand for equality does not make the demand non-racial," the Caste War rebels fought for "an end to discrimination against their kind" (personal communication, February 18, 2018, emphasis there). I would argue instead that such a demand is not racial but anti-racial. Beyond this, as shown in Chapter 13, the rebels were quite a heterogeneous "kind" and membership was apparently not defined by descent or phenotype.

Civil War, Ideology and Motivation

Letters to adversaries or conflict mediators may of course be insincere. Thus, establishing whether the facts support the racial war thesis calls for a closer look at rebel deeds. Indeed, a few sources suggest that the rebels treated Indian and vecino prisoners differently. The vecino Anastasio Durán, captured by the kruso'b in Tunkas in 1861, declared after his return to the government-controlled area eleven months later that he and his fellow prisoners had to break stones for eight days after their arrival in Chan Santa Cruz. The kruso'b then singled out the seventy-five white and mestizo captives and killed them on the outskirts of the town. Indian captives, on the other hand, were baptized according to the kruso'b ritual and assigned to break more stones. They were subsequently obliged to work on ranches belonging to rebel chiefs. According to Durán's statement, he survived by presenting himself as Indian. He did not mention how he substantiated this claim. Beyond that, he described the kruso'b minister or "tata Polin" as "a white man, a dodderer of elevated stature," thereby casting doubt on the assumption that rebels rejected non-Indians unreservedly.[23] Pedro Hernández, a muleteer caught by the rebels, reported after his escape in the same year that "the barbarians put almost all their white prisoners to the sword ... sparing only women." At the same time, he added that several white prisoners (Gerardo Castillo, a musician named Martinez and several other musicians) were still alive in Chan Santa Cruz.[24]

Events surrounding the political turmoil among the kruso'b in the early 1860s could also be read as an indication of rebel racist attitudes. In late 1863, Venancio Puc is reported to have demanded the slaying of all white prisoners in the name of the cross and the raid of frontier settlements to kill more of them "for it was decreed by God that not a single white person was to be left alive."[25] These were not his words, however, but those of a vecino captive writing on behalf of two of Puc's rivals (Zapata and Santos), who had just overthrown and killed Puc, and were attempting to justify their actions vis-à-vis the British in Belize, as mentioned in the previous chapter.[26] The statement of Esteban Cen, who was a rebel

---

[23] Noticias que emite el C. Anastasio Durán ..., *LRP*, September 5, 1862, 1–3.

[24] F. Pren to Gobernador, Sotuta, February 14, 1862, *EN*, February 19, 1862, 2.

[25] D. Zapata, L. Santos, G. del Castillo to the superintendent of Belize, January 1, 1864, Archives of Belize R. 84, cited in Sullivan 2004:87; see also Dumond 1997:254–255 for longer quotations from the document.

[26] Comisión del gobierno de Yucatán ..., Mérida, June 13, 1864, *LNE*, June 24, 1864, 1. See Sullivan (2004:220 n. 21) for the authorship of Gerardo del Castillo, a captive musician. Sullivan suggests that Zapata and "all the white male prisoners he had

Part VI: Intricacies of Caste War Violence

captive for a couple of weeks in 1879, seems to be a clear hint of racial considerations among the kruso'b. According to the Yucatecan official who interrogated him, Cen claimed that "rebellious Indians have orders not to mistreat in any way those who belong to their race and live in our towns, to see if blandishment and good treatment would motivate them to embrace the banner of the rebellion, and that whites should be finished off without any mercy."[27] Whether these orders genuinely existed, we cannot say. If they did, they were not obeyed. The assault on the town of Tahdziu and the rancho Katbé in late February 1879, in the course of which Cen was abducted, affected Indians and vecinos alike.[28] Contrary to the report containing Cen's statement, the kruso'b did not slay all the vecinos in the assaulted settlements.

A major drawback with Cen's and similar statements is that we only have access to the Spanish translations of Maya originals. We cannot therefore be sure of the Maya terms used for friend and foe. In the surviving Maya correspondence, at least, rebels rarely employed terms referring to skin color to designate their adversaries. The only instances I know of are three notes written to rebel commander Pedro Chuc in Chikindzonot between late July and September 1847. The author (Máximo Huchim in two cases, no originator for the third) designates enemies as "zacpipoil uinicoob" (pale humans), "zac maaxoob" (white persons) and "zac maax uinicoob," (white person humans).[29] While these terms could be read as references to a racial type, the author contrasts them with a social category – "otsil uinic" (poor people) – casting doubt on the real meaning of the aforementioned categories.[30] In any case, for the most part the rebels employed the ethnically neutral terms *enemigo*

---

protected" (2004:87) were killed. The letter from the commission merely speaks of "unfortunate prisoners" but makes no reference to their ethnic category or skin color. Another source suggests that the "50 Spaniards and 20 Indians" who had fled with Zapata from Chan Santa Cruz were killed with him (E. Burke to secretario colonial, Corosal, April 4, 1864, *LNE*, April 25, 1864, 3). However, the letter refers to them as his companions (*compañeros*) without clarifying whether they were followers or prisoners.

[27] Declaración de José Estevan Cen, Mérida, April 11, 1879, AGEY, PE, CLM, box 207bis.

[28] J.D. Capetillo, to Gobernador, Tekax, February 12, 1879, *NE*, February 28, 1879, 2–3; Relacion de las personas del pueblo de Tahdziu que han sido saqueadas en la invasion de los indios sublevados el 24 de Febrero próximo pasado, N. Novelo, Peto, March 1, 1879, *RP*, March 5, 1879, 2.

[29] García y García (1865:vii) suggested that Indians referred to "individuals of the European race" as "sac maax," which he translates as "white monkey." However, no other source or context is given.

[30] M. Huchim to P. Chuc, n.p., July 27 and September 15, 1847, Letter to P. Chuc, n.p., August 20, 1847, all in CAIHDY, M, XLI.1847–1849/1.

Civil War, Ideology and Motivation 259

(enemy) and, less often, ts'ul (foreigner/gentleman/rich man) to refer to their adversaries. As mentioned earlier, they usually identified themselves with terms alluding to religious ties (cristiano'b, kruso'b) or social position (otsilo'b). This also holds true for masewalo'b, which described the common people but was not an ethnic category.[31] While contemporary Yucatecan officials and numerous later scholars generally translated ts'ul and masewal as "white" and "Indian," respectively, these renderings are problematic since ts'ul and masewal alluded to differences in lifestyle and status, and expressed social distance to the speaker.[32]

Widespread racist attitudes and deeds among the rebels are highly improbable for several reasons.[33] As already mentioned, the contending parties, government troops and rebels, were composed of people from both legal and racial categories. Many kruso'b leaders were non-Indians. Esteban Cen, for example, had to work on the ranch of rebel captain Vitoriano Vitorín, who was considered a vecino in contemporary Yucatecan society, thereby further questioning the racist interpretation of his report by the Yucatecan interrogator. In fact, a substantial number of non-Indians lived among the rebels most or all of the time and included leaders, the rank and file, and captives. Deserters from central Mexico or Yucatán, vecinos who joined the rebels or were captured, black lumbermen and Chinese contract laborers who had fled Belize and their descendants were all assimilated into kruso'b society. In 1888, for example, a visitor to the kruso'b village of Chunculché found "several purely white people, some with fair hair." "These people," he added, "speak only the Indian language – 'Maya' – and in dress and manner, and so far as I could judge, in ideas, are exactly the same as the Indians by whom they were surrounded."[34] A common way of life rather than phenotypic

---

[31] For the use of these terms, see several letters from rebel leaders in Chi Poot (1982:230, 240, 243); E. Aké to P. Pech, Uayma, December 27, 1849, CGC:59; F. Chan et al. to J.M. Barrera, Cruzchén, April 22, 1850, CAIHDY, M, XLII.1850–1866/011; P. Balam to General J.F. Tun Cantón, Cauil Akal, May 13, 1855, CAIHDY, M, XLII.1850–1866/ 27; J.C. Poot to L. Canul, Noh Cah Sta. Cruz, November 18, 1882, ACASY, box 3, dossier 35, file 2; Sullivan (1989:118). See also Dumond (1997:123–124) for masewal and ts'ul as neither ethnic nor racial categories.

[32] See the references on social categories in Chapter 3. For the translation of ts'ul and masewal as white and Indian, cf., for example, Bricker 1981:187–218 and the documents published in CGC.

[33] See extended discussions of the issue and further references in Gabbert (2004b:97–104) and Restall and Gabbert (2017:102–104, 109–118).

[34] Miller 1889:28. See also F. Gil to Gobernador, Tekax, May 20, 1868, *RP*, May 20, 1868, 1. In 1869, seventy-seven to eighty Chinese lived in Chan Santa Cruz (Lieutenant Governor to Governor, Jamaica, September 16, 1869, R. 98, ABH:315).

260   *Part VI: Intricacies of Caste War Violence*

features determined membership of the we-group.[35] Dumond has succinctly pinpointed why this was so, summarizing the effects of centuries of miscegenation and cultural borrowing:

> With the borderlines muddied between "Indian" and "Spaniard" in a social sense if not a legal one; with half or more of all *vecinos* able to count a mother, a grandmother, or both, who had been legally Indian before marriage; with affective relations thus made ambiguous; and with Maya the real native language of all campesinos, inclusion of *vecinos* among the rebels was inevitable.[36]

As shown in Chapter 17, not only individuals categorized as white or mestizo but also Indians were victims of kruso'b attacks. Neither did the rebels slay all the vecinos in the towns they occupied. The government endeavored to conceal this fact fearing a broad coalition of the lower classes, namely, legal Indians and vecinos, against elite policies. As mentioned earlier, it consistently denigrated rebels as barbarous Indians who threatened civilization in general and non-Indians in particular. That the government knew better is clearly shown in a document from December 1847 submitted to the chamber of deputies in secret session, since the Governor considered it "inconvenient" that the real insurgent program be made public. It clarifies that tax reduction was the genuine aim of the rebellion and thus attractive to Indians and non-Indians alike, in turn magnifying the threat to the government:

> Convinced that the Indian rebel program is obviously not to destroy other races ... but to liberate everyone from the poll tax ... proved by the fact that vecinos in occupied villages were not killed if they surrendered, His Excellency is of the opinion that it will spread and find proselytes among the Indians in every district in the state ... but also among proletarians of other races renowned for their dislike of the poll tax.[37]

That the Yucatecan elite was still apprehensive about an alliance between the lower classes and the kruso'b ten years later is confirmed in a statement by Governor Pantaleón Barrera. Complaining that rebel emissaries were even found roaming around Mérida, he declared that "there is no shortage of notorious ignoramuses who are reviving the frauds that gave rise to the Indian revolt of 1847 and convincing the gullible masses that what Indians want is a change of government."[38]

---

[35] See also the evidence in Gann (1926:246–247) and Villa Rojas (1945:48, 95).
[36] Dumond 1997:408–409, his emphasis.
[37] A la comisión de puntos constitucionales, Mérida, December 26, 1847, AGEY, PE, G, box 65.
[38] Proclama de Pantaleon Barrera, Mérida, September 30, 1857, GS, October 2, 1857, 1.

Civil War, Ideology and Motivation

Although the evidence presented so far conflicts with the alleged racist or exterminatory attitude of the kruso'b, male vecino prisoners did in fact run a higher risk of being killed. This was most likely a consequence of their class position and lack of practical skills rather than their skin color. Whereas many legal vecinos resembled the bulk of Indians in both language and way of life, as argued, the number of upper-class individuals was of course higher in the former group. The elite, easily recognizable by their Spanish and their clothes, probably experienced more hostility from rebels than lower-class vecinos. Beyond that, they were ill-suited to agricultural or construction work and thus more of a burden than an asset unless they had special skills, such as the ability to play an instrument. Of the prisoners captured in Dzitas and Pisté in 1862, General Castillo remarked that "almost all of these unfortunates perished, among them numerous families whose education made it impossible for them, without dying, to carry out the hard work they [the rebels] imposed on them."[39] For reasons best known to themselves, holding the life of an elite prisoner to ransom never became standard practice with the kruso'b.

As far as can be deduced from Juan de la Cruz's letters and the statements of rebel leaders, kruso'b ideology fostered continuation of the struggle against Yucatecans. In addition, there are indications of dehumanization of the enemy. According to the reports of escaped captives, Bernardino Cen, for example, was selected to lead the assaults on the Yucatecan frontier in 1871, since "he was the most suitable, as he himself said, to make a good harvest of squash (or heads), intending with this phrase to inspire courage and faith in his subordinates."[40] Extermination of the enemy, however, was apparently not encouraged and would have conflicted with the self-image of the rebels as devout Christians. As mentioned earlier, one proclamation of the cross criticized the slaughter of fellow Christians who had surrendered as a "grave sin".[41] Other utterances suggest that the rebels never intended to kill all non-Indians. In 1869, for example, Crescencio Poot and other rebel leaders directed a letter at the Yucatecans requesting them to relinquish combat. While the lives of those who surrendered peacefully to the kruso'b were to be spared, those who decided to continue fighting would be killed:

Today I am in this town with those loyal to our father to fight with those who want to, for this we are [here]; whoever is found in combat will die [todo el que caiga en accion de guerra morirá]; [but] we will gladly take in those who come to us in

---

[39] GCY:119.   [40] La guerra de casta, RP, March 29, 1871, 2–3.
[41] Proclama de Juan de la Cruz, Balamna, October 15, 1850, CAIHDY, M, XLII.1850–1866/12.

peace. . . . [W]e are soldiers of our Most Holy Cross and of the Three persons [the Holy Trinity], whom we respect and venerate. No one was killed where we passed; only those we saw died [Por donde hemos pasado no se ha matado á nadie; solamente han muerto los que hemos visto]. We do not borrow, we have troops and ammunition to burn you all, even for ten years. We will soon burn Mérida. We will gladly accept whoever wants to surrender. . . . You have July, August and September to surrender; consideration will cease on October 1st; we will take in all those who wish to surrender, be they Indian [indio], white or black [negro]. . . . Of those who fail to surrender, I will pierce the muzzle [hocico] the way it is performed on cattle and hang them wherever I like. Soldiers, I speak to you; he who comes to defeat us, deluded by government deceit, will be killed, and thus the fool will die.[42]

To conclude, the lines of conflict did not correspond to skin color or a legal category and there is little evidence that physical features were important in determining rebel behavior. The rare explicit categorizing of Blacks in rebel discourse probably reflected the long history of legal discrimination of people of African descent in the Spanish and British colonies, and their status as slaves. Slavery had finally been abolished in Mexico in 1829 and in Belize in 1838, but continued in Puerto Rico and Cuba until 1873 and 1886, respectively. In addition, it is possible that a number of people of African descent stood out physically from the rest of the population. However, Blacks were mentioned in the context of demanding equal rights and some even became kruso'b leaders, thereby proving the absence of discrimination. There was no clear distinction between legal Indians and vecinos in terms of skin color, hair texture or physiognomy with the result that people in both categories were considered masewalo'b. While the few sources that explicitly mention Blacks (box) distinguish them from the masewalo'b, the former were easily integrated into the in-group as otsilo'b. What separated them all from ts'ulo'b was not phenotype but a way of life. Class was a complicated matter. While the insurgents initially included wealthy individuals such as Jacinto Pat and other batabo'b, social differentiation among the kruso'b diminished in later years. Equality was cherished in theory if not always in practice, as shown by the attempt of various leaders to monopolize certain revenues. Being a Maya speaker and poor did not suffice, however, to save someone from capture or death at the hands of the kruso'b. Those living in the government-controlled area were seen as potential enemies and hence legitimate targets for assault.

---

[42] J.C. Poot, J.A. Cobá, A. Ek, C. Novelo, T. Moreno, A. Chablé, J. Aguilar, Tibolon, July 1, 1869, *EP*, July 27, 1869, 3–4. Since the published text was a translated version, the terms used in the Maya original were probably masewal, ts'ul and box.

Civil War, Ideology and Motivation

Racist thinking, in contrast, clearly permeated Yucatecan elite discourse in the nineteenth century and contributed to the slander of Caste War rebels as ferocious savages. While racist discourse may have helped to mobilize Spanish-speaking urban dwellers against the rebels, it is doubtful that it had much impact on the behavior of government troops in campaign, since army and National Guard units included many legal Indians. Thus, racist considerations on both sides had little effect on the use of violence on the ground, which for the most part followed the logics of caudillo politics and factional conflict. The lines between friend and foe did not separate groups that differed in phenotype, legal or racial category or class but ran between the heterogeneous followers of the leaders, regardless of whether these were Yucatecan politicians or kruso'b chiefs.

19

Kruso'b and Soldiers: Parallels and Contrasts

Although Caste War rebels were frequently despised as "barbarians" or "savages," their culture, their society and their military organization were strongly reminiscent of rural Yucatán. A contemporary observer in the 1860s stressed that kruso'b had a "similar degree of cultivation" to people living in the government-controlled area, as they shared the same language, customs and dress. Kruso'b soldiers were "not savage warriors with bodies daubed with colors and adorned with feathers." They were "organized in corps or battalions, and their chiefs and officers, while lacking knowledge of military science, have long practice in waging war."[1] Not unlike army detachments, some rebel combat units included tambours and cornets.[2] As has been shown, the similarities between the Yucatecan population in general, National Guard units in particular and the kruso'b frequently made it difficult to distinguish friend from foe. In addition, kruso'b raiding parties deliberately dressed as soldiers and entered Yucatecan towns without resistance on several occasions (e.g., Tekax in 1857 and Tunkas in 1861). In the latter case, kruso'b leader Claudio Novelo even greeted familiar inhabitants of the town cordially and invited them to take part in a "political plan" proclaimed in Campeche. Although this was nothing more than a trick to prevent the resistance of the inhabitants, it demonstrates that an alliance of pronunciados and kruso'b was still deemed

[1] GCY:129.
[2] J. Orihuela to General en Jefe, Valladolid, August 30, 1855, *EO*, September 18, 1855, 1–3; N. Novelo to Gobernador, Dzonotchel, January 12, 1863, *EN*, January 23, 1863, 1; C. Montes de Oca to Gobernador, Tekax, January 7, 1863, *EN*, January 9, 1863, 1.

Kruso'b and Soldiers: Parallels and Contrasts 265

conceivable at that time.[3] Yucatecan soldiers likewise attempted to deceive their enemies by posing as rebel combatants.[4]

Kruso'b and soldiers were both victims and perpetrators of internal and external violence. They employed force to attack the enemy, defend themselves, appropriate valuable commodities (food, booty) and take prisoners. During expeditions, the army's course of action greatly resembled kruso'b raids on Yucatán's frontier. Soldiers and rebels used similar tactics on their thrusts into enemy territory, mostly assaulting settlements with surprise attacks. As shown above, looting was a key incentive for both soldiers and kruso'b when it came to combat. Prisoners were often sold or employed as laborers. While soldiers handed over prisoners as farm workers to local hacienda owners and agents active in the so-called slave trade with Cuba or as domestics for wealthy urban households, kruso'b leaders exploited captive labor to construct public buildings or work on their farms and in their households. Soldiers and rebels sold captive children as criados, the former to Yucatecans, the latter to Belizians. Army and militia officers and kruso'b leaders naturally had more options to make a profit from these ventures than the rank and file.

Both rebels and government forces rarely distinguished clearly between combatants and non-combatants. At first glance, the killing of non-combatants, particularly women, children and the old, seems cruel and senseless. These deeds may lose some of their apparent irrationality, however, when the purposes of violence and warfare are considered. As mentioned in Chapter 17, the rebels employed a strategy of terror to induce inhabitants of frontier settlements to abandon their homes, thereby expanding the no-man's-land between rebel territory and areas under government control. The government forces, for their part, tried to violently purge the buffer zone of peasants living there beyond state control in order to establish more precise boundaries to the rebels and thus ease their persecution. Beyond that, women and children pose an indirect threat as the potential backbone of both emotional and economic support for the enemy.[5] Destroying this cornerstone would contribute to weakening the foe.

---

[3] GCY:111–112, 116–117, 170–171; J.M Avila to Gobernador, Tekax, September 27, 1857, AGEY, PE, M, box 198, file 56; M. Barbachano: Sobre la última correria de los bárbaros, *EC*, September 11, 1861, 3–4.

[4] See, for example, M. Micheltorena to MGM, Mérida, December 31, 1850, AHM, XI/481.3/2914.

[5] Riches 1986:5, 6 n. 5.

266   *Part VI: Intricacies of Caste War Violence*

Most of the killing in the war occurred in hand-to-hand fighting or during assaults. The machete was employed in combat and as an execution tool by both rebels and government forces.[6] Slaying opponents with several machete blows was likewise standard practice in acts of violence unrelated to the war.[7] The prominence of this weapon was not only due to weather conditions characterized by heavy rains in parts of the year and constantly high degrees of humidity that often made firearms unreliable or useless, but reflected a peasant culture shared by most fighters. The machete was the all-round tool everyone learned to use from an early age.

These similarities notwithstanding, major differences existed between government forces and rebels. Army soldiers and militiamen constituted a significant segment of Yucatecan society but were a minority in the adult male population. Even at the height of the war, most Yucatecan men did not participate in the fighting. Furthermore, Yucatán was part of a larger polity – Mexico – for most of the period. While the Yucatecan state government could thus count on financial and military assistance, the Mexican administration also had a modicum of influence on the direction of the war. Although trade with Belize was essential to the rebels, the British had no say in their internal affairs. The kruso'b resembled a warrior society, particularly for the first three or four decades of the war, when combat against government forces was frequent and booty a major revenue. All men of a specific age took part in defensive action and joined raiding expeditions to Yucatecan settlements. Fighting their enemies, either as assault or defense, was vital to the perseverance of rebel society in political and economic terms. Hence, warfare was much more prevalent among the rebels in the form of concrete action, folklore and the socializing of future generations than the struggle against them was for most Yucatecans. Indeed, training to kill was possibly inherent in kruso'b socialization practices, as the report of children participating in the slaughter of the Bacalar captives in 1858 indicates.

While the army sought to defend the towns and cantonments, kruso'b generally withdrew with little or no fighting when their strongholds were assaulted in an effort to encircle the attackers. This probably reflected differences in the importance attributed to concentrated settlements in both societies. While Yucatecans considered towns and cities as the center of their civilization and the preferred abode of the elite, kruso'b society

---

[6] See, for example, R. Díaz de la Vega to MGM, Peto, May 11, 1852, AHM, XI/481.3/3300; Baqueiro 1990, 5:173.

[7] See, for example, Asesinato en el Partido de los Chenes, *EP*, May 25, 1869, 4.

Kruso'b and Soldiers: Parallels and Contrasts 267

was significantly less stratified and had a far more rural focus. Kruso'b society was not devoid of ranking, however, albeit less rigid than Yucatecan hierarchies. One important exception was the Speaking Cross, which claimed to be and often was the unquestioned authority but not always, as the putsch of Generals Zapata and Santos shows. The mechanisms of order and obedience were most pronounced in regular army units. Militiamen at least had a say in electing their field officers. Among the kruso'b, companies also chose their corporals. It seems that leaders could not simply order an assault on Yucatecans but had to motivate their followers to cooperate. Moreover, as seen earlier, the rank and file had the power to alter the target during expeditions.

Internal violence occurred in both groups, although the underlying causes differed. Force was a means of preventing desertion for government forces as much as for kruso'b. While it merely served to *maintain* obedience of subalterns to superiors in army and militia units, violence was vital among the rebels to *establishing* and upholding the political hierarchy. Government forces were, in principle, based on established, formalized hierarchies of obedience and command, whereas kruso'b caudillism, characterized by a high degree of patrimonialization, was structurally more volatile. As argued in Chapter 15, violence was inherent in caudillo politics. What is more, leadership changes are to be expected in a political system where charisma plays a significant role. A leader's death and major changes in the group situation, such as the need to tap new resources to finance campaigns, are critical moments. As Klaus Schlichte argues, gaining permanent control over a wider area can also cause problems for the established leadership: "The charismatic quality is at risk when armed groups achieve territorial control because of the requirements of everyday life policies contradict unrealistic expectations."[8] If the leader proved unable to meet basic needs of the inhabitants in the area, such as food and safety, his reputation would be seriously damaged. Due to these structural weaknesses, the readiness to use violence had to be demonstrated more frequently among the kruso'b than among government forces if leadership positions were to be maintained.

Kruso'b and Yucatecans also differed in terms of prisoners and their significance for both societies. Yucatecan landowners saw in rebel captives a welcome addition to the hacienda labor force. The latter, however, did not constitute a major demographic factor in regional society. Things were quite different among the kruso'b. Female captives and children

---

[8] Schlichte 2009:114.

played a crucial role in the reproduction of rebel society, balancing the heavy population losses resulting from army attacks, disease, hunger and flight. This is reminiscent of the situation in colonial Yucatán, when Indians who had fled beyond the area controlled by the Spanish abducted women during their raids on frontier settlements.[9]

---

[9] Scholes and Roys 1968:306–308, 334–335, 344.

20

Caste War Casualties

The Caste War was without doubt a bitter and violent conflict that claimed numerous victims and led to the abandonment of many settlements, notably in the central part of the peninsula. The reasons for these deaths were manifold. People of both sexes and all age groups perished in battle or during assaults by rebel or government forces, died of starvation or, weakened by hunger and privation, succumbed to epidemics and disease. The quantification of casualties and their more or less exact attribution to specific causes is, however, not an easy task. According to several sources, between 1846 and 1862 alone, the state of Yucatán (without the area of what became the state of Campeche in 1857) lost 174,209 inhabitants or 41.24 percent of the population and a third or 1,057 of its "most agricultural and productive" localities (*poblaciones*); in other words 24 towns, 216 haciendas and 817 ranchos.[1] Other sources estimate the population decline in the peninsula at over 300,000, which amounts to half the number of pre-war inhabitants.[2] This data is not reliable and most of the vast population loss resulted from dispersion, retreat to areas beyond government control or emigration to Belize.[3]

---

[1] García y García 1865:ix-x; Editorial, *RP*, September 11, 1867, 3–4. According to Rodriguez Losa (1989:211–212), the territory of Campeche had lost 10,177 inhabitants between 1846 and 1862. The additional number of 184,386 inhabitants amounts to a total loss of 36.54 percent of the peninsula's pre-war population.

[2] Dictamen de las comisiones primera de guerra y defensa contra los bárbaros sobre la pacificacion de Yucatán, Mexico, 1873, CAIHDY, F, XXV.1873/5; see also Regil and Peón 1853:291.

[3] For thorough discussions of demographic processes in Caste War Yucatán, see Remmers (1981:310–324) and Rodríguez Losa (1989).

270   *Part VI: Intricacies of Caste War Violence*

The most trustworthy data on Caste War casualties comes from government documents that reported the damage inflicted by kruso'b assaults on Yucatecan towns, haciendas and hamlets. We are in possession of numerous lists detailing the number of dead and wounded, and often their names, gender and age. Sullivan estimates that the rebels killed at least 1,800 and captured between 680 and 1,300 people on their forays into the area around the Yucatecan frontier between 1853 and 1899 alone.[4] I counted approximately 220 instances of offensive rebel military action between 1847 and 1901. Information on the number of victims was available in 152 of these cases and suggests that at least 4,000 to 5,000 Yucatecans – men, women and children – were killed during the attacks.[5] Militia and army losses during government thrusts into rebel territory are not included. Things are much more complicated when it comes to accounts of army losses in service. Dispatches tend not to supply the exact number of dead or wounded. Officers reporting to their superiors carefully selected their information. General Díaz de la Vega, for example, revealed enemy losses in detail in a letter to the minister of defense but remained suspiciously vague about his own casualties.[6] Although occasionally the extreme imbalance between army losses and the number of slain enemies can be explained by the element of surprise or more advanced weaponry, it does tend to jeopardize the credibility of the accounts.

Aggregated data on casualties among the military or rebel combatants is negligible. Reed suggests, however, that government forces lost about a thousand men in 1854–5, half of whom may have been killed in action and "hundreds more died of cholera or were disabled with wounds."[7] Ten percent of the 15,000 soldiers serving in 1849 were hospitalized with illness or injuries.[8] In my detailed computation at least 1,056 soldiers were killed during army attacks on the rebels between 1847 and the end of the nineteenth century.[9] Rugeley asserts that poor nutrition, disease and

---

[4] Sullivan 1997a, I:4.

[5] See Appendix 1. I found concrete figures for 3,433 dead. In seven cases, the sources stated that there had been "several" victims, which I counted as four in each case. In seven other instances, the sources mention that "many" people had died, which I assessed as ten in each case resulting in a total of 3,531. Between 500 and 1,200 victims of the Tekax assault in 1857 and "most" of the 1,800 defenders of Ticul in 1848 must be added to this figure.

[6] R. Díaz de la Vega to MGM, Peto, May 11, 1852, AHM, XI/481.3/3300.

[7] Reed 2001:185. He unfortunately does not give any sources for his statement.

[8] S. López de Llergo to MGM, Mérida, October 12, 1849, AHM, XI/481.3/2914.

[9] See Appendix 2. The numbers given in the sources amount to 1,030 dead soldiers. The figure 26 must be added to these for the four instances where the documents speak of

Caste War Casualties

epidemics claimed more casualties among soldiers than the actual fighting. He provides a list of their calamities, which could certainly be likewise applied to the rebels:

The difficulties and deprivations of service invited an enormous variety of physical hardships, including respiratory infections, hernias, destroyed muscle tissues, and reproductive organs, malaria and mosquito-borne infections, rheumatism, heart disease, fractured spines, eye inflammations, hematosis and varicose veins, faces mangled by bullet, and wounds in all possible parts of the body.[10]

In fact, plans for a major offensive against Chan Santa Cruz in 1866 calculated expected losses from illness alone to be a quarter of the troops.[11] Some areas were particularly conducive to health dangers, including those with a humid climate favorable to fevers and exposed locations close to rebel territory. Lack of medical treatment and provisions added to the burden. The garrison at Bacalar, for example, was tantamount to a suicide mission for all these reasons. Late 1849 saw over 200 of the 1,000-strong garrison defeated by illness and the death of the only doctor available.[12] From a company of seventy-eight US mercenaries sent there by the Yucatecan government, only twenty-six returned in 1850.[13] Food deprivation, lack of medical treatment and exposure to inclemency caused mortality rates to run high among the soldiers, sometimes reaching more than 80 percent. General Díaz de la Vega considered the climate of Bacalar "so deadly that it not even spares the natives and residents of the place." Those who arrived from other places "suffer constantly and are exposed to loss of life from the many and severe diseases." It is therefore no surprise that from a battalion of 100 men sent to Bacalar only 17 survived their stay.[14] Between April 1849 and September 1851, 601 soldiers died there. In addition, 43 officers, sergeants and corporals, and 194 soldiers deserted.[15]

"several" soldiers lost and the one case where they state that "many" had been killed. No data is given for 91 of the 307 cases.

[10] Rugeley 2009:72.

[11] Informe sobre el plan de campaña del Gral. Castillo, J.L. Uraya to Emperador, n.p., [November 27] 1865, AGN, G, SI, vol. 44, file 69.

[12] S. López de Llergo to MGM, Mérida, October 12, 1849, AHM, XI/481.3/2914.

[13] M. Micheltorena to MGM, Mérida, August 5, 1850, AHM, XI/481.3/2914.

[14] R. Díaz de la Vega to MGM, Mérida, June 26, 1851, AHM, XI/481.3/3256. See also M. Micheltorena to MGM, Mérida, October 31, 1850, AHM, XI/481.3/2914; R. Díaz de la Vega to MGM, March 26, 1852, AHM, XI/481.3/3300.

[15] Correspondencia del Siglo, SDN, September 17, 1851, 3.

272   *Part VI: Intricacies of Caste War Violence*

A look at the demography gives some general clues to kruso'b living conditions and their mortality rate. The somewhat scant information on the rebel population consists mostly of rough estimates and is often conflicting. In the absence of reliable statistics, and given the highly mobile population, it is extremely difficult to identify the precise reasons for varying figures. Dumond provides the most thorough discussion of rebel demography. He suggests 100,000 as a reasonable figure for the approximately 30,000 rebel combatants and their families in the spring of 1848, after they had conquered much of the peninsula. This figure probably dropped to about 25,000 in the 1860s, following the rebel retreat to the southeast and the defection of major groups in the south in 1853 and in the north in 1859. In the 1870s and 1880s, the kruso'b population varied between 9,000 and 15,000 people. Around 1900, the figure was between 5,000 and 6,600 kruso'b.[16] It is more than likely that war casualties constitute only a minor portion of the population decline. Dumond argues plausibly that the kruso'b population failed to reproduce. Possible reasons are defection, epidemics, other diseases, hunger, high infant mortality, internal faction fighting and the dead resulting from combat with government forces.[17] The sources indicate the frequent scarcity of food, particularly in the early 1850s, when kruso'b were subjected to almost constant persecution by the army.[18] Dysentery, fevers, infections caused by sand fleas (tetanus), and other ills wreaked havoc among the rebels.[19]

The biggest challenge is calculating rebel casualties. We have almost no detailed accounts of combat with government forces and only a few of the assaults on Yucatecan settlements from the kruso'b perspective that allow for reliable quantification of their losses. Government accounts may be inflated to boast of army successes or underrate rebel casualties due to the latter's custom of carrying their dead and injured off the battlefield. In

---

[16] Dumond 1997:130–131, 409–412.   [17] Dumond 1997:413–416.

[18] See, for example, M. Micheltorena to MGM, Mérida, April 24, 1851, AHM, XI/481.3/3257; J.E. Rosado to CGE, Cruzchén, May 6, 1851, AHM, XI/481.3/3258; R. Díaz de la Vega to MGM, Mérida, June 12, 1851, AHM, XI/481.3/3256; R. Díaz de la Vega to MGM, Mérida, June 26, 1851, AHM, XI/481.3/3257; M.F. Peraza to General en Jefe, Valladolid, April 3, 1855, *EO*, April 20, 1855, 1–3; M.F. Peraza to Comandante General, Valladolid, October 28, 1857, *GS*, November 4, 1857, 1.

[19] Correspondencia, *RP*, August 5, 1874, 4. Chan Santa Cruz was hit by a severe cholera epidemic in 1853, for example (J.M. Esquivel to SGG, Sotuta, November 16, 1853, AGEY, PE, SP, box 211, file 17; J.M. Covian to General en Jefe, Peto, November 26, 1853 and M.F. Peraza to General en Jefe, Valladolid, November 28, 1853, both in *ER*, December 9, 1853, 2–3).

Caste War Casualties 273

other words, traces of blood left by dead or wounded kruso'b are often the only indication of the losses incurred.

Distinguishing civilians from combatants among the rebel casualties is a formidable task for at least two reasons. Firstly, as in most civil wars, the lines between the two groups were blurred. Insurgent groups habitually lacked formally defined membership and hiding among civilians may have been insurgent tactics. Secondly, the killing of non-combatants found in no-man's-land beyond the government domain or in rebel territory could be disguised as combat procedure in army reports. The sources suggest that killings indicated in official reports as the result of combat with armed kruso'b had often taken place in the form of surprise attacks on unsuspecting peasant villages in no-man's-land or rebel territory.[20] In late June and early July 1850, for example, Lieutenant Colonel O'Horan and 700 soldiers undertook an excursion to Santa Rosa and Bacalar, far beyond the Yucatecan frontier. His forces attacked eighteen alleged rebel settlements, killing 108 men and 9 women, and taking 218 prisoners of both sexes and different ages. No more than four soldiers were injured. The exact circumstances are not given in most cases so that it remains unclear whether the killings took place during combat or not. A report on one of these incidents on the way from Colohcheakal to Tzucacab, for example, dryly remarks: "three rebels and two women received death."[21] In September of the same year, Captain Pérez attacked several hamlets in the territory beyond the frontier, killed twenty-six alleged rebels and took an equal number of "prisoners of both sexes and different ages." Only one of his 200 soldiers was slightly injured in the expedition.[22] Sullivan calculates that at least 547 kruso'b were killed and 1,413 caught by government forces between February 1853 and April 1855 alone.[23] In compliance with Yucatecan sources, almost 7,000 rebels (men, women and children) were killed during government attacks between 1847 and the end of the nineteenth century.[24]

While lack of sources makes a reliable calculation of rebel casualties during the war impossible, existing documentation permits an informed

[20] Cámara Zavala 1928, part 10.
[21] M. Micheltorena to MGM, Mérida, July 30, 1850, AHM, XI/481.3/2914.
[22] M. Micheltorena to MGM, Mérida, October 12, 1850, AHM, XI/481.3/2914.
[23] Sullivan 1997a, II:5 cuadro 2.
[24] See Appendix 2. The sources indicate 6,763 dead enemies. The figure 100 must be added for cases where the documents mention "several" (ten instances) or "many" (six instances). We have no data on the number of rebels killed in 53 of the 307 cases. Rebels killed during the campaign of General Bravo are not included.

274   *Part VI: Intricacies of Caste War Violence*

guess as to kruso'b losses during their offensive operations against Yucatecan settlements in the second stage of the conflict. Sullivan estimates that between 300 and 600 kruso'b warriors died during their assaults on the Yucatecan frontier from 1853 to 1899. Given that the dead and those captured by government forces amounted to no more than 12 percent in the worst cases, these losses do not appear overwhelming.[25] According to my count, the rebels lost more than 1,500 men in the course of their offensive actions between 1847 and 1901.[26] Similar to government forces, rebel casualties were not only due to combat. Illness resulting from diet deficiency, exhaustion and poor drinking water on the march were more often the cause of death than the fighting itself.

In most respects, the first phase of the Caste War up to the end of 1848 resembled the other large-scale revolts and civil wars that plagued Yucatán and Mexico for much of the nineteenth century. As mentioned earlier, engagements frequently took place between relatively large bodies of combatants. Places in settled parts of the peninsula in or around the towns, villages and haciendas were the typical theaters of battle. Conditions changed dramatically, however, in the second phase of the war when, with the exception of kruso'b assaults on Yucatecan frontier settlements, most of the fighting occurred in the dense jungle of the peninsula's southeast. Here the climate and general living conditions were particularly harsh. Access to food and clean drinking water constituted a serious problem, particularly during campaigns, with medical treatment by doctors rarely available for the injuries or illnesses of the soldiers and healers (h-meno'b) among the rebels. It can be assumed therefore that the share of casualties as a direct result of fighting, the scale of which had been reduced, probably declined in relation to those that resulted from illness, lack of food and water and exhaustion. Detailed knowledge of the southeastern jungle gave the kruso'b an edge in this respect. While the rebels faced a limited risk of dying in the course of their assaults on the Yucatecan frontier between 1853 and 1899, army unit operations beyond the government-controlled area had become quite perilous, particularly since the mid-1850s when rebel society had

---

[25] Sullivan 1997a, I:4, II:5.

[26] See Appendix 1. The numbers of rebels killed are reported for 76 of the 220 cases, amounting to 1,485 dead. I estimated rebel losses at four when the sources spoke of "several" rebels killed and ten when they indicated that "many" had died. To the resulting number of 1,533 dead, a portion of the 250 to 300 rebels injured and killed at Yaxcabá in 1848 must be added.

Caste War Casualties

consolidated and their military expertise increased. Several major army thrusts (e.g., 1854, 1856, 1860) ended in complete disaster.

As mentioned, battles between large masses of combatants only occurred at the beginning of the war. Most of the fighting after that took place in the form of raids and surprise attacks on Yucatecan cantonments, towns, villages, haciendas and hamlets or rebel settlements. On the whole, casualty rates for this type of fighting were low, with the number of dead generally below ten in most single instances. However, since army thrusts and rebel raiding expeditions affected more than one settlement as a rule, casualties often added up to several dozen dead.[27] Surprise attacks on or sieges of major settlements, massacres of fleeing adversaries or the slaughtering of captives led to higher numbers of victims in exceptional cases, that is, dozens or even hundreds of human casualties. Probably more than 1,000 men, women and children, for example, were slain by the rebels during their assault on Tekax on September 14, 1857.[28]

---

[27] See Appendix 1 and 2.

[28] J.M. Avila to Gobernador, Tekax, September 17, 1857, AGEY, PE, M, box 198, file 38; J. Cadenas to MGM, Mérida, September 30, 1857, AHM, XI/481.3/4264; ABH:199.

21

The Caste War in Broader Perspective

As argued in the Introduction, the Caste War stands out from the numerous other rebellions and civil wars that haunted Mexico in the nineteenth century due to its duration, its magnitude and its consequences.[1] The most intensive phase lasted several years, from 1847 to the mid-1850s, a period comparable only to several Yaqui rebellions in northern Mexico, the Reform War (1857 to 1861) and the struggles against the French Intervention and the Mexican Empire of Maximilian (1861–7). While war-related casualties added up to hundreds or even several thousands in most other conflicts, they probably amounted to tens of thousands in the Caste War and the last two cases mentioned.[2] Apart from the Yaqui rebellions, the Caste War was the only rural uprising that led to the establishment of independent rebel polities lasting more than a few months or years. Contrary to other rural insurgents such as those of Guerrero between 1842 and 1846, Caste War rebels did not apparently link their struggle to national politics of the day after 1848 by explicitly adopting the political discourse of liberals or conservatives, for example, or siding with one party or another.[3] This may reflect Yucatán's relative

[1] Since a thorough comparative study of the numerous rebellions and civil wars in Mexico during that period would exceed the scope of this book, the following remarks seek merely to highlight some particularities of the Caste War and its similarities to other uprisings as stimulation for further studies in this direction.

[2] Cf. the estimates on battle-related deaths for several wars and major uprisings in nineteenth-century Mexico in Dixon and Reid Sarkees (2016:37–55, 63–64, 66–68, 70). Scheina estimates that French, Austrian and Mexican conservatives lost more than 33,000 lives during the French Intervention and Liberals "undoubtedly lost more" (2003:311).

[3] For the Guerrero uprising, see Guardino 1995, especially pp. 207–212.

The Caste War in Broader Perspective

geographical and, to a certain extent, political isolation from the rest of Mexico, the rebels' closeness to the British in Belize and their effort to maintain autonomy.

Leaving these particularities aside for the moment, it is evident that many features of the Caste War were far from unique but mirrored widespread patterns of violence, politics and state-building in Latin America. Political instability, gross inequality, a lingering racist ideology and rivalry for power, not least to access revenues in the context of an economy slow to recover, shaped the background against which the Caste War and other revolts and civil strifes evolved. Given the weakness of formal institutions, caudillism became the dominant pattern of politics and rule for decades after Independence, not only among Yucatecan factions and kruso'b but all over Mexico and beyond. Robert L. Scheina has rightfully chosen *The Age of the Caudillo* as a subtitle for the first book in his series on Latin America's Wars dedicated to the nineteenth century.[4] The period of endemic pronunciamientos and civil wars in Mexico first came to an end in 1877, when Oaxacan caudillo General Porfirio Díaz defeated his rivals politically and militarily. During his presidency, the country experienced three decades of relative peace, economic development and the strengthening of central state power under the control of an authoritarian and, where necessary, repressive regime. It was in this context that government forces finally conquered kruso'b territory in 1901.

Besides the dynamics inherent in caudillo politics – rivalry for leadership and lack of institutionalized succession procedures – violence among and between contending parties and against non-combatants was fostered by additional features in the Caste War, as in many other nineteenth-century insurrections. The use of force was widespread in the recruitment of soldiers all over Latin America. Recruitment was uneven and unfair. Thus, alleged vagabonds or men in poor condition and the rural poor bore most of the burden of military service in standing armies and militias. No wonder desertion was rampant and exemplary punishments deemed necessary to maintain discipline.[5]

Warfare was often cruel, with the summary execution of prisoners, the sacking of towns and haciendas and the burning of buildings. Massive battles were comparatively rare and fighting occurred mostly in the course of assaults. Even in large-scale civil wars, guerilla tactics remained the most common form of fighting, which, along with counter-insurgency

---

[4] Scheina 2003. See also Lynch 1992.   [5] Deas 2002:86–89.

278   *Part VI: Intricacies of Caste War Violence*

operations, also affected countless non-combatants.[6] Given the limited capacity of governments and insurgent leaders to secure regular combatant provisioning, commandeering or plundering resources was indispensable in many cases. This in turn further increased civilian deprivation and suffering. Whether the acquisition of goods by force counted as a legal requisition or outright robbery lay in the eye of the beholder. In addition, both governments and insurgents tended to rely on bandits to fight against their adversaries and, as Paul Vanderwood put it for the Mexican Reform War, "differences between soldier, bandit, patriot and avenger simply disappeared."[7]

As mentioned in Chapter 18, characterization of the Yucatán uprising of 1847 as a caste or race war was far from unique. On the whole, elites widely interpreted the social structure of their societies in terms of race in nineteenth-century Latin America, tying in with colonial policies and legislation, and increasingly coined in the language of (pseudo-)science. The period was the heyday of "scientific" racism in many parts of the world. Mexico was no exception. Indians and non-Indians were seen as the main social and racial categories in most of the former Spanish colonies. Even wealthy and educated Indians were liable to become suspect, as shown by the ruthless persecution of caciques in the initial months of the Caste War. Denigrating views and practices were not confined to legal Indians but applied to the (rural) lower classes in general. In many instances, peasants and farm workers were referred to as Indians irrespective of descent or culture, equating race and economic position.[8] As these constituted the vast majority of the population, elites considered unrest among them a major threat to the established order. Against this backdrop, the trope of the caste war became a common means to delegitimize social protest and disturbances as attacks on "civilization" by "barbarous" Indians.

Religion played a key role in many rural uprisings in nineteenth-century Mexico.[9] It served to justify the insurgent cause in the eyes of the world or to legitimize leaders vis-à-vis their followers. Leaders often backed their claims to command by asserting privileged access to

---

[6] For the Mexican Reform War (1857–61) and the French Intervention (1861–7), see Scheina 2003:298–299, 302, 303–305, 308–309.

[7] Vanderwood 1984:49; see also pp. 42, 48–55.

[8] The relation of race and class concepts in the nineteenth century is discussed in Gabbert (2007).

[9] For a brief discussion of various uprisings and their religious aspects, see, for example, Barabas 1989. Vanderwood (1998) provides a detailed study of one of these movements.

The Caste War in Broader Perspective 279

supernatural forces and presented their decisions as based on God's revelations. Rebels repeatedly styled themselves as the true believers. Millenarist elements in rebel beliefs helped to keep fighters in the struggle. As already mentioned, talking idols were, for example, an integral part of the insurgent cult in the War of St. Rose in Chamula, Chiapas (1867–70).[10] Promises that believers would be immune to rifle fire or restored to life if killed in battle were attempts to raise the fighting spirit of the rebels.[11]

The lower classes bore the brunt of casualties and suffering in the Caste War as in most other violent conflicts of the period. They were over-represented in the rank and file of army and National Guard units and rebel ranks alike and, if non-combatants, ran a far greater risk of falling prey to assault. While haciendas and towns held the promise of more booty for the raiders, they were better protected than the isolated peasant homesteads, hamlets or villages. Hence, as we saw, rebels killed numerous Maya speakers during their assaults. Politicians in Mérida and Campeche were absorbed in their internal power struggles and – when the existential threat of rebel victory was averted in the second half of 1848 – content to protect the mainstay of elite economic interests, that is, the large towns, cities and henequen plantations in the peninsula's west and northwest. Neither were they greatly concerned that the border areas were being ravaged by rebel assaults or that military garrisons along the front line suffered from lack of food, adequate clothing and often pay, and were haunted by disease of all kinds. Although the border area was constantly threatened by kruso'b attacks up to the 1870s, it seemed sufficiently remote and uninteresting from the elite perspective in Mérida and Campeche to allow frontier cantonments to be stripped of countless troops on several occasions to act as fighting power in the factional struggles in the west. Yucatecan elites were thus quite typical in their disregard for the fate of the lower classes in nineteenth-century Latin America.

The Caste War example confirms key findings of recent empirical research and theoretical efforts to understand violence in civil wars and insurgencies. Of particular importance are the peculiarities of factional

---

[10] For summary accounts of the movement, see Reina 1980:45–57, Bricker 1981:119–125, Barabas 1989:211–216, 228–229 and Köhler 1999.
[11] See, for example, Barabas 1989:215; Vanderwood 1998:4. Hoffman (2011) offers an interesting interpretation of this kind of war magic based on material from Sierra Leone and Liberia suggesting that it should be seen as a creative method of dealing with the existential uncertainties of warfare.

conflict such as the confrontation of collectivities that crosscut other cleavages (e.g., class and ethnicity) and the key role of material benefits and personal loyalties between leaders and followers in the recruitment of conflict groups. In many cases people pursued their own idiosyncratic interests and, if circumstances required, changed sides. Hence, political ideology and the "master cleavage" (Kalyvas) cannot always account for civil war violence. Beyond this, the use of physical force is often contingent on short-term necessities such as scarcity of supplies to feed troops or captives. Think of the collapse of peace negotiations with the kruso'b in Yucatán in 1851 as the result of the frontier garrisons' rejection of a ceasefire, which would have called a halt to thrusts into rebel territory to garner corn.

While the Yucatán Caste War was depicted by Yucatecan and Mexican elites as the existential struggle of civilization against barbarism in the nineteenth century, it was vindicated after the Mexican Revolution as an exemplary agrarian struggle by the indigenous people against Ladino exploiters. More recently, the conflict has been reappraised as a Mayan ethnic liberation war against the Spanish-speaking oppressors. Beyond their obvious differences, these interpretations have at least two features in common. All of them interpret the war as a struggle between good and bad, glorifying one side or the other as heroic, depending on their ideological leanings and contemporary circumstances. In addition, all of them tend to neglect the countless deaths and distress suffered on the "bad" side.[12] If this book helps to remind us that, similar to other wars, the Caste War took the lives of many, most of them innocent people, on both sides of the front and in the buffer zone in between, it has served its purpose.

---

[12] This critique obviously does not apply to more recent historical studies such as those of Paul Sullivan, Terry Rugeley or Don Dumond, frequently cited in this text, all of whom have greatly contributed to a more balanced interpretation of the conflict.

Appendices

Abbreviations

Places	CSC	Chan Santa Cruz
	CSC-O	attacks from CSC del Oriente/Mabén
	h.	hacienda
	r.	rancho
People	ch	child
	CS	cosaco
	f	female
	HD	hidalgo
	I	Indian
	m	male
	P	prisoner
	R	presentado
	S	soldier
	V	vecino
	t	toddler
	Z	seized
Booty	@	arrobas
	$	pesos
	es	escopeta (shotgun, fowling piece)
Sources	CGE	Comandante General del Estado
	GDE	Gobernador del Estado
	JP	Jefatura Política
	MGM	Ministro de Guerra y Marina
	SGG	Secretaría General de Gobierno
General	n.d.	no data

APPENDIX 1 *Rebel and Kruso'b Attacks*

Date	Place	Leader, strength	Yucatecans				Rebels			Sources/Remarks
			injured	dead	captive	Booty	injured	dead	captive	
30/7/47	Tepich	Chi+200	–	22–23V	–	n.d.	–	–	–	GCY:30; Baqueiro 1990, 1:237 (25–30 vecino families killed)
early Aug. 47	Ekpedz	4–500	–	several	–	n.d.	–	–	–	Baqueiro 1990, 2:12–13
12/8/47	r.Yaxché	n.d.	2fV	1mV	–	60 ounces gold, jewelry, clothes	–	–	–	Baqueiro 1990, 2:14/ women probably raped
Aug. 47	h.Acanbalán, r.San Fernando	Chan+B. Novelo +200	–	several mfchl+V	–	oratory ornaments +jewelry	–	–	–	Baqueiro 1990, 2:17; Ancona 1879/80, 4:36–37
Oct. 47	Tixcacalcupul	Indians of Muchucux	–	most residents	–	n.d.	–	–	–	Ancona 1879/80, 4:86; Baqueiro 1990, 2:244/ town burned
10/11/47	Tihosuco	J. Pat?+1,500–2,000	n.d.	n.d.	n.d.	200,000 cargas corn, livestock, 16,000$	–	–	–	GCY:35; Baqueiro 1990, 2:49
27/11/47	Tinum	300	n.d.	25	1ml	livestock	n.d.	n.d.	n.d.	*LU* 7/12/47/ houses burned
5/12/47	Chemax	4,000	2V, 1IS	1	n.d.	n.d.	n.d.	n.d.	n.d.	F. Domínguez Sosa to E. Rosado, Chemax, Dec. 5, 1847, AGEY, PE, G, box 65; E. Rosado, Valladolid, Dec. 9, 1847, AGEY, PE, G, box 64/ 45 houses burned
Dec. 47	r.Cehac	n.d.	n.d.	1mV	several f	n.d.	n.d.	n.d.	–	Ancona 1879/80, 4:87
19/12/47	Xcan, Chancenote	n.d.	1fV	1mV+1ch	2 girls	n.d.	n.d.	n.d.	n.d.	Letter from V. Rivero, Valladolid, Dec. 19, 1847, AGEY, PE, G, box 65
29/12/47	Tikuch	n.d.	n.d.	n.d.	–	n.d.	several	several	–	Ancona 1879/80, 4:87–89
5, 19–24/12/47	Ichmul	Ve+6–10,000	>100S	>80	n.d.	n.d.	n.d.	19ml	–	GCY:36; Baqueiro 1990, 2:65, 67; Ancona 1879/80, 4:64–65; Clodfelter 2002:338 (1000 dead Yucatecans)
28/12/47	Kancabzonot, Santa María, Yaxuná	n.d.	6–8V	–	–	n.d.	–	–	–	Baqueiro 1990, 2:92
Jan. 48	Kankabchén (5/1), Sacalaca, Petuillo, Dzitnup, Dzonotchel	Barrera+100	n.d.	4mV	several	n.d.	–	–	–	P. Badillo to Obispo, Peto, Jan. 11, 1848, AHAY, G, I, box 227, file 3; *LU*, Jan. 15, 1848; Baqueiro 1990, 2:70
3/1/48	Tikuch	n.d.	30S	18S	n.d.	n.d.	n.d.	n.d.	n.d.	Baqueiro 1990, 2:109–110

Date	Place								Source
4/1/48	Cacalchén, h.Xul, Kancabdzonot	n.d.	n.d.	n.d.	n.d.	n.d.	n.d.	n.d.	Baqueiro 1990, 2:93/ burned
9/1/48	Uayma	n.d.	n.d.	n.d.	n.d.	n.d.	15m	n.d.	Baqueiro 1990, 2:112
16/1/48	Tixcacaltuyú	n.d.	1S	1S	n.d.	n.d.	1	n.d.	Baqueiro 1990, 2:94
20?/1/48	r.Santa Cruz, h.Xbach, r.Nohitza	Tee+300	>1mV	>1mV	n.d.	–	–	–	GDE to Comandante en gefe, division en operaciones, Maxcanú, Jan. 21, 1848, AGEY, PE, G, box 67
26/1-6/2/48	Peto	Chi, Pat+2-3,000	22S	98+many	n.d.	n.d.	n.d.	n.d.	Baqueiro 1990, 2:79, 272, 274-275, 284; GCY:40 (strength 15,000 during siege)
early Feb. 48	Thul, Ticum, Caxaituk, San Antonio	n.d.	n.d.	n.d.	n.d.	n.d.	n.d.	n.d.	Baqueiro 1990, 2:87
1/2/48	Chancenote	1-2,000	n.d.	18S+several families	n.d.	n.d.	n.d.	n.d.	Baqueiro 1990, 2:117; Ancona 1879/80, 4:93 n. 7
12/2/48	Yaxcabá	great numbers	n.d.	n.d.	n.d.	n.d.	n.d.	n.d.	GCY:40; Baqueiro 1990, 2:96-97
16/2/48	r.Sacsucil	n.d.	n.d.	36mf	n.d.	n.d.	n.d.	n.d.	Baqueiro 1990, 2:89/burned
17/2/48	Polyuc, Cancabchén, Yalkukul	n.d.	n.d.	1mV	>30 mostly women	n.d.	n.d.	n.d.	GDE to Gefe de division en operaciones, Maxcanú, Feb. 17, 1848, AGEY, PE, G, box 67
27/2/48	Macmay	n.d.	n.d.	12	n.d.	n.d.	n.d.	n.d.	GDE to Comandante en gefe, division de operaciones, Maxcanú, Feb. 27, 1848, AGEY, PE, G, box 67
18/1-14/3/48	Valladolid	12-15,000	n.d.	>400m+many fch	n.d.	huge	n.d.	n.d.	Baqueiro 1990, 2:113,130; GDE to Comandante General de Marina de la Havana, Maxcanú, March 21, 1848, AGEY, PE, G, box 67; S. Molas to CGE, Tizimín, Sept. 22, 1849, AGEY, PE, M, box 168, file 17 (rebel losses 35 dead and injured)
Jan. 48	Popolá	n.d.	n.d.	1mI	n.d.	n.d.	n.d.	n.d.	Baqueiro 1990, 2:114
29/2-10/3/48	Sotuta	Chi?+5-6,000	>40	2S	n.d.	n.d.	n.d.	n.d.	Ancona 1879/80, 4:81-83; Baqueiro 1990, 2:97, 100; CGY:51/burned
24/3/48	Sacalum	n.d.	1S	several	n.d.	n.d.	n.d.	n.d.	Ancona 1879/80, 4:123
2/4/48	Tunkás	n.d.	1S	n.d.	n.d.	n.d.	1	n.d.	JP de Izamal to SGG, Izamal, April 2, 1848, AGEY, PE, box 67
10/4/48	Bacalar	Pec+10,000	n.d.	n.d.	n.d.	n.d.	n.d.	n.d.	M. Estevas to the Superintendent, Bar of San Antonio, April 20, 1848, and Superintendent to Officer Commanding Troops, April 23, 1848, both in ABH:106; Baqueiro 1990, 2:160-161; 3:147-149; Dumond 1997:127 (siege April 16-20)

(continued)

Date	Place	Leader, strength	Yucatecans			Booty	Rebels			Sources/Remarks
			injured	dead	captive		injured	dead	captive	
late April 48	Tipikal	n.d.	–	1V	–	n.d.	–	–	–	A. Rejon to SGG, Mérida, May 10, 1848, AGEY, PE, G, box 67
27/4/48	Hopelchén	"a white man" +2–3,000	n.d.	1m	n.d.	–	–	n.d.	–	P. Ramos to SGG, May 2 and 6, 1848, both in AGEY, PE, G, box 67
May 48	Dzilam	n.d.	n.d.	n.d.	n.d.	n.d.	n.d.	several	n.d.	Baqueiro 1990, 2:193
May 48	Sitilpech	n.d.	n.d.	n.d.	n.d.	n.d.	n.d.	36	n.d.	Baqueiro 1990, 2:194
3/5/48	Maní	n.d.	n.d.	>100mf	n.d.	n.d.	n.d.	n.d.	n.d.	A. Rejon to SGG, Mérida, May 10, 1848, AGEY, PE, G, box 67; GCY:55 (burned down); Baqueiro 1990, 2:181 (>200 Yucatecans dead)
3/5/48	r.Nohbec	n.d.	–	–	3mI+3fI	n.d.	–	–	–	J. Falavera to SGG, Ticul, May 3, 1848, AGEY, PE, J, box 67
early May 48	Ich-Ek	1,000	n.d.	3V	n.d.	n.d.	–	–	–	P. Ramos to SGG, Campeche, May 6, 1848, AGEY, PE, G, box 67
4/5/48	r.Halal	n.d.	several	n.d.	n.d.	n.d.	–	–	–	J. Falavera to SGG, Ticul, May 4, 1848, AGEY, PE, J, box 67
4/5/48	Bolonchén	n.d.	n.d.	n.d.	n.d.	n.d.	–	–	–	P. Ramos to SGG, Campeche, May 6, 1848, AGEY, PE, G, box 67
12/5/48	Tekax	J.Pat+sizable forces	n.d.	n.d.	n.d.	n.d.	n.d.	n.d.	n.d.	GCY:55
May? 48	Panaba	Huchim+200	n.d.	many	n.d.	n.d.	–	–	–	Juicio contra conspiradores, Sisal 1848, AGEY, PE, J, box 69
19/5/48	Tekanto, Teya	n.d.	n.d.	n.d.	n.d.	n.d.	–	–	–	A. de Zepeda to SGG, Motul, May 19, 1848, AGEY, PE, G, box 67/ burned
16–26/5/48	Ticul, Muna, Sacalum	J. Pat+24,000	>62S+1mI	>4S+several families	n.d.	n.d.	several	>31	–	Baqueiro 1990, 2:185, 186, 188, 191
20–28/5/48	Ticul	24,000	n.d.	most of the 1,800 defenders	n.d.	n.d.	n.d.	n.d.	n.d.	Clodfelter 2002:338; Baqueiro 1990, 2:184; GCY:56
mid-May 48	Sitilpech, Tepakán	n.d.	n.d.	4S	n.d.	n.d.	n.d.	30	n.d.	Baqueiro 1990, 2:196
20–29/5/48	Izamal and environs	B. Novelo, Huchim +huge number	several S	several S	–	n.d.	n.d.	n.d.	n.d.	GCY:55; Baqueiro 1990, 2:191, 195, 199–200/more than 350 soldiers dead, injured or dispersed,
18/6/48	Hampolol	n.d.	16S	4–5	n.d.	n.d.	n.d.	many	n.d.	Baqueiro 1990, 3:9
7/7/48	Homún, Cuzamá, Huhí	n.d.	n.d.	n.d.	n.d.	n.d.	n.d.	many	n.d.	Ancona 1879/80, 4:152
19?/7/48	Tecoh	n.d.	n.d.	n.d.	n.d.	n.d.	n.d.	>40	n.d.	Baqueiro 1990, 3:9; Ancona 1879/80, 4:151

18–19/7/48	Tunkas	Gutierrez	8S	n.d.	n.d.	n.d.	n.d.	>50	n.d.	GCY:62; Baqueiro 1990, 3:13
21/7/48	Sacalum	J. Pat	12	1S	n.d.	n.d.	19	14	–	J.D. Zetina to General en Gefe, Sacalum, July 22–24, 1848, AGEY, PE, M, box 165, file 52; Baqueiro 1990, 3:19–20
Aug. 48	Huhí	n.d.	n.d.	n.d.	n.d.	n.d.	n.d.	7	–	Baqueiro 1990, 3:25
8?/8/48	Dzitás	n.d.	n.d.	17S	–	n.d.	n.d.	n.d.	n.d.	Baqueiro 1990, 3:74
8–19/9/48	Yaxcabá	Chi, Pec, Chan, Poot, Cahum +5,000	n.d.	>5S	n.d.	–	–	250–300 injured and dead	–	Baqueiro 1990, 3:58, 61, 65; Ancona 1879/80, 4:175–179/taken by rebels, reconquered 30/9/48
15/9/48	Tixcacaltuyú, Mopilá	huge masses	n.d.	n.d.	n.d.	n.d.	n.d.	n.d.	n.d.	Ancona 1879/80, 4:177
20/9/48	Sotuta	5,000	4S	n.d.	n.d.	n.d.	n.d.	4	n.d.	Baqueiro 1990, 3:66
Oct. 48	Loché	n.d.	2	8	n.d.	n.d.	n.d.	n.d.	–	Baqueiro 1990, 3:80
6/10–11/11/48	Tekax	Barrera, M. Pat +4,500–5,000	97S	22S	–	n.d.	n.d.	25	–	Baqueiro 1990, 3:81, 83–85, 87–91
22/12/48–30/4/49	Tihosuco	J. Pat	50S	8S	–	n.d.	n.d.	n.d.	–	Baqueiro 1990, 3:112–115
17 Jan.–April 49	Sabán sieged	Barrera, Espadas, Encalada	n.d.	1S	n.d.	n.d.	n.d.	n.d.	n.d.	Baqueiro 1990, 3:116
15/2/49	Sacalaca	n.d.	n.d.	n.d.	n.d.	n.d.	n.d.	n.d.	n.d.	GCY:74/attacked, abandoned by soldiers and restored
late Feb. 49	Oxkutzcab	n.d.	12	7	–	n.d.	n.d.	n.d.	–	GCY:74/attacked, Indians repelled
31/3/49	Xcupil	n.d.	1S	–	–	n.d.	n.d.	10	–	Baqueiro 1990, 3:118–119
April 49	Tihosuco, Sabán	n.d.	31S	9S	n.d.	n.d.	n.d.	n.d.	n.d.	Baqueiro 1990, 3:190; GCY:73/sieged, T. 9 months, S. 1 year
19/5/49	Becanchén	n.d.	n.d.	8	–	–	several	7	–	Letter to Comandante de la 1a division, Tekax, May 21, 1849, AGEY, PE, M, box 168, file 60
2/5–29/8/49	Bacalar	n.d.	>24	>43S	–	n.d.	many	>36	>1	J.D. Zetina to CGE, Bacalar, June 24, 1849, *BOGY*, July 10, 1849, 1–4; GCY:77/ sieged
Sept. 49	Santa Elena	indios of Moreno +Nohayin	–	1S+1V	3 families	n.d.	n.d.	n.d.	–	Baqueiro 1990, 3:201
late 49	Chunchintok	indios of Nohayim	4S	6S	–	n.d.	n.d.	n.d.	–	Baqueiro 1990, 3:233
late 49	Tituc	n.d.	n.d.	331	n.d.	n.d.	n.d.	n.d.	n.d.	Clodfelter 2002:338
March 50	Espita	Huchim+150 +50 ligeros	n.d.	n.d.	–	n.d.	n.d.	n.d.	–	Baqueiro 1990, 4:13–14/attack repelled
8/3/50	Tixcacalcupul	Chi, Poot	8S	–	–	n.d.	n.d.	n.d.	–	Baqueiro 1990, 4:17–18
March 50	Cenotillo	n.d.	4S+1f	1S	–	n.d.	n.d.	1	–	Baqueiro 1990, 4:19
30/3–9/4/50	Cavil, Sabán, Excovil, Tixcacal	huge mass	4	3	–	n.d.	some	22	–	Yucatán, diversos encuentros, n.p., n.d. [April 1850], AHM, XI/481.3/2914

(*continued*)

Date	Place	Leader, strength	Yucatecans			Booty	Rebels			Sources/Remarks
			injured	dead	captive		injured	dead	captive	
30/6/50	Ekpedz	Matias Uh+large number	6S+2f	1S	–	n.d.	16	6	–	M. Micheltorena to MGM, Mérida, July 16 and Oct. 10, 1850, both in AHM, XI/481.3/2914
16/7/50	Kaua	Chulim	1S	11S	–	n.d.	n.d.	9	–	Baqueiro 1990, 4:90
23/7/50	Kaua	sizable number	10S+1f	1S+1fch+1m	–	n.d.	n.d.	9	–	M. Micheltorena to MGM, Mérida, July 31, 1850, AHM, XI/481.3/2914
15/10/50	Chichimilá	sizable number	3S+2mI	1mI	–	n.d.	n.d.	n.d.	–	M. Micheltorena to MGM, Mérida, Oct. 19, 1850, AHM, XI/481.3/2914
29/10/50	Calotmul	Chan+200 armed +many unarmed	4S	–	–	n.d.	n.d.	>9	–	M. Micheltorena to MGM, Mérida, Nov. 2, 1850, AHM, XI/481.3/2914
4/11/50	Tekax	200	5S+2f	5S+1f	–	trade goods, arms	some	n.d.	–	M. Micheltorena to MGM, Mérida, Nov. 8, 1850, AHM, XI/481.3/2914
22/11/50	Bolonchénticul	Góngora, Chan +500	11	8m+1f+1t	5fI voluntary	clothing, liquor, soap	n.d.	13 (incl. P. Chan)	–	Comandancia General de Yucatán to MGM, Mérida, Nov. 28, 1850, and M. Micheltorena to MGM, Mérida, Dec. 11, 1850, both in AHM, XI/481.3/2914; Baqueiro 1990, 4:113–114
1/1/51	Xul	n.d.	–	–	several families	n.d.	many	4	–	M. Micheltorena to MGM, Mérida, Jan. 18, 1851, AHM, XI/481.3/3255
4/1/51	Kampocolché	n.d.	32S	4S	–	n.d.	n.d.	>97	–	M. Micheltorena to MGM, Mérida, Jan. 10, 1851, AHM, XI/481.3/3255; Baqueiro 1990, 4:121–122
24/1/51	Kampocolché	huge masses	2S	1S	–	–	many	21	2	M. Micheltorena to MGM, Mérida, Jan. 31, 1851, AHM, XI/481.3/3257
10/2/51	cantón Ox	huge number	–	–	–	–	3	7	the 3 injured	M. Micheltorena to MGM, Mérida, Feb. 18, 1851, AHM, XI/481.3/3258
19–20/3/51	Kampocolché	>1,000	5	–	–	–	n.d.	80 (incl. R. Chan, C. Cahum)	10	M. Micheltorena to MGM, March 28, 1851, AHM, XI/481.3/3257
20/3/–April? 51	Macanché	n.d.	2	2	–	–	n.d.	12	2mV+1mI +6f	M. Micheltorena to MGM, Mérida, May 5, 1851, AHM, XI/481.3/3257/ sieged
28/3/51	Bacalar	Pec+800	11S	1S	6S	51 firearms	many	132	–	R. Díaz de la Vega to MGM, Mérida, June 13, 1851, AHM, XI/481.3/3256
19/12/51	Tihosuco	Cocom+100+?	6S+1m+2f	1mV	n.d.	n.d.	n.d.	42	–	R. Díaz de la Vega to MGM, Tihosuco, Jan. 29, 1852, AHM, XI/481.3/3300; Baqueiro 1990, 4:168; Cámara Zavala 1928, part 2
March 52	Dzibalchén	Cocom	n.d.	n.d.	several families	n.d.	n.d.	n.d.	n.d.	Baqueiro 1990, 4:174

March 52	Tekax	May	n.d.	n.d.	n.d.	n.d.	n.d.	n.d.	n.d.	n.d.	Baqueiro 1990, 4:174
23/4/52	r.Chumvec+environs	200	n.d.	various m+ch	various f,	n.d.	–	–	–		Cámara Zavala 1928, part 11
June 52	Xcohil, Nohyaxché, Kampocolché, Tepich	Vargues+sizable number	18S	–	several m+f+3S	n.d.		n.d.	28	–	E. Rosado to General en Jefe, Peto, June 8 and 12, 1852, both in AGEY, PE, M, box 179, files 77–79; GCY:91; Baqueiro 1990, 4:174-175
31/7/52	Oxkutzcab	May+400	1S	1S+1mV	–	–		many	10	–	R. Díaz de la Vega to MGM, Mérida, Aug. 2, 1852, AHM, XI/481.3/3300
13/9/52	Chiquindzonot	n.d.	n.d.	n.d.	n.d.	n.d.		several	several	8	J.D. Pasos to SGG, Sotuta, Sept. 16, 1852, AGEY, PE, M, box 180, file 38; R. Díaz de la Vega to MGM, Mérida, Oct. 4, 1852, AHM, XI/481.3/3300
12?/10/52	Xcan	C.+B. Novelo	n.d.	n.d.	–	booty lost		n.d.	21	4	R. Díaz de la Vega to MGM, Mérida, Oct. 30, 1852, AHM, XI/481.3/3300
18/10/52	Hool	n.d.	n.d.	4m							R. Carvajal to SGG, Campeche, Oct. 18, 1852, AGEY, PE, G, box 67
20/10/52	cantón Chemax	sizable number	6	n.d.	n.d.	n.d.		n.d.	25	–	R. Díaz de la Vega to MGM, Mérida, Oct. 30, 1852, AHM, XI/481.3/3300
1853	Sacalaca, Sabán, Tituc, Uaymex, Polyuc et al.	n.d.	n.d.	n.d.	large number	huge		n.d.	n.d.	–	GCY:94
1853	Tiholop	n.d.	n.d.	n.d.	at least 1mV	n.d.		n.d.	n.d.	n.d.	P.A. Gonzalez to GDE, Yokdzonot, Dec. 12, 1854, EO, Jan. 2, 1855, 1–2
May 53	r.San Pedro	n.d.	n.d.	16mV+1fI	4mV+ several mI	n.d.		n.d.	n.d.	–	E. Rosado to GDE, Peto, May 17, 1853, AGEY, PE, G, box 94
15, 17/5/53	Temoson, Tesoco	n.d.	n.d.	1mI	n.d.	n.d.		n.d.	n.d.	n.d.	M. Cepeda Peraza to General en Jefe de la Division Vega, Valladolid, May 17, 1853, AGEY, PE, M, box 182, file 19
May 53	several around Valladolid	n.d.	n.d.	n.d.	several mI+ families	n.d.		n.d.	15	–	R. Díaz de la Vega to MGM, Peto, May 27, 1853, AHM, XI/481.3/3300
7/7/53	Tixcacalcupul	500	n.d.	n.d.	n.d.	n.d.		2	25	–	Sullivan 1997, I:4
July 53	Tikuch	n.d.	3S	–	–	–		n.d.	10	3	R. Díaz de la Vega to MGM, Mérida, Aug. 13, 1853, AHM, XI/481.3/3696
mid-9/53	Tituc, Peto+environs	n.d.	1S	>12S+ numerous families	n.d.	n.d.		n.d.	n.d.	n.d.	Baqueiro 1990, 4:223
9–12/53	Tihosuco, Ichmul, Chikindzonot, Sacalaca, Dzonotchel, Tadzibichén, Sabán, Tixcacaltuyú, Yaxcabá, Santa María	n.d.	n.d.	large number	several	trade goods		n.d.	n.d.	n.d.	Baqueiro 1990, 4:199–200; Ancona 1879/80, 4:350/burned

(continued)

Date	Place	Leader, strength	Yucatecans			Booty	Rebels			Sources/Remarks
			injured	dead	captive		injured	dead	captive	
Jan. 54	Río Lagartos	n.d.	n.d.	n.d.	n.d.	n.d.	n.d.	n.d.	n.d.	Rugeley 2009:116
18/7/54	Sacalaca	n.d.	n.d.	n.d.	2mI+1fI	n.d.	n.d.	n.d.	n.d.	Relacion nominal de las personas que se llevaron los bárbaros…, April 9, 1855, AGEY, PE, CP, box 65, file 21
22/7/54	Tihosuco	500	–	–	–	–	n.d.	14	4	J.M. Novelo to General en Jefe de la division, Peto, July 23, 1854, *EO*, Aug. 18, 1854, 1
6–9/9/54	Peto, Yaxcabá, Tiholop, Ichmul, Yacalkab, Dzonotchel	800	n.d.	13	26mV+12fV +27mI+25fI +11ch	n.d.	n.d.	15	–	Sullivan 1997a, I:4; GCY:103; J.D. Castro to GDE, Izamal, Sept. 12, 1854, *EO*, Sept. 22, 1854, 2; Relacion nominal de las personas que se llevaron los bárbaros…, April 9, 1855, AGEY, PE, CP, box 65, file 21
24/10/54	Tihosuco	300	n.d.	n.d.	n.d.	n.d.	n.d.	9	–	Sullivan 1997a, I:4
1–2/11/54	Tekom, Kaua	300	n.d.	>20mf	n.d.	n.d.	5	9	–	Sullivan 1997a, I:4; A.Pat et al. to GDE, Valladolid, Dec. 19, 1854, AGEY, PE, G, box 98; M.F. Peraza to General en Jefe de la division Cadenas, Valladolid, Jan. 12, 1855, *EO*, Jan. 23, 1855, 1–3 (gives early Dec.)
9–10/1/55	way to Pachmul	200	8S	5S	–	8 horses	several	1 or more	–	P.A. Gonzalez to GDE, Yokdzonot, Jan. 25, 1855, *EO*, Feb. 16, 1856, 1–3/assault on 42 soldiers and 6 hidalgos
11/2/55	Peto, San Pedro, Bulu-Kax, Suná, Poluincil, Pocol	300	n.d.	>60mfVI+7S	many	rich booty	n.d.	18	–	G. Ruiz to SGG, Tekax, Feb. 14, 1855, AGEY, PE, M, box 185, files 57 and 59; Relacion…ataque a la villa de Peto, Feb. 13, 1855, AGEY, PE, G, box 120, exp. 14; J. Rivas to GDE, Mérida, March 9, 1855, AGEY, PE, M, box 186, file 33; GCY:105
21/2/55	Pachmul	large group	18S	28S	n.d.	n.d.	n.d.	n.d.	–	J.M. Novelo to General en Jefe, Pachmul, Febrero 22, 1855, *EO*, March 20, 1855, 2; Baqueiro 1990, 4:230 (80 casualties)
25/2/55	Xocen, Xocom	100	–	1f	–	–	–	2	–	M.F. Peraza to General en Jefe de la division Ampudia, Valladolid, Feb. 27, 1855, *EO*, March 9, 1855, 3–4
12/3/55	r.Noh-cut	30	2mI	–	–	–	–	–	–	L. Gutierrez to Comandante General y en Jefe, Valladolid, March 15, 1855, *EO*, March 30, 1855, 3

late Dec. 55	Becanchén	n.d.	n.d.	>16mf+18I	–	trade goods	–	–	–	Movimiento de los Bárbaros, UL, Dec. 28, 1855, 4
10/1/56	cantón Calotmul	300	2S+2f	1S			many	8	–	M.F. Peraza to CGE, Valladolid, Jan. 12 and 15, 1856, both in AGEY, PE, G, M, box 103
21/4/56	Kancabdzonot	400	14	65f+17m		n.d.	n.d.	n.d.	–	J.M. Esquivel to GDE, Sotuta, April 25, 1856, GS, April 30, 1856, 2–3
21/4/56	Tijolop and pozo	400	n.d.	>43mf		n.d.	n.d.	n.d.	–	J.M. Esquivel to GDE, Sotuta, April 25, 1856, GS, April 30, 1856, 3
22/4/56	Yaxcabá, h.Xul	400	1	1S+4ch+21f+19		rich booty	1	3	–	J.M. Esquivel to GDE, Sotuta, April 25, 1856, GS, April 30, 1856, 3; J.G. Rejon to GDE, Sotuta, April 23, 1856, GS, April 28, 1856, 2; GCY:1106; Baqueiro 1990, 4:260
23/4/56	Tihosuco, h.Balche	n.d.	5S	–		n.d.	some	n.d.	n.d.	J.M. Novelo to GDE, Peto, April 24, 1856, GS, April 30, 1856, 2/h.Balche burned
4/56	Tixcacalcupul, Kaua	n.d.	–	11mf		n.d.	sizable	sizable	n.d.	Baqueiro 1990, 4:262
April 56	partidos Peto and Sotuta	n.d.	n.d.	>200mf		n.d.	n.d.	n.d.	n.d.	C. Baqueiro to GDE, Hopelchen, May 2, 1856, AGEY, PE, G, box 104
mid-July 56	r.Isla Blanca	Yam, José Pat+60	n.d.	3		n.d.	–	–	n.d.	M.F. Peraza to CGE, Valladolid, July 15, 1856, AGEY, PE, G, box 103
July? 56	Xcan	n.d.	n.d.	n.d.	5ml+ families		n.d.	n.d.	n.d.	M.F. Peraza to GDE, Valladolid, July 18, 1856, AGEY, PE, G, box 103
20/9/56	Ichmul	n.d.	n.d.	1fV		n.d.	n.d.	n.d.	–	GCY:1106/burned
20/10/56	Tixcacalcupul	C. Novelo, Poot +1,000	5	–		–	several	several	n.d.	M.F. Peraza to CGE, Valladolid, Oct. 21, 1856, GS, Oct. 24, 1856, 2–3; M.F. Peraza to CGE, Valladolid, Oct. 23, 1856, GS, Oct. 29, 1856, 1–2/rebels "completely destroyed"
21/10/56	Kaua	large number	2	1S+11fch		n.d.	n.d.	n.d.	–	M.F. Peraza to CGE, Valladolid, Oct. 22, 1856, GS, Oct. 29, 1856, 1/burned
26/10/56	Tihosuco	Poot+200	2S	–		–	n.d.	>1	1	J.M. Novelo to CGE, Peto, Oct. 28, 1856, GS, Oct. 31, 1856, 1
22/11/56	Tihosuco	n.d.	22S+1f	9S		n.d.	–	10	2	J.M. Novelo to GDE, Peto, Nov. 27, 1856, GS, Dec. 3, 1856, 1; Sullivan 1997a, I:4 (20 rebel losses)
late 56 or early 57	Nohhá	n.d.	n.d.	n.d.		n.d.	n.d.	n.d.	n.d.	La Redaccion, GS, Jan. 12, 1857, 3/victims V and I
16/2/57 CSC-O	Kikil, r.Kankanjaas	Sánchez+300 Tun+30	1m	1mI	various mf	trade goods	n.d.	7	1	La Redacción, GS, Feb. 25, 1857, 4; M.F. Peraza to CGE, Valladolid, Feb. 27, 1857, GS, March 4, 1857, 1

(continued)

Date	Place	Leader, strength	Yucatecans			Booty	Rebels			Sources/Remarks
			injured	dead	captive		injured	dead	captive	
1–2/8/57	Chikindzonot, Ekpedz, r.Ticul	60+unarmed	n.d.	>78mfIV	n.d.	virgin and saints from church	n.d.	n.d.	n.d.	J.M. Esquivel to GDE, Sotuta, Aug. 5, 1857, GS, Aug. 10, 1857, 1; J.M. Novelo to CGE, Peto, Aug. 4, 1857, AGEY, PE, M, box 197, file 2 (1,000 rebels)/houses burned
13/9/57	Tihosuco, Sacalaca, Ichmul	300	n.d.	n.d.	n.d.	–	n.d.	2	n.d.	J.M. Novelo to GDE, Peto, Sept. 14, 1857, GS, Sept. 18, 1857, 3 Sullivan 1997a, I:4
14–15/9/57	Tekax	Zapata+3–700	n.d.	500–1,200 chmfVI	several	n.d.	several	18	1	J.M. Avila to GDE, Tekax, Sept. 17, 1857, AGEY, PE, M, box 198, file 38; J. Cadenas to MGM, Sept. 28, 1857, AHM, XI/481.3/3783; J. Cadenas to MGM, Mérida, Sept. 30, 1857, AHM, XI/481.3/4264; M.F. Peraza to CGE, Valladolid, Sept. 22, 1857, GS, Sept. 28, 1857, 1; M. F. Peraza to CGE, Valladolid, Oct. 16, 1857, GS, Oct. 21, 1857, 3; GCY:110–111, 169; Aldherre and Mendiola 1869:78 (>2,000mf in Tekax and other towns and hamlets)
15/10/57	Chichimilá	n.d.	3	3	n.d.	n.d.	many	8 (incl. 2nd chief Juan Poot)	1	A última hora, GS, Oct. 19, 1857, 4; M.F. Peraza to CGE, Valladolid, Oct. 16, 1857, GS, Oct. 21, 1857, 3; Sullivan 1997a, I:4 (12 rebel losses)
28/11/57	Tixcacal	80	–	1f	–	–	n.d.	2	–	M.F. Peraza to CGE, Valladolid, Dec. 1, 1857, GS, Dec. 7, 1857, 1
21/2/58	Bacalar	500–600	n.d.	50S+200chmf	13	n.d.	–	–	–	"Sucesos de Bacalar," Mérida, March 29, 1858, AHM, XI/481.3/6288; T.R. Estéves to GDE, Punta Consejo, March 3, 1858, GS, March 31, 1858, 1–2; M. F. Peraza to MGM, Mérida, March 31, 1858, AHM, XI/481.3/6444; Declaracion de José Cen, Valladolid, April 5, 1858, GS, April 7, 1858, 2–3; Sullivan 1997a, I:4; Superintendent to Governor, Jamaica, March 13, 1858, R. 55, ABH:203 (1,600 rebels, victims mostly women)

Date	Location									Source
7/3/58	Dzonot	n.d.	n.d.	n.d.	2	n.d.	n.d.	n.d.	n.d.	F. Ruiz to GDE, Tizimín, June 8, 1858, *GS*, July 11, 1858,
1/4/58	Valladolid, r. Xnohbuktun	C. Novelo, Poot, Dzul, Balam +300->1,000	33mfVI	4S+1f	n.d.	n.d.	many	12	n.d.	M.F. Peraza to MGM, Mérida, April 3, 1858 and J. Baca to GDE, Valladolid, April 1, 1858, both in AHM, XI/481.3/6444; J. Martínez Vaca, Valladolid, April 1, 1858, *GS*, April 4, 1858, 1–2; Declaracion de José Cen, Valladolid, April 5, 1858, *GS*, April 7, 1858, 2–3; Buhler 1975:11 (commanders C. Poot, L. Santos, B. Novelo, 200 rebel losses)
1/4/58	Xocen	n.d.	n.d.	30mft	n.d.	n.d.	n.d.	>4	1	J. Martínez Vaca to GDE, Valladolid, April 5, 1858, *GS*, April 9, 1858, 1; J. Martínez Baca to GDE, Valladolid, April 9, 1858, AGEY, PE, M, box 201, file 9; Sullivan 1997a, I:4 (58 dead Yucatecans in Valladolid and Xocen), X. almost completely burned
early June 58	r.Botija	n.d.	1mV	–	1fV	n.d.	–	–	2	F. Ruiz to GDE, Tizimín, June 8, 1858, *GS*, July 11, 1858, 1
July 58	Chancenote, Xcan	Batun, Ayala+300	n.d.	n.d.	n.d.	n.d.	n.d.	n.d.	n.d.	J. Martínez Vaca to GDE, Valladolid, July 27, 1858, *GS*, July 30, 1858, 1
20–21/8/58	r.Pusjabin	n.d.	n.d.	51mfchVI	n.d.	n.d.	n.d.	n.d.	n.d.	Relacion de los sirvientes … asesinados …, Peto, Aug. 24, 1858, *GS*, Aug. 27, 1858, 2
21/8/58	Peto, Temozón	Poot, Gonzalez, Castillo, Vitorin, Tzuc, C. Novelo	50	10S+3-4f+49mf in T	several	–	>90	40	n.d.	F. Pren to GDE, Peto, Aug. 21, 1858, *GS*, Aug. 21, 1858, 2; J.M. Novelo, to GDE, Peto, Aug. 24, 1858, *GS*, Aug. 30, 1858, 2
17/11/58	r.Chicibchulul, r.Xtcan	n.d.	3mf	4f+1m	n.d.	n.d.	n.d.	n.d.	–	P. Acereto to GDE, Espita, Nov. 18, 1858, *EC*, Nov. 26, 1858, 1
19–20/12/58	Tacchevichén, Tixcacal, Tiholop, Sotuta	n.d.	3	131	1fI	trade goods, cattle, horses	2	2	–	La situacion, *EC*, Dec. 27, 1858, 4; R. Salazar to GDE, Sotuta, Dec. 24, 1858 and J.C. Salazar to General en Jefe, Sotuta, Dec. 25, 1858, both in *EC*, Dec. 29, 1858, 2/ not included victims in r.Kukul, r.Sisbic and Sotuta
early Jan. 59	r.Xcampech, r.Xkantun	n.d.	n.d.	1m	n.d.	n.d.	–	–	–	M. Sierra Arce to GDE, Tizimín, Jan. 10, 1859, *EC*, Jan. 17, 1859, 1
31/1/59	r.Tzamá	60	–	4mft	19	n.d.	some	n.d.	–	P. Acereto to General en Jefe, Valladolid, Feb. 4, 1859, AGEY, PE, M, box 202, file 19
8/2/59	r.Bodzil, r.Sodzil	25	2mV	1mI	1m	n.d.	–	–	–	M. Sierra Arce to GDE, Tizimín, Feb. 9, 1859, *EC*, Feb. 16, 1859, 1

(*continued*)

Date	Place	Leader, strength	Yucatecans			Booty	Rebels			Sources/Remarks
			injured	dead	captive		injured	dead	captive	
8/2/59 CSC-O	Sucopo	Valle+150	1S+2mV	1mI	–	–	various	1	–	L. Irigoyen to MGM, Mérida, Feb. 18, 1859, AHM, XI/481.3/7112; M. Sierra Arce to GDE, Tizimín, Feb. 9, 1859, *EC*, Feb. 16, 1859, 1/12 houses and audiencia burned
20/2/59	partido Ticul	n.d.	–	–	1fI+3 boys	–	–	–	–	B. Cuevas to GDE, Ticul, Feb. 22, 1859, *EC*, Feb. 23, 1859, 3
24/2/59	r.Yokdzonot	n.d.	3mI+1fI	3mI+5fI+2	–	n.d.	–	–	–	M. Sierra Arce to GDE, Tizimín, Feb. 25, 1859, *EC*, Feb. 28, 1859, 2
26/2/59 CSC-O	Susula, Oxcal	many	2m	1mV+2m	–	n.d.	–	–	–	L.Irigoyen to MGM, Mérida, March 4, 1859, AHM, XI/481.3/7125
27/3/59	r.Xkuxché, r. Xacabchén, r. Chunyá, r. Xtulim	n.d.	1mV	n.d.	12	n.d.	2	n.d.	–	P. Acereto to GDE, Valladolid, March 29, 1859 and J.M. Iturralde to GDE, Valladolid, March 31, 1859, both in *EC*, April 1, 1859, 1–2
17/7/59	Tiholop	600	1S	–	–	–	n.d.	5	–	J.D. Zetina to General en Jefe, Peto, July 19, 1859, *EC*, July 22, 1859, 1–2
17/7/59	Yaxcabá	n.d.	12mV+3mI +1fV +1ch	6mV+2mI+2fV	–	n.d.	n.d.	12	–	Relacion de los individuos muertos y heridos, Mérida, July 16, 1859, and L. Irigoyen to MGM, Mérida, July 19, 1859, both in AHM, XI/481.3/7199
21?/7/59	Ichmul	2–400	4S	2m	–	n.d.	n.d.	7	–	J.D. Zetina to General en Jefe, Peto, July 21, 1859, *EC*, July 25, 1859, 1; Letters from J.D. Zetina to General en Jefe, Peto, July 25 and 26, 1859, both in *EC*, Aug. 1, 1859, 1–2; Sullivan 1997a, I:4 (37 rebel losses)
6/8/59	r.Chan-Hunuku, h.Kampepen	25+20	3mV	43mI+2fV+1fI	1m+8f+3t	n.d.	–	–	–	L. Irigoyen to MGM, Mérida, Aug. 17, 1859, AHM, XI/481.3/7504; J.M. Iturralde to General en Jefe, Valladolid, Aug. 9, 1859, *EC*, Aug. 12, 1859, 1–2
22/6/60	Ekpedz	n.d.	n.d.	n.d.	all families	n.d.	–	–	–	GCY:116
1/7/60	cantón Sacalaca	n.d.	n.d.	22m+32f	–	n.d.	–	–	–	GCY:116/all vecinos enclosed in a house and than burned
31/7/60	r.Hobonil	n.d.	n.d.	2mV+2mI+3fI +1f	n.d.	n.d.	–	–	–	F. Ramírez to GDE, Peto, Aug. 1, 1860, *EC*, Aug. 8, 1860, 1
31/7/60	r.Op	n.d.	n.d.	6	n.d.	n.d.	–	–	–	F. Ramírez to GDE, Peto, Aug. 7, 1860, *EC*, Aug. 8, 1860, 1

31/7/60	Tzucacab	n.d.	1mV+1fl2ml+2fV	3mV+1ml+3fl	n.d.	n.d.	–	–	–	F. Ramirez to GDE, Peto, Aug. 7, 1860, EC, Aug. 8, 1860, 1
20/6/61	Tixcacal	large number	2S	2S	2ml+11f+7t	n.d.	n.d.	>3	–	General en Jefe to MGM, Mérida, June 25, 1861, AHM, XI/481.4/8429
22–23/6/61	Tihosuco, Ekpedz, r. Sihomal, r.Yaxché, r.S.Magdalena, r. Has	n.d.	1ml	7ml+5fl+3ch	many families	n.d.	–	n.d.	–	J.M. Esquivel to GDE, Sotuta, June 24, 1861, EC, July 1, 1861, 2; Relacion de las personas asesinadas…, Peto, June 29, 1861, EC, July 3, 1861, 2
1/7/61	Sacalaca	n.d.	n.d.	13mV+2ml +23fV+6fl	n.d.	n.d.	n.d.	n.d.	n.d.	Relacion de las personas sacrificadas…, Peto, July 4, 1861, EC, July 8, 1861, 2
7/9/61	Tunkas	C. Novelo, Poot, Briceño+300	80–150 (2 in town, rest on the way back)	250–500mfVl	47,000 (25,000 pesos cash) 100 mules, 4,000 trade goods	–	–	–	–	Sobre la última correria de los bárbaros, EC, Sept. 11, 1861, 3–4; Noticias que emite el C. Anastasio Durán…, LRP, Sept. 5, 1862, 1–3; Baqueiro 1990, 5:163; GCY:118
7–12/9/61	Chan Dzonot, Kaxpich, Yaxhá, Xpac, Nohinza, Santa Cruz Román	n.d.	n.d.	200	n.d.	n.d.	n.d.	n.d.	n.d.	GCY:117–118/burned, all inhabitants taken
28/7/62	Pisté	B. Novelo+400–500	n.d.	7mf	83mf	n.d.	n.d.	–	–	L. Irigoyen to MGM, Mérida, Aug. 7, 1862, AHM, XI/481.4/8772; Sullivan 1997, I:4
28/8/62	Dzitas, Mascab-pixoy, S.Antonio, Doholku, Santa Rita, Makulam, Santa Bárbara, San Francisco, San Román	Poot+6–700	4–1S	33mf	n.d.	n.d.	n.d.	–	–	L. Irigoyen to MGM, Mérida, Aug. 30, 1862, AHM, XI/481.4/8772; Baqueiro 1990, 5:199–200/73 houses burned
3/9/62	crucero Sahcabá	n.d.	5S	12S	n.d.	100 guns	n.d.	7	–	L. Irigoyen to MGM, Valladolid, Sept. 10, 1862, AHM, XI/481.4/8772
Sept. 62	r.Labchén, h. Canasuytún	n.d.	many	almost all residents	cattle, horses	–	–	–	–	Baqueiro 1990, 5:203, 205; GCY:122/burned
28/10/62	Dzitas, Kahuá, Pitón, Xlabchén, Kanasuytún, San Román, San Antonio, Kaxacpech, Kanisté, Tepakán, Cuctub, Sabchén, San Lorenzo, San José	>2000	38	10	>200 heads of cattle	n.d.	n.d.	n.d.	n.d.	Sullivan 1997, I:4; Villalobos González 2006:282; N. Novelo to GDE, Peto, Nov. 25, 1862, AGEY, PE, G, box 131

(continued)

APPENDIX I (*continued*)

			Yucatecans					Rebels			
Date	Place	Leader, strength	injured	dead	captive	Booty	injured	dead	captive	Sources/Remarks	
29/10/62	Yaxché, Holkolben, Maitun	Zapata, Cen, Canul +500–1000	n.d.	n.d.	10mf	70 cattle, horses and 15 beasts	–	–	–	D. Peniche to GDE, Espita, Nov. 1 and 3, 1862, *EN*, Nov. 5, 1862, 1–2; F. Zavala, to General en Jefe, Valladolid, Nov. 10, 1862, *EN*, Nov. 14, 1862, 2	
1/11/62	r.Labchén, h. Cauasuytun	n.d.	n.d.	>15ml	n.d.	n.d.	n.d.	n.d.	n.d.	Rugeley 2009:174	
31/12/62	Tikuch r.Xkuil, Becanchén	Poot, Manzanillo +230–300	–	–	2mV+several f	n.d.	–	–	–	C.M. de Oca to GDE, Tekax, Jan. 1 and 4, 1863, *EN*, Jan. 9, 1863, 1; R. Lopez to General en Jefe, Peto, Jan. 4, 1863, *EN*, Jan. 9, 1863, 1	
23–24/9/63	r.Xmabén, Libre Unión	2,000	n.d.	1f	several	n.d.	–	–	–	M. Rodriguez Solis to Jefe Supremo de Armas, Izamal, Sept. 23 and 24, *LNE*, Sept. 25, 1863, 2; Sullivan 1997a.I:4	
13/11/63	Chemax	150–200	n.d.	n.d.	n.d.	n.d.	n.d.	n.d.	n.d.	F. Canton to Jefe Superior de las Armas, Valladolid, Nov. 13, 1863, *LNE*, Nov. 16, 1863, 1–2	
12/2/64	Kanxoc	Ueh+30–40	1ml	2ml	4ml	n.d.	1	1 (B.Ueh)	1	F.A. Canton to Prefecto, Valladolid, Feb. 12, 1864, *LNE*, Feb. 15, 1864, 1; N. Ontiveros to Prefecto, Valladolid, Feb. 12, 1864, *LNE*, Feb. 17, 1864, 1	
23/2/64	Dzonotchel	250	n.d.	n.d.	>1ml	n.d.	n.d.	n.d.	n.d.	J.E. Tejero to Prefecto, Peto, March 26, 1864, AGEY, PE, M, box 225, file 91; A. Sandoval to General en Jefe, Peto, June 12, 1864, *LNE*, June 17, 1864, 1	
16/10/64	Tekom	100	n.d.	2ml+3fI+3ch	n.d.	n.d.	n.d.	n.d.	n.d.	F. Canton, Valladolid, Oct. 16, 1864 and Lista de los individuos asesinados, Chichimilá, Oct. 18, 1864, both in *LNE*, Oct. 21, 1864, 2	
28–29/11/64	Yaxché, Xcimé, Huchim, Chunhuas, Kakalná, Thuul, Acum, Tzuacacab, Ekbalam, Haxché, Xkanan, Chacsikin, Tahdziu, Tixhualajtun, San Miguel Buenavista, Timul, Tepich, Santa Clara	Poot, Cen+600	39mfVI	55mfVI	many	17 mules	n.d.	n.d.	n.d.	Relacion de los muertos y heridos, Peto, Nov. 29, 1864, Relacion de los muertos y heridos, Peto, Dec. 1, 1864, La Redacción and Los indios bárbaros, all in *LNE*, Dec. 3, 1864, 2–4; GCY:134; Aldherre and Mendiola 1869:76; Sullivan 1997a, I:4	

						weapons, munition			
13–19/6/65	Dzonot, Tihosuco	2,000	>608	>438	n.d.		–	200	J. Salazar Ilarrequi to MGM, Ticul, June 22 and 23, 1865, both in AHM, XI/481.4/9976/ J. Salazar Ilarregui to J.D. Peza, Mérida, June 24, 1865, CAIHDY, M, XLVII.1864/21 (304 army losses)
7/9/65	sabanas Calotmul	n.d.	18	15	n.d.	n.d.	n.d.	n.d.	S. Castillo to MGM, Mérida, Sept. 15, 1865, AHM, XI/481.4/9987
27/11/ 2/12–4/12/65	Sahcabá, Senotillo, r. Xluch, Pisté	C. Novelo, Poot, Cen, Dzul +600–1,600	19mVI	14mVI+1f1+2ch	2ml	n.d.	21	11	Guerra de castas, PODM, Dec. 4, 1865, 3; F. Cantón to GDE, Valladolid, Dec. 3, 1865; AGEY, PE, M, box 242, file 46; D. Soberanis to Prefecto, Senotillo, Dec. 2, 1865, PODM, Dec. 6, 1865, 1; Noticias de los indios rebeldes, PODM, Dec. 18, 1865, 4
6/12/65	Fuerte Carolina	<2000	118	108	–	–	n.d.	n.d.	A. Sandoval to General en Jefe, Fuerte de Carolina, Dec. 6, 1865, AGEY, PE, M, box 242, file 54/rebel losses higher than those of soldiers
April 66	ranchos Calotmul, Canalum, Chulul, San Juan, Chan Yaxché, Yaxché, NohYaxché	200	n.d.	3m+2f	several men	45 mules+40–59 horses	–	–	D. Valencia to Prefecto, Peto, April 21, 1866, AGN, G, legajo 2001, box 2497, file 3
11/8/66	close Xcabil (SW Tihosuco)	800	n.d.	22	478 missing	–	n.d.	n.d.	Comandancia superior de la 7a division, Mérida, Aug. 11, 1866, Periódico Oficial, Aug. 13, 1866, in AGN, G, legajo 2001, box 2497, file 2
3/8–23/9/66	Tihosuco (sieged)	Cen+3,000	n.d.	n.d.	n.d.	n.d.	150–200	>33	D. Traconis to General en Jefe, Tihosuco, Sept. 18, 1866, GC, Sept. 25, 1866, 2; La guerra de casta, RP, March 29, 1871, 2–3; Sullivan 1997a, I.4
18/12/66	near Tixcacalcupul	200–300	n.d.	n.d.	4	n.d.	–	–	Sullivan 1997a, I.4; F. Cantón to Prefecto, Valladolid, Jan. 29, 1867, AGEY, PE, CI, box 268, file 58
mid-Jan. 67	ranchos Acum, Oxuas, Thul, Kakalná, Kanalum	n.d.	n.d.	1m	1ch	n.d.	–	–	F. Navarrete to Comisario Imperial, Ticul, Jan. 19, 1867, and Comisario Imperial to jefe de las lineas de oriente y sur, Ticul, Jan. 22, 1867, both in CAIHDY, M, XLVI.1864, 60 and 63

(continued)

Date	Place	Leader, strength	Yucatecans				Rebels			Sources/Remarks
			injured	dead	captive	Booty	injured	dead	captive	
24–28/6/67	Coloxché, Ticum, Tixcuytun, Tixmeuac, Tixcacal, Tixcacaltuyú, Tacchibchén, Cantamec, finca Jesus Maria	Poot+600	5S	6S+15mf	several families	30 cattle, many horses, 3–4 donkeys, loot	many	17	n.d.	F. Medina to GDE, Ticul, June 25, 1867, *RP*, June 28, 1867, 1; L. Espinosa to GDE, Tekax, July 3, 1867, *RP*, July 12, 1867, 2; E. Esquivel to GDE, Sotuta, June 29, 1867, *RP*, July 2, 1867, 1–2 (1,500 rebels)
15/8/67	Tixualahtun	100	2mI+ several mfch	–	–	n.d.	n.d.	5	–	T. Correa to GDE, Valladolid, Aug. 15, 1867, *RP*, Aug. 18, 1867, 1; Villalobos González 2006:283 (60 Yucatecans killed)
7/3/69	Xul	n.d.	n.d.	32S	n.d.	n.d.	n.d.	n.d.	–	J.A. Cepeda Peraza to GDE, Tekax, March 7, 10 and 11, 1869, *RP*, March 12 and 15, 1869; Sullivan 1997a, I:4 (60 Yucatecans killed)
1–3/7/69	Tacchibichén, Yaxcabá, Tzalam, Tiholop, ranchos close to Tunkas, Tibolon, Tzucacab, h. Nohdzonot, Sotuta	1,000	n.d.	140S+1mV +2fV+1f	3f+2t+3ch	silver crown	n.d.	n.d.	n.d.	Letters to GDE, July 2 and 3, 1869, *RP*, July 5, 1869, 2; Los bárbaros en el Oriente, *EP*, July 9, 1869, 4; M.M. Mendoza to Obispo, Sotuta, July 8, 1869, and J.Y. Castro to Obispo, Tixcacaltuyú, July 26, 1869 both in AHAY, G, I, box 228, file 4; Sullivan 1997a, I:4
7/7/69	Chacsikin	1,000	n.d.	n.d.	n.d.	n.d.	several	1	–	N. Novelo to GDE, Tzucacab, July 7, 1869, *RP*, July 12, 1869, 1
12/1/70	Kaua, Uayma, Kapchén, Huaymil, Xanlá, Cisil, Nohakaucab, Santa Lucía, Muchncux, Sorila, Santa María, Xlabchén, Xclopxul, Xhacabá, Canahltun	n.d.	n.d.	n.d.	159	50 horses, 82 pigs	n.d.	n.d.	n.d.	Villalobos González 2006:283
16/1/70	r.Sac-akal, h.Xkanlol, r.Sinabilá, Yaxpeheché, Kantun-balam et al.	200	5S	1S	n.d.	80–100 beasts	–	–	–	N. Novelo to GDE, Tekax, Jan. 17, 1870, *RP*, Jan. 21, 1870, 2; M. Galera to GDE, Tekax, Jan. 18, 1870, *RP*, Jan. 21, 1870, 1–2; Villalobos González 2006:284 (8 Yucatecans killed)
23/8/70	Chichimilá	Poot, C. Novelo +7–800	1mV+2mI	5mI+1mV+4S	3mI+3fI+2fV	n.d.	n.d.	some	–	D. Traconis to GDE, Valladolid, Aug. 26, 1870, *RP*, Aug. 29, 1870, 1; Lo de Chichimila, *RP*, Sept. 5, 1870, 3–4

18–19/12/70	Thul, Caxaytuk, Nohtunich, Ticum, Tixcuytun, Xaya, Nenelá, Tacchibichén	Poot+4–500	2S	3S+4	8	n.d.	17	19	–	J.A. Cepeda Peraza to GDE, Tekax, Dec. 19, 1870, J.M. Diaz to GDE, Sotuta, Dec. 20, 1870 and M. Galera to GDE, Tekax, Dec. 21, 1870, all in *RP*, Dec. 21, 1870, 2–3; J. Y. Castro to Obispo, Tixcacaltuyú, Jan. 7, 1871, AHAY, G, I, box 228, file 4; Sullivan 1997a, I:4; J.C. Poot to I. Chablé, Gran pueblo Santa Cruz, Dec. 28, 1870, *RM*, March 1, 1871, 3 (176 Yucatecans killed)
22/12/70	h. Katbé, r.Napoot	n.d.	–	–	–	several horses	–	–	–	J.A. Cepeda Peraza to GDE, Tekax, Dec. 23, 1870, *RP*, Dec. 26, 1870, 1
1–2/7/71	Chemax	n.d.	4S	3mI+1S	n.d.	n.d.	n.d.	7	–	D. Traconis to GDE, Valladolid, July 4,1871, AGEY, PE, M, box 293, file 40; A. Espinosa to GDE, Valladolid, July 4, 1871, *RP*, July 7, 1871, 2; M. Cicerol to Coronel del Batallon 5° de la GN, Mérida, July 20, 1871, *RP*, July 22, 1871, 1/almost all houses burnt
3–4/2/72	Tahdziu, Tixhualahtun, San José, r.Carolina, Santa Barbara, Santa Rita, Sacakal, Santa Teresa	Poot+600	2S+2mI+1fI	2S+3HD+1mI +1mV	3mI+3fI	n.d.	–	several	–	J. Vazquez to GDE, Peto, Feb. 6 and 10, 1872, both in AGEY, PE, CO, box 297, file 6; Villalobos Gónzalez 2006:284
72?	Tekax	n.d.	n.d.	n.d.	several	n.d.	n.d.	n.d.	n.d.	N. Urcelay to General en Jefe, Isla Mujeres, Aug. 19, 1872, *RP*, Aug. 26, 1872, 1
20/11/72	Yaxleulá, Santa Cruz, Xkeuil, Cauahaltun	large number	n.d.	3mI	21mI+29fI	n.d.	–	–	–	F. Piña to GDE, Sotuta, Nov. 27, 1872, *RM*, Dec. 1, 1872, 2/places are ranchos in Yaxcabá area
11–12/1/73	Ebtun, Kaua, Uayma, Kopcheen, Haymil, Xanlá, Cisil, Nohkaucab, Santa Lucia, Muchucux, Sodzilá, Santa Maria, Xlabechén, Xlopxul, Sahcabá, Canahaltun	Poot, Moguel +300–1,000	6+4S	7+1S	164mfch	50 horses, 82 pigs, 3 pans for sugar making	n.d.	n.d.	–	F. Canton to GDE, Valladolid, Jan. 18, 1873, *RP*, Jan. 24, 1873, 1; C. Moreno Navarrete to GDE, Valladolid, Jan. 25, 1873, *RP*, Jan. 29, 1873, 1; Relacion de personas llevadas, Jan. 31, 1873, *RM*, Jan. 31, 1873, 2–3; Correspondencia, P. Bolio, Izamal, *RM*, May 2, 1873, 3; F. Díaz to CGE, Valladolid, July 29, 1874, AGEY, PE, M, box 311, file 44; F. Canton to GDE, Tizimín, Jan. 14, 1873, AGEY, PE, M, box 302, file 48 (heavy rebel losses at Kaua)
6/2/73	Xnapot	n.d.	n.d.	n.d.	1nV	n.d.	n.d.	n.d.	n.d.	R. Bolio, to GDE, Tekax, June 30, 1873, *RM*, July 4, 1873, 2; see also Katbé

(*continued*)

Date	Place	Leader, strength	Yucatecans			Booty	Rebels			Sources/Remarks
			injured	dead	captive		injured	dead	captive	
6/2/73	r.Katbé, r.San Gregorio	300	–	–	1mV	4 cattle, 1 pig	1–2	–	–	D. Valencia to GDE, Tekax, Feb. 12, 1873, *RP*, Feb. 14, 1873, 1/Katbé burned
27/10/73	Dzonotchel	Poot+2–300	–	2mI	1f+1mI	n.d.	n.d.	n.d.	n.d.	Declaracion de Mónica May, Peto, Aug. 1, 1874, AGEY, PE, CO, box 310, file 86; Correspondencia, *RP*, Aug. 19, 1874, 2
27/10/73	Tekax	large number	1S	2S	1S+3 families	n.d.	n.d.	n.d.	–	G. Ruiz to GDE, Tekax, Oct. 29, 1873, *RP*, Oct. 31, 1873, 1
26/7/74	Balché, Kankabchén, San José	Poot, Vitorin, Moreno+200	4mI	2mV+3mI	5mI+6fI+2mV	n.d.	–	–	–	S. Piña to GDE, Peto, July 28, 1874, AGEY, PE, M, box 311, file 42; N. Novelo to GDE, Peto, Feb. 26, 1879, *RP*, March 3, 1879, 2–3
8/10/75	Ayin and surroundings	Tzuc+60	–	1mI	1m+2f+3ch	5 horses	–	–	–	R.A. Perez to GDE, Peto, Oct. 12 and 16, 1875, *RP*, Oct. 15 and 20, 1875, 1; S. Piña to GDE, Peto, March 11, 1876, *RP*, March 17, 1876, 1
12/10/75	Xuxub	Cen, Juan Pat+90	1mV+2S	4mV+13mf	all peons and families	n.d.	–	20–21	3 (2 injured)	B.M. Montilla to GDE, Puntachen, Oct. 15 and 18, 1875, *RP*, Oct. 20, 1875, 1, 4; D. Sierra, Dzilan, Oct. 19, 1875, *RP*, Oct. 22, 1875, 1; D.S. Osorio to GDE, Tizimín, Nov. 20, 1875, *RP*, Nov. 22, 1875, 1; Causa contra Encarnacion Cahum..., Mérida, May 29, 1876, *RP*, June 2, 1876, 1; Sullivan 1997a, I:4 (42 Yucatecans killed)
11/2/79	Katbé	>400	2mV+2mI +1fI	1mI+many	1mV	n.d.	–	–	–	J.D. Capetillo to GDE, Tekax, Feb. 12, 1879, *RP*, Feb. 14, 1879, 2–3; Existencia de la guerra de castas, *NE*, Jan. 3, 1882, 2
24/2/79	Tahdziu	Chuc+300	–	2mI, 2mV	5mI+2fV+5t	20 mules, 4 cattle	n.d.	10	–	J.D. Capetillo to GDE, Tekax, Feb. 25, 1879, *NE*, March 7, 1879, 3; J.D. Capetillo to GDE, Tekax, Feb. 26, 1879, AGEY, PE, JP Tekax, box 210B; Relacion de personas saqueadas..., Peto, March 1, 1879, *RP*, March 5, 1879, 2; Relacion de los muertos..., Peto, March 11, 1879, *RP*, March 14, 1879, 1; J.M. Iturralde to GDE, Valladolid, March 23, 1888, *RP*, April 6, 1888, 3; Sullivan 1997a, I:4

6–7/2/86	Tixualahtun, Dzonotchel	400–1,000	8S	–	–	–	40	30	–	Los indios sublevados, *RP*, Feb. 8 and 10, 1886, 1; La Razon del Pueblo, *RP*, April 5, 1886, 1; J.M. Iturralde to GDE, Valladolid, March 23, 1888, *RP*, April 6, 1888, 3 (R.Tex+200 rebels)
early April 88	camps of Urcelay on coast between Cozumel and Isla Mujeres	rebels from Tulum	n.d.	100	n.d.	n.d.	n.d.	n.d.	n.d.	Dumond 1997:358

APPENDIX 2 *Attacks by Government Forces*

Date	Place	Leader, Strength	Enemies				Yucatecan losses			Sources/Remarks
			injured	dead	captive	Booty	injured	dead	captive	
27–28/7/47	Tepich, Ekpedz	Trujeque+100 several V	several f	6m	n.d.	n.d.	–	–	–	GCY:30/women raped
4/8/47	environs Tepich	Pacheco, Beitia	n.d.	n.d.	n.d.	n.d.	1	5	–	Baqueiro 1990, 2:110
7/8/47	Tepich	Ongay+>200	n.d.	12m	n.d.	n.d.	5	4	–	Baqueiro 1990, 2:110–11/m, f, ch burned
9/8/47	r.Chunbob	Ongay+250	n.d.	n.d.	n.d.	n.d.	11	several	–	Baqueiro 1990, 2:13
Aug. 47	Xcá	Cámara, Zavala +200	n.d.	n.d.	n.d.	n.d.	7–12	8	–	Baqueiro 1990, 2:17; Ancona 1879/80, 4:36
early Aug. 47	Cochatún	O'Horan+150	n.d.	n.d.	n.d.	n.d.	2	several	–	Baqueiro 1990, 2:19
25/8/47	Xcanul	Heredia	n.d.	30–32	–	n.d.	17	1	–	Baqueiro 1990, 2:16, 241–243; Ancona 1879/80, 435
24/11/47	Sacalaca	Baqueiro+200	n.d.	12ml	n.d.	n.d.	n.d.	n.d.	–	Baqueiro 1990, 2:63
late Nov. 47	Ichmul	Baqueiro	n.d.	>100ml	n.d.	n.d.	n.d.	n.d.	n.d.	Baqueiro 1990, 2:64
mid-Dec. 47	Chemax	Irabién+150	n.d.	n.d.	n.d.	n.d.	36	–	–	Baqueiro 1990, 2:107/injured not in combat
late Dec. 47	Tiholop	1,500	n.d.	several	several	n.d.	n.d.	n.d.	n.d.	GCY:37
29/12/47	Kancabdzonot	Castillo	n.d.	n.d.	n.d.	n.d.	several	several	–	Baqueiro 1990, 2:292
Jan. 48	Canakón	Díaz	n.d.	n.d.	n.d.	n.d.	n.d.	n.d.	n.d.	Baqueiro 1990, 2:95/heavy defeat
8/1/48	Ebtún	Rivero	n.d.	n.d.	n.d.	1 cattle, horses, many mules	10	5	–	Baqueiro 1990, 2:111–112
9/1/48	h.San Lorenzo	Rivero+200	n.d.	n.d.	n.d.	n.d.	5	4	–	Baqueiro 1990, 2:112
11/1/48	Tahchibichén	170	n.d.	n.d.	n.d.	n.d.	n.d.	n.d.	n.d.	Baqueiro 1990, 2:293
20/1/48	Dzonotchel	Ongay, Baqueiro +500	n.d.	several	–	n.d.	–	–	–	Baqueiro 1990, 70–71; GCY:37
15/2/48	Chichmilá	n.d.	n.d.	n.d.	n.d.	n.d.	n.d.	n.d.	n.d.	GCY:45/burned
18/2/48	Becanchén	Pérez	n.d.	8+several P killed	n.d.	n.d.	n.d.	n.d.	n.d.	Baqueiro 1990, 2:90
20/2/48	Dzitnup	Rivero+300	n.d.	n.d.	n.d.	–	15–20	30–40	–	Baqueiro 1990, 2:119–120/sortie from Valladolid
26/2/48	Cantamayec	García	n.d.	n.d.	n.d.	n.d.	6	2	–	Baqueiro 1990, 2:88
24/3/48	h.Suná	González+250	several	15	–	supplies	n.d.	n.d.	n.d.	Ancona 1879/80, 4:123
14/4/48	Komchén	n.d.	n.d.	n.d.	4	n.d.	–	–	–	A. Marcin to CGE, Campeche, April 16, 1848, AGEY, PE, G, box 74

Date	Place	Forces								Source
20–27/5/48	Hopelchén	Barrera+500	n.d.	n.d.	152	powder+160 guns	n.d.	n.d.	n.d.	Baqueiro 1990, 2:166–167; GCY:69
10/6/48	Tunkas	Gutierrez+1,200 +200HD	n.d.	n.d.	n.d.	n.d.	n.d.	n.d.	n.d.	Ancona 1879/80, 4:140
17/6/48	Zavala	Valencia+125	n.d.	120	n.d.	n.d.	n.d.	n.d.	n.d.	Ancona 1879/80, 4:150
19/6/48	Sotuta	Pasos	n.d.	100	n.d.	supplies	n.d.	n.d.	n.d.	Ancona 1879/80, 4:151
20/6/48	Cenotillo	Vergara+400	n.d.	100	n.d.	n.d.	n.d.	n.d.	n.d.	Ancona 1879/80, 4:140
2/7/48	Cenotillo	Peniche, Vergara +600+400	n.d.	42	–	>30 horses, 18 pigs, supplies, 17 guns	2	2	–	J. Mendes to Comandante en Jefe, 4a division, Tunkas, July 3, 1848, AGEY, PE, G, box 68; Ancona 1879/80, 4:142
2/7/48	Sotuta	Pasos	n.d.	200	n.d.	n.d.	n.d.	n.d.	n.d.	Ancona 1879/80, 4:152
3/7/48	Dzitás	Méndez, Peniche	n.d.	42	n.d.	n.d.	n.d.	n.d.	n.d.	GCY:63; Ancona 1879/80, 4:142 (19/7/48)
4/7/48	Hocabá	n.d.	n.d.	300	n.d.	n.d.	n.d.	n.d.	n.d.	GCY:63
7/7/48	Zuctuc	Baqueiro	n.d.	>52	–	n.d.	5	5	4	J. Cadenas to General en Gefe, Campeche, July 7, 1848, AGEY, PE, G, box 68
7/7/48	Cantamayec	Pasos	several	40	–	n.d.	n.d.	n.d.	n.d.	Ancona 187980, 4:152
7/7/48	Ticul	Cetina+1,024	n.d.	>51	n.d.	n.d.	n.d.	n.d.	n.d.	GCY:60; Baqueiro 1990, 3:7; Ancona 1879/80, 4:144
8/7/48	h.Sacakal	Cetina, Ruiz	n.d.	many	n.d.	much corn	11	5	n.d.	Baqueiro 1990, 3:19; Ancona 1879/80, 4:145–146
10/7/48	Maní	Cetina	n.d.	197	many	n.d.	n.d.	n.d.	n.d.	GCY:61; Baqueiro 1990, 7 (>200 rebels killed)
10/7/48	Tunkás	Peniche+1,200	n.d.	several	several	n.d.	n.d.	n.d.	n.d.	GCY:61; Baqueiro 1990, 3:8
15/7/48	Bolonchénticul	700	n.d.	many	n.d.	n.d.	n.d.	n.d.	n.d.	GCY:71
17/7/48	Zavala	Valencia+125	n.d.	120	n.d.	37 horses, supplies	n.d.	n.d.	n.d.	GCY:62; Baqueiro 1990, 3:8
18/7/48	Hopelchén	n.d.	n.d.	2	6f+2ch	n.d.	n.d.	n.d.	n.d.	J. Cadenas to General en Gefe, Campeche, July 22, 1848, AGEY, PE, G, box 68
mid-July? 48	Xcupil	P.Barrera	n.d.	n.d.			12	2	–	Baqueiro 1990, 3:12
19/7/48	Sotuta	Pasos	n.d.	105mfch	102f	n.d.	n.d.	n.d.	n.d.	GCY:62; Baqueiro 1990, 3:8, 23 (120 rebels killed)
27/7/48	Mama	González	n.d.	many	n.d.	n.d.	n.d.	n.d.	n.d.	Ancona 1879/80, 4:153
Aug. 48	Dzibalchén	n.d.	n.d.	several	3	n.d.	15	3	–	Baqueiro 1990, 3:46
11/8/48	h.Xocneceh, Yotholim, Oxkutzcab	Pren, Cetina+560	n.d.	n.d.	n.d.	n.d.	n.d.	n.d.	n.d.	Ancona 1879/80, 4:147–148
19/8/48	Tekax	Ruíz, Ramírez, Novelo, Cetina	n.d.	several	n.d.	n.d.	21	4	–	Baqueiro 1990, 3:22–23; Ancona 1879/80, 4:149/prisoners cruelly killed
19/8/48	Teabo	Pasos	n.d.	n.d.	n.d.	n.d.	n.d.	n.d.	n.d.	Ancona 1879/80, 4:153
19/8/48	Yotholim, Oxkutzcab	Cetina+560	n.d.	>40	n.d.	n.d.	n.d.	n.d.	n.d.	Ancona 1879/80, 4:148; GCY:66

(continued)

APPENDIX 2 (*continued*)

Date	Place	Leader, Strength	Enemies				Yucatecan losses			Sources/Remarks
			injured	dead	captive	Booty	injured	dead	captive	
24/8/48	Yaxcabá	Díaz+300	n.d.	>40	n.d.	n.d.	n.d.	n.d.	n.d.	Ancona 1879/80, 4:154; GCY:66
9/9/48	Sucilá	Molas	n.d.	n.d.	n.d.	n.d.	n.d.	n.d.	n.d.	Ancona 1879/80, 4:172/heavy rebel losses
9/9/48	Tixcacaltuyú, Tabi, Cantamayec, Tahchibichén	González, Valencia, Salazar	n.d.	n.d.	57mf	n.d.	6	1	–	Baqueiro 1990, 3:68–69
12/9/48	Tinum	Vergara	n.d.	n.d.	n.d.	n.d.	n.d.	n.d.	n.d.	Ancona 1879/80, 4:173
18, 20/9/48	Kaua, Uayma	Vergara	n.d	n.d.	n.d.	n.d.	n.d	n.d.	n.d.	Ancona 1879/80, 4:174
17–23/10/48	Bolonchén, Yaxché, Xul, Santa Elena	León+700	n.d.	n.d.	n.d.	n.d.	several	1	–	Baqueiro 1990, 3:85–87
3–5/11/48	Tizimín	Cepeda	n.d.	many	n.d.	n.d.	n.d.	n.d.	n.d.	Ancona 1879/80, 4:181–182
24, 26/11/48	Canakom, Tiholop	Méndez+1,000	n.d.	n.d.	n.d.	n.d.	6	3	–	Baqueiro 1990, 3:95/advance on Peto
28/11/48	Tixmehuac	González	n.d.	n.d.	n.d.	n.d.	16	7	–	Baqueiro 1990, 3:96/advance on Peto
29/11/48	Tzucacab	Cetina+1,000	n.d.	30	n.d.	n.d.	5	1	–	Baqueiro 1990, 3:94/advance on Peto
30/11–3/12/48	Tadziú, Peto, Tzucacab, Dzonotchel, Ichmul	Rosado, Cetina+a few 1,000	n.d.	n.d.	n.d.	n.d.	30	8	–	GCY:66–67; Baqueiro 1990, 3:97
12/12/48	Tihosuco	Méndez, Cetina	–	–	–	n.d.	–	–	–	GCY:68/occupied without resistance, rebels establish siege
mid 12/48	Telá, Culumpich, Ekpedz	n.d.	several	–	1	n.d.	59	4	–	Baqueiro 1990, 3:109–112
26/12/48	Valladolid	n.d.	–	–	–	n.d.	–	–	–	GCY:68/occupied without resistance
29/4–4/5/49	r.Tajasal, Bacalar	Cetina, Rosado, González+800	many	n.d.	n.d.	n.d.	20	8	–	Letter of T. Encalada, Bacalar, May 8, 1849, AHAY, G, I, box 227, file 6; Baqueiro 1990, 3:150–157
May–Sept. 49	Chenes (various places)	Baqueiro, Trujillo	n.d.	n.d.	210	650 cargas maize	7	4	–	Baqueiro 1990, 202–203/caudillos Julián Uitz and Benito Chim first caught and later shot
Aug. 49	surroundings Tihosuco	Novelo+300, Acosta+300	n.d	n.d.	n.d.	n.d.	>25	several	n.d	Baqueiro 1990, 3:178–182/75 soldiers dead or dispersed
Aug.? 49	advance on Tituc	Pasos+535	n.d.	n.d.	n.d.	n.d.	40	75+11 muleteers	n.d.	Baqueiro 1990, 3:186
Aug.? 49	Chevalan, Muchucux, Sabán	n.d	n.d.	n.d.	n.d	n.d.	15	2	n.d.	Baqueiro 1990, 3:188/thrusts for provisions
15, 22, 29/8/49	surroundings Sabán (r.Chanxcenil)	Pren+400, Valencia, Pacheo	n.d.	heavy losses	n.d.	n.d.	38	4	n.d	Baqueiro 1990, 3:193–195

14/9/49	surroundings Sabán (Cab, San Antonio)	Pren+500	n.d.	17	several P	many mules, 70es	13	2	n.d	Baqueiro 1990, 3:199–200
late 49/early 50	Komchén	Maldonado	n.d.	>100m	n.d.	n.d.	n.d.	n.d.	n.d.	Baqueiro 1990, 4:73
early 50	Xcopoil, Suytún et al.	Molas+1,000	n.d	n.d.	20P+150R	20 guns	16	5	–	Baqueiro 1990, 4:11
Feb. 50	Kéken, Chekubul, Nohalal, Pixoiakal	Acosta+320	n.d	208	300fP+31mP	112es, 45 guns, powder, 165 horses	9	2	–	Baqueiro 1990, 4:50–52/captains I. May and F. Tuz killed, captain P. Moo caught
Feb. 50	r.Kanchoch, r.Petac	Baqueiro	n.d	6	11P+112mf	n.d.	n.d.	n.d.	n.d.	Baqueiro 1990, 4:54
Feb. 50	Tepich, Yokdzonot et al.	Ruz	n.d	n.d	71P	40 guns, 25 horses	n.d.	n.d.	n.d.	Baqueiro 1990, 4:25–26
Feb. 50	Humtichmul, Santa Rosa	n.d	n.d.	n.d.	309	n.d.	n.d.	n.d.	n.d.	GCY:81
mid-Feb. 50	r.Tzel-Actum	Molas, Gutiérrez	n.d.	24	2P+144Z	n.d	n.d.	n.d.	n.d.	Baqueiro 1990, 4:16
15/2/50	Yaxcopoil	Ontiveros	n.d	8	n.d.	iron, munition	n.d.	n.d.	n.d.	Baqueiro 1990, 4:17
16/2/50	Xcanul	González+300	n.d	n.d.	800P+R	n.d.	2	–	–	Baqueiro 1990, 4:24
March 50	villages south of Tihosuco	Gónzalez	n.d.	n.d	883P	n.d.	n.d.	n.d.	n.d.	Baqueiro 1990, 4:66; GYC:80 (833)
March 50	r.Chanaychén, San Fernando, Xcayil et al.	Ontiveros+250	n.d.	n.d.	3P+85R	14 guns	several	8	n.d.	Baqueiro 1990, 4:19–21
March 50	Kanxoc	Irabién	n.d.	4	n.d.	n.d.	n.d.	n.d.	n.d.	Baqueiro 1990, 4:22
March 50	Tekom, Xcenil, Chanchén, Chunox, Xcojil	Alfaro, Reyes, Roca	n.d.	n.d.	115P+40Z	3 es, 3 mules, 2 horses	2	n.d.	n.d.	Baqueiro 1990, 4:31
March 50	Xmabén	Roca, Maldonado	n.d	n.d.	>100mfZ	33 horses	n.d.	n.d.	n.d.	Baqueiro 1990, 4:33
1–6/3/50	Xmabén	Baqueiro	n.d.	10	124P	70 guns, 30 pounds powder	3	2	n.d	Baqueiro 1990, 4:55–56, 66
1/3/50	28 localities south of Tihosuco	Maldonado, Ruz +>500	n.d.	2	309Z	powder, 115 horses, 18 guns, 22es	n.d.	n.d.	n.d.	Baqueiro 1990, 4:27–28/caudillos J.B. Victorim and A. Cham killed
March 50	Xuncloc	Maldonado+160	n.d.	n.d.	>200mfP	53 horses	n.d.	n.d.	n.d.	Baqueiro 1990, 4:35
31/3–3/4/50	Tzuhcum, Nohpop, Xmabén	Maldonado+290	n.d.	2	1P+90mfZ	supplies, 18 mules, 15 horses	4	–	–	M. Micheltorena to MGM, Mérida, April 13, 1850, AHM, XI/481.3/2914
April 50	Chancanab, Kantemó	Gamboa	n.d.	n.d.	200Z+several P	3@ powder, 20 mules, 16 horses, tobacco	n.d.	n.d.	n.d.	Baqueiro 1990, 4:44–45

(continued)

Date	Place	Leader, Strength	Enemies			Booty	Yucatecan losses			Sources/Remarks
			injured	dead	captive		injured	dead	captive	
early April 50	Chikindzonot	n.d.	n.d.	3	n.d	n.d.	n.d.	n.d.	n.d.	M. Micheltorena to MGM, Mérida, April 5, 1850, AHM, XI/481.3/2914
3–6/4/50	Chanay Chén, San Fernando, Nohcacab	Ontiveros+250	several	10	3P+85Z	3 guns, 11 es, powder, 7 mules, 18 horses	3	2	–	M. Micheltorena to MGM, Mérida, April 12, 1850, AHM, XI/481.3/2914
20/4/50	Tixcacal area	López+100, Navarrete+100	n.d.	9	34Z	134 sack maize, 5 mules, 8 horses	2	–	–	M. Micheltorena to MGM, Mérida, May 1, 1850, AHM, XI/481.3/2914
21/4/50	Chanchén et al.	Maldonado+160	–	–	48P+200mfIVZ	20 mules, 33 horses, salt	1	–	–	M. Micheltorena to MGM, Mérida, April 26, 1850, AHM, XI/481.3/2914
22/4/50	Santa Rosa et al.	Rivascacho+300	n.d.	73	45P+94mfZ	54 beasts, 6 cargas sugar, iron, copper, 43 guns	–	–	–	M. Micheltorena to MGM, Mérida, May 8, 1850, AHM, XI/481.3/2914
22–27/4/50	Santa Rita et al.	Peniche+150	n.d.	11	41mfP	n.d.	–	–	–	M. Micheltorena to MGM, Mérida, May 6, 1850, AHM, XI/481.3/2914
29/4/50	Kanxoc	Yrabien+100	n.d.	6	1P	n.d.	–	–	–	M. Micheltorena to MGM, Mérida, May 3, 1850, AHM, XI/481.3/2914
28/4–6/5/50	Chumpich, Macanché, Xuechil, Chun Kulché	Baqueiro	several	48	119mfPR	109 beasts, 21 es, 1 gun	10	6	–	Reports from incursions, n.p., n.d. [May 1850] and Relación de los muertos y heridos, canton de Iturbide, Macanché, May 9, 1850, AHM, XI/481.3/2914
May 50	Kantemó, r.Tzucxeb	Vázquez	n.d.	36	2P	2es, 1 gun	9	2	–	Baqueiro 1990, 4:46–47
May 50	r.Keken, r.Xcancep	Alvarez, Sandoval	n.d.	2	1P	n.d.	–	–	–	Baqueiro 1990, 4:48
7–11/5/50	Haas, Bohchén, Santa Rosa et al.	Maldonado+260	many	72	21P+217ZR	38 guns, 35 es, 14 cargas beans, 13 mules, 42 horses	3	–	–	M. Micheltorena to MGM, Mérida, May 20, 1850, AHM, XI/481.3/2914; Baqueiro 1990, 4:43–44, 69, 73 (+100 rebels killed in Komchén)
10/5/50	Chemax	230	n.d.	19	2P+49Z	1 mule, 2 horses	–	–	–	M. Micheltorena to MGM, Mérida, May 30, 1850, AHM, XI/481.3/2914
mid-May 50	Chancenote et al.	n.d.	n.d.	57	n.d.	11 mules, 36 horses, maize	–	–	–	M. Micheltorena to MGM, Mérida, May 16, 1850, AHM, XI/481.3/2914

26/5/50	Dzooc	Iman+100	n.d.	4	4P+35mfZ	2 guns, 2 es, 70 cargas maize	–	–	–	M. Micheltorena to MGM, Mérida, June 20, 1850, AHM, XI/481.3/2914
27/5/50	surroundings of Kampocolché	Roca+100	n.d.	12	2P+71mfZ	1 gun, 3 es, 20 mules, 41 horses, 20 cargas beans	–	–	–	M. Micheltorena to MGM, Mérida, June 20, 1850, AHM, XI/481.3/2914
27/5/50	thrust from Chandzonot, Tekom	Pacheco+136	n.d.	n.d.	59	4 guns, 5 mules, 7 horses	1	–	–	M. Micheltorena to MGM, Mérida, June 20, 1850, AHM, XI/481.3/2914
28/5/50	thrust from Chandzonot, Tekom	Vega+80	n.d.	9	–	1 gun	3	–	–	M. Micheltorena to MGM, Mérida, June 20, 1850, AHM, XI/481.3/2914
1/6/50	r.Chpil	Guerra+176	n.d.	15	4mP	3 es, 16 beasts	–	–	–	M. Micheltorena to MGM, Mérida, June 20, 1850, AHM, XI/481.3/2914
12, 14/6/50	thrusts from Tihosuco	Roca+160, Molina +150	n.d.	12	1P	4 guns, 160 cargas maize	3	2	–	M. Micheltorena to MGM, Mérida, June 20, 1850, AHM, XI/481.3/2914
15/6/50	thrust from Tekom	n.d.	n.d.	17	–	110 cargas maize, 5 es, 4 mules, 4 horses	3	–	–	M. Micheltorena to MGM, Mérida, June 20, 1850, AHM, XI/481.3/2914
16/6/50	r.Xpechil	Cervera+100	n.d.	–	40P	2 guns, 9 boilers, 7 horses	–	–	–	M. Micheltorena to MGM, Mérida, June 20, 1850, AHM, XI/481.3/2914
16/6/50	thrusts from Kampocolché	Roca	n.d.	2	3P+34VZ	159 cargas maize, 2 guns	1	–	–	M. Micheltorena to MGM, Mérida, June 20, 1850, AHM, XI/481.3/2914
June 50	thrusts from Valladolid	Acereto	n.d.	14	11mfP+167IVZ	12 guns, 132 cargas maize, 1 mule, 5 horses, 8 beasts	4	1	–	M. Micheltorena to MGM, Mérida, July 1, 1850, AHM, XI/481.3/2914
June 50	Cruzchén, Ixil, Chanchén	Ruz+300	n.d.	13	6P+1 family	1@ powder, 25 cargas maize, 5 mules, 13 horses	n.d.	n.d.	n.d.	Baqueiro 1990, 4:87–88
June 50	Nohmiguel	Vargas+150	n.d.	8–12	n.d.	15 cargas maize	2–3	1–2	–	Baqueiro 1990, 4:88–89
30/6/50	Nenelá, Dzemajas	Covian+16+25	n.d.	1	1fP+3mP	8 guns, 10 es	–	–	–	M. Micheltorena to MGM, Mérida, July 16, 1850, AHM, XI/481.3/2914
25/6–3/7/50	Tzucchil et al.	Novelo+340	n.d.	11	39P+228mfZ	3@ powder, 23 beasts, 38 guns	–	–	–	M. Micheltorena to MGM, Mérida, July 16, 1850, AHM, XI/481.3/2914

(continued)

Date	Place	Leader, Strength	Enemies			Booty	Yucatecan losses			Sources/Remarks
			injured	dead	captive		injured	dead	captive	
3/7/50	r.Santa Cruz	Suarez+25+25	n.d.	–	4fP+1c	n.d.	–	–	–	M. Micheltorena to MGM, Mérida, July 16, 1850, AHM, XI/481.3/2914
5/7/50	thrust from Tizimín	Romero+200	n.d.	18	>13mfchZ	55 beasts	–	1	–	M. Micheltorena to MGM, Mérida, July 16, 1850, AHM, XI/481.3/2914
10/7/50	n.d.	Ruz+350	n.d.	13	6mP+1 family	1@ powder, 125 cargas maize, 6 mules, 13 horses	1	1	–	M. Micheltorena to MGM, Mérida, July 16, 1850, AHM, XI/481.3/2914/ cabecilla Paulin Santolo and family captured
10/7/50	thrusts from Tihosuco	Roca, Reyes+160 +160	n.d.	3	147PZR	7 guns, 11 mules, 5 cargas beans	1	2	–	M. Micheltorena to MGM, Mérida, July 16, 1850, AHM, XI/481.3/2914
11/7/50	thrust from Kankabchén	Coral+100	n.d.	–	–	86 cargas maize	3	–	–	M. Micheltorena to MGM, Mérida, July 16, 1850, AHM, XI/481.3/2914
11/7/50	n.d.	Varguez	n.d.	26	–	9 guns, 15 cargas maize, 14 mules and horses	–	–	–	M. Micheltorena to MGM, Mérida, July 16, 1850, AHM, XI/481.3/2914
26/6–18/7/50	expedition to Bacalar	O'Horan+700	n.d.	108m+9f	218mfP	83 guns, 34 mules and horses, 28 boilers, 2 rosaries, rings etc.	2	–	–	M. Micheltorena to MGM, Mérida, July 30, 1850, AHM, XI/481.3/2914/ 18 places attacked
16/7/50	r.Xpalla	Garcia+150	n.d.	4m	10P+53mfZ	4 mules, 2 horses	–	–	–	M. Micheltorena to MGM, Mérida, July 31, 1850, AHM, XI/481.3/2914
16/7/50	Macanché et al.	Escalante+300	n.d.	15m	69mfZ	4 guns, 100 cargas maize	1	1	–	M. Micheltorena to MGM, Mérida, July 31, 1850, AHM, XI/481.3/2914
22/7/50	r.Xcopoil	Reyes+125	–	6m	17mfZ	4 guns	–	–	–	M. Micheltorena to MGM, Mérida, July 31, 1850, AHM, XI/481.3/2914
29/7–12/8/50	thrusts from Kanxoc, Xcohil, Becanchén, Ticacal,	various	n.d.	58	114P+133Z	70 guns, munition, 21 mules, 44 pigs, 23 horses, sugar, salt, >67 cargas maize	5	–	–	Comandancia General de Yucatán to MGM, Mérida, Aug. 17, 1850, AHM, XI/481.3/2914

15–30/8/50	thrusts from Tixcacalcupul, Kankabchén, Becanchén, Tixcacal, Kampocolché, Xul, Sabán	various	n.d.	105	>33P+270ZI +10ZV	49 guns, 17 horses, 29 mules, 37 pigs, 85 cargas maize	12	1	–	Comandancia General de Yucatán to MGM, Mérida, Sept. 4, 1850, AHM, XI/481.3/ 2914
6/9/50	thrust from Bacalar	Perez+100, Flores +100	n.d.	2	–	n.d.	4	1	–	M. Micheltorena to MGM, March 26, 1851, AHM, XI/481.3/3257
7–16/9/50	thrusts from Peto, Becanchén, San Antonio, Xcohil, Tizimín, Tixcacal	various	n.d.	114	54P+158mfZI +7ZV	29 cargas maize, 56 bags of maize cobs, 80 guns, 19 mules, 1 horse, 16 pigs	31	6	–	Comandancia General de Yucatán to MGM, Mérida, Sept. 21, 1850, AHM, XI/481.3/ 2914
18/9/50	thrust from San Antonio	50	n.d.	5	2P+4fZ	maize	–	–	–	M. Micheltorena to MGM, Mérida, Oct. 12, 1850, AHM, XI/481.3/2914
27/9/50	Chaquin	Avila+154	n.d.	21	1P	106 bags maize cobs, 2 guns	1	–	–	M. Micheltorena to MGM, Mérida, Oct. 12, 1850, AHM, XI/481.3/2914
28/9/50	thrust from Becanchén	Perez+200	n.d.	26	26mfP	11 guns, 10 horses, 60 bags maize cobs	1	–	–	M. Micheltorena to MGM, Mérida, Oct. 12, 1850, AHM, XI/481.3/2914
16–30/9/50	36 hamlets in the southeast, Chanchén et al.	Novelo+151+11CS +21HD	n.d.	–	13mP+16mfZ	25 guns, lead, iron, 28 horses	–	–	–	M. Micheltorena to MGM, Mérida, Oct. 10, 1850, AHM, XI/481.3/2914; see also Baqueiro 1990, 4:107–109
Oct. 50	thrust from Valladolid	Novelo+175	n.d.	11	129mfP	12 beasts, 13 guns	3	–	–	M. Micheltorena to MGM, Mérida, Oct. 21, 1850, AHM, XI/481.3/2914
4/10/50	Mabén	n.d.	n.d.	4	2mP	n.d.				Comandancia General de Yucatán to MGM, Mérida, Oct. 14, 1850, AHM, XI/481.3/ 2914
11, 15/10/50	r.Xtocmó (Bacalar)	Flores+200	n.d.	1	–	2 es	2	–	–	M. Micheltorena to MGM, March 26, 1851, AHM, XI/481.3/3257
18/10/50	thrust from Iturbide	n.d.	n.d.	3	–	n.d.	1	–	–	Comandancia General de Yucatán to MGM, Merida, Oct. 18, 1850, AHM, XI/481.3/ 2914

(continued)

Date	Place	Leader, Strength	Enemies			Booty	Yucatecan losses			Sources/Remarks
			injured	dead	captive		injured	dead	captive	
mid-Oct. 50	Tzuktuk	112+8CS+6HD	n.d.	–	92mfZ	35 horses	1	–	–	Comandancia General de Yucatán to MGM, Mérida, Oct. 25, 1850, AHM, XI/481.3/2914
23/10/50	Haydzonot	100	n.d.	7	8P+9Z	1 mule	1	–	–	Comandancia General de Yucatán to MGM, Mérida, Oct. 24, 1850, AHM, XI/481.3/2914
24/10/50	Macanché	Reyes+125	n.d.	6	–	n.d.	–	1	–	M. Micheltorena to MGM, Mérida, Oct. 31, 1850, AHM, XI/481.3/2914
27/10/50	Chunhuhub	n.d.	n.d.	7	50Z	14 guns, 4 mules, 2 horses	2	–	–	M. Micheltorena to MGM, Mérida, Nov. 21, 1850, AHM, XI/481.3/2914
early Nov. 50	thrust from Nohyaxché	Dominguez+75 +20HD	n.d.	6	60mfZ	29 mules, 18 horses	–	–	–	M. Micheltorena to MGM, Mérida, Nov. 15, 1850, AHM, XI/481.3/2914
1/11/50	Polyuc	Castillo+80	n.d.	32	31mfP	n.d.	–	–	–	M. Micheltorena to MGM, Mérida, Nov. 15, 1850, AHM, XI/481.3/2914
3/11/50	r.Dumuncan	Sabido+100	n.d.	2	6IP+1VP	n.d.	–	–	–	M. Micheltorena to MGM, Mérida, Nov. 15, 1850, AHM, XI/481.3/2914
3/11/50	Laguna (Chenes)	Montero+170	n.d.	14	251mfP	7 mules, 7 horses	–	–	–	M. Micheltorena to MGM, Mérida, Nov. 18, 1850, AHM, XI/481.3/2914
5–8/11/50	Cruzakal, aguada Pich, Nohchul	Pardenilla, Reyes	n.d.	27	–	n.d.	–	–	–	M. Micheltorena to MGM, Mérida, Nov. 16, 1850, AHM, XI/481.3/2914
6/11/50	r.San Felipe	García+80	n.d.	1	4mfP	n.d.	1	–	–	M. Micheltorena to MGM, Mérida, Nov. 15, 1850, AHM, XI/481.3/2914
8–13/11/50	Chehunkuk	Garcia	n.d.	40mIV	56mfP	21 guns, beasts, horses	5	1	–	M. Micheltorena to MGM, Mérida, Nov. 22, 1850, AHM, XI/481.3/2914
9/11/50	Polyuc, Chunhuhub	Castillo+75	n.d.	5	11Z	1 mule, 1 horse	–	–	–	M. Micheltorena to MGM, Mérida, Nov. 21, 1850, AHM, XI/481.3/2914
15/11/50	thrust from Nohyaxché	Paredes+70+12HD	n.d.	6	1VP+60Z	17 mules, 9 horses	1	–	–	M. Micheltorena to MGM, Mérida, Nov. 21, 1850, AHM, XI/481.3/2914
27/10–17/11/50	thrust from Valldolid to east coast	Ruz+190+30HD	n.d.	41	77P+227mfZ +13IVR	45 mules, 36 horses	4	4	–	S. López de Llergo to MGM, Mérida, Nov. 23, 1850, AHM, XI/481.3/2914
15–19/11/50	Chunchacté, Sithbatab	Pinela	several	13	6P+several families Z	n.d.	n.d.	n.d.	n.d.	S. López de Lergo to MGM, Mérida, Dec. 3, 1850, AHM, XI/481.3/2914

20/11/50	Cruzakal	Pérez+100	n.d.	22	n.d.	n.d.	3	–	–	S. López de Llergo to MGM, Mérida, Nov. 27, 1850, AHM, XI/481.3/2914
21–26/11/50	thrust from Nohyaxché to Xtucichén	Dominguez+90+12CS+20HD	n.d.	n.d.	192mfZ	guns, powder, 51 mules and horses	2	–	–	M. Micheltorena to MGM, Mérida, Dec. 10, 1850, AHM, XI/481.3/2914
late Nov. 50	thrust from Xmabén	Montero+175	n.d.	14	several P+many families Z	n.d.	n.d.	n.d.	n.d.	Baqueiro 1990, 4:114/caudillo Antonio Mazón and secretary caught
30/11/50	Chankiní et al.	Garcia	n.d.	5	47mfP	4 guns+powder	–	–	–	M. Micheltorena to MGM, Mérida, Dec. 11, 1850, AHM, XI/481.3/2914
2/12/50	Macanché	n.d.	n.d.	17 incl. José Z. May	n.d.	n.d.	–	7	–	M. Micheltorena to MGM, Mérida, Dec. 11, 1850, AHM, XI/481.3/2914
3/12/50	Nohbec (excursion from Bacalar)	n.d.	n.d.	3	42mfZ+3R	n.d.	–	–	–	M. Micheltorena to MGM, Mérida, March 26, 1851, AHM, XI/481.3/3257
6/12/50	thrust from Kampocolché	Castillo	n.d.	2	1P+55mfZ	n.d.	–	–	–	Comandancia General de Yucatán to MGM, Mérida, Dec. 14, 1850, AHM, XI/481.3/2914
7–21/12/50	Pixoy, Santa Rosa et al.	Perez	several	35	11mP	12 es, 4 guns, 4 mules, 4 horses, 11 comales, 1 coffee pot	–	1	–	M. Micheltorena to MGM, Mérida, Dec. 31, 1850, AHM, XI/481.3/2914
11/12/50	Yoknicte, Yoknaranja, San José, Chulim	Vargas+200	n.d.	79	30P, 130mfZ	n.d.	2	–	–	M. Micheltorena to MGM, Mérida, Jan. 18, 1851, AHM, XI/481.3/3255
20/12/50	thrust from Nohyaxché	n.d.	n.d.	10	–	n.d.	–	–	–	Comandancia General de Yucatán to MGM, Mérida, Dec. 28, 1850, AHM, XI/481.3/2914
19–27/12/50	thrust from Chemax	Ontiveros	n.d.	21	84mfPZ	3 es	–	1	–	M. Micheltorena to MGM, Mérida, Jan. 18, 1851, AHM, XI/481.3/3255
28/12/50	thrust from San Antonio	30	n.d.	13	35mfZ	6 guns	–	–	–	M. Micheltorena to MGM, Mérida, Jan. 18, 1851, AHM, XI/481.3/3255
late Dec. 50	thrust from Valladolid	Acereto+100+12CS+16HD	n.d.	58	15P+several families Z	19 guns, 4@ powder, 11 mules, 18 horses	1	1	–	M. Micheltorena to MGM, Mérida, Jan. 18, 1851, AHM, XI/481.3/3255
late Dec. 50	Chicilá (Río Lagartos)	n.d.	n.d.	28	29	n.d.	–	–	–	M. Micheltorena to MGM, Mérida, Jan. 16, 1851, AHM, XI/481.3/3255
31/12/50	Yalahau et al.	Pérez+100	n.d.	45	51P+99Z	40 mules and horses,	2	2	–	M. Micheltorena to MGM, Mérida, Jan. 23, 1851, AHM, XI/481.3/3255
Jan. 51	thrust to southeast	Novelo+15+15	n.d.	4	–	6 mules, 4 horses	–	–	–	M. Micheltorena to MGM, Mérida, Jan. 22, 1851, AHM, XI/481.3/3255

(continued)

Date	Place	Leader, Strength	Enemies			Booty	Yucatecan losses			Sources/Remarks
			injured	dead	captive		injured	dead	captive	
4/1/51	Numkan-chochó	Monjarte+40	n.d.	4	11mP+16f	n.d.	–	–	–	M. Micheltorena to MGM, Mérida, Jan. 18, 1851, AHM, XI/481.3/3255
9–10/1/51	r.Xyumchén	Buendia+100	n.d.	8	5P	n.d.	1	1	–	M. Micheltorena to MGM, Mérida, Jan. 13, 1851, AHM, XI/481.3/3255
11/1/50	Chachalal, Yokdzonot	Romero	n.d.	7	6P+families	n.d.	1	–	–	M. Micheltorena to MGM, Mérida, Jan. 18, 1851, AHM, XI/481.3/3255
12/1/51	r.Nohmun	n.d.	n.d.	2	1mI+3fI+ch all Z	4 horses	–	–	–	M. Micheltorena to MGM, Mérida, Jan. 22, 1851, AHM, XI/481.3/3255/ looking for maize
12–31/1/51	Xcan et al. (Espita)	Manrique+180	n.d.	8	2P+60Z	n.d.	1	–	–	M. Micheltorena to MGM, Mérida, March 7, 1851, AHM, XI/481.3/3258
21/1/51	Chuntzacan	Montero+120 +60HD	n.d.	30	153Z	24 horses	–	–	–	M. Micheltorena to MGM, Mérida, Feb. 4, 1851, AHM, XI/481.3/3257
22/1/51	Mabén, r.Tacotzimin	Vargas+150	12	10	11P+7mZ+20 families Z	n.d.	1 (by accident)	–	–	M. Micheltorena to MGM. Mérida, Feb. 10, 1851, AHM, XI/481.3/3257
25/1/51	Pixoy, Chuch (Nohyaxché)	Dominguez+60	n.d.	3	30Z	n.d.	–	–	–	M. Micheltorena to MGM, Mérida, Feb. 5, 1851, AHM, XI/481.3/3258
27/1/51	San Pastor (excursion from Bacalar)	Ongay+35	n.d.	n.d.	–	–	–	10	–	M. Micheltorena to MGM, March 26, 1851, AHM, XI/481.3/3257
30/1/51	h.Sahcab	Garza+20	n.d.	4	–	n.d.	1	1	–	M. Micheltorena to MGM, Mérida, Feb. 7, 1851, AHM, XI/481.3/3258
31/1/51	r.Taychén (cantón Santa Cruz)	Yrabien+90	n.d.	14	–	1 mule, 1 mare	–	–	–	M. Micheltorena to MGM, Mérida, Feb. 10, 1851, AHM, XI/481.3/3257
1–7/2/51	Macanché, Xkomchehuas	Cachon, Pérez +100+80	n.d.	9	13P+30fIZ	8 pounds powder	–	–	–	M. Micheltorena to MGM, Mérida, Feb. 18, 1851, AHM, XI/481.3/3258
5/2/51	r.Yokdzonot	Pinzon	n.d.	17	9P+54Z	6 guns	–	–	–	M. Micheltorena, to MGM, Feb. 11, 1851, AHM, XI/481.3/3257
12–13/2/51	r.Chanchén (cantón Santa Cruz)	90	n.d.	4	2P	n.d.	n.d.	n.d.	n.d.	M. Micheltorena to MGM, Mérida, Feb. 26, 1851, AHM, XI/481.3/3258
15/2/51	Cobá	Ontiveros+120	n.d.	10	1P	4 mules, 1 horse	3	–	–	M. Micheltorena to MGM, March 7, 1851, AHM, XI/481.3/3258

18/2/51	thrust from Nohyaxché	90+9CS	n.d.	11	106Z	34 beasts	–	1	–	M. Micheltorena to MGM, March 8, 1851, AHM, XI/481.3/3258
25/2/51	Xcan	Romero+200	n.d.	17	20P+30mR +families	20 beasts with maize	–	–	–	M. Micheltorena to MGM, Mérida, March 4, 1851, AHM, XI/481.3/3258
late Feb. 51	r.Motul (excursion from Chemax)	55	n.d.	–	1P	2 mules	–	–	–	M. Micheltorena to MGM, Mérida, Feb. 26, 1851, AHM, XI/481.3/3258
1/3/51	thrust from Santa Cruz	Yravien+90	n.d.	6	2P	6 horses	–	2	–	M. Micheltorena to MGM, March 12, 1851, AHM, XI/481.3/3258
3/3/51	thrust from San Antonio	102	n.d.	18	3P+59ZR	n.d.	n.d.	n.d.	n.d.	M. Micheltorena to MGM, Mérida, April 16, 1851, AHM, XI/481.3/3257
11/3/51	San Miguel	Maldonado	n.d.	3	2P+9Z	n.d.	n.d.	n.d.	n.d.	M. Micheltorena to MGM, Mérida, April 16, 1851, AHM, XI/481.3/3257
17/3/51	thrust	n.d.	n.d.	10	–	8 guns, 20 beasts	–	1	–	M. Micheltorena to MGM, Mérida, April 1, 1851, AHM, XI/481.3/3257
20/3/51	r.Kanhá	Espinoso+50	n.d.	19	8P	n.d.	–	2	–	M. Micheltorena to MGM, Mérida, April 14, 1851, AHM, XI/481.3/3257
21/3/51	thrust from Hobonox	Pacheco+58	n.d.	8	52IZ	n.d.	–	–	–	M. Micheltorena to MGM, Merida, April 3, 1851, AHM, XI/481.3/3256
21/3–17/4/51	thrusts from Cruzchén	Ruz+100	n.d.	67	>89P+350Z	200 beasts, 25 guns, 6 @ powder, 700 cargas maize	1	–	–	M. Micheltorena to MGM, Mérida, April 23, 1851, AHM, XI/481.3/3257
23/3/51	CSC	Novelo+150+20CS	n.d.	>19	2,000Z	23 guns+es, powder, 20 mules and horses	3	–	–	M. Micheltorena to MGM, Mérida, April 2, 1851, AHM, XI/481.3/3257/ Manuel Nauat killed
25/3/51	Piyox (excursion from Nohyaxché)	Manzanero+82	1	6	1P	8 mules, 10 horses	–	–	–	M. Micheltorena to MGM, Mérida, April 7, 1851, AHM, XI/481.3/3257
27/3/51	thrusts from Kaua and Tekax	Pérez+120	n.d.	2	33Z	n.d.	n.d.	n.d.	n.d.	M. Micheltorena to MGM, April 5, 1851, AHM, XI/481.3/3257
3–11/4/51	thrusts from Sabán, Kancabchén, Tobonox	Molina, Reyes+60 +10HD+100 +40	n.d.	37	7P+31Z	5 guns, 9 horses	–	2	–	M. Micheltorena to MGM, Mérida, April 19, 1851, AHM, XI/481.3/3257
5/4/51	Akalcay (Kancabchén)	n.d.	n.d.	2	10P	6 horses	–	–	–	M. Micheltorena to MGM, Mérida, April 10, 1851, AHM, XI/481.3/3257
8/4/51	Tizimín	60	n.d.	2	5P+5IR +families	n.d.	n.d.	n.d.	n.d.	M. Micheltorena to MGM, Mérida, April 14, 1851, AHM, XI/481.3/3257
12–15/4/51	Yaxché, Kampeheche, Cameh (Xmabén)	100	n.d.	7	40Z	4 horses	n.d.	n.d.	n.d.	M. Micheltorena to MGM, Mérida, May 12, 1851, AHM, XI/481.3/3257

(continued)

Date	Place	Leader, Strength	Enemies				Booty	Yucatecan losses			Sources/Remarks
			injured	dead	captive			injured	dead	captive	
15/4/51	Zucera, Cun-limon (San Antonio)	Méndez+125	n.d.	25	205Z	57 beasts and horses	–	–	–	M. Micheltorena to MGM, Mérida, May 1, 1851, AHM, XI/481.3/3256
20–22/4/51	thrust from Kampocolché	Maldonado+240 +10CS	n.d.	1	14P+60mfZ	20 guns, 2 mules	3	–	–	M. Micheltorena to MGM, Mérida, May 6, 1851, AHM, XI/481.3/3257
22/4/–2/5/51	La Laguna, Chanchén, Lochhá, Oxpe-akal, Kanemo, Yalac	Guerra+180	n.d.	17	48P+128Z	9 es, 34 horses, 6 mules	3S+1HD	–	–	M. Micheltorena to MGM, Mérida, May 9, 1851, AHM, XI/481.3/3257
1/5/51	thrust from Kampocolché	Maldonado+96	n.d.	3	58Z	4 guns, 2 horses	–	–	–	M. Micheltorena to MGM, Mérida, April 11, 1851, AHM, XI/481.3/3257
early May 51	Chumpich (Xmabén)	140	n.d.	4	48Z	6 horses	1	–	–	M. Micheltorena to MGM, Mérida, May 12, 1851, AHM, XI/481.3/3257
early May 51	Chultan, Zucera	140	n.d.	2	26P+230mfchZ	14 guns, powder	n.d.	n.d.	n.d.	M. Micheltorena to MGM, Mérida, May 19, 1851, AHM, XI/481.3/3257
3–4/5/51	CSC	González+123 +30CS+10HD	n.d.	26	81P	21 guns, 7 mules	14	7	–	Baqueiro 1990, 4:125–127
May 51	thrust from Cruzchén	Ruz+150	n.d.	28	58P+130R	n.d.	n.d.	n.d.	n.d.	R. Díaz de la Vega to MGM, Mérida, June 5, 1851, AHM, XI/481.3/3256/ wife, daughter and daughter-in-law of B. Novelo captured
4–23/5/51	thrust from Tizimín	300	n.d.	–	>800mfZ	28 es, 8 guns, 31 mules and horses	n.d.	n.d.	n.d.	M. Micheltorena to MGM, Mérida, June 2, 1851, AHM, XI/481.3/3257
7–9/5/51	San Miguel, San Cristoval	Alfaro+30	n.d.	–	5P+6Z	n.d.	–	–	–	M. Micheltorena to MGM, Mérida, May 17, 1851, AHM, XI/481.3/3257
13, 14, 18/5/51	thrust from San Antonio	n.d.	n.d.	–	305ZR	n.d.	n.d.	n.d.	n.d.	M. Micheltorena to MGM, Mérida, June 2, 1851, AHM, XI/481.3/3257
16–23/5/51	CSC	Maldonado+120	n.d.	15	4P+61Z	12 guns, 5 mules, 2 horses	1	–	–	M. Micheltorena to MGM, Mérida, June 2, 1851, AHM, XI/481.3/3257
19/5/51	thrust from Tizimín	n.d.	n.d.	–	50P+400Z	n.d.	8	1	–	R. Díaz de la Vega to MGM, Mérida, July 14, 1851, AHM, XI/481.3/3256
13–15/6/51	r.Dzonot, CSC, r. Nohsas	Novelo+410+10CS	n.d.	27	3P+91Z	n.d.	4	2	–	R. Díaz de la Vega to MGM, Mérida, June 30, 1851, AHM, XI/481.3/3256
23/6–7/7/51	CSC	Pérez, Pazos+190 +100	n.d.	1	19mfP+92mfZ	11 guns	2	–	–	J.D. Pasos to CGE, Peto, July 5 and 8, 1851, AGEY, PE, M, box 175, files 64 and 80

Date	Target	Leader								Source
28/6/51	Labcah	Correa	n.d.	–	33P	n.d.	2	1	–	R. Díaz de la Vega to MGM, Mérida, June 28, 1851, AHM, XII/481.3/3256
end of June 51	thrust from Kampocolché	Tejero+100	n.d.	7	22R	22 cargas maize	–	1	–	R. Díaz de la Vega to MGM, Mérida, July 5, 1851, AHM, XII/481.3/3256
early July 51	Macanché	Acosta	n.d.	4	3fP	n.d.	3	1	–	R. Díaz de la Vega to MGM, Mérida, July 5, 1851, AHM, XII/481.3/3256
3–17/7/51	Macanché, Cruzchén	Rosado, Rejón+30	n.d.	6	28P+189Z+11R	n.d.	n.d.	n.d.	n.d.	R. Díaz de la Vega to MGM, Mérida, July 23, 1851, AHM, XII/481.3/3257
12/7/51	thrust from Chemax	Novelo, Ozorio	n.d.	5	22Z	15 guns	n.d.	n.d.	n.d.	R. Díaz de la Vega to MGM, Mérida, July 16, 1851, AHM, XII/481.3/3257
19–21/7/51	Chumcilché et al.	Ruelas	n.d.	3	22P+86mfchZ	n.d.	2	1	–	R. Díaz de la Vega to MGM, Mérida, July 29, 1851, AHM, XII/481.3/3257
July 51	to Bacalar, Palmira	Roca	n.d.	–	185mfP	n.d.	n.d.	n.d.	n.d.	R. Díaz de la Vega to MGM, July 28, 1851, AHM, XII/481.3/3257/ Baqueiro 1990, 4:161 (300mfZ)
late Aug. 51	several thrusts	various	n.d.	1	1P+7fZ	n.d.	3	–	–	R. Díaz de la Vega to MGM, Mérida, Aug. 1851, AHM, XII/481.3/3259
early Sept. 51	r.Santa Lucia	N. Aguilar+50	n.d.	3	2P+22Z	n.d.	1	–	–	R. Díaz de la Vega to MGM, Sept. 17, 1851, AHM, XII/481.3/3259
Sept. 51	way to Bacalar	Novelo+600	several	several	4P+93Z+their families	n.d.	10	8	–	R. Díaz de la Vega to MGM, Mérida, Sept. 26, 1851, AHM, XII/481.3/3257
21/11/51	Cabechén	Maldonado	n.d.	9	7P	2 guns, 4 es	n.d.	n.d.	n.d.	Campaña contra los indios ..., n.p., n.d., AHM, XII/481.3/3300
1/1/52	Komchén	Reyes	n.d.	15	10P	n.d.	n.d.	n.d.	n.d.	Campaña contra los indios ..., n.p.,n.d., AHM, XII/481.3/3300
1/1/52	Kancabacal (Chenes)	Pacheco	n.d.	n.d.	n.d.	3 guns	n.d.	n.d.	n.d.	Campaña contra los indios ..., n.p., n.d., AHM, XII/481.3/3300
1/1/52	Chunhuas, Lochhá	Maldonado	n.d.	2m	17P+13omfZ	17 es, 9 mules	n.d.	n.d.	n.d.	Campaña contra los indios ..., n.p., n.d., AHM, XII/481.3/3300
27/11/52	Lochhá	Maldonado	n.d.	10	1P+44mfZ	6 guns	n.d.	n.d.	n.d.	Campaña contra los indios ..., n.p., n.d., AHM, XII/481.3/3300
27/11/52	Chenes	Roca+150	n.d.	46	14P	5 guns, 16 es	n.d.	n.d.	n.d.	Campaña contra los indios ..., n.p., n.d., AHM, XII/481.3/3300
late Jan. 52	Hancal-akal, Mesapich +26 places	Espinosa+200	n.d.	80	12P+56fchZ	13 es, 6 guns	–	1	–	R. Díaz de la Vega to MGM, Tihosuco, Jan. 29, 1852, AHM, XII/481.3/3300
21/2/52	Lochhá, Balché	Ruiz	several	>9	many P, many mfR	many arms	n.d.	n.d.	n.d.	R. Díaz de la Vega to MGM, Peto, May 11, 1852, AHM, XII/481.3/3300
19/2/–27/4/52	thrust to CSC	Díaz de la Vega+600 +50 dragoons	n.d.	296	985mP+832fP	213 guns, 490 es, powder	n.d.	n.d.	n.d.	Relacion de los muertos, prisioneros y recogidos ..., R. Díaz de la Vega, Peto, May 11, 1852, AHM, XII/481.3/3300; Cámara Zavala 1928, part 3

(continued)

| Date | Place | Leader, Strength | Enemies | | | Booty | Yucatecan losses | | | Sources/Remarks |
			injured	dead	captive		injured	dead	captive	
22–23/2/52	Zucun, Xmakulán, CSC	Díaz de la Vega	n.d.	3	5P+40mflZ	n.d.	–	–	–	Cámara Zavala 1928, parts 4, 5, 9
4/3/52	Yokdzonot	Solis+30	n.d.	2	3P	n.d.		1	–	C. Gonzalez to R. Díaz de la Vega, Sabán, March 19, 1852, AGEY, PE, M, box 178, file 95
17/3/52	Chichanhá	Baqueiro	n.d.	several	n.d.	n.d.	several	–	–	R. Díaz de la Vega to MGM, Peto, May 11, 1852, AHM, XI/481.3/3300/ Cámara Zavala 1928, part 10 (2/4/52)
22/3/52	r.Tanviz	Bonilla+60	n.d.	4	1P	3 guns	–	–	–	S. Medina to CGE, Kancabchén, March 28, 1852, AGEY, PE, M, box 178, file 99
1–19/4/52	Haas, Sacvecan, Siismuk	Díaz de la Vega	n.d.	–	several mfP	n.d.	–	1	–	Cámara Zavala 1928, part 11
21/4/52	Macanché, Keken, Akalnel Lochhá	Ruiz	several	many	many P+Z	n.d.	1	–	–	R. Díaz de la Vega to MGM, Peto, May 11, 1852, AHM, XI/481.3/3300; Cámara Zavala 1928, part 11; Baqueiro 1990, 4:173–174
22/4/52	r.Xtuitz, r.Akabchén	Zavala+25	n.d.	8	7	5 guns	–	–	–	S. Lopez de Llergo to GDE, May 9, 1852, AGEY, PE, M, box 179, file 43
24/4/52	Halal	Meso, Garcia	n.d.	21	several P	n.d.	1	–	–	Cámara Zavala 1928, part 11
late May– early June 52	Macanché	Ruiz	n.d.	12	16mP+21 families Z	n.d.	–	–	–	Division Vega to MGM, Peto, June 3 and 14, 1852, AGEY, PE, M, box 179, files 58 and 87.
early June 52	r.Yocmajas, r.Poop, Tusik	Gamboa+30, Iturraran	n.d.	several	17mP+2f	n.d.	–	–	–	E. Rosado to General an Jefe, Peto, June 8, 1852, AGEY, PE, M, box 179, file 79
18/6/52	CSC	Novelo	n.d.	18	–	150 guns	n.d.	n.d.	n.d.	R. Díaz de la Vega to MGM, Peto, June 26, 1852, AHM, XI/481.3/3300/ V. Pec and J.B. Yam killed
22/6/–22/7/ 52	excursions from Bacalar	Novelo	n.d.	46	several P and Z	n.d.	15	3	–	R. Díaz de la Vega to MGM, Mérida, July 31, 1852, AHM, XI/481.3/3300
4/7/52	r.Hacch	Loria+16	n.d.	2	1P	1 gun	n.d.	n.d.	n.d.	R. Díaz de la Vega to MGM, Peto, July 5, 1852, AHM, XI/481.3/3300
6–7/8/52	r. Dzonot, CSC	Manrique	n.d.	19	4P+80fZ +25mZ	1 gun, 6 es	2	–	–	R. Díaz de la Vega to MGM, Mérida, Aug. 18, 1852, AHM, XI/481.3/3300
early Nov. 52	Becanchén	Falcon+60	n.d.	10	36mfP	n.d.	–	–	–	R. Díaz de la Vega to GDE, Mérida, Nov. 9, 1852, AGEY, PE, M, box 180, file 35
early Dec. 52	Xcan	Carrillo+80	several	20	–	–	–	–	–	R. Díaz de la Vega to GDE, Mérida, Nov. 9, 1852, AGEY, PE, M, box 180, file 35

July–Sept. 52	various	several	n.d.	252	221P	101 guns	–	–	–	Anaya to General en Jefe, Mérida, Oct. 7, 1852, AHM, XI/481.3/3300
17/12/52	Lochhá	Blanco+50	n.d.	12	–	n.d.	1	1	–	R. Díaz de la Vega to MGM, Merida, Dec. 18, 1852, AHM, XI/481.3/3300
9–12/2/53	Champop, CSC, Xtinta, Pachmul	Reyes	n.d.	95	17P	n.d.	–	–	–	J.E. Rosado to General en Jefe, Ichmul, Feb. 27, 1853, ER, May 11, 1853, 1
spring 53	Puerto de la Ascensión	Iturrarán+100	n.d.	several	n.d.	n.d.	n.d.	n.d.	n.d.	GCY:92; Baqueiro 1990, 4:185
17/3–19/5/53	excursions from Nohjalal	Novelo+200	n.d.	238	573mfPZ	84 guns, 14 mules and horses	n.d.	n.d.	n.d.	J. E. Rosado to General en Gefe, Peto, May 24, 1853, AGEY, PE, M, box 182, file 34
20/4 – 14/5/53	Mesapich et al.	Baqueiro+130	n.d.	39	28mP+46f	27 guns, 3 horses	4	–	–	R. Díaz de la Vega to MGM, Mérida, May 17, 1853, AHM, XI/481.3/3505
28/4/53	CSC	Ruz+300	n.d.	n.d.	n.d.	n.d.	n.d.	n.d.	n.d.	GCY:102
July 53	Navalam, Mabén et al.	several units	several	66	47P+114mfZ +125R	18 guns	n.d.	n.d.	n.d.	R. Díaz de la Vega to MGM, Mérida, Aug. 13, 1853, AHM, XI/481.3/3696
mid-Aug. 53	Santa María, h.Mabén	Osorio	–	5	6m+6fP	n.d.	–	–	–	M.F. Peraza to GDE, Valladolid, Aug. 19, 1853, ER, Aug. 26, 1853, 4
late 53	Xcabil	Dominguez, Sandoval	n.d.	22	n.d.	n.d.	n.d.	n.d.	n.d.	Baqueiro 1990, 4:201
Dec. 53	Tizimín	Pérez+200	–	220–300	–	n.d.	–	–	–	Cronica, ER, Dec. 12, 1853, 4; Pérez Alcala 1880:75–82
18/3/–8/4/54	Kankabchén, r.Yokinic, CSC del Este	Dominguez, Vergara+225 +100	several	18	16mfPZ	12 guns	5	1	–	R. Díaz de la Vega to MGM, Mérida, April 28, 1854, AHM, XI/481.3/3696
22/5/54	CSC	Ruz, Vergara+365	n.d.	n.d.	n.d.	n.d.	n.d.	many	n.d.	GCY:102–103/army completely beaten, Ruz, Vergara and many soldiers died from cholera
2–3/12/54	CSC, Xunantunich	González+600	n.d.	10	22mfZ	13 guns	4	2	–	P.A. Gonzalez to GDE, Yokdzonot, Dec. 12, 1854, EO, Jan. 2, 1855, 1–2; GCY:94
5–8/12/54	excursions from Yokdzonot	various	20	3	10mfZ	30 demijohns liquor, 3 of honey, 2 of butter, 5 boxes sugar, tobacco	5	1	–	P.A. Gonzalez to GDE, Yokdzonot, Dec. 14, 1854, EO, Jan. 5, 1855, 1–3
6–29/12/54	excursion from Tixcacal	Aguilar+110	many	28	44PZR	5 guns	–	–	–	M.F. Peraza to General en Jefe, Valladolid, Jan. 12, 1855, EO, Jan. 23, 1856, 1–3
11/12/54	environs CSC	Pacheco, Ocampo +100	n.d.	2	5mfP	3 guns 1 es, 1 pig, many chicken	–	1	–	P.A. Gonzalez to GDE, Yokdzonot, Dec. 14, 1854, EO, Jan. 5, 1855, 1–3
16/12/54	r.Nohhalal	Maldonado+300 +12CS	n.d.	20	n.d.	13 guns, 4@ powder	3	1	–	J.M. Novelo to General en Jefe, Pachmul, Jan. 2, 1855, EO, Jan. 23, 1855, 3–4

(continued)

Date	Place	Leader, Strength	Enemies			Booty	Yucatecan losses			Sources/Remarks
			injured	dead	captive		injured	dead	captive	
31/12/54-4/1/55	r.Chunkulche and environs	Pacheco	n.d.	2	15P+24mfchZ	n.d.	2	3	–	P.A. Gonzalez to GDE, Yokdzonot, Jan. 25, 1855, *EO*, Feb. 16, 1856, 1–3
2/12/54-2/1/55	evirons Pachmul	Novelo	n.d.	63	296mfPZ	42 firearms, 23 beasts	n.d.	14–15	n.d.	J.M. Novelo to General en Jefe, Pachmul, Jan. 2, 1855, *EO*, Jan. 23, 1855, 3–4; Baqueiro 1990, 4:227–229
Jan. 55	excursions from Chunkulché	Gonzalez	n.d.	n.d.	192Z	n.d.	n.d.	n.d.	n.d.	P.A. Gonzalez to GDE, Chunkulché, Feb. 1, 1855, *EO*, March 6, 1855, 3–4
4?/1/55	Yokdzonot	Suarez	n.d.	2	17mfZ	n.d.	1	–	–	P.A. Gonzalez to GDE, Yokdzonot, Jan. 25, 1855, *EO*, Feb. 16, 1856, 1–3
10–15/1/55	Chunkulché et al.	Pacheco+200	n.d.	4	1P+4mfZ	2 guns	2	1	–	P.A. Gonzalez to GDE, Yokdzonot, Jan. 25, 1855, *EO*, Feb. 16, 1856, 1–3
18/1/55	environs Yokdzonot	Gonzalez+200	n.d.	2	–	1 gun	2	–	–	P.A. Gonzalez to GDE, Yokdzonot, Jan. 25, 1855, *EO*, Feb. 16, 1856, 1–3
Jan. 55	aguada Sayabsin, Polyuc	Herrera+100	n.d.	8	49mfZ	n.d.	n.d.	n.d.	n.d.	J.M. Novelo to General en Jefe, Pachmul, Jan. 27, 1855, *EO*, March 16, 1855, 2
27/2–3/4/55	to puerto de Ascencion et al.	Dominguez+96	n.d.	11	2mfP+>40ZR	5 guns, wax	–	–	–	M.F. Peraza to General en Jefe, Valladolid, April 3, 1855, *EO*, April 20, 1855, 1–3
mid-March 55	r.Hon	González+264	n.d.	45mfchP	–	n.d.	n.d.	n.d.	n.d.	P.A. Gonzalez to GDE, Ichmul, March 14, 1855, *EO*, March 27, 1855, 2/P died of thirst
5/2/55	r.Xlabehem, Sahcabchén	Suarez	n.d.	4	51mfZ	n.d.	–	1	–	P.A. Gonzalez to GDE, Chunkulché, Feb. 7, 1855, AGEY, PE, G, box 100
late March 55	Pakchén, Bolonná, Chan Mabén	Correa	many	30–31	–	n.d.	n.d.	n.d.	n.d.	M.F. Peraza to General en Jefe, division Ampudia, Valladolid, March 30, 1855, AGEY, PE, G, box 100
10/4/55	Mabén	Xuluc+55HD	n.d.	n.d.	n.d.	2 guns, clothing	n.d.	n.d.	n.d.	M.F. Peraza to General en Jefe de la division Ampudia, Valladolid, April 21, 1855, *EO*, May 1, 1855, 1–2
8?/5/55	r.Xcekul, r.Nohtook	Rodriguez+73 +6HD	n.d.	24	–	n.d.	2	–	–	M.F. Peraza to General en Jefe, division Ampudia, Valladolid, May 9, 1855, *EO*, May 15, 1855, 2–3
Aug. 55	Pacchén	Braga+40	many	28	–	n.d.	8	–	–	J. Orihuela to General en Jefe, division Ampudia, Valladolid, Aug. 30, 1855, *EO*, Sept. 18, 1855, 1–3

Date	Place	Force								Source
21/1–19/2/56	Chancah-xaan, Muchí	Rodriguez+80 +12HD	many	10	several mfP	n.d.	1	–	–	M.F. Peraza to CGE, Valladolid, Feb. 22, 1856, AGEY, PE, G, box 103
16/4/56	Nohyaxché	Maldonado, Domínguez +232+400	n.d.	n.d.	n.d.	n.d.	n.d.	211	n.d.	GCY:106; Baqueiro 1990, 4:258–259/ expedition of Maldonado defeated
4/7/56	Nabalam	Xuluc+40HD	–	–	5m+4fIP	n.d.	–	–	–	M.F. Peraza to CGE, Valladolid, July 4, 1856, AGEY, PE, G, box 103
15/8/–17/10/56	Chunyá, CSC et al.	Acereto	many	>200	15mP+52fP	22 guns	n.d.	n.d.	n.d.	M.F. Peraza to CGE, Valladolid, Oct. 17, 1856, GS, Oct. 22, 1856, 1–2
1/9/56	Diz Akal	40HD+10V	n.d.	n.d.	3mIP+4fP+2c	n.d.	n.d.	n.d.	n.d.	M. Martin to GDE, Valladolid, Sept. 1, 1856, AGEY, PE, G, box 103
22/3–26/5/57	thrust from Valladolid	Acereto	>61	61	19mP+many fP	27 guns etc.	3	–	–	M.F. Peraza to CGE, Valladolid, May 26, 1857, UL, June 2, 1857, 1–2
23/3/57	Mabén, Petzimin	Vargas	n.d.	3	8P+3mR+8fR	3 guns, machetes, clothing	n.d.	n.d.	n.d.	M.F. Peraza to CGE, Valladolid, April 7, 1857, GS, April 13, 1857, 3
late March 57	r.Navalam	Xuluc	n.d.	3	6P+3fZ	3 guns	–	–	–	M.F. Peraza to CGE, Valladolid, April 30, 1857, GS, March 6, 1857, 2–3
11, 17/5/57	Nabalam	Ruz+20	n.d.	1	3R+families	maize	–	–	–	M.F. Peraza to CGE, Valladolid, May 23, 1857, GS, May 29, 1857, 1
late Oct. 57	Maven	Xuluc	n.d.	4	3P	1 es	n.d.	n.d.	n.d.	M.F. Peraza to CGE, Valladolid, Oct. 28, 1857, GS, Nov. 4, 1857, 1
2/12/57	Maven	Xuluc+40HD	several	5	3P+2mR +families	n.d.	–	–	–	J.M. Covian to General en Jefe, Valladolid, Dec. 11, 1857, GS, Dec. 18, 1857, 1–2
2/4/58	Chunkuché	n.d.	n.d.	2	8P	n.d.	n.d.	n.d.	n.d.	F. Ruíz to GDE, Tizimín, April 2, 1858, GS, April 9, 1858, 1–2
17/4/58	Komchéchén	Bacelis+50 pacíficos	n.d.	13	–	n.d.	–	1	–	J.M. Novelo to GDE, Peto, April 17, 1858, AGEY, PE, G, M, box 115
19/1/59	r.Yokdzonot	Aguilar	n.d.	–	–	food	1S+1HD	–	–	Celo de las autoridades, EC, Jan. 24, 1859, 4
12/2/–5/3/59	excursion from Tizimín	Canto	n.d.	11	7P	5 guns	2	–	–	L. Irigoyen to MGM, Mérida, March 11, 1859, AHM, XI/481.3/ 7114
14/4/59	r.Yokdzonot	Medina	n.d.	5m+3f	–	6 guns	1	1	–	P. Acereto to GDE, Valladolid, April 14, 1859, EC, April 20, 1859, 1
22/5/59	r.Yokdzonot	Aguilar+209 +60HD	n.d.	3	6fI	n.d.	1	–	–	P. Acereto to GDE, Valladolid, May 17 and 23, 1859, EC, May 20 and 30, 1859, 1
1–23/1/60	CSC	Acereto+2,200 +650HD	n.d.	n.d.	several	n.d.	n.d	>60	n.d.	Baqueiro 1990, 5:117–127; Reed 1964:178; Aldherre and Mendiola 1869:78–79 (1,500 S and HD killed)
8/9/62	crucero Sahcabá	Lopez	n.d.	7	–	n.d.	5	12	n.d.	L. Irigoyen to MGM, Valladolid, Sept. 10, 1862, AHM, XI/481.4/8772

(continued)

Date	Place	Leader, Strength	Enemies			Booty	Yucatecan losses			Sources/Remarks
			injured	dead	captive		injured	dead	captive	
29/6/64	Kampocolché	500+200HD	n.d.	n.d.	n.d.	n.d.	n.d.	n.d.	n.d.	La Redacción, *LNE*, July 1, 1864, 3
17/10/64	thrust from Valladolid	Alcocer	n.d.	2mI	4mIP	n.d.	n.d.	n.d.	n.d.	Relacion de los indígenas prisioneros y muertos, Valladolid, Oct. 18, 1864, *LNE*, Oct. 21, 1864, 2
May–June 65	Dzonot, Kampocolché	Galvez+1,400	n.d.	>200	n.d.	n.d.	>104	>400	n.d.	J.S. Ilarrequi to MGM, Ticul, June 22, 1865, AHM, XI/481.4/9976; J.S. Ilarregui to J. de Dios Peza, Mérida, June 24, 1865, CAIHDY, M, XLVII.1864, 21; Aldherre and Mendiolea 1869:80; GCY:135–137
March 70	Cobá	Traconis	n.d.	n.d.	5mIP+4fIP	n.d.	n.d.	n.d.	n.d.	D. Traconis to GDE, Valladolid, April 11, 1870, AGEY, PE, M, box 290, file 16
21/1/–7/2/71	Tulum, Muyil, Chun Pom	Traconis+1,000 +300HD	n.d.	85	2mIP+3fIP+5ch	14 guns	7	1	–	Movimiento militar, *RP*, Jan. 25, 1871, 4; Relacion de prisioneros, Valladolid, Feb. 7, 1871, *RP*, Feb. 15, 1871, 1; D. Traconis to GDE, Xocen, Feb. 6,1871, AGEY, PE, M, box 293, file 40; Diario de la columna de operaciones, Valladolid, Feb. 20, 1871, *RM*, Feb. 26, 1–2 and March 1, 1871, 2; José Maria Muñoz, Report ..., June 2, 1882, TULAL, M 26, box 2, folder 14
31/7–14/8/ 72	San Antonio	Urcelay	n.d.	6	–	n.d.	–	–	–	Itinerario ..., Isla Mujeres, Aug. 19, 1872, *RP*, Aug. 26 and 28, 1872
1899–1901	CSC	Bravo								campaign of general Ignacio Bravo

APPENDIX 3 *Kruso'b Attacks on Pacífico groups*

| Date | Place | Strength | Pacíficos | | | Booty | Kruso'b | | | Sources/Remarks |
			injured	dead	captive		injured	dead	captive	
early Oct. 51	Chichanhá	Barrera+>400	n.d.	n.d.	several	n.d.	n.d.	n.d.	n.d.	Noticias de la campaña, *SDN*, Oct. 8, 1851, 4; Ancona 1879/80, 4:324 (strength 500)
26/12/52	Chichanhá	C. Pech, J.I. Pat	n.d.	many	n.d.	n.d.	n.d.	n.d.	n.d.	Baqueiro 1990, 4:178
Aug. 53	Xcansus, Xpetentulix, Yakal-Ingles, Chanchén, Pachá, Santo Domingo	n.d.	n.d.	many f+ch	n.d.	n.d.	n.d.	n.d.	n.d.	J.M. Novelo to General en Jefe, division Ampudia, Peto, March 31, 1855, AGEY, PE, M, box 186, file 93/burned
late Dec. 55	Macanché, Lochhá, Saczucil, Becanchén, Xbudzil	n.d.	n.d.	>34mf	many	trade goods	n.d.	n.d.	n.d.	Movimiento de los Bárbaros, *UL*, Dec. 28, 1855, 4; J.M. Novelo to GDE, Peto, Dec. 29,1855, AGEY, PE, G, box 103; C. Baqueiro to GDE, Hopelchen, Jan. 7, 1856, AGEY, PE, G, box 104;
early May 57	Petenkax	300	n.d.	n.d.	n.d.	n.d.	several	2	–	A última hora, *GS*, March 6, 1857, 4
Nov. 58	southern pacífico area	n.d.	n.d.	286mf	500mf	n.d.	n.d.	n.d.	–	J.T. Briceño to GDE, Chanzut., Nov. 15, 1858, *EC*, Nov. 24, 1858, 1; J. Escalante to GDE, Tekax, Nov. 16, 1858, *EC*, Nov. 22, 1858, 1; Baqueiro 1990, 4:85
8/3/59	surroundings Xbudzil	n.d.	n.d.	several	several	400 cargas maize	n.d.	n.d.	n.d.	G. Ruiz to GDE, Peto, March 12, 1859, *EC*, March 16, 1859, 1
June 60	Chichanhá	n.d.	n.d.	several mf	several f+ch	n.d.	n.d.	n.d.	n.d.	Crown Surveyor to Superintendent, July 6, 1860, R. 71, ABH:230.
Dec. 60	Yakalcab	n.d.	n.d.	the captive mf	360mfch	n.d.	n.d.	n.d.	n.d.	J.A. Loesa, Aug. 26, 1861, Archives of Belize, Record 74, 174–175, in Rugeley 2001b:79–80; M. Medina to P. García, Hopelchén, Dec. 22, 1860, *EP*, Dec. 25, 1860, 1
April 61	Chichanhá	n.d.	n.d.	18	n.d.	n.d.	n.d.	n.d.	n.d.	Cal 1983:101

(*continued*)

Date	Place	Strength	Pacíficos			Booty	Kruso'b			Sources/Remarks
			injured	dead	captive		injured	dead	captive	
3/1/63	Lochhá, Noj-Gantemó	Poot+2–600	many	15mf	many	60 cattle, many mules, trade goods worth 10,000$	–	1	–	M. Barbosa to GDE de Campeche, Mesapich, Jan. 4, 1863, *EP*, Jan. 20, 1863, 1; C. Montes de Oca to GDE, Tekax, Jan. 7, 1863 and R. Lopez to General en Jefe, Peto, Jan. 4, 1863, both in *EN*, Jan. 9, 1863, 1; N. Novelo to GDE, Peto, Jan. 7 and 12, 1863, *EN*, Jan. 12 and 23, 1863, 1
18–27/6/67	Macanché, Lochhá, Chanchum-pich, Noh-Ayin; Xmabén	Poot, Cen +400–1,000	4S	>5m	n.d.	700$	–	–	–	A. Huchim to R. Calderon, Macanché, June 30, 1867, *EP*, July 9, 1867, 2–3; Los Indios, *RP*, July 23, 1867, 2; J.L. Santini to GDE, Noh-Ayin, July 26, 1867, *RP*, Aug. 9, 1867, 2–3; J. Chable to GDE, Chunchintoc, July 30, 1867, *EP*, Aug. 6, 1867, 2; F. Medina to GDE, Ticul, Aug. 2, 1867, *RP*, Aug. 9, 1867, 1; Declaracion de Pablo Encalada, Campeche (part 2), Aug. 12, 1867, *EP*, Sept. 27, 1867, 1/Chanchumpich burned
early Jan. 68	Icaiché	n.d.	n.d.	n.d.	n.d.	n.d.	n.d.	>50	n.d.	N. Novelo to GDE, Tekax, March 4, 1868, *RP*, March 9, 1868, 1
12/6/68	Macanché	n.d.	n.d.	n.d.	n.d.	n.d.	n.d.	n.d.	n.d.	N. Novelo to GDE, Tekax, June 26, 1868, *RP*, July 1, 1868, 1
Oct. 69	Xmabén	people of Chunxan	n.d.	n.d.	n.d.	n.d.	n.d.	n.d.	n.d.	Sullivan 1997a, I:5
5/7/72	Kantunilkin, Chunchacal-has	Pomol+300	n.d.	12	11+ several families incl. 50t in Ch.	silver plate from church in K., 2 bulls	2	20	–	N. Urcelay to General en Jefe, Isla Mujeres, Aug. 19, 1872, *RP*, Aug. 26, 1872, 1; Itinerario ..., D. Peniche, Isla Mujeres, Aug. 19, 1872, *RP*, Aug. 26 and 28, 1872; Lista de los individuos ..., *RP*, Nov. 22, 1872, 1; Sullivan 1997a, I:4/91 houses burnt

Bibliography

ABBREVIATIONS

CGE	Comandante General del Estado
MG	Ministro de Guerra
MGM	Ministro de Guerra y Marina
MGO	Ministro de Gobernación
SGG	Secretaría General de Gobierno

ARCHIVES

ACASY Archivo Carrillo y Ancona del Seminario de Yucatán, Conkal
AGEC Archivo General del Estado de Campeche, Campeche
    AH Archivo Histórico
    AM Asuntos Militares
    G Gobernación
    PY Período Yucateco, 1820–1857
AGEY Archivo General del Estado de Yucatán, Mérida
    J Justicia
        PN Penal
    PE Poder Ejecutivo
        C Correspondencia
        CI Comisaría Imperial
        CLM Colonias Militares
        CP Censos y Padrones
        G Gobernación
        GM Guerra y Marina
        GN Guardia Nacional
        J Justicia
        JP Jefatura Política

Bibliography

M	Milicia
ODG	Oficina del Gobernador
P	Población
PM	Presidencia Municipal
SM	Servicios Militares
SP	Salud Pública

AGN Archivo General de la Nación, México, D.F.
 G Gobernación
 SI Segundo Imperio

AHAY Archivo Histórico del Arzobispado de Yucatán, Conkal
 G Gobierno
 I Inventarios
 O Obispos

AHM Archivo Histórico Militar, México, D.F.

CAIHDY Centro de Apoyo a la Investigación Histórica de Yucatán, Mérida
 F Folletos
 M Manuscritos

TNA The National Archives, Kew
 CO Colonial Office

TULAL Tulane University, Latin American Library, New Orleans
 M-26 Manuscripts Collection 26 (Yucatán)
 MIC Microfilm Collection

PRINTED SOURCES

ABH *Archives of British Honduras.* Vol. 3: From 1841 to 1884, edited by John Alder Burdon. London: Sifton Praed & Co. 1935.

APP *Colección de leyes, decretos y órdenes o acuerdos de tendencia general del poder legislativo del estado libre y soberano de Yucatán.* 3 vols, edited by Alonzo Aznar Pérez and Rafael Pedrera. Mérida: Imprenta del Editor 1849–51.

CGC *Correspondencia de la Guerra de Castas,* edited by Fidelio Quintal Martín. Mérida: Universidad Autónoma de Yucatán 1992.

DAME *Demography and Parish Affairs in Yucatan, 1797–1897. Documents from the Archivo de la Mitra Emeritense Selected by Joaquín de Arrigunaga Peón,* edited by Carol Streichen Dumond and Don E. Dumond (University of Oregon Anthropological Papers No. 27). Eugene 1982.

DHY *Documentos para la Historia de Yucatán.* 3 vols, edited by France V. Scholes, C.R. Menéndez, J.I. Rubio Mañé and E.B. Adams. Mérida: Compañía Tipográfica Yucateca 1936/38.

EA *Colección de leyes, decretos, órdenes y demás disposiciones de tendencia general, expedidas por el poder legislativo del estado de Yucatán.* Vol. 1, edited by Eligio Ancona. Mérida: Imprenta de "El Eco de Comercio" 1882.

EHRY Cited numbers follow pages in Baqueiro 1990.

Bibliography 323

GCY   *Guerra de Castas en Yucatán: su origen, sus consecuencias y su estado actual* [1866], edited and transcribed by Melchor Campos García. Mérida: Universidad Autónoma de Yucatán 1997.

GG   *Recopilación de leyes, decretos y órdenes, expedidas en Yucatán, desde el año de 1851 en adelante.* Vol. 1, edited by Apolinar García y García. Mérida: Imprenta Manuel Aldana Rivas 1865.

PG   *Colección de leyes, decretos y órdenes del augusto congreso del estado libre y soberano de Yucatán.* 2 vols, edited by José María Peón and Isidro Gondra. Mérida: Lorenzo Seguí 1832.

SGY   Secretaría General de Gobierno, Yucatán: Memoria leída ante el augusto congreso extraordinario de Yucatán, por el secretario general de gobierno el día 18 de septiembre de 1846. Mérida.

PERIODICALS

BOGY   *Boletin Oficial del Gobierno de Yucatan*, Mérida
DO   *Diario Oficial*, Mérida
DY   *Diario de Yucatán*, Mérida
EC   *El Constitucional*, Mérida
EE   *El Estandarte*, San Luis Potosí
EF   *El Fenix*, Campeche
EN   *El Espíritu Nacional*, Mérida
EO   *El Orden*, Mérida
EP   *El Espíritu Público*, Campeche
ER   *El Regenerador*, Mérida
GC   *La Guerra de Castas*, Mérida
GS   *Las Garantías Sociales*, Mérida
LD   *La Discusión*, Campeche
LNE   *La Nueva Época*, Mérida
LRP   *La Razón de los Pueblos*, Mérida
LU   *La Unión*, México, D.F.
MR   *El Monitor Republicano*, México, D.F.
NE   *La Nueva Era*, Campeche
PODM   *Periódico Oficial del Departamento de Mérida*, Mérida
RM   *Revista de Mérida*, Mérida
RP   *La Razón del Pueblo*, Mérida
RY   *Revista Yucateca*, Mérida
SDN   *El Siglo Diez y Nueve*, México, D.F.
UL   *La Unión Liberal*, Campeche

BOOKS AND ARTICLES

Adorjan, Michael, Tony Christensen, Benjamin Kelly and Dorothy Pawluch (2012): "Stockholm Syndrome as Vernacular Resource." *The Sociological Quarterly* 53 (3):454–74.

324   *Bibliography*

Adrian, H. (1924): "Einiges über die Maya-Indianer von Quintana Roo." *Zeitschrift der Gesellschaft für Erdkunde zu Berlin* (5–7):235–47.

Alavi, Hamza (1987): Village Factions. In *Peasants and Peasant Societies*, edited by Teodor Shanin. [2nd edition]. London: Penguin, pp. 346–56.

Aldherre, Fed and M. Mendiolea (1869): "Los indios de Yucatán." *Boletín de la Sociedad Mexicana de Geografía y Estadística*, IIa época 1:73–81.

Álvarez Cuartero, Izaskun (2002): "Indios mayas en Cuba. Algunas reflexiones sobre su comercio." *Balauarte* 3: 121–41.

Ancona, Eligio (1879/80): *Historia de Yucatán desde la época más remota hasta nuestros días*. Mérida: Imprenta de M. Heredia Argüelles. Vols. 3 and 4 [facsimile edition, Universidad de Yucatán: Mérida 1978].

Angel, Barbara (1997): "Choosing Sides in War and Peace: The Travels of Herculano Balam among the Pacíficos del Sur." *The Americas* 53 (4):525–49.

Anonymous (1878): Report on Rebel Military Capacity. In *Maya Wars: Ethnographic Accounts from Nineteenth-Century Yucatán*, edited by Terry Rugeley. Norman: University of Oklahoma Press 2001, pp. 88–94.

Arnold, Channing and Frederick J. Tabor Frost (1909): *The American Egypt: A Record of Travel in Yucatan*. London: Hutchinson.

Baberowski, Jörg (2016): *Räume der Gewalt*. Bonn: Bundeszentrale für politische Bildung.

Baerlein, Henry (1913): *Mexico: The Land of Unrest. Being Chiefly an Account of What Produced the Outbreak in 1910, Together with the Story of the Revolutions Down to This Day*. London: Herbert and Daniel.

Bakewell, Peter (2004): *A History of Latin America: C. 1450 to the Present*. Oxford: Blackwell.

Balandier, Georges (1986): "An Anthropology of Violence and War." *International Social Science Journal* 38 (110):499–511.

Bandura, Albert (1999): "Moral Disengagement in the Perpetration of Inhumanities." *Personality and Social Psychology Review* 3 (3):193–209.

Baqueiro, Serapio (1989 [1887]): "Un estudio biográfico de Crescencio Poot." *Boletín de la Escuela de Ciencias Antropológicas de la Universidad de Yucatán* 16 (96):15–33.

(1990): *Ensayo histórico sobre las revoluciones de Yucatán desde el año de 1840 hasta 1864*. 5 vols. [original 1878, 1879, and 1887]. Mérida: Universidad Autónoma de Yucatán.

Barabas, Alicia Mabel (1979): "Colonialismo y racismo en Yucatán: Una aproximación histórica y contemporánea." *Revista Mexicana de Ciencias Políticas y Sociales* 25 (97):105–40.

(1989): *Utopías Indias: Movimientos socio-religiosos en México*. México, D.F.: Grijalbo.

Baranda, Joaquín (1867): "Los indios." *El Espíritu Público*, August 16:1.

Bartolomé, Miguel Alberto (1988): *La dinámica social de los mayas de Yucatán: Pasado y presente de la situación colonial*. México, D.F.: Instituto Nacional Indigenista.

Bartolomé, Miguel Alberto and Alicia Mabel Barabas (1977): *La resistencia maya: Relaciones interétnicas en el oriente de la península de Yucatán*. México, D. F.: Instituto Nacional de Antropología e Historia.

Bibliography

325

Baumann, Marcel M. (2009): "Understanding the Other's 'Understanding' of Violence: Legitimacy, Recognition, and the Challenge of Dealing with the Past in Divided Societies." *International Journal of Conflict and Violence* 3 (1):107–23.

Bazant, Jan (1991): From Independence to the Liberal Republic, 1821–1867. In *Mexico since Independence*, edited by Leslie Bethell. Cambridge: Cambridge University Press, pp. 1–48.

Bellingeri, Marco (1995): Las ambigüedades del voto en Yucatán. Representación y gobierno en una formación interétnica 1812–1829. In *Historia de las elecciones en Iberoamérica, siglo XIX: De la formación del espacio político nacional*, edited by Antonio Annino. México, D.F.: Fondo de Cultura Económica, pp. 227–90.

Berzunza Pinto, Ramón (1965): *Guerra social en Yucatán*. [new edition 2001]. México, D.F.: Costa-Amic.

Betancourt Pérez, Antonio and José Luis Sierra Villarreal (1989): *Yucatán: Una historia compartida*. México, D.F.: Secretaria de Educación Pública, Instituto Mora, Gobierno del Estado de Yucatán.

Bracamonte, Pedro (1993): *Amos y sirvientes: Las haciendas de Yucatán, 1789–1860*. Mérida: Universidad Autónoma de Yucatán.

(1994): *La memoria enclaustrada: Historia indígena de Yucatán, 1750–1915*. México, D.F.: Centro de Investigaciones y Estudios Superiores en Antropología Social and Instituto Nacional Indigenista.

Bricker, Victoria R. (1981): *The Indian Christ, the Indian King: The Historical Substrate of Maya Myth and Ritual*. Austin: University of Texas Press.

Buhler, Richard (1975): *"A Refugee of the War of the Castes Makes Belize His Home": The Memoirs of J.M. Rosado*. Belize: Belize Institute for Social Research and Action (BISRA).

Buisson, Inge (1978): "Gewalt und Gegengewalt im 'Guerra de Castas' in Yukatan, 1847–1853." *Jahrbuch für Geschichte von Staat, Wirtschaft und Gesellschaft Lateinamerikas* 15:7–27.

Bustillos Carrillo, Antonio (1957): *Los mayas ante la cultura y la revolución de México*. México, D.F.: Talleres Lito-Tipogr. de S. Turanzas del Valle, Suc.

Busto, Emiliano (1880): *Estadística de la República Mexicana: Estado que guardan la agricultura, indústria, minería y comercio*. 3 vols. México, D.F.: Imprenta Ignacio Cumplido.

Cal, Angel E. (1983): Anglo Maya Contact in Northern Belize: A Study of British Policy toward the Maya during the Caste War of Yucatán, 1847–1872. Master of Arts thesis, Department of History, University of Calgary.

(1991): Rural Society and Economic Development: British Mercantile Capital in Nineteenth-century Belize. Ph.D. dissertation. University of Arizona.

Cámara Zavala, Felipe de la (1928): "Las memorias inéditas de D. Felipe de la Cámara Zavala. Relación circunstanciada de la expedición practicada por el gral. don Rómulo Díaz de la Vega ... desde el 15 de diciembre de 1851." *Diario de Yucatán* (12 de agosto – 21 de octubre).

Cárdenas, Lázaro (1972): *Ideario político*. México, D.F.: Era.

Careaga Viliesid, Lorena (1990): *Quintana Roo: Una historia compartida*. México, D.F.: Instituto de Investigaciones Dr. José María Luis Mora.

Bibliography

(1998): *Hierofanía combatiente: Lucha, simbolismo y religiosidad en la Guerra de Castas.* Chetumal: Universidad de Quintana Roo.

Carrillo y Ancona, Crescencio (1871): Guerra de castas. In *Yucatán: Textos de su historia*, edited by Antonio Pérez Betancourt and Rodolfo Ruz Menéndez. 2 vols. México, D.F.: Secretaria de Educación Pública, Instituto Mora, Gobierno del Estado de Yucatán, 1988, vol. 2, pp. 61–72.

(1950): Los mayas de Yucatán: Estudio histórico sobre la raza indígena de Yucatán [1865]. In *Los mayas de Yucatán*, edited by Crescencio Carrillo y Ancona. Mérida, pp. 29–69.

Castro, Inés de (2001): Die Geschichte der sogenannten *Pacíficos del Sur* während des Kastenkrieges von Yucatán: 1851–1895. Ph.D. dissertation. Universität Bonn.

Chagnon, Napoleon A. (1983): *Yanomamö: The Fierce People.* [3rd revised edition]. New York: Holt, Rinehart and Winston.

Chi Poot, María Bonifacia, ed. (1982): *Medio siglo de resistencia armada maya: Fuentes documentales*, vol. 4. [Etnolingüística 27] México, D.F.: Secretaria de Educación Pública and Instituto Nacional Indigenista.

Chust, Manuel and José Antonio Serrano Ortega (2007): Milicia y revolución liberal en España y en México. In *Las armas de la Nación: Independencia y ciudadanía en Hispanoamérica (1750–1850)*, edited by Manuel Chust and Juan Marchena. Madrid: Iberoamericana, pp. 81–110.

Cline, Howard F. (1947): "The 'Aurora Yucateca' and the Spirit of Enterprise in Yucatan, 1821–1847." *The Hispanic American Historical Review* 27 (1):30–60.

(1948a): "The Sugar Episode in Yucatan, 1825–1850." *Inter-American Economic Affairs* 1 (4):79–100.

(1948b): "The Henequen Episode in Yucatan." *Inter-American Economic Affairs* 2 (2):30–51.

(1950): "Related Studies in Early Nineteenth Century Yucatecan Social History. Part II: The War of the Castes and its Consequences and V: Regionalism and Society in Yucatan, 1825–1847." Microfilm Collection of Manuscripts on Middle American Cultural Anthropology No. XXXII. University of Chicago Library.

Clodfelter, Michael (2002): *Warfare and Armed Conflict: A Statistical Reference NJ to Casualty and Other Figures.* [2nd edition]. Jefferson, NC: McFarland.

Cockroft, James D. (1990): *Mexico: Class Formation, Capital Accumulation, and the State.* [Revised edition]. New York: Monthly Review Press.

Cohen, Ronald (1984): Warfare and State Formation: Wars Make States and States Make Wars. In *Warfare, Culture, and Environment*, edited by R. Brian Ferguson. Orlando, FL: Academic Press, pp. 329–58.

Collins, Randall (2008): *Violence: A Micro-Sociological Theory.* Princeton, NJ: Princeton University Press.

(2009): "Micro and Macro Causes of Violence." *International Journal of Conflict and Violence* 3 (1):9–22.

CORDEMEXX (1980): *Diccionario Maya Cordemex. Maya – español, español – maya.* Director Alfredo Barrera Vásquez. Mérida: Ediciones Cordemex.

Coronil, Fernando and Julie Skurski (1991): "Dismembering and Remembering the Nation: The Semantics of Political Violence in Venezuela." *Comparative Studies in Society and History* 33 (2):288–337.

Bibliography

Coser, Lewis A. (1956): *The Functions of Social Conflict*. Glencoe, IL.: The Free Press.

(1967): *Continuities in the Study of Social Conflict*. New York: The Free Press.

Daly, Martin and Margo Wilson (1988): *Homicide*. New York: Adine de Gruyter.

Das, Veena (2008): "Violence, Gender, and Subjectivity." *Annual Review of Anthropology* 37:283–99.

De Waal, Frans B.M. (2013): Foreword. In *War, Peace, and Human Nature: The Convergence of Evolutionary and Cultural Views*, edited by Douglas P. Fry. New York: Oxford University Press, pp. xi–xiv.

Deas, Malcolm (2002): The Man on Foot: Conscription and the Nation-State in Nineteenth-Century Latin America. In *Studies in the Formation of the Nation-State in Latin America*, edited by James Dunkerley. London: Institute of Latin American Studies, pp. 77–93.

Depalo, William A. Jr. (1997): *The Mexican National Army, 1822–1852*. College Station: Texas A&M University Press.

Dixon, Jeffrey S. and Meredith Reid Sarkees (2016): *Guide to Intra-State Wars: An Examination of Civil Wars 1816–2014*. London: Sage.

Ducey, Michael T. (2001): "Indian Communities and Ayuntamientos in the Mexican Huasteca: Sujeto Revolts, Pronunciamientos and Caste War." *The Americas* 57 (4):525–50.

Dumond, Don E. (1977): Independent Maya of the Late Nineteenth Century: Chiefdoms and Power Politics. In *Anthropology and History in Yucatan*, edited by Grant D. Jones. Austin: University of Texas Press, pp. 103–38.

(1985): "The Talking Crosses of Yucatan: A New Look at their History." *Ethnohistory* 32 (4):291–308.

(1997): *The Machete and the Cross: Campesino Rebellion in Yucatan*. Lincoln & London: University of Nebraska Press.

Durham, William H. (1976): "Resource Competition and Human Aggression, Part 1." *Quarterly Review of Biology* 51:385–415.

Dutt, Rajeshwari (2012): Managing the Interstices: Cacique Politics in Late Colonial and Early National Yucatán. Ph.D. dissertation. Carnegie Mellon University.

Edgerton, Robert B. (2000): *Warrior Women: The Amazons of Dahomey and the Nature of War*. Boulder, CO: Westview Press.

Eisner, Manuel (2009): "The Uses of Violence: An Examination of Some Cross-Cutting Issues." *International Journal of Conflict and Violence* 3 (1):40–59.

Ellis, Stephen (1995): "Liberia 1989–1994: A Study of Ethnic and Spiritual Violence." *African Affairs* 94 (375):165–97.

Elwert, Georg (1997): Gewaltmärkte: Beobachtungen zur Zweckrationalität der Gewalt. In *Soziologie der Gewalt*, edited by Trutz von Trotha. Kölner Zeitschrift für Soziologie und Sozialpsychologie Sonderheft 37. Opladen: Westdeutscher Verlag, pp. 86–101.

Ember, Carol R. and Melvin Ember (1994): "War, Socialization, and Interpersonal Violence: A Cross-Cultural Study." *The Journal of Conflict Resolution* 38 (4):620–46.

Escalante Gonzalbo, Fernando (1993): *Ciudadanos imaginarios: memorial de los afanes y desventuras de la virtud y apología del vicio triunfante en la*

República Mexicana; tratado de moral pública. México, D.F.: El Colegio de México.

Fallaw, Ben (1995): Peasants, Caciques, and Camarillas: Rural Politics and State Formation in Yucatán, 1924–1940. Ph.D. dissertation. Department of History, University of Chicago.

(1997): "Cárdenas and the Caste War That Wasn't: State Power and Indigenismo in Post-Revolutionary Yucatán." *The Americas* 53 (4):551–77.

Farriss, Nancy M. (1984): *Maya Society under Colonial Rule*. Princeton, NJ: Princeton University Press.

Feldman, Allen (1991): *Formations of Violence. The Narrative of the Body and Political Terror in Northern Ireland*. Chicago, IL: University of Chicago Press.

Ferguson, R. Brian (1984): Introduction: Studying War. In *Warfare, Culture, and Environment*, edited by R. Brian Ferguson. Orlando, FL: Academic Press, pp. 1–81.

Flores, Jorge (1961): "La vida rural en Yucatán en 1914." *Historia Mexicana* 10 (3):471–83.

Fowler, Henry A. (1879): *A Journey Across the Unknown Portion of British Honduras*. Belize City: Government Press.

Fowler, Will (1995): "Dreams of Stability: Mexican Political Thought during the 'Forgotten Years.' An Analysis of the Beliefs of the Creole Intelligentsia (1821–1853)." *Bulletin of Latin American Research* 14 (3):287–312.

Ed. (2010a): *Forceful Negotiations: The Origins of the Pronunciamiento in Nineteenth-Century Mexico*. Lincoln & London: University of Nebraska Press.

(2010b): Introduction: The Nineteenth-Century Practice of the Pronunciamiento and Its Origins. In *Forceful Negotiations: The Origins of the Pronunciamiento in Nineteenth-Century Mexico*, edited by Will Fowler. Lincoln & London: University of Nebraska Press, pp. i–xxxix.

Ed. (2012a): *Malcontents, Rebels, and Pronunciados: The Politics of Insurrection in Nineteenth-Century Mexico*. Lincoln & London: University of Nebraska Press.

(2012b): Introduction: Understanding Individual and Collective Insurrectionary Action in Independent Mexico, 1821–1876. In *Malcontents, Rebels, and Pronunciados: The Politics of Insurrection in Nineteenth-Century Mexico*, edited by Will Fowler. Lincoln & London: University of Nebraska Press, pp. i–xxxvi.

Gabbert, Wolfgang (1997): Ethnicity and Forms of Resistance: The Caste War of Yucatán in Regional Perspective. In *Resistencia y Adaptación Nativas en las Tierras Bajas Latinoamericanas*, edited by Maria Susana Cipolletti. Quito: Abya-Yala, pp. 205–32.

(2001): "Social Categories, Ethnicity, and the State in Yucatán, México." *Journal of Latin American Studies* 33 (3):459–84.

(2004a): Was ist Gewalt? Anmerkungen zur Bestimmung eines umstrittenen Begriffs. In *Anthropologie der Konflikte: Georg Elwerts konflikttheoretische Thesen in der Diskussion*, edited by Julia Eckert. Bielefeld: Transcript Verlag, pp. 88–111.

Bibliography

(2004b): "Of Friends and Foes: The Caste War and Ethnicity in Yucatán." *Journal of Latin American Anthropology* 9 (1):90–118.

(2004c): *Becoming Maya: Ethnicity and Social Inequality in Yucatán since 1500.* Tucson: University of Arizona Press.

(2005): Flux and Stability in Nineteenth-Century Kruso'b Political Organization. In *Los buenos, los malos y los feos: Poder y resistencia en América Latina,* edited by Nikolaus Böttcher, Isabel Galaor and Bernd Hausberger. Madrid & Frankfurt: Iberoamericana & Vervuert, pp. 309–23.

(2007): Vom (internen) Kolonialismus zum Multikulturalismus: Kultur, Ethnizität und soziale Ungleichheit. In *Achsen der Ungleichheit: Zum Verhältnis von Klasse, Geschlecht und Ethnizität,* edited by Cornelia Klinger, Gudrun-Axeli Knapp and Birgit Sauer. Frankfurt & New York: Campus, pp. 116–30.

(2014): El desafío de los caudillos: La economía política de los kruso'b en el siglo XIX. In *El pueblo Maya del siglo XIX: Perspectivas arqueológicas e históricas,* edited by Susan Kepecs and Rani T. Alexander. Cuadernos del Centro de Estudios Mayas, No. 40. México, D.F.: Universidad Nacional Autónoma de México, pp. 35–51.

(2015): Imagining a Nation: Elite Discourse and the Native Past in Nineteenth-Century Mexico. In *Globalized Antiquity: Uses and Perceptions of the Past in South Asia, Mesoamerica, and Europe,* edited by Ute Schüren, Daniel Segesser and Thomas Späth. Berlin: Reimer, pp. 189–210.

Galtung, Johan (1969): "Violence, Peace, and Peace Research." *Journal of Peace Research* 6 (3):167–91.

(1990): "Cultural Violence." *Journal of Peace Research* 27 (3):291–305.

Gann, Thomas W. (1918): *The Maya Indians of Southern Yucatan and Northern British Honduras.* (Smithsonian Institution. Bureau of American Ethnology Bulletin 64) Washington, DC: Government Printing Office.

(1924): *In an Unknown Land.* New York: Charles Scribner's Sons.

(1926): *Ancient Cities and Modern Tribes: Exploration and Adventure in Maya Lands.* New York: Charles Scribner's Sons.

García y García, Apolinar (1865): *Historia de la guerra de castas de Yucatán, sirviéndole el prólogo una reseña de los usos, costumbres e inclinaciones peculiares de los indígenas.* Mérida: Tipografía de Manuel Aldana Rivas.

Gill, Christopher (2001): The Intimate Life of the Family: Patriarchy and the Liberal Project in Yucatán, Mexico, 1860–1915. Ph.D. dissertation. Yale University.

Gluckman, Max (1955): "The Peace in the Feud." *Past and Present* 8:1–14.

Gobierno del Estado (1871a): *Código civil del Estado de Yucatan.* Mérida: Imprenta del Gobierno.

(1871b): *Código penal del estado de Yucatan.* Mérida: Imp. Literaria dirigida por Gil Canto.

Goldschmidt, Walter (1989): Inducement to Military Participation in Tribal Societies. In *The Anthropology of War and Peace,* edited by Paul R. Turner and David Pitt. Granby, MA: Bergin & Garvey, pp. 15–31.

González Navarro, Moisés (1970): *Raza y tierra. La guerra de castas y el henequén.* México, D.F.: El Colegio de México.

Bibliography

(1976): "Las guerras de castas." *Historia Mexicana* 26 (1):70–106.

Granado Baeza, Bartolomé del (1989): "Los indios de Yucatán. Informe dado por el cura de Yaxcabá D. Bartolomé del Granado Baeza, en contestación al interrogatorio de 36 preguntas, circulado por el ministro de ultramar, sobre el manejo, vida y costumbres de los indios, que acompañó el Illmo. Sr. Obispo á la diputacion provincial [1813]." *Revista de la Universidad Autónoma de Yucatán* 4 (168):52–63.

Grossman, Dave (1996): *On Killing: The Psychological Cost of Learning to Kill in War and Society*. New York: Back Bay Books.

Grube, Nikolai (1998): Freiheit und Sklaverei. Die Konstruktion prophetischer Geschichte bei den Cruzoob-Maya von Quintana Roo, Mexiko. Unpublished habilitation thesis. Universität Bonn.

Guardino, Peter (1995): "Barbarism or Republican Law? Guerrero's Peasants and National Politics, 1820–1846." *The Hispanic American Historical Review* 75 (2):185–213.

(2005): *The Time of Liberty: Popular Political Culture in Oaxaca, 1750 – 1850*. Durham, NC: Duke University Press.

Güémez Pineda, José Arturo (1987): Resistencia indígena en Yucatán: El caso del abigeato en el distrito de Mérida, 1821–1847. Tésis de licenciatura. Facultad de Ciencias Antropológicas, Universidad Autónoma de Yucatán.

(2005a): *Mayas, gobierno y tierras frente a la acometida liberal en Yucatán, 1812–1847*. Zamora & Mérida: El Colegio de Michoacán and Universidad Autónoma de Yucatán.

(2005b): "Ciudadanía indígena y representación en Yucatán, 1825–1847." In *Encrucijadas de la ciudadanía y la democracia, Yucatán 1812–2004*. Mérida: Ediciones de la Universidad Autónoma de Yucatán, pp. 83–108.

(2010): Municipalización y guerra de castas: testimonios de la restricción a la libertad civil maya en Yucatán, 1847–1869. In *Republicanismos emergentes: continuidades y rupturas en Yucatán y Puebla, 1786–1869*, edited by Melchor Campos García. Mérida: Ediciones de la Universidad Autónoma de Yucatán, pp. 197–242.

Hallpike, Christopher R. (1977): *Bloodshed and Vengeance in the Papuan Mountains: The Generation of Conflict in Tauade Society*. Oxford: Clarendon Press.

Harrison, Simon (2002): War, Warfare. In *The Routledge Encyclopedia of Social and Cultural Anthropology*, edited by Alan Barnard and Jonathan Spencer. Hoboken: Taylor and Francis, pp. 561–2.

Heller, Carl Bartholomaeus (1853): *Reisen in Mexiko in den Jahren 1845–1848*. Leipzig: Wilhelm Engelmann.

Hicken, Allen (2011): "Clientelism." *Annual Review of Political Science* 14:289–310.

Hinton, Alexander L. (1996): "Agents of Death: Explaining the Cambodian Genocide in Terms of Psychosocial Dissonance." *American Anthropologist* 98 (4):818–31.

Hinz, Armin (2011): Physische, soziale und symbolische Räume in Quintana Roo, Mexiko: Ist der yucatekische 'Kastenkrieg' (1847–1901) ein 'Erinnerungsort'? In *Erinnerungsorte in Mesoamerika*, edited by Lars

Bibliography

Frühsorge, Armin Hinz, Jessica Jacob, Annette Kern and Ulrich Wölfel. Aachen: Shaker, pp. 193–248.

(2013): Gelebte Geschichte und praktizierte Erinnerungskultur: Die Fiesta von Tixcacal Guardia in Quintana Roo, Mexiko. Ph.D. dissertation. Fachbereich Kulturgeschichte und Kulturkunde. Universität Hamburg.

Hoffman, Danny (2011): *The War Machines: Young Men and Violence in Sierra Leone and Liberia*. Durham, NC: Duke University Press.

Hostettler, Ueli (1996): Milpa Agriculture and Economic Diversification: Socioeconomic Change in a Maya Peasant Society of Central Quintana Roo, 1900-1990s. Ph.D. dissertation. Universität Bern.

Hughbank, Richard J. and Dave Grossman (2013): The Challenge of Getting Men to Kill: A View from Military Science. In *War, Peace, and Human Nature: The Convergence of Evolutionary and Cultural Views*, edited by Douglas P. Fry. New York: Oxford University Press, pp. 495–513.

Jenkins, Richard (1997): *Rethinking Ethnicity: Arguments and Explorations*. Thousand Oaks & New Delhi: Sage.

Jones, Grant D. (1974): "Revolution and Continuity in Santa Cruz Maya Society." *American Ethnologist* 1 (4):659–83.

(1978): "Belize, Santa Cruz and Yucatan: The 1884 Articles of Peace." *Belizean Studies* 6 (2):1–9.

Joseph, Gilbert M. (1980): Revolution from Without: The Mexican Revolution in Yucatan, 1910–1940. In *Yucatán: A World Apart*, edited by Edward H. Moseley and Edward Terry. Tuscaloosa: University of Alabama Press, pp. 142–71.

Joseph, Gilbert M. and Allen Wells (1988): "El monocultivo henequenero y sus contradicciones. Estructura de dominación y formas de resistencia en las haciendas yucatecas a fines del Porfiriato." *Siglo XIX* 3 (6):215–77.

(1990): Yucatán: Elite Politics and Rural Insurgency. In *Provinces of the Revolution: Essays on Regional Mexican History*, edited by Thomas Benjamin and Mark Wasserman. Albuquerque: University of New Mexico Press, pp. 93–131.

Jost, John T., Alison Ledgerwood and Curtis D. Hardin (2008): "Shared Reality, System Justification, and the Relational Basis of Ideological Beliefs." *Social and Personality Psychology Compass* 2 (1):171–86.

Kalyvas, Stathis N. (2005): Warfare in Civil Wars. In *Rethinking the Nature of War*, edited by Isabelle Duyvesteyn and Jan Angstrom. Abingdon: Frank Cass, pp. 88–108.

(2006): *The Logic of Violence in Civil Wars*. Cambridge: Cambridge University Press.

Katz, Friedrich (1959): "Plantagenwirtschaft und Sklaverei: Der Sisalanbau auf der Halbinsel Yucatan bis 1910." *Zeitschrift für Geschichtswissenschaft* 7 (5):1002–27.

Keegan, John (2001): *Die Kultur des Krieges*. Reinbek: Rowohlt.

Kelman, Herbert (1973): "Violence without Moral Constraint." *Journal of Social Issues* 29 (4):25–61.

Köhler, Ulrich (1999): *Der Chamula-Aufstand in Chiapas, Mexiko, aus der Sicht heutiger Indianer und Ladinos*. Münster: Lit.

Bibliography

Koos, Carlo (2015): What Do We Know about Sexual Violence in Armed Conflicts? Recent Empirical Progress and Remaining Gaps in Peace and Conflict Research. *GIGA Working Paper*, No. 275.

Krohn-Hansen, Christian (1997): "The Anthropology and Ethnography of Political Violence (Review Essay)." *Journal of Peace Research* 34 (2):233–40.

Lapointe, Marie (1983): *Los mayas rebeldes de Yucatán*. Zamora: El Colegio de Michoacán.

Lemarchand, René and Keith Legg (1972): "Political Clientelism and Development: A Preliminary Analysis." *Comparative Politics* 4 (2):149–78.

Lifton, Robert Jay (1996): "The Psychology of Violence." *The Mount Sinai Journal of Medicine* 63 (2):90–6.

Lorenz, Konrad (1974): *Das sogenannte Böse: Zur Naturgeschichte der Aggression*. München: dtv.

Lozoya, Jorge Alberto (1968): "Un guión para el estudio de los ejércitos mexicanos del siglo diecinueve." *Historia Mexicana* 17 (4):553–68.

Lüdtke, Alf (1983): Herrschaft, Leiden, 'Körpersprache'? Formen direkter und 'sanfter' Gewalt in der bürgerlichen Gesellschaft. In *Gewalt in der Geschichte*, edited by Jörg Calliess. Düsseldorf: Schwann, pp. 271–95.

Lynch, John (1992): *Caudillos in Spanish America, 1800–1850*. Oxford: Oxford University Press.

Maler, Teobert ([1886–93] 1997): *Península Yucatán*, edited by Hanns J. Prem. Berlin: Gebr. Mann Verlag.

Martínez de Arredondo, Francisco (1841): "Viaje á Bolonchen-Ticul." *El Museo Yucateco* 1:217–21.

Méndez, Santiago (1870): "Noticia sobre las costumbres, trabajos, idioma, indústria, fisonomia etc, de los indios de Yucatán …. In García y Cubas, Antonio: Materiales para formar la estadística general de la República Mexicana." *Boletín de la Sociedad Mexicana de Geografia y Estadística* 2 (2):374–87.

Menéndez, Carlos R. (1923): *Historia del infame y vergonzoso comercio de indios vendidos a los esclavistas de Cuba por los políticos yucatecos desde 1848 hasta 1861. Justificación de la revolución indígena de 1847. Documentos irrefutables que lo comprueban*. Mérida: Talleres Gráficos de "La Revista de Mérida."

——— (1932): *Las memorias de d. Buenaventura Vivó y La venta de indios yucatecos en Cuba. Apéndice a la historia de aquel infame y vergonzoso tráfico, con nuevos e interesantes datos y comentarios*. Mérida: Talleres de la Compañia Tipográfica Yucateca.

Métraux, Alfred (1949): Warfare, Cannibalism, and Human Trophies. In *Handbook of South American Indians*, edited by Julian H. Steward. Washington, DC: Smithsonian Institution: Bureau of American Ethnology, vol. 5, pp. 383–409.

Miller, William (1889): "A Journey from British Honduras to Santa Cruz, Yucatan." *Proceedings of the Royal Geographical Society*, n.s. 2:23–8.

Molina Solís, Juan Francisco (1927): *Historia de Yucatán desde la independencia hasta la época actual*. 2 vols. Mérida: Talleres Gráficos de "La Revista de Mérida".

Montalvo Ortega, Enrique (1988): Revolts and Peasant Mobilizations in Yucatán: Indians, Peons, and Peasants from the Caste War to the Revolution. In *Riot,*

Bibliography

Rebellion, and Revolution. Rural Social Conflict in Mexico, edited by Friedrich Katz. Princeton, NJ: Princeton University Press, pp. 295–317.

Montes, Brian (2009): Memories of War: Race, Class, and the Production of Post Caste War Maya Identity in East Central Quintana Roo. Ph.D. dissertation. University of Illinois.

Mora, José María Luis ([1836] 1965): *México y sus revoluciones.* 3 vols. México, D.F.: Porrua.

Morelet, Arthur (1872): *Reisen in Central-Amerika.* Jena: Costenoble.

Mühlenpfordt, Eduard ([1844] 1969): *Versuch einer getreuen Schilderung der Republik Mexiko.* Einleitung Ferdinand Anders. Um eine Einleitung vermehrter Nachdruck der 1844 bei C.F. Kius, Hannover, erschienenen Ausgabe. Graz: Vol. 1. Akademische Druck- u. Verlagsanstalt.

Murphy, William P. (2003): "Military Patrimonialism and Child Soldier Clientelism in the Liberian and Sierra Leonean Civil Wars." *African Studies Review* 46 (2):61–87.

Negrín Muñoz, Alejandro (1991): *Campeche: una historia compartida.* México, D.F.: Gobierno del Estado de Campeche and Instituto Mora.

Nicholas, Ralph W. (1965): Factions: A Comparative Analysis. In *Political Systems and the Distribution of Power,* edited by Michael Banton. London: Tavistock Publications, vol. 2, pp. 21–61.

Norman, B. M. (1843): *Rambles in Yucatan Including a Visit to the Remarkable Ruins of Chi-Chen, Kabah, Zayi, Uxmal & c.* [2nd edition]. New York: J. and H. Langley.

Ohmstede, Antonio (1988): "Política indigenista en el México del siglo XIX (1800–1857)." *Papeles de la Casa Chata* 3 (4):11–23.

Orlove, Benjamin S. (1978): Systems of Production and Indian Peasant Insurrections: A General Discussion and Three Specific Cases. In *Actes du XVIIe Congrès International des Amèricanistes.* Paris: Société des Américanistes, vol. 3, pp. 127–44.

Otterbein, Keith F. (2000): "Killing of Captured Enemies: A Cross-cultural Study." *Current Anthropology* 41 (3):439–43.

Paoli Bolio, Francisco José (2015): *La Guerra de Castas en Yucatán.* Mérida: Dante.

Patch, Robert W. (1990): Decolonización, el problema agrario y los orígenes de la guerra de castas, 1812–1847. In *Sociedad, estructura agraria y estado en Yucatán,* edited by Othón Baños Ramírez. Mérida: Universidad Autónoma de Yucatán, pp. 45–95.

Peniche Rivero, Piedad (1993): Mujeres de la Guerra de Castas: una crítica feminista. In *Tesoros del archivo,* edited by Piedad Peniche Rivero, Jorge Canto Alcocer and Rosa Elena Solís Blanco. Mérida: Gobierno del Estado de Yucatán, pp. 101–4.

(1999): "La comunidad doméstica de la hacienda henequenera de Yucatán, México, 1870–1915." *Mexican Studies/Estudios Mexicanos* 15 (1):1–33.

Pérez Alcalá, Felipe (1880): *Guerra social en Yucatan: Ensayos biográficos.* Mérida: Comercio.

Quintal Martín, Fidelio (1986): "Proceso y ejecución de Manuel Antonio Ay Tec caudillo campesino de Chichimilá, Yucatán." *Boletín de la Escuela de Ciencias Antropológicas de la UADY* 13 (76):21–43.

334 Bibliography

(1988): "Inicio interpretativo de la correspondencia en maya sobre la 'guerra de castas' (1842–1866)." *Revista de la Universidad Autónoma de Yucatán* 3 (165):3–19.

Reed, Nelson (1964): *The Caste War of Yucatán*. Stanford, CA: Stanford University Press.

(1997a): "Mosquetes y machetes. Reseña militar de la guerra de castas de Yucatán." *Unicornio* (Supplement of Por Estó!):3–9 (October 26).

(1997b): "Juan de la Cruz, Venancio Puc, and the Speaking Cross." *The Americas* 53 (4):497–523.

(1997c): "White and Mestizo Leadership of the Cruzoob." *Saastun. Revista de Cultura Maya* 0 (1):63–88.

(2001): *The Caste War of Yucatán*. [2nd revised edition]. Stanford, CA: Stanford University Press.

Regil, José M. and Alonso Manuel Péon (1853): "Estadística de Yucatán." *Boletín de la Sociedad Mexicana de Geografía y Estadística*, Ia época 3:237–340.

Reina, Leticia (1980): *Las rebeliones campesinas en México, 1819–1906*. México, D.F.: Siglo Veintiuno Editores.

Remmers, Lawrence J. (1981): Henequen, the Caste War and the Economy of Yucatan, 1846–1883: The Roots of Dependence in a Mexican Region. Ph.D. dissertation. University of California.

Restall, Matthew (1997): *The Maya World*. Stanford, CA: Stanford University Press.

(2009): *The Black Middle: Africans, Mayas, and Spaniards in Colonial Yucatan*. Stanford, CA: Stanford University Press.

Restall, Matthew and Wolfgang Gabbert (2017): Maya Ethnogenesis and Group Identity in Yucatán, 1500–1900. In *"The Only True People": Linking Maya Identities Past and Present*, edited by Bethany J. Beyyette and Lisa J. LeCount. Boulder: University of Colorado Press, pp. 91–130.

Riches, David (1986): The Phenomenon of Violence. In *The Anthropology of Violence*, edited by David Riches. Oxford: Blackwell, pp. 1–27.

Richter, Daniel K. (1992): *The Ordeal of the Longhouse: The Peoples of the Iroquois League in the Era of European Colonization*. Williamsburg, VA: University of North Carolina Press.

Richthofen, Emil Karl Freiherr von (1859): *Die äußeren und inneren politischen Zustände der Republik Mexico seit deren Unabhängigkeit bis auf die neueste Zeit*. Berlin: Deckersche Geheime Ober-Hofbuchdruckerei.

Riekenberg, Michael (1998): Kriegerische Gewaltakteure in Lateinamerika im frühen 19. Jahrhundert. In *Kulturen der Gewalt. Ritualisierung und Symbolisierung von Gewalt in der Geschichte*, edited by Rolf Peter Sieferle and Helga Breuninger. Frankfurt: Campus, pp. 195–214.

Robins, Nicholas A. (2005): *Native Insurgencies and the Genocidal Impulse in the Americas*. Bloomington: Indiana University Press.

Rodríguez Losa, Salvador (1989): *Geografía política de Yucatán. Tomo II. División territorial, gobierno de los pueblos y población, 1821–1900*. Mérida: Ediciones de la Universidad Autónoma de Yucatán.

Rodriguez Piña, Javier (1987–88): "Guerra de castas y azúcar: el comercio de indígenas mayas con Cuba (1848–1861)." *Anales del Caribe* 7–8:28–93.

Bibliography

Rogers, E. (1885): "British Honduras: Its Resources and Development." *Journal of the Manchester Geographical Society* 1:197–227.

Rosado Rosado, Georgina and Landy Santana Rivas (2008): "María Uicab: reina, sacerdotisa y jefa militar de los mayas rebeldes de Yucatán (1863–1875)." *Mesoamérica* 29 (50):112–39.

Roys, Ralph (1972): *The Indian Background of Colonial Yucatan.* [1st edition 1943]. Norman: University of Oklahoma Press.

Rufin, Jean-Cristophe (1999): Kriegswirtschaft in internen Konflikten. In *Ökonomie des Bürgerkrieges*, edited by Francois Jean and Jean-Cristophe Rufin. Hamburg: Hamburger Edition, pp. 15–46.

Rugeley, Terry (1995): "The Maya Elites of Nineteenth-Century Yucatán." *Ethnohistory* 42 (3):477–93.

(1996): *Yucatán's Maya Peasantry & the Origins of the Caste War.* Austin: University of Texas Press.

(1997): "Rural Political Violence and the Origins of the Caste War." *The Americas* 53 (4):469–96.

(2001a): *Of Wonders and Wise Men: Religion and Popular Cultures in Southeast Mexico, 1800–1876.* Austin: University of Texas Press.

(2001b): *Maya Wars: Ethnographic Accounts from Nineteenth-Century Yucatán.* Norman: University of Oklahoma Press.

(2009): *Rebellion Now and Forever: Mayas, Hispanics, and Caste War Violence in Yucatán, 1800–1880.* Stanford, CA: Stanford University Press.

Sapper, Karl (1895): "Die unabhängigen Indianerstaaten von Yucatan." *Globus* 67 (13):197–201.

Scheina, Robert L. (2003): *Latin America's Wars. Vol 1: The Age of the Caudillo, 1791–1899.* Washington, DC: Brassey's.

Schiefenhövel, Wulf (1995): Aggression und Aggressionskontrolle am Beispiel der Eipo aus dem Hochland von West-Neuguinea. In *Töten im Krieg*, edited by Heinrich von Stietencron and Jörg Rüpke. Freiburg i.Br., München: Alber, pp. 339–62.

Schlichte, Klaus (2009): *In the Shadow of Violence: The Politics of Armed Groups.* Frankfurt: Campus.

Scholes, France V. and Ralph Roys (1968): *The Maya Chontal Indians of Acalan-Tixchel: A Contribution to the History and Ethnography of the Yucatan Peninsula* Norman: University of Oklahoma Press.

Schüren, Ute (2003): Los mayas pacíficos de los Chenes ayer y hoy. In *El reloj chenero*, edited by Mario H. Aranda González. Campeche: Gobierno del Estado, Universidad Autónoma de Campeche, pp. 155–65.

Scott, James C. (1972): "Patron-Client Politics and Political Change in Southeast Asia." *American Political Science Review* 66 (1):91–114.

(1989): Everyday Forms of Resistance. In *Everyday Forms of Peasant Resistance*, edited by Forrest D. Colburn. New York: M.E. Sharpe, pp. 3–33.

Seifert, Ruth (1995): Der weibliche Körper als Symbol und Zeichen: Geschlechtsspezifische Gewalt und die kulturelle Konstruktion des Krieges. In *Gewalt im Krieg: Ausübung, Erfahrung und Verweigerung von Gewalt in Kriegen des 20. Jahrhunderts*, edited by Andreas Gestrich. (Jahrbuch für Historische Friedensforschung 4). Münster: Lit, pp. 13–33.

Bibliography

(1996): "The Second Front: The Logic of Sexual Violence in Wars." *Women's Studies International Forum* 19 (1/2):35–43.

Sierra O'Reilly, Justo ([1848–51] 1994): *Los indios de Yucatán.* 2 vols. Mérida: Universidad Autónoma de Yucatán.

Simmel, Georg ([1908] 1995): Der Streit. In *Soziologie. Untersuchungen über die Formen der Vergesellschaftung,* edited by Otthein Rammstedt. Georg Simmel Gesamtausgabe. Frankfurt: Suhrkamp, pp. 284–382.

Sluka, Jeffrey, A. (1992): The Anthropology of Conflict. In *The Paths to Domination, Resistance, and Terror,* edited by Carolyn Nordstrom and Jo Ann Martin. Berkeley: University of California Press, pp. 18–36.

Sofsky, Wolfgang (1996): *Traktat über die Gewalt.* Frankfurt: Fischer.

Sorokin, Pitirim A. (1942): *Man and Society in Calamity.* New York: E.P. Dutton.

Stephens, John L. ([1841] 1969): *Incidents of Travel in Central America, Chiapas and Yucatan.* 2 vols. New York: Dover.

([1843] 1963): *Incidents of Travel in Yucatan.* 2 vols. New York: Dover.

Strickon, Arnold (1965): "Hacienda and Plantation in Yucatan." *América Indígena* 25 (1):35–63.

Stuart, William T. (1972): The Explanation of Patron-Client Systems: Some Structural and Ecological Perspectives. In *Structure and Process in Latin America: Patronage, Clientage and Power Systems,* edited by Arnold Strickon and Sidney M. Greenfield. Albuquerque: University of New Mexico Press, pp. 19–42.

Suárez Molina, Victor M. (1977): *La evolución económica de Yucatán a través del siglo XIX.* 2 vols. México, D.F.: Ediciones de la Universidad de Yucatán.

Suárez y Navarro, Juan ([1861] 1993): Informe sobre las causas y carácter de los frecuentes cambios políticos ocurridos en el Estado de Yucatán. In *La guerra de castas.* México, D.F.: CONACULTA, pp. 147–431.

Sullivan, Paul (1984): Contemporary Yucatec Maya Apocalyptic Prophecy: The Ethnographic and Historical Context. Ph.D. dissertation. John Hopkins University.

(1989): *Unfinished Conversations: Mayas and Foreigners between Two Wars.* Berkeley: University of California Press.

(1997a): "Para qué lucharon los mayas rebeldes?" *Unicornio* (Supplement of Por Estó!), parts I:3–9 (August 3) and II:3–9 (August 10).

(1997b): "The Search of Peace Between Yucatán and the Rebel Maya, 1876–1886." *Saastun* 0 (3):3–46.

(2004): *Xuxub Must Die: The Lost Histories of a Murder on the Yucatan.* Pittsburgh, PA: University of Pittsburgh Press.

Sweeney, Lean (2006): *La supervivencia de los bandidos. Los mayas icaichés y la política fronteriza del sureste de la península de Yucatán, 1847–1904.* Mérida: UNAM.

Taylor, William B. (1979): *Drinking, Homicide and Rebellion in Colonial Mexican Villages.* Stanford, CA: Stanford University Press.

Thomson, Guy P. C. (1991): "Popular Aspects of Liberalism in Mexico, 1848–1888." *Bulletin of Latin American Research* 10 (3):265–92.

Tiesler, Vera (2001): "La muerte del General Bernadino Cen, líder de la Guerra de Castas." *Temas Antropológicos* 23 (1):83–99.

Bibliography 337

Trotha, Trutz von (1997): Einleitung. Zur Soziologie der Gewalt. In *Soziologie der Gewalt*, edited by Trutz von Trotha. Kölner Zeitschrift für Soziologie und Sozialpsychologie Sonderheft 37. Opladen: Westdeutscher Verlag, pp. 9–56.

Unzueta Reyes, Victoria (2006): La permanencia del fuero de antiguo régimen en la sociedad mexicana decimonónica: el fuero militar en la segunda mitad del siglo XIX. In *Cultura política en América: variaciones regionales y temporales*, edited by Ricardo Forte and Natalia Silva Prado. México, D.F.: Universidad Metropolitana, Unidad Iztapalapa, pp. 87–104.

(2009): Corte Interamericano de Derechos Humanos. Rosendo Radilla Pacheco (Caso 12.511) contra los Estados Unidos Mexicanos, Amicus Curiae preparado por Dra. Victoria Livia Unzueta Reyes, 21 de julio (www.senado .gob.mx/comisiones/justicia/docs/Justicia_Militar/Acad_MesaIII_VUR.pdf; accessed 21/3/2017).

Valentino, Benjamin, Paul Huth and Dylan Balch-Lindsay (2004): "'Draining the Sea': Mass Killing and Guerrilla Warfare." *International Organization* 58 (2):375–407.

Vanderwood, Paul J. (1984): "El bandidaje en el siglo XIX: una forma de subsistir." *Historia Mexicana* 34 (1):41–75.

(1998): *The Power of God against the Guns of Government: Religious Upheaval in Mexico at the Turn of the Nineteenth Century*. Stanford, CA: Stanford University Press.

Villa Rojas, Alfonso (1945): *The Maya of East Central Quintana Roo*. Washington, DC: Carnegie Institution.

Villalobos González, Martha Herminia (2006): *El bosque sitiado: asaltos armados, concesiones forestales y estrategias de resistencia durante la Guerra de Castas*. México, D.F.: Centro de Investigaciones y Estudios Superiores en Antropología Social.

Wallace, Anthony F. C. (1972): *The Death and Rebirth of the Seneca*. New York: Vintage Books.

Weingrod, Alex (1968): "Patrons, Patronage, and Political Parties." *Comparative Studies in Society and History* 10 (4):377–400.

Wells, Allen (1984): Yucatán: Violence and Social Control on Henequen Plantations. In *Other Mexicos: Essays on Regional Mexican History, 1876–1911*, edited by Thomas Benjamin and William McNellie. Albuquerque: University of New Mexico Press, pp. 213–41.

(1985): *Yucatán's Gilded Age: Haciendas, Henequen and International Harvester, 1860–1915*. Albuquerque: University of New Mexico Press.

(1996): "Forgotten Chapters of Yucatán's Past: Nineteenth-Century Politics in Historiographical Perspective." *Mexican Studies/Estudios Mexicanos* 12 (2):195–229.

Wilhelm, Burkhard, ed. (1997): *Indios rebeldes? El fin de la Guerra de Castas en Yucatán vista por El Estandarte de San Luis Potosí*. San Luis Potosí: Lascasiana.

Wolf, Eric and Edward C. Hansen (1967): "Caudillo Politics: A Structural Analysis." *Comparative Studies in Society and History* 9 (2):168–79.

Zimmerman, Charlotte (1965): "The Hermeneutics of the Maya Cult of the Holy Cross." *Numen* 12 (2):139–59.

Index

Acereto, Pedro 80, 222, 229
adultery 204
Aké, José María
    death of 201
alcohol 39
    and violence 24, 183, 238
army, Mexican 46, 54
atrocities 3, 26, 27, 55–57, 69, 195
    by government forces 138–144
    by kruso'b 215, 233–234
Ay, Manuel Antonio 62

Bacalar 70, 141, 215, 271
    conquered by kruso'b 236–238, 266
    conquered by rebels 68
    rebel attacks on 80, 169
banditry 45
    sanctions for 46
Baqueiro, Romualdo 141
Baqueiro, Serapio 250
Barbachano, Miguel 51, 61, 65, 149
Barrera, Agustín 229
Barrera, José María 69, 70, 150, 160, 182, 184
    and Speaking Cross 150
    death of 185
Barrera, Pantaleón 260
Barret, Domingo 61
batabo'b 43, 51, 173, 181, 262
Batún, Nicolás 171
Belize 79, 174, 197, 226
    and Caste War rebels 88, 152
    and end of slavery 262

status of 87
Blacks
    among kruso'b 262
Bravo, Ignacio 85
Bricker, Victoria 165
buffer zone 175, 265
    as target of government forces 120
    attractions of 120
    raided by kruso'b 214

Cab, Hilario
    death of 201
Cahum, Luciano 228
Campeche
    opposition to independence 61
    separation from Yucatán 77, 193
    siege of city 55
cantones 68
Canul, José María
    death of 201
Canul, Luciano
    death of 201
Careaga Viliesid, Lorena 163
casta
    meaning of the term 2
Caste War 2
    and ideology 251–252
    and peace talks 69, 122, 150, 197, 198, 202
    and personal gain 126, 248
    battles 68
    costs of 75, 83
    depicted as race war 9, 63, 64, 252–255

Index

interpretation of 6, 48, 151, 280
origins of 62
Caste War rebels 2, *see also kruso'b*
and rent collection 157–158, 194, 198,
199–200, 201
and trade with Belize 152, 155, 156, 188,
220, 248, 266
armament of 89, 152, 207–210
demands of 255–256
losses of 208, 272–274
non-Indians among 149–150, 259
number of 66, 70
organization of 147
self-designation of 71, 150
tactics of 68, 117, 216
Castillo, Severo del 3, 81, 95, 140, 213, 215,
221, 223
categories, ethnic or social 33–34, 41,
see also masewal; ts'ul
used by Caste War rebels 258–259
caudillo politics 176–181, 184, 202
Cen, Bernardino 174, 187, 188, 197, 198,
232
death of 198, 220
personality of 182, 261
Cetina, José Dolores 65, 76, 141, 143
Chablé, Juan 185
Chan Hunuku
kruso'b attack on 208, 217, 234
Chan Santa Cruz 71, 79, 161, 174, 186,
187, 188, 190, 205, 219, 220, 222,
225, 227, 228, 229
and Tulum 190, 201
attacks on 71, 74, 80, 85, 123, 160, 164,
228, 271
crafts in 155
Chan, Florentino 70, 173, 184, 192
Chan, José Luciano 171
Chancah Veracruz 171
Chemax 68
Chenes region 31, 151
Chi, Cecilio 63, 140, 173
death of 70
Chi, Juan 142
Chichanhá 73, 141
Chichimilá 63
Chinese
living among kruso'b 259
Chuc, Juan
death of 199
Chunpom 82, 171, 198

civil war
and violence 28
in Yucatán 55
Corozal 155, 166, 168, 174
cortes (Spanish national assembly) 256
Coser, Lewis 18

desertion *see also* government forces
from government forces 45
Díaz de la Vega, Rómulo 23, 72, 94, 112,
141, 270
Díaz, Porfirio 85, 201, 277
Dumond, Don 6, 165, 183, 196
on rebel demography 272
on rebel organization 171
Dzitas
kruso'b attack on 261
Dzonot
battle of 81, 113, 140
Dzonotchel 213
kruso'b attack on 230
Dzul, Aniceto 88, 198, 200, 204
death of 201
Dzul, Pedro 185

Ekpedz
kruso'b attack on 223
elections 51
Elwert, Georg 18
Empire, Mexican 46
and Caste War 80
Encalada, Pablo 226, 228
Espadas, Antonio 230, 250

factionalism 51
flogging 40, 41, 108, 109, 111, 193
among the kruso'b 203
fuero militar 144

Galtung, Johan 15
government forces *see also* army, Mexican;
Indians; National Guard; prisoners
and abuse of soldiers 111, 125
and abuse of town residents 118
and desertion 112–116, 209
and lack of arms 77
and lack of supplies 111, 121–123
and looting 125, 265
and prisoners 125, 127–137
and scorched-earth policy 121, 144
armament of 88

340 *Index*

government forces (cont.)
  enlistment in 109
  losses of 81, 85
  organization of 112–116
  strategy of 80, 85, 123
  strength of 66, 93
Great Britain
  and Mexico 87
guerillas
  tactics of 55
Guerra de Reforma 46, 276

Hansen, Edward 176, 184
hidalgos 66, 83
homicide
  sanctions for 44

Icaiché 214
Ichmul 68
independence 1, 48, 51
  of Yucatán 50, 55, 61
Indians 39, 165
  as soldiers in civil wars 62
  in government forces 97–103
  legal status of 33
instability, political
  reasons for 50
Izamal 66, 170

Jones, Grant 196
Juárez, Benito 55

Kalyvas, Stathis 3, 145, 251
  and joint production of violence 249–250
Kampepén
  kruso'b attack on 217
Kampocolché 70, 80, 161
Kancabchén 77
  kruso'b attack on 212, 230
Kantunilkin 171
  kruso'b attack on 217
Kaua 153
killing
  inhibition to 24
kruso'b 2, 79, 113, 264, *see also* Caste War
    rebels
  and deserters 114, 150, 259
  and dislike of taxes 168, 193
  and guard service 171
  and local conflicts 232
  and looting 152–154, 219, 265

and prisoners 218–226
and trade with Yucatecans 231
assaults on Yucatán 83–84
ideology of 255–263
motivations for killing 239–245
origins of 151
political organization of 173–191
politics and religion among 191
raids on pacíficos 214
sanctions among 206
victims of 216–218
kruso'b leaders 165
  and religion 196
  and wealth 196, 200
  economic activities of 182, 222
  power struggles among 175–176,
    181–182, 192–203

Laws and Customs of War
  declaration on 139
Lochhá 73, 229
  kruso'b attack on 218, 238
Loesa, José 227
López de Llergo, Sebastián 64, 122

Mabén 171
Macanché 73
Manzanilla, Secundino 230
masewal 34, 259
May, Zacarías 185
Méndez, Santiago 51, 62, 231
Mesapich 73
Micheltorena, Manuel 68, 112, 154
Miller, William 172
Molas, Sebastián 142
Muyil 82, 175

Ná, José 187
  death of 194
National Guard 49, 94, 264, 279
  and exemptions from service 106
  and lack of training 216
  Indians in 263
  organization of 53
  origins of 53
Nauat, Manuel
  death of 162
Novelo, Bonifacio 72, 150, 182, 184, 187,
    197, 204, 218
  death of 187, 189
Novelo, Claudio 264

Index

death of 188
Novelo, Juan María 160

Ontiveros, Juan 230
Otterbein, Keith 216

pacíficos del norte 78
pacíficos del sur 73, 82, 97, 113
Pat, Jacinto 64, 65, 150, 173, 182, 221, 228
    death of 70, 192, 193
Pat, Juan de la Cruz 232
patron-client relations 51
Pec, Venancio 70
Pech, Luciano
    death of 200
Peón Contreras, Juan 200
Pérez Virgilio, Narciso 142
Peto 77, 166
    rebel attacks on 217
Pisté
    kruso'b attack on 218, 261
Polyuc 215
Poot, Crescencio 82, 182, 187, 188, 190,
        197, 218, 228, 229, 238, 250, 261
    and rupture with Cen 198
    death of 199
population
    decline of 2
prisoners 265, *see also* government forces;
        kruso'b; *vecinos*; women
    abused by government forces 128–132,
        139–140
    and Stockholm syndrome 230
    children as 226
    integration into kruso'b society 231
    sanctions for 127
    significance of 267
    sold to Cuba 132–138
    treatment by kruso'b 205, 214, 218–231,
        257
    treatment of 3, 216
pronunciamiento 49
Puc, José María 201
Puc, Venancio 185, 193, 194, 204, 227
    and killing of prisoners 257
    death of 194
punishment, corporal 44, 111

race war 6
racism 278
rape 21, 63, 143, 234–236

Rean, Pastora
    wife of Crescencio Poot 228
rebellions
    in Yucatán 76
rebels *see* Caste War rebels; *kruso'b*
Reed, Nelson 5, 167, 186, 215
    model of kruso'b organization 162–164
refugees
    in Belize 65, 154
    internal 66
Riches, David 18
Río Hondo 214
Rosado, José Eulogio 23
Rugeley, Terry 6, 7, 139, 165, 168,
        270

Sabán 70, 213
Sacalaca 213
San Antonio Muyil 82, 171
Sánchez, Apolinar 167
Santa María 213
Santos, Leandro 185, 187, 196, 267
    death of 197
    putsch against Puc 194
Schlichte, Klaus 159, 267
soldiers
    loyalty of 54
Speaking Cross 2, 9, 11, 150, 245, 267
    and folk religiosity 170
    and political organization 111, 160
    functions of 71, 169–170, 251
    messages of 161, 167, 169, 184
    origins of 71, 160–162
    structure of the cult 173
Stephens, Robert
    killed in Xuxub 232
Sullivan, Paul 7, 165, 190, 199, 211, 256,
        257
    on Yucatecan losses 270

Tahdzibichén 213
Tahdziu
    kruso'b attack on 258
Tec, José Dolores 193
Tekax 141, 151
    kruso'b attack on 230, 235, 264
Tekom 250
Tepich 63, 140, 234
Ticul 66
Tiholop
    kruso'b attack on 227

Tihosuco 23, 67, 68, 70, 77, 81, 229
  rebel attacks on 213
  rebellion in 112
  siege of 82
Tixcacal Guardia 171
Tixcacaltuyú 213
Tizimín 142
  rebellion in 76
Traconis, Daniel 82, 189
Treaty of Tzucacab 65
ts'ul 34, 259
Tulum 82, 171, 198
  as cult center 188–190
  kruso'b attack on 200
Tunkas
  kruso'b attack on 170, 213, 219, 223, 264
  prisoners from 225, 227
Tzuc, José María 73
Tzuc, Juan Tomás 204

Uayma 153
Uch, Clemente 142
Uicab, María 188
Urcelay, Nicolás 82

Valladolid 67, 151
  rebel attacks on 114, 175, 204
  siege of 68
vecinos 6, 149
  as kruso'b prisoners 261
Villa Rojas, Alfonso 171, 174, 190
Villalobos González, Martha 7, 189
violence
  and dehumanization 25
  and emotions 21–22, 29, 44, 216

and norms 139
and space 117–121
definition of 15
domestic 40, 43
functions of 18–19, 248
internal
  and hierarchy 267
reasons for 58
routinization of 25
socialization for 19–20
Vitorín, Vitoriano 259

Wolf, Eric 176, 184
women
  and status among rebels 5, 189
  as kruso'b prisoners 221, 228
  as victims 25, 217

Xkanhá 73
Xuluc, Isabel 200
Xuxub 198
  kruso'b attack on 220, 232

Yama, Felipe
  death of 201
Yaxcabá 213
  kruso'b attack on 208
  rebel losses at 274
Yucatán
  economy of 35–37, 76

Zapata, Dionisio 185, 187, 193, 267
  death of 197, 257
  putsch against Puc 194

Other Books in the Series (continued from page ii)

102. *Indian and Slave Royalists in the Age of Revolution*, Marcela Echeverri
101. *Indigenous Elites and Creole Identity in Colonial Mexico, 1500–1800*, Peter Villella
100. *Asian Slaves in Colonial Mexico: From Chinos to Indians*, Tatiana Seijas
99. *Black Saint of the Americas: The Life and Afterlife of* Martín de Porres, Celia Cussen
98. *The Economic History of Latin America since Independence, Third Edition*, Victor Bulmer-Thomas
97. *The British Textile Trade in South American in the Nineteenth Century*, Manuel Llorca-Jaña
96. *Warfare and Shamanism in Amazonia*, Carlos Fausto
95. *Rebellion on the Amazon: The Cabanagem, Race, and Popular Culture in the North of Brazil, 1798–1840*, Mark Harris
94. *A History of the Khipu*, Galen Brokaw
93. *Politics, Markets, and Mexico's "London Debt," 1823–1887*, Richard J. Salvucci
92. *The Political Economy of Argentina in the Twentieth Century*, Roberto Cortés Conde
91. *Bankruptcy of Empire: Mexican Silver and the Wars between Spain, Britain, and France, 1760–1810*, Carlos Marichal
90. *Shadows of Empire: The Indian Nobility of Cusco, 1750–1825*, David T. Garrett
89. *Chile: The Making of a Republic, 1830–1865: Politics and Ideas*, Simon Collier
88. *Deference and Defiance in Monterrey: Workers, Paternalism, and Revolution in Mexico, 1890–1950*, Michael Snodgrass
87. *Andrés Bello: Scholarship and Nation-Building in Nineteenth-Century Latin America*, Ivan Jaksic
86. *Between Revolution and the Ballot Box: The Origins of the Argentine Radical Party in the 1890s*, Paula Alonso
85. *Slavery and the Demographic and Economic History of Minas Gerais, Brazil, 1720–1888*, Laird W. Bergad
84. *The Independence of Spanish America*, Jaime E. Rodríguez
83. *The Rise of Capitalism on the Pampas: The Estancias of Buenos Aires, 1785–1870*, Samuel Amaral
82. *A History of Chile, 1808–2002, Second Edition*, Simon Collier and William F. Sater
81. *The Revolutionary Mission: American Enterprise in Latin America, 1900–1945*, Thomas F. O'Brien
80. *The Kingdom of Quito, 1690–1830: The State and Regional Development*, Kenneth J. Andrien
79. *The Cuban Slave Market, 1790–1880*, Laird W. Bergad, Fe Iglesias García, and María del Carmen Barcia
78. *Business Interest Groups in Nineteenth-Century Brazil*, Eugene Ridings

77. *The Economic History of Latin America since Independence, Second Edition*, Victor Bulmer-Thomas

76. *Power and Violence in the Colonial City: Oruro from the Mining Renaissance to the Rebellion of Tupac Amaru (1740–1782)*, Oscar Cornblit

75. *Colombia before Independence: Economy, Society and Politics under Bourbon Rule*, Anthony McFarlane

74. *Politics and Urban Growth in Buenos Aires, 1910–1942*, Richard J. Walter

73. *The Central Republic in Mexico, 1835–1846, 'Hombres de Bien' in the Age of Santa Anna*, Michael P. Costeloe

72. *Negotiating Democracy: Politicians and Generals in Uruguay*, Charles Guy Gillespie

71. *Native Society and Disease in Colonial Ecuador*, Suzanne Austin Alchon

70. *The Politics of Memory: Native Historical Interpretation in the Colombian Andes*, Joanne Rappaport

69. *Power and the Ruling Classes in Northeast Brazil, Juazeiro and Petrolina in Transition*, Ronald H. Chilcote

68. *House and Street: The Domestic World of Servants and Masters in Nineteenth-Century Rio de Janeiro*, Sandra Lauderdale Graham

67. *The Demography of Inequality in Brazil*, Charles H. Wood and José Alberto Magno de Carvalho

66. *The Politics of Coalition Rule in Colombia*, Jonathan Hartlyn

65. *South America and the First World War: The Impact of the War on Brazil, Argentina*, Peru and Chile, Bill Albert

64. *Resistance and Integration: Peronism and the Argentine Working Class, 1946–1976*, Daniel James

63. *The Political Economy of Central America since 1920*, Victor Bulmer-Thomas

62. *A Tropical Belle Epoque: Elite Culture and Society in Turn-of-the-Century Rio de Janeiro*, Jeffrey D. Needell

61. *Ambivalent Conquests: Maya and Spaniard in Yucatan, 1517–1570, Second Edition*, Inga Clendinnen

60. *Latin America and the Comintern, 1919–1943*, Manuel Caballero

59. *Roots of Insurgency: Mexican Regions, 1750–1824*, Brian R. Hamnett

58. *The Agrarian Question and the Peasant Movement in Colombia: Struggles of the National Peasant Association, 1967–1981*, Leon Zamosc

57. *Catholic Colonialism: A Parish History of Guatemala, 1524–1821*, Adriaan C. van Oss

56. *Pre-Revolutionary Caracas: Politics, Economy, and Society 1777–1811*, P. Michael McKinley

55. *The Mexican Revolution, Volume 2: Counter-Revolution and Reconstruction*, Alan Knight

54. *The Mexican Revolution, Volume 1: Porfirians, Liberals, and Peasants*, Alan Knight

53. *The Province of Buenos Aires and Argentine Politics, 1912–1943*, Richard J. Walter

52. *Sugar Plantations in the Formation of Brazilian Society: Bahia, 1550–1835*, Stuart B. Schwartz
51. *Tobacco on the Periphery: A Case Study in Cuban Labour History, 1860–1958*, Jean Stubbs
50. *Housing, the State, and the Poor: Policy and Practice in Three Latin American Cities*, Alan Gilbert and Peter M. Ward
49. *Unions and Politics in Mexico: The Case of the Automobile Industry*, Ian Roxborough
48. *Miners, Peasants and Entrepreneurs: Regional Development in the Central Highlands of Peru*, Norman Long and Bryan Roberts
47. *Capitalist Development and the Peasant Economy in Peru*, Adolfo Figueroa
46. *Early Latin America: A History of Colonial Spanish America and Brazil*, James Lockhart and Stuart B. Schwartz
45. *Brazil's State-Owned Enterprises: A Case Study of the State as Entrepreneur*, Thomas J. Trebat
44. *Law and Politics in Aztec Texcoco*, Jerome A. Offner
43. *Juan Vicente Gómez and the Oil Companies in Venezuela, 1908–1935*, B. S. McBeth
42. *Revolution from without: Yucatán, Mexico, and the United States, 1880–1924*, Gilbert M. Joseph
41. *Demographic Collapse: Indian Peru, 1520–1620*, Noble David Cook
40. *Oil and Politics in Latin America: Nationalist Movements and State Companies*, George Philip
39. *The Struggle for Land: A Political Economy of the Pioneer Frontier in Brazil from 1930 to the Present Day*, J. Foweraker
38. *Caudillo and Peasant in the Mexican Revolution*, D. A. Brading, ed.
37. *Odious Commerce: Britain, Spain and the Abolition of the Cuban Slave Trade*, David Murray
36. *Coffee in Colombia, 1850–1970: An Economic, Social and Political History*, Marco Palacios
35. *A Socioeconomic History of Argentina, 1776–1860*, Jonathan C. Brown
34. *From Dessalines to Duvalier: Race, Colour and National Independence in Haiti*, David Nicholls
33. *Modernization in a Mexican ejido: A Study in Economic Adaptation*, Billie R. DeWalt.
32. *Haciendas and Ranchos in the Mexican Bajío, Léon, 1700–1860*, D. A. Brading
31. *Foreign Immigrants in Early Bourbon Mexico, 1700–1760*, Charles F. Nunn
30. *The Merchants of Buenos Aires, 1778–1810: Family and Commerce*, Susan Migden Socolow
29. *Drought and Irrigation in North-east Brazil*, Anthony L. Hall
28. *Coronelismo: The Municipality and Representative Government in Brazil*, Victor Nunes Leal
27. *A History of the Bolivian Labour Movement, 1848–1971*, Guillermo Lora

26. *Land and Labour in Latin America: Essays on the Development of Agrarian Capitalism in the Nineteenth and Twentieth Centuries,* Kenneth Duncan and Ian Rutledge, eds.

25. *Allende's Chile: The Political Economy of the Rise and Fall of the Unidad Popular,* Stefan de Vylder

24. *The Cristero Rebellion: The Mexican People Between Church and State, 1926–1929,* Jean A. Meyer

23. *The African Experience in Spanish America, 1502 to the Present Day,* Leslie B. Rout, Jr.

22. *Letters and People of the Spanish Indies: Sixteenth Century,* James Lockhart and Enrique Otte, eds.

21. *Chilean Rural Society from the Spanish Conquest to 1930,* Arnold J. Bauer

20. *Studies in the Colonial History of Spanish America,* Mario Góngora

19. *Politics in Argentina, 1890–1930: The Rise and Fall of Radicalism,* David Rock

18. *Politics, Economics and Society in Argentina in the Revolutionary Period,* Tulio Halperín Donghi

17. *Marriage, Class and Colour in Nineteenth-Century Cuba: A Study of Racial Attitudes and Sexual Values in a Slave Society,* Verena Stolcke

16. *Conflicts and Conspiracies: Brazil and Portugal, 1750–1808,* Kenneth Maxwell

15. *Silver Mining and Society in Colonial Mexico: Zacatecas, 1546–1700,* P. J. Bakewell

14. *A Guide to the Historical Geography of New Spain,* Peter Gerhard

13. *Bolivia: Land, Location and Politics Since 1825,* J. Valerie Fifer, Malcolm Deas, Clifford Smith, and John Street

12. *Politics and Trade in Southern Mexico, 1750–1821,* Brian R. Hamnett

11. *Alienation of Church Wealth in Mexico: Social and Economic Aspects of the Liberal Revolution, 1856–1875,* Jan Bazant

10. *Miners and Merchants in Bourbon Mexico, 1763–1810,* D. A. Brading

9. *An Economic History of Colombia, 1845–1930,* W. P. McGreevey

8. *Economic Development of Latin America: Historical Background and Contemporary Problems,* Celso Furtado and Suzette Macedo

7. *Regional Economic Development: The River Basin Approach in Mexico,* David Barkin and Timothy King

6. *The Abolition of the Brazilian Slave Trade: Britain, Brazil and the Slave Trade Question, 1807–1869,* Leslie Bethell

5. *Parties and Political Change in Bolivia, 1880–1952,* Herbert S. Klein

4. *Britain and the Onset of Modernization in Brazil, 1850–1914,* Richard Graham

3. *The Mexican Revolution, 1910–1914: The Diplomacy of Anglo-American Conflict,* P. A. R. Calvert

2. *Church Wealth in Mexico: A Study of the 'Juzgado de Capellanias' in the Archbishopric of Mexico 1800–1856,* Michael P. Costeloe

1. *Ideas and Politics of Chilean Independence, 1808–1833,* Simon Collier